BARRON'S

AP*

COMPUTER SCIENCE A

7TH EDITION

Roselyn Teukolsky, M.S.
Formerly, Ithaca High School
Ithaca, New York

BARRON'S

About the Author:

Roselyn Teukolsky has an M.S. degree from Cornell University, and has been teaching programming and computer science since 1980. She has published articles in *The Mathematics Teacher* and in the National Council of Teachers of Mathematics Yearbook. She is the author of Barron's *ACT Math and Science Workbook* and co-author of Barron's *SAT 2400: Aiming for the Perfect Score*. She has received the Edyth May Sliffe Award for Distinguished Mathematics Teaching and the Alfred Kalfus Distinguished Coach Award from the New York State Math League (NYSML).

All inquiries should be addressed to:
Barron's Educational Series, Inc.
250 Wireless Boulevard
Hauppauge, New York 11788
www.barronseduc.com

ISBN: 978-1-4380-0594-2
ISBN (with CD-ROM): 978-1-4380-7553-2

ISSN (Print): 2169-5571
ISSN (Print with CD-ROM): 2169-558X

PRINTED IN THE UNITED STATES OF AMERICA
9 8 7

10%
POST-CONSUMER
WASTE
Paper contains a minimum
of 10% post-consumer
waste (PCW). Paper used
in this book was derived
from certified, sustainable
forestlands.

Contents

Barron's Essential 5

As you review the content in this book to work toward earning that **5** on your AP Computer Science A exam, here are five things that you **MUST** know above everything else:

1 **The Basics.** Every AP exam question uses at least one of these:
- Types and Identifiers (p. 60)
- Operators (p. 63)
- Control structures (p. 69)

2 **Objects, Classes, and Inheritance.** You may have to write your own class. You'll definitely need to interpret at least one class that's given.
- Methods (p. 95)
- Subclasses (p. 131)
- Abstract classes (p. 142)
- Interfaces (p. 144)

3 **Lists and Arrays.** Learn to manipulate a list. Search, delete an item, insert an item. It seems as if every second question on the AP exam uses a list!
- One-dimensional arrays (p. 233)
- ArrayLists (p. 244)

4 **Two-dimensional Arrays.** Learn to manipulate a matrix. This topic has become more prominent on the AP exam in recent years.
- Two-dimensional arrays (p. 249)
- Row-column traversal (p. 251)
- for-each loop traversal (p. 251)
- Row-by-row array processing (p. 251)

5 **Sorting and Searching.** Know these algorithms!
- Selection Sort (p. 324)
- Insertion Sort (p. 325)
- Merge Sort (p. 325)
- Binary Search (p. 329)

Preface

This book is aimed at students reviewing for the AP Computer Science A exam. It would normally be used at the completion of an AP course. However, it contains a complete summary of all topics for the exam, and it can be used for self-study if accompanied by a suitable textbook.

The book provides a review of object-oriented programming, algorithm analysis, and data structures. It can therefore be used as a supplement to first-year college courses where Java is the programming language and as a resource for teachers of high school and introductory college courses.

This seventh edition includes all features of Java that will be tested on the AP exam.

The AP Computer Science Development Committee is placing greater emphasis on two-dimensional arrays. As a result, the following new sections have been added:

- using a for-each loop traversal
- treating a matrix as an array of arrays

All students should be able to create, initialize, modify, and traverse two-dimensional arrays. More questions on two-dimensional arrays have been added for this edition.

The GridWorld Case Study is gone! Starting in May 2015 there will be no questions on GridWorld. All GridWorld questions in the practice exams have been replaced by new questions, both multiple-choice and free-response.

The AP Computer Science Labs were developed as a replacement for GridWorld. However, there will be no questions on the specific content of the labs on the AP exam. Instead, there will be questions that test the concepts developed in the labs.

This seventh edition has a new chapter that summarizes the labs and highlights the concepts that are emphasized in them. The chapter contains a new section of multiple-choice questions based on these concepts. A new symbol in the margin, as shown here, is used throughout the book to draw attention to these concepts.

Another topic that is gone is the Comparable interface, which will no longer be tested on the AP exam. Students will, however, be expected to understand how the compareTo method is used for type String.

The style of all questions and examples in the book has been revamped to better reflect the style of recent exams.

There are three complete practice exams. The exams follow the format of the AP exam, with multiple-choice and free-response sections. One exam is presented after the introduction to the book for possible use as a diagnostic test. A diagnostic chart accompanies this test. Detailed solutions with explanations are provided for all exams. Two additional exams are provided on the optional CD-ROM. This edition contains several new questions. There is no overlap of questions between the exams.

Note that the scoring worksheets that accompany each exam, in both the book and CD-ROM, have been updated in this edition. They reflect the new College Board policy of not penalizing students for wrong answers on the multiple-choice section.

ACKNOWLEDGMENTS

I owe thanks to many people who helped in the creation of this book.

I am most grateful to my excellent editor, Linda Turner, of Barron's, for her friendly guidance and moral support throughout this project, over many years. I also thank all the other members of the Barron's staff who worked on the production of the book.

I am grateful to Steven Andrianoff and David Levine of St. Bonaventure University, New York, for their outstanding workshops that gave me a leg up in computer science. Many ideas from their Java workshops found their way into early editions of this book.

Thanks also to Robert Glen Martin for invaluable advice and suggestions.

Many thanks to the four wonderful students who helped me check the new questions for this edition: Lilia Escobedo, Rob Schlom, Irene Yoon, and Aryeh Zax.

Thank you to all of the computer science teachers throughout the country who took time to write to me with suggestions for the new edition, including my colleague at Ithaca High School, Fred Deppe.

A very special thank you to Judy Hromcik and Chris Nevison, who went way beyond the call of duty to help me with this new edition.

My husband, Saul, continues to be my partner in this project—typesetting the manuscript, producing the figures, and giving advice and moral support every step of the way. This book is dedicated to him.

Roselyn Teukolsky
Ithaca, NY
July 2014

Introduction

Computer Science: The boring art
of coping with a large number of trivialities.
—*Stan Kelly-Bootle*, The Devil's DP Dictionary *(1981)*

GENERAL INFORMATION ABOUT THE EXAM

The AP Computer Science exam is a three-hour written exam. No books, calculators, or computers are allowed! The exam consists of two parts that have equal weight:

- Section I: 40 multiple-choice questions in 1 hour and 30 minutes.

- Section II: 4 free-response questions in 1 hour and 30 minutes.

Section I is scored by machine—you will bubble your answers with a pencil on a mark-sense sheet. Each question correctly answered is worth 1 point. There are no deductions for incorrect answers, and a question left blank is ignored.

Section II is scored by human readers—you will write your answers in a booklet provided. Free-response questions typically involve writing methods in Java to solve a given problem. Sometimes there are questions analyzing algorithms or designing and modifying data structures. You may be asked to write or design an entire class. To ensure consistency in the grading, each grader follows the same rubric, and each of your four answers may be examined by more than one reader. Each question is worth 9 points, with partial credit awarded where applicable. Your name and school are hidden from the readers.

Your raw score for both sections is converted to an integer score from 1 to 5, where 1 represents "Not at all qualified" and 5 represents "Extremely well qualified." Be aware that the awarding of AP credit varies enormously from college to college. The exam covers roughly a one-semester introductory college course.

The language of the AP exam is Java. Only a subset of the Java language will be tested on the exam. In writing your solutions to the free-response questions, however, you may use any Java features, including those that are not in the AP subset. For a complete description of this subset, see the College Board website at *http://www.collegeboard.com/student/testing/ap/subjects.html*. **Every language topic in this review book is part of the AP Java subset unless explicitly stated otherwise. Note that the entire subset is covered in the book.**

For both the multiple-choice and free-response sections of the exam, there will be a quick reference in the appendix. You can look at this ahead of time at *http://apcentral. collegeboard.com/apc/public/repository/ap_comp_sci_a_quick_reference.pdf*.

The quick reference contains The standard Java interfaces and classes with lists of their required methods.

> Note the new times for Sections I and II starting in 2016.

> There is no penalty for wrong answers on the multiple-choice section.

HINTS FOR TAKING THE EXAM

The Multiple-Choice Section

- Since there are no deductions for wrong answers, you should guess when you've eliminated what you can.

- You have a little less than two minutes per question, so don't waste time on any given question. You can always come back to it if you have time at the end.

- Seemingly complicated array questions can often be solved by hand tracing the code with a small array of two or three elements. The same is true for matrices.

- Many questions ask you to compare two pieces of code that supposedly implement the same algorithm. Often one program segment will fail because it doesn't handle endpoint conditions properly (e.g., num == 0). *Be aware of endpoint conditions throughout the exam.*

- Since the mark-sense sheet is scanned by machine, make sure that you erase completely if you change an answer.

The Free-Response Section

- Each free-response question is worth 9 points. Take a minute to read through the whole exam so that you can start with a question that you feel confident about. It gives you a psychological leg up to have a solid question in the bag.

- Don't omit a question just because you can't come up with a complete solution. Remember, partial credit is awarded. Also, if you can't do part (a) of a question, don't omit part (b)—they are graded independently.

- In writing solutions to a question, you must use the public methods of classes provided in that question wherever possible. If you write a significant chunk of code that can be replaced by a call to one of these methods, you will probably not receive full credit for the question.

- If an algorithm is suggested to solve a problem, just follow it. Don't reinvent the wheel.

- Don't waste time writing comments: the graders generally ignore them. The occasional brief comment that clarifies a segment of code is OK.

- Points are not deducted for inefficient code unless efficiency is an issue in the question.

- Most of the standard Java library methods are not included in the AP subset. They are accepted on the exam if you use them correctly. However, there is always an alternative solution that uses the AP subset and you should try to find it.

- Don't cross out an answer until you have written a replacement. Graders are instructed not to read anything crossed out, even if it would have gotten credit.

- Have some awareness that this section is graded by humans. It is in your interest to have the graders understand your solutions. With this in mind,

  - Use a sharp pencil, write legibly, space your answers, and indent correctly.
  - Use self-documenting names for variables, methods, and so on.

- Use the identifiers that are given in a question. You will lose usage points if you persist in using the wrong names.
- Write clear readable code. This is your goal. Don't write one obscure convoluted statement when you can write two short clear statements. The APCS exam is not the place to demonstrate that you're a genius.

HOW TO USE THIS BOOK

Each chapter in the book contains a comprehensive review of a topic, multiple-choice questions that focus on the topic, and detailed explanations of answers. These focus questions help you to review parts of the Java subset that you should know. A few questions are not typical AP exam questions—for example, questions that test low-level details of syntax. Most of the focus questions, however, and all the multiple-choice questions in the practice exams are representative of actual exam questions.

You should also note that several groups of focus questions are preceded by a single piece of code to which the questions refer. Be aware that the AP exam will usually restrict the number of questions per code example to two.

In both the text and questions/explanations, a special code font is used for parts of the text that are Java code.

```
//This is an example of code font
```

A different font is used for pseudo-code.

< Here is pseudo-code font. >

A small number of optional topics that are not part of the AP Java subset are included in the book because they are useful in the free-response questions. Sections in the text and multiple-choice questions that are optional topics are clearly marked as such. Some sections are marked by a lightning bolt, as shown here in the margin. This means wake up! Here is a concept that is likely to be tested on the AP exam because it was emphasized in the new AP Computer Science labs.

Three complete practice exams are provided in the book. One exam is at the start of the book and may be used as a diagnostic test. It is accompanied by a diagnostic chart that refers you to related topics in the review book. The other two exams are at the end of the book. There are two additional exams on the optional CD-ROM provided with the book.

Each of the five exams has an answer key, complete solutions and explanations for the free-response questions, and detailed explanations for the multiple-choice questions. There is no overlap in the questions.

An answer sheet is provided for the Section I questions of each exam. When you have completed an entire exam, and have checked your answers, you may wish to calculate your approximate AP score. Use the scoring worksheet provided on the back of the answer sheet.

An appendix at the end of the book provides a glossary of computer terms that occasionally crop up on the exam.

A final hint about the book: Try the questions before you peek at the answers. Good luck!

PRACTICE EXAM ONE / DIAGNOSTIC TEST

The exam that follows has the same format as that used on the actual AP exam. There are two ways you may use it:

1. As a diagnostic test before you start reviewing. Following the answer key is a diagnostic chart that relates each question to sections that you should review. In addition, complete explanations are provided for each solution.
2. As a practice exam when you have completed your review.

   Complete solutions with explanations are provided for the free-response questions.

Answer Sheet: Practice Exam One

1. Ⓐ Ⓑ Ⓒ Ⓓ Ⓔ
2. Ⓐ Ⓑ Ⓒ Ⓓ Ⓔ
3. Ⓐ Ⓑ Ⓒ Ⓓ Ⓔ
4. Ⓐ Ⓑ Ⓒ Ⓓ Ⓔ
5. Ⓐ Ⓑ Ⓒ Ⓓ Ⓔ
6. Ⓐ Ⓑ Ⓒ Ⓓ Ⓔ
7. Ⓐ Ⓑ Ⓒ Ⓓ Ⓔ
8. Ⓐ Ⓑ Ⓒ Ⓓ Ⓔ
9. Ⓐ Ⓑ Ⓒ Ⓓ Ⓔ
10. Ⓐ Ⓑ Ⓒ Ⓓ Ⓔ
11. Ⓐ Ⓑ Ⓒ Ⓓ Ⓔ
12. Ⓐ Ⓑ Ⓒ Ⓓ Ⓔ
13. Ⓐ Ⓑ Ⓒ Ⓓ Ⓔ
14. Ⓐ Ⓑ Ⓒ Ⓓ Ⓔ

15. Ⓐ Ⓑ Ⓒ Ⓓ Ⓔ
16. Ⓐ Ⓑ Ⓒ Ⓓ Ⓔ
17. Ⓐ Ⓑ Ⓒ Ⓓ Ⓔ
18. Ⓐ Ⓑ Ⓒ Ⓓ Ⓔ
19. Ⓐ Ⓑ Ⓒ Ⓓ Ⓔ
20. Ⓐ Ⓑ Ⓒ Ⓓ Ⓔ
21. Ⓐ Ⓑ Ⓒ Ⓓ Ⓔ
22. Ⓐ Ⓑ Ⓒ Ⓓ Ⓔ
23. Ⓐ Ⓑ Ⓒ Ⓓ Ⓔ
24. Ⓐ Ⓑ Ⓒ Ⓓ Ⓔ
25. Ⓐ Ⓑ Ⓒ Ⓓ Ⓔ
26. Ⓐ Ⓑ Ⓒ Ⓓ Ⓔ
27. Ⓐ Ⓑ Ⓒ Ⓓ Ⓔ
28. Ⓐ Ⓑ Ⓒ Ⓓ Ⓔ

29. Ⓐ Ⓑ Ⓒ Ⓓ Ⓔ
30. Ⓐ Ⓑ Ⓒ Ⓓ Ⓔ
31. Ⓐ Ⓑ Ⓒ Ⓓ Ⓔ
32. Ⓐ Ⓑ Ⓒ Ⓓ Ⓔ
33. Ⓐ Ⓑ Ⓒ Ⓓ Ⓔ
34. Ⓐ Ⓑ Ⓒ Ⓓ Ⓔ
35. Ⓐ Ⓑ Ⓒ Ⓓ Ⓔ
36. Ⓐ Ⓑ Ⓒ Ⓓ Ⓔ
37. Ⓐ Ⓑ Ⓒ Ⓓ Ⓔ
38. Ⓐ Ⓑ Ⓒ Ⓓ Ⓔ
39. Ⓐ Ⓑ Ⓒ Ⓓ Ⓔ
40. Ⓐ Ⓑ Ⓒ Ⓓ Ⓔ

How to Calculate Your (Approximate) AP Computer Science Score

Multiple Choice

Number correct (out of 40) = _____   ⟸ Multiple-Choice Score

Free Response

Question 1 _____
(out of 9)

Question 2 _____
(out of 9)

Question 3 _____
(out of 9)

Question 4 _____
(out of 9)

Total _____ × 1.11 = _____   ⟸ Free-Response Score
(Do not round.)

Final Score

_____   +   _____   =   _____
Multiple-   Free-   Final Score
Choice   Response   (Round to nearest
Score   Score   whole number.)

Chart to Convert to AP Grade
Computer Science

Final Score Range	AP Grade[a]
62–80	5
47–61	4
37–46	3
29–36	2
0–28	1

[a]The score range corresponding to each grade varies from exam to exam and is approximate.

Practice Exam One
COMPUTER SCIENCE
SECTION I

Time—1 hour and 30 minutes
Number of questions—40
Percent of total grade—50

Directions: Determine the answer to each of the following questions or incomplete statements, using the available space for any necessary scratchwork. Then decide which is the best of the choices given and fill in the corresponding oval on the answer sheet. Do not spend too much time on any one problem.

Notes:
- Assume that the classes in the Quick Reference have been imported where needed.
- Assume that variables and methods are declared within the context of an enclosing class.
- Assume that method calls that have no object or class name prefixed, and that are not shown within a complete class definition, appear within the context of an enclosing class.
- Assume that parameters in method calls are not `null` unless otherwise stated.

1. Consider this inheritance hierarchy, in which Novel and Textbook are subclasses of Book.

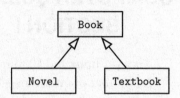

Which of the following is a *false* statement about the classes shown?
(A) The Textbook class can have private instance variables that are in neither Book nor Novel.
(B) Each of the classes—Book, Novel, and Textbook—can have a method computeShelfLife, whose code in Book and Novel is identical, but different from the code in Textbook.
(C) If the Book class has private instance variables title and author, then Novel and Textbook cannot directly access them.
(D) Both Novel and Textbook inherit the constructors in Book.
(E) If the Book class has a private method called readFile, this method may not be accessed in either the Novel or Textbook classes.

2. A programmer is designing a program to catalog all books in a library. He plans to have a Book class that stores features of each book: author, title, isOnShelf, and so on, with operations like getAuthor, getTitle, getShelfInfo, and setShelfInfo. Another class, LibraryList, will store an array of Book objects. The LibraryList class will include operations such as listAllBooks, addBook, removeBook, and searchForBook. The programmer plans to implement and test the Book class first, before implementing the LibraryList class. The programmer's plan to write the Book class first is an example of
   (A) top-down development.
   (B) bottom-up development.
   (C) procedural abstraction.
   (D) information hiding.
   (E) a driver program.

3. The color of a pixel can be represented using the RGB (Red, Green, Blue) color model, which stores values for red, green, and blue, each ranging from 0 to 255. How many bits (binary digits) would be needed to represent a color in the RGB model?
   (A) 8
   (B) 16
   (C) 24
   (D) 32
   (E) 40

GO ON TO THE NEXT PAGE.

Questions 4–5 refer to the Card and Deck classes shown below.

```
public class Card
{
    private String suit;
    private int value;       //0 to 12

    public Card(String cardSuit, int cardValue)
    { /* implementation */ }

    public String getSuit()
    { return suit; }

    public int getValue()
    { return value; }

    public String toString()
    {
        String faceValue = "";
        if (value == 11)
            faceValue = "J";
        else if (value == 12)
            faceValue = "Q";
        else if (value == 0)
            faceValue = "K";
        else if (value == 1)
            faceValue = "A";
        if (value >= 2 && value <= 10)
            return value + " of " + suit;
        else
            return faceValue + " of " + suit;
    }
}

public class Deck
{
    private Card[] deck;
    public final static int NUMCARDS = 52;

    public Deck()
    { ...

    /** Simulate shuffling the deck. */
    public void shuffle()
    { ...

    //Other methods are not shown.
}
```

4. Which of the following represents correct /* *implementation* */ code for the constructor in the Card class?

   (A) ```
suit = cardSuit;
value = cardValue;
```

   (B) ```
cardSuit = suit;
cardValue = value;
```

   (C) `Card = new Card(suit, value);`

   (D) `Card = new Card(cardSuit, cardValue);`

   (E) ```
suit = getSuit();
value = getValue();
```

5. Consider the implementation of a writeDeck method that is added to the Deck class.

   ```
/** Write the cards in deck, one per line. */
public void writeDeck()
{
    /* implementation code */
}
```

   Which of the following is correct /* *implementation code* */?

   I `System.out.println(deck);`

   II ```
for (Card card : deck)
    System.out.println(card);
```

   III ```
for (Card card : deck)
    System.out.println((String) card);
```

   (A) I only
   (B) II only
   (C) III only
   (D) I and III only
   (E) II and III only
```

6. Refer to the following method that finds the smallest value in an array.

```
/** Precondition: arr is initialized with int values.
 *  @param arr the array to be processed
 *  @return the smallest value in arr
 */
public static int findMin(int[] arr)
{
    int min = /* some value */;
    int index = 0;
    while (index < arr.length)
    {
        if (arr[index] < min)
            min = arr[index];
        index++;
    }
    return min;
}
```

Which replacement(s) for /* *some value* */ will always result in correct execution of the findMin method?

   I Integer.MIN_VALUE

  II Integer.MAX_VALUE

 III arr[0]

(A) I only
(B) II only
(C) III only
(D) I and III only
(E) II and III only

7. Consider the following loop, where n is some positive integer.

```
for (int i = 0; i < n; i += 2)
{
    if (/* test */)
        /* perform some action */
}
```

In terms of n, which Java expression represents the maximum number of times that /* *perform some action* */ could be executed?

(A) n / 2
(B) (n + 1) / 2
(C) n
(D) n - 1
(E) (n - 1) / 2

8. A method is to be written to search an array for a value that is larger than a given item and return its index. The problem specification does not indicate what should be returned if there are several such values in the array. Which of the following actions would be best?

(A) The method should be written on the assumption that there is only one value in the array that is larger than the given item.
(B) The method should be written so as to return the index of every occurrence of a larger value.
(C) The specification should be modified to indicate what should be done if there is more than one index of larger values.
(D) The method should be written to output a message if more than one larger value is found.
(E) The method should be written to delete all subsequent larger items after a suitable index is returned.

9. When will method whatIsIt cause a stack overflow (i.e., cause computer memory to be exhausted)?

```
public static int whatIsIt(int x, int y)
{
    if (x > y)
        return x * y;
    else
        return whatIsIt(x - 1, y);
}
```

(A) Only when $x < y$
(B) Only when $x \leq y$
(C) Only when $x > y$
(D) For all values of x and y
(E) The method will never cause a stack overflow.

10. The boolean expression a[i] == max || !(max != a[i]) can be simplified to
(A) a[i] == max
(B) a[i] != max
(C) a[i] < max || a[i] > max
(D) true
(E) false

11. Suppose the characters $0, 1, \ldots, 8, 9, A, B, C, D, E, F$ are used to represent a hexadecimal (base-16) number. Here $A = 10, B = 11, \ldots, F = 15$. What is the largest base-10 integer that can be represented with a two-digit hexadecimal number, such as 14 or 3A?
(A) 32
(B) 225
(C) 255
(D) 256
(E) 272

12. Consider a Clown class that has a default constructor. Suppose a list ArrayList<Clown> list is initialized. Which of the following will *not* cause an IndexOutOfBoundsException to be thrown?

(A) for (int i = 0; i <= list.size(); i++)
        list.set(i, new Clown());

(B) list.add(list.size(), new Clown());

(C) Clown c = list.get(list.size());

(D) Clown c = list.remove(list.size());

(E) list.add(-1, new Clown());

Refer to the following class for Questions 13 and 14.

```
public class Tester
{
    private int[] testArray = {3, 4, 5};

    /** @param n an int to be incremented by 1 */
    public void increment (int n)
    { n++; }

    public void firstTestMethod()
    {
        for (int i = 0; i < testArray.length; i++)
        {
            increment(testArray[i]);
            System.out.print(testArray[i] + " ");
        }
    }

    public void secondTestMethod()
    {
        for (int element : testArray)
        {
            increment(element);
            System.out.print(element + " ");
        }
    }
}
```

13. What output will be produced by invoking `firstTestMethod` for a `Tester` object?
    (A) 3 4 5
    (B) 4 5 6
    (C) 5 6 7
    (D) 0 0 0
    (E) No output will be produced. An `ArrayIndexOutOfBoundsException` will be thrown.

14. What output will be produced by invoking `secondTestMethod` for a `Tester` object, assuming that `testArray` contains 3,4,5?
    (A) 3 4 5
    (B) 4 5 6
    (C) 5 6 7
    (D) 0 0 0
    (E) No output will be produced. An `ArrayIndexOutOfBoundsException` will be thrown.

Questions 15–17 refer to the Point, Quadrilateral, and Rectangle classes below:

```
public class Point
{
    private int xCoord;
    private int yCoord;

    //constructor
    public Point(int x, int y)
    {
        ...
    }

    //accessors

    public int get_x()
    {
        ...
    }

    public int get_y()
    {
        ...
    }

    //Other methods are not shown.

}

public abstract class Quadrilateral
{
    private String labels;    //e.g., "ABCD"

    //constructor
    public Quadrilateral(String quadLabels)
    { labels = quadLabels; }

    public String getLabels()
    { return labels; }

    public abstract int perimeter();
    public abstract int area();
}
```

```
public class Rectangle extends Quadrilateral
{
    private Point topLeft;    //coords of top left corner
    private Point botRight;   //coords of bottom right corner

    //constructor
    public Rectangle(String theLabels, Point theTopLeft, Point theBotRight)
    { /* implementation code */ }

    public int perimeter()
    { /* implementation not shown */ }

    public int area()
    { /* implementation not shown */ }

    //Other methods are not shown.
}
```

15. Which statement about the `Quadrilateral` class is *false*?
    (A) The `perimeter` and `area` methods are abstract because there's no suitable default code for them.
    (B) The `getLabels` method is not abstract because any subclasses of `Quadrilateral` will have the same code for this method.
    (C) If the `Quadrilateral` class is used in a program, it *must* be used as a super-class for at least one other class.
    (D) No instances of a `Quadrilateral` object can be created in a program.
    (E) Any subclasses of the `Quadrilateral` class *must* provide implementation code for the `perimeter` and `area` methods.

16. Which represents correct /* *implementation code* */ for the `Rectangle` constructor?

    I `super(theLabels);`

    II `super(theLabels, theTopLeft, theBotRight);`

    III `super(theLabels);`
    `   topLeft = theTopLeft;`
    `   botRight = theBotRight;`

    (A) I only
    (B) II only
    (C) III only
    (D) I and II only
    (E) II and III only

GO ON TO THE NEXT PAGE.

17. Refer to the Parallelogram and Square classes below.

```
public class Parallelogram extends Quadrilateral
{
    //Private instance variables and constructor are not shown.
    ...

    public int perimeter()
    { /* implementation not shown */ }

    public int area()
    { /* implementation not shown */ }
}

public class Square extends Rectangle
{
    //Private instance variables and constructor are not shown.
    ...

    public int perimeter()
    { /* implementation not shown */ }

    public int area()
    { /* implementation not shown */ }
}
```

Consider an ArrayList<Quadrilateral> quadList whose elements are of type Rectangle, Parallelogram, or Square.
Refer to the following method, writeAreas:

```
/** Precondition:  quadList contains Rectangle, Parallelogram, or
 *                  Square objects in an unspecified order.
 *  @param quadList the list of quadrilaterals
 */
public static void writeAreas(List<Quadrilateral> quadList)
{
    for (Quadrilateral quad : quadList)
        System.out.println("Area of " + quad.getLabels()
            + " is " + quad.area());
}
```

What is the effect of executing this method?
(A) The area of each Quadrilateral in quadList will be printed.
(B) A compile-time error will occur, stating that there is no area method in abstract class Quadrilateral.
(C) A compile-time error will occur, stating that there is no getLabels method in classes Rectangle, Parallelogram, or Square.
(D) A NullPointerException will be thrown.
(E) A ClassCastException will be thrown.

18. Refer to the doSomething method:

```
// postcondition
public static void doSomething(List<SomeType> list, int i, int j)
{
    SomeType temp = list.get(i);
    list.set(i, list.get(j));
    list.set(j, temp);
}
```

Which best describes the *postcondition* for doSomething?
(A) Removes from list the objects indexed at i and j.
(B) Replaces in list the object indexed at i with the object indexed at j.
(C) Replaces in list the object indexed at j with the object indexed at i.
(D) Replaces in list the objects indexed at i and j with temp.
(E) Interchanges in list the objects indexed at i and j.

19. Consider the NegativeReal class below, which defines a negative real number object.

```
public class NegativeReal
{
    private Double negReal;

    /** Constructor. Creates a NegativeReal object whose value is num.
     *  @param num   a negative real number
     */
    public NegativeReal(double num)
    { /* implementation not shown */ }

    /** @return the value of this NegativeReal */
    public double getValue()
    { /* implementation not shown */ }

    /** @return this NegativeReal rounded to the nearest integer */
    public int getRounded()
    { /* implementation */ }
}
```

Here are some rounding examples:

Negative real number	Rounded to nearest integer
−3.5	−4
−8.97	−9
−5.0	−5
−2.487	−2
−0.2	0

Which /* *implementation* */ of getRounded produces the desired postcondition?
(A) return (int) (getValue() - 0.5);
(B) return (int) (getValue() + 0.5);
(C) return (int) getValue();
(D) return (double) (getValue() - 0.5);
(E) return (double) getValue();

GO ON TO THE NEXT PAGE.

20. Consider the following method.

```
public static void whatsIt(int n)
{
    if (n > 10)
        whatsIt(n / 10);
    System.out.print(n % 10);
}
```

What will be output as a result of the method call `whatsIt(347)`?
(A) 74
(B) 47
(C) 734
(D) 743
(E) 347

21. A large list of numbers is to be sorted into ascending order. Assuming that a "data movement" is a swap or reassignment of an element, which of the following is a *true* statement?
    (A) If the array is initially sorted in descending order, then insertion sort will be more efficient than selection sort.
    (B) The number of comparisons for selection sort is independent of the initial arrangement of elements.
    (C) The number of comparisons for insertion sort is independent of the initial arrangement of elements.
    (D) The number of data movements in selection sort depends on the initial arrangement of elements.
    (E) The number of data movements in insertion sort is independent of the initial arrangement of elements.

22. Refer to the definitions of `ClassOne` and `ClassTwo` below.

```
public class ClassOne
{
    public void methodOne()
    {
        ...
    }

    //Other methods are not shown.
}

public class ClassTwo extends ClassOne
{
    public void methodTwo()
    {
        ...
    }

    //Other methods are not shown.
}
```

Consider the following declarations in a client class. You may assume that `ClassOne` and `ClassTwo` have default constructors.

```
ClassOne c1 = new ClassOne();
ClassOne c2 = new ClassTwo();
```

Which of the following method calls will cause an error?

   I `c1.methodTwo();`

  II `c2.methodTwo();`

 III `c2.methodOne();`

(A) None
(B) I only
(C) II only
(D) III only
(E) I and II only

23. Consider the code segment

```
if (n == 1)
    k++;
else if (n == 4)
    k += 4;
```

Suppose that the given segment is rewritten in the form

```
if (/* condition */)
    /* assignment statement */;
```

Given that n and k are integers and that the rewritten code performs the same task as the original code, which of the following could be used as
    (1) /* *condition* */   and   (2) /* *assignment statement* */?

(A) (1) n == 1 && n == 4   (2) k += n

(B) (1) n == 1 && n == 4   (2) k += 4

(C) (1) n == 1 || n == 4   (2) k += 4

(D) (1) n == 1 || n == 4   (2) k += n

(E) (1) n == 1 || n == 4   (2) k = n - k

24. Which of the following will execute *without* throwing an exception?

```
 I String s = null;
   String t = "";
   if (s.equals(t))
       System.out.println("empty strings?");
```

```
II String s = "holy";
   String t = "moly";
   if (s.equals(t))
       System.out.println("holy moly!");
```

```
III String s = "holy";
    String t = s.substring(4);
    System.out.println(s + t);
```

(A) I only
(B) II only
(C) III only
(D) I and II only
(E) II and III only

25. Three numbers a, b, and c are said to be a *Pythagorean Triple* if and only if the sum of the squares of two of the numbers equals the square of the third. A programmer writes a method `isPythTriple` to test if its three parameters form a Pythagorean Triple:

```java
//Returns true if a * a + b * b == c * c; otherwise returns false.
public static boolean isPythTriple(double a, double b, double c)
{
    double d = Math.sqrt(a * a + b * b);
    return d == c;
}
```

When the method was tested with known Pythagorean Triples, `isPythTriple` sometimes erroneously returned `false`. What was the most likely cause of the error?

(A) Round-off error was caused by calculations with floating-point numbers.
(B) Type `boolean` was not recognized by an obsolete version of Java.
(C) An overflow error was caused by entering numbers that were too large.
(D) `c` and `d` should have been cast to integers before testing for equality.
(E) Bad test data were selected.

26. Refer to the following class, containing the `mystery` method.

```java
public class SomeClass
{
    private int[] arr;

    /** Constructor. Initializes arr to contain nonnegative
     *  integers k such that 0 <= k <= 9.
     */
    public SomeClass()
    { /* implementation not shown */ }

    public int mystery()
    {
        int value = arr[0];
        for (int i = 1; i < arr.length; i++)
            value = value * 10 + arr[i];
        return value;
    }
}
```

Which best describes what the `mystery` method does?
(A) It sums the elements of arr.
(B) It sums the products `10*arr[0]+10*arr[1]+···+10*arr[arr.length-1]`.
(C) It builds an integer of the form $d_1 d_2 d_3 \ldots d_n$, where $d_1 = $ `arr[0]`, $d_2 = $ `arr[1]`, $\ldots$, $d_n = $ `arr[arr.length-1]`.
(D) It builds an integer of the form $d_1 d_2 d_3 \ldots d_n$, where $d_1 = $ `arr[arr.length-1]`, $d_2 = $ `arr[arr.length-2]`, $\ldots$, $d_n = $ `arr[0]`.
(E) It converts the elements of arr to base-10.

GO ON TO THE NEXT PAGE.

Questions 27 and 28 refer to the search method in the Searcher class below.

```
public class Searcher
{
    private int[] arr;

    /** Constructor. Initializes arr with integers. */
    public Searcher()
    { /* implementation not shown */ }

    /** Precondition:  arr[first]...arr[last] sorted in ascending order.
     *  Postcondition: Returns index of key in arr. If key not in arr,
     *                 returns -1.
     */
    public int search(int first, int last, int key)
    {
        int mid;
        while (first <= last)
        {
            mid = (first + last) / 2;
            if (arr[mid] == key)        //found key, exit search
                return mid;
            else if (arr[mid] < key)  //key to right of arr[mid]
                first = mid + 1;
            else                        //key to left of arr[mid]
                last = mid - 1;
        }
        return -1;                      //key not in list
    }
}
```

27. Which assertion is true just before each execution of the while loop?
    (A) arr[first] < key < arr[last]
    (B) arr[first] ≤ key ≤ arr[last]
    (C) arr[first] < key < arr[last] or key is not in arr
    (D) arr[first] ≤ key ≤ arr[last] or key is not in arr
    (E) key ≤ arr[first] or key ≥ arr[last] or key is not in arr

28. Consider the array a with values as shown:

    4, 7, 19, 25, 36, 37, 50, 100, 101, 205, 220, 271, 306, 321

    where 4 is a[0] and 321 is a[13]. Suppose that the search method is called with
    first = 0 and last = 13 to locate the key 205. How many iterations of the while
    loop must be made in order to locate it?
    (A) 3
    (B) 4
    (C) 5
    (D) 10
    (E) 13

29. Consider the following `RandomList` class.

```
public class RandomList
{
    private int[] ranList;

    public RandomList()
    { ranList = getList(); }

    /** @return array with random Integers from 0 to 100
     *    inclusive */
    public int[] getList()
    {
        System.out.println("How many integers? ");
        int listLength = IO.readInt();      //read user input
        int[] list = new int[listLength];
        for (int i = 0; i < listLength; i++)
        {
            /* code to add integer to list */
        }
        return list;
    }

    /** Print all elements of this list. */
    public void printList()
    { ...
}
```

Which represents correct /* *code to add* integer *to* list */?

(A) `list[i] = (int) (Math.random() * 101);`

(B) `list.add((int) (Math.random() * 101));`

(C) `list[i] = (int) (Math.random() * 100);`

(D) `list.add(new Integer(Math.random() * 100))`

(E) `list[i] = (int) (Math.random() * 100) + 1;`

GO ON TO THE NEXT PAGE.

30. Refer to method `insert` described here. The `insert` method has two string parameters and one integer parameter. The method returns the string obtained by inserting the second string into the first starting at the position indicated by the integer parameter pos. For example, if `str1` contains `xy` and `str2` contains `cat`, then

```
insert(str1, str2, 0)   returns   catxy
insert(str1, str2, 1)   returns   xcaty
insert(str1, str2, 2)   returns   xycat
```

Method `insert` follows:

```
/** Precondition:   0 <= pos <= str1.length().
 *  Postcondition:  If str1 = a_0 a_1 ... a_{n-1} and str2 = b_0 b_1 ... b_{m-1},
                    returns a_0 a_1 ... a_{pos-1} b_0 b_1 ... b_{m-1} a_{pos} a_{pos+1} ... a_{n-1}
public static String insert(String str1, String str2, int pos)
{
    String first, last;
        /* more code */
    return first + str2 + last;
}
```

Which of the following is a correct replacement for /* *more code* */?

(A)
```
first = str1.substring(0, pos);
last = str1.substring(pos);
```

(B)
```
first = str1.substring(0, pos - 1);
last = str1.substring(pos);
```

(C)
```
first = str1.substring(0, pos + 1);
last = str1.substring(pos + 1);
```

(D)
```
first = str1.substring(0, pos);
last = str1.substring(pos + 1, str1.length());
```

(E)
```
first = str1.substring(0, pos);
last = str1.substring(pos, str1.length() + 1);
```

GO ON TO THE NEXT PAGE.

31. A matrix (two-dimensional array) is declared as

```
int[][] mat = new int[2][3];
```

Consider the following method:

```
public static void changeMatrix(int[][] mat)
{
    for (int r = 0; r < mat.length; r++)
        for (int c = 0; c < mat[r].length; c++)
            if (r == c)
                mat[r][c] = Math.abs(mat[r][c]);
}
```

If mat is initialized to be

```
-1 -2 -6
-2 -4  5
```

which matrix will be the result of a call to changeMatrix(mat)?

(A) 1 -2 -6
    -2 4 5

(B) -1 2 -6
     2 -4 5

(C) -1 -2 -6
    -2 -4 -5

(D) 1 2 -6
     2 4 5

(E) 1 2 6
     2 4 5

GO ON TO THE NEXT PAGE.

Use the following program description for Questions 32–34.

A programmer plans to write a program that simulates a small bingo game (no more than six players). Each player will have a bingo card with 20 numbers from 0 to 90 (no duplicates). Someone will call out numbers one at a time, and each player will cross out a number on his card as it is called. The first player with all the numbers crossed out is the winner. In the simulation, as the game is in progress, each player's card is displayed on the screen.

The programmer envisions a short driver class whose main method has just two statements:

```
BingoGame b = new BingoGame();
b.playBingo();
```

The BingoGame class will have several objects: a Display, a Caller, and a PlayerGroup. The PlayerGroup will have a list of Players, and each Player will have a BingoCard.

32. The relationship between the PlayerGroup and Player classes is an example of
    (A) an interface.
    (B) encapsulation.
    (C) composition.
    (D) inheritance.
    (E) independent classes.

33. Which is a reasonable data structure for a BingoCard object? Recall that there are 20 integers from 0 to 90 on a BingoCard, with no duplicates. There should also be mechanisms for crossing off numbers that are called, and for detecting a winning card (i.e., one where all the numbers have been crossed off).

```
I  int[] bingoCard;   //will contain 20 integers
                //bingoCard[k] is crossed off by setting it to -1.
   int numCrossedOff;   //player wins when numCrossedOff reaches 20.

II boolean[] bingoCard;  //will contain 91 boolean values, of which
                         //20 are true. All the other values are false.
                         //Thus, if bingoCard[k] is true, then k is
                         //on the card, 0 <= k <= 90. A number k is
                         //crossed off by changing the value of
                         //bingoCard[k] to false.
   int numCrossedOff;   //player wins when numCrossedOff reaches 20.

III ArrayList<Integer> bingoCard;  //will contain 20 integers.
         //A number is crossed off by removing it from the ArrayList.
         //Player wins when bingoCard.size() == 0.
```

    (A) I only
    (B) II only
    (C) III only
    (D) I and II only
    (E) I, II, and III

34. The programmer decides to use a List<Integer>, which is implemented as an ArrayList<Integer>, to store the numbers to be called by the Caller:

```
public class Caller
{
    private List<Integer> numbers;

    public Caller()
    {
        numbers = getList();
        shuffleNumbers();
    }

    /** @return the numbers 0...90 in order */
    private List<Integer> getList()
    { /* implementation not shown */ }

    /** Shuffle the numbers. */
    private void shuffleNumbers()
    { /* implementation not shown */ }
}
```

When the programmer tests the constructor of the Caller class, she gets a NullPointerException. Which could be the cause of this error?

(A) The Caller object in the driver class was not created with new.

(B) The programmer forgot the return statement in getList that returns the list of Integers.

(C) The declaration of numbers is incorrect. It needed to be

```
private List<Integer> numbers = null;
```

(D) In the getList method, an attempt was made to add an Integer to an ArrayList that had not been created with new.

(E) The shuffleNumbers algorithm went out of range, causing a null Integer to be shuffled into the ArrayList.

35. Consider method `findSomething` below:

```
/** Precondition: a.length is equal to b.length. */
public static boolean findSomething(int[] a, int[] b)
{
    for (int aValue: a)
    {
        boolean found = false;
        for (int bValue: b)
        {
            if (bValue == aValue)
                found = true;
        }
        if (!found)
            return false;
    }
    return true;
}
```

Which *best* describes what method `findSomething` does? Method `findSomething` returns true only if
(A) Arrays a and b contain identical elements in the same order.
(B) Arrays a and b contain identical elements in reverse order.
(C) Arrays a and b are permutations of each other.
(D) Array a contains at least one element that is also in b.
(E) Every element of array a is also in b.

36. Consider a program that has a two-dimensional array mat of int values. The program has several methods that change mat by reflecting elements of mat across a mirror placed symmetrically on the matrix. Here are five such methods:

```
                                              2 4 6          2 4 2
    mirrorVerticalLeftToRight    transforms   1 3 5    to    1 3 1
                                              8 9 0          8 9 8


                                              2 4 6          6 4 6
    mirrorVerticalRightToLeft    transforms   1 3 5    to    5 3 5
                                              8 9 0          0 9 0


                                              2 4 6          2 4 6
    mirrorHorizontalTopToBottom  transforms   1 3 5    to    1 3 5
                                              8 9 0          2 4 6


                                              2 4 6          8 9 0
    mirrorHorizontalBottomToTop  transforms   1 3 5    to    1 3 5
                                              8 9 0          8 9 0


                                              2 4 6          2 4 6
    mirrorDiagonalRightToLeft    transforms   1 3 5    to    4 3 5
                                              8 9 0          6 5 0
```

Consider the following method that transforms the matrix in one of the ways shown above:

```java
public static void someMethod(int[][] mat)
{
    int height = mat.length;
    int numCols = mat[0].length;
    for (int col = 0; col < numCols; col++)
        for (int row = 0; row < height/2; row++)
            mat[height - row - 1][col] = mat[row][col];
}
```

Which method described above corresponds to someMethod?
(A) mirrorVerticalLeftToRight
(B) mirrorVerticalRightToLeft
(C) mirrorHorizontalTopToBottom
(D) mirrorHorizontalBottomToTop
(E) mirrorDiagonalRightToLeft

Refer to the following for Questions 37 and 38.

A word creation game uses a set of small letter tiles, all of which are initially in a tile bag. A partial implementation of a `TileBag` class is shown below.

```
public class TileBag
{
    //tiles contains all the tiles in the bag
    private List<Tile> tiles;
    //size is the number of not-yet-used tiles
    private int size;

    //Constructors and other methods are not shown.
}
```

Consider the following method in the `TileBag` class that allows a player to get a new tile from the `TileBag`.

```
public Tile getNewTile()
{
    if (size == 0)  //no tiles left
        return null;
    int index = (int) (Math.random() * size);
    size--;
    Tile temp = tiles.get(index);
    /* code to swap tile at position size with tile at position index */
    return temp;
}
```

37. Which /* *code to swap tile at position* `size` *with tile at position* `index` */ performs the swap correctly?

 (A) `tiles.set(size, temp);`
    `tiles.set(index, tiles.get(size));`

 (B) `tiles.set(index, tiles.get(size));`
    `tiles.set(size, temp);`

 (C) `tiles.swap(index, size);`

 (D) `tiles.get(size, temp);`
    `tiles.get(index, tiles.set(size));`

 (E) `tiles.get(index, tiles.set(size));`
    `tiles.get(size, temp);`

38. Which is *true* about the `getNewTile` algorithm?
 (A) The algorithm allows the program to keep track of both used and unused tiles.
 (B) The `tiles` list becomes one element shorter when `getNewTile` is executed.
 (C) The algorithm selects a random `Tile` from all tiles in the list.
 (D) The `tiles` list has used tiles in the beginning and unused tiles at the end.
 (E) The `tiles` list contains only tiles that have not been used.

39. Consider the following two classes.

```
public class Bird
{
    public void act()
    {
        System.out.print("fly ");
        makeNoise();
    }

    public void makeNoise()
    {
        System.out.print("chirp ");
    }
}

public class Dove extends Bird
{
    public void act()
    {
        super.act();
        System.out.print("waddle ");
    }

    public void makeNoise()
    {
        super.makeNoise();
        System.out.print("coo ");
    }
}
```

Suppose the following declaration appears in a class other than `Bird` or `Dove`:

```
Bird pigeon = new Dove();
```

What is printed as a result of the call `pigeon.act()`?
(A) `fly`
(B) `fly chirp`
(C) `fly chirp waddle`
(D) `fly chirp waddle coo`
(E) `fly chirp coo waddle`

Diagnostic Test

40. Consider a method `partialProd` that returns an integer array prod such that for all k, prod[k] is equal to arr[0] * arr[1] * ⋯ arr[k]. For example, if arr contains the values {2,5,3,4,10}, the array prod will contain the values {2,10,30,120,1200}.

```java
public static int[] partialProd(int[] arr)
{
    int[] prod = new int[arr.length];
    for (int j = 0; j < arr.length; j++)
        prod[j] = 1;
    /* missing code */
    return prod;
}
```

Consider the following two implementations of /* *missing code* */.
Implementation 1

```java
for (int j = 1; j < arr.length; j++)
{
    prod[j] = prod[j - 1] * arr[j];
}
```

Implementation 2

```java
for (int j = 0; j < arr.length; j++)
    for (int k = 0; k <= j; k++)
    {
        prod[j] = prod[j] * arr[k];
    }
```

Which of the following statements is *true*?
(A) Both implementations work as intended but Implementation 1 is faster than Implementation 2.
(B) Both implementations work as intended but Implementation 2 is faster than Implementation 1.
(C) Both implementations work as intended and are equally fast.
(D) Implementation 1 doesn't work as intended because the elements of prod are incorrectly assigned.
(E) Implementation 2 doesn't work as intended because the elements of prod are incorrectly assigned.

END OF SECTION I

COMPUTER SCIENCE
SECTION II

Time—1 hour and 30 minutes
Number of questions—4
Percent of total grade—50

Directions: SHOW ALL YOUR WORK. REMEMBER THAT
PROGRAM SEGMENTS ARE TO BE WRITTEN IN Java.

Write your answers in pencil only in the booklet provided.

Notes:

- Assume that the classes in the Quick Reference have been imported where needed.

- Unless otherwise stated, assume that parameters in method calls are not null and that methods are called only when their preconditions are satisfied.

- In writing solutions for each question, you may use any of the accessible methods that are listed in classes defined in that question. Writing significant amounts of code that can be replaced by a call to one of these methods may not receive full credit.

---

1. This question manipulates one-dimensional and two-dimensional arrays. In part (a) you will write a method to reverse elements of a one-dimensional array. In parts (b) and (c) you will write methods to reverse elements of a two-dimensional array.

    (a) Consider the following incomplete `ArrayUtil` class, which contains a static `reverseArray` method.

```
public class ArrayUtil
{
    /** Reverses elements of array arr.
     * Precondition: arr.length > 0.
     * Postcondition: The elements of arr have been reversed.
     * @param arr the array to manipulate
     */
    public static void reverseArray(int[] arr)
    { /* to be implemented in part (a) */ }

    //Other methods are not shown.
}
```

GO ON TO THE NEXT PAGE.

Write the `ArrayUtil` method `reverseArray`. For example, if `arr` is the array {2,7,5,1,0}, the call to `reverseArray` changes `arr` to be {0,1,5,7,2}.

Complete method `reverseArray` below.

```
/** Reverses elements of array arr.
 *  Precondition: arr.length > 0.
 *  Postcondition: The elements of arr have been reversed.
 *  @param arr the array to manipulate
 */
public static void reverseArray(int[] arr)
```

(b) Consider the following incomplete `Matrix` class, which represents a two-dimensional matrix of integers. Assume that the matrix contains at least one integer.

```
public class Matrix
{
    private int[][] mat;

    /** Constructs a matrix of integers. */
    public Matrix (int[][] m)
    {  mat = m; }

    /** Reverses the elements in each row of mat.
     *  Postcondition: The elements in each row have been reversed.
     */
    public void reverseAllRows()
    { /* to be implemented in part (b) */ }

    /** Reverses the elements of mat.
     *  Postcondition:
     *    - The final elements of mat, when read in row-major order,
     *      are the same as the original elements of mat when read
     *      from the bottom corner, right to left, going upward.
     *    - mat[0][0] contains what was originally the last element.
     *    - mat[mat.length-1][mat[0].length-1] contains what was
     *      originally the first element.
     */
    public void reverseMatrix()
    { /* to be implemented in part (c) */ }

    //Other instance variables, constructors and methods are not shown
}
```

Write the `Matrix` method `reverseAllRows`. This method reverses the elements of each row. For example, if `mat1` refers to a `Matrix` object, then the call `mat1.reverseAllRows()` will change the matrix as shown below.

	Before call					**After call**			
	0	1	2	3		0	1	2	3
0	1	2	3	4	0	4	3	2	1
1	5	6	7	8	1	8	7	6	5
2	9	10	11	12	2	12	11	10	9

In writing `reverseAllRows`, you *must* call the `reverseArray` method in part (a). Assume that `reverseArray` works correctly regardless of what you wrote in part (a).

Complete method `reverseAllRows` below.

```
/** Reverses the elements in each row of mat.
 * Postcondition: The elements in each row have been reversed.
 */
public void reverseAllRows()
```

(c) Write the `Matrix` method `reverseMatrix`. This method reverses the elements of a matrix such that the final elements of the matrix, when read in row-major order, are the same as the original elements when read from the bottom corner, right to left, going upward. Again let `mat1` be a reference to a `Matrix` object. The the call `mat1.reverseMatrix()` will change the matrix as shown below.

	Before call			**After call**	
	0	1		0	1
0	1	2	0	6	5
1	3	4	1	4	3
2	5	6	2	2	1

In writing `reverseMatrix`, you *must* call the `reverseAllRows` method in part (b). Assume that `reverseAllRows` works correctly regardless of what you wrote in part (b).

Complete method `reverseMatrix` below.

```
/** Reverses the elements of mat.
 * Postcondition:
 *    - The final elements of mat, when read in row-major order,
 *      are the same as the original elements of mat when read
 *      from the bottom corner, right to left, going upward.
 *    - mat[0][0] contains what was originally the last element.
 *    - mat[mat.length-1][mat[0].length-1] contains what was
 *      originally the first element.
 */
public void reverseMatrix()
```

GO ON TO THE NEXT PAGE.

2. A text-editing program uses a `Sentence` class that manipulates a single sentence. A sentence contains letters, blanks, and punctuation. The first character in a sentence is a letter, and the last character is a punctuation mark. Any two words in the sentence are separated by a single blank. A partial implementation of the Sentence class is as follows.

```java
public class Sentence
{
    /** The sentence to manipulate */
    private String sentence;

    /** @return an ArrayList of integer positions containing a
     *    blank in this sentence. If there are no blanks in the
     *    sentence, returns an empty list.
     */
    public List<Integer> getBlankPositions()
    { /* to be implemented in part (a) */ }

    /** @return the number of words in this sentence
     *    Precondition:  Sentence contains at least one word.
     */
    public int countWords()
    { /* to be implemented in part (b) */ }

    /** @return the array of words in this sentence
     *    Precondition:
     *      - Any two words in the sentence are separated by one blank.
     *      - The sentence contains at least one word.
     *    Postcondition: String[] returned containing the words in
     *                   this sentence.
     */
    public String[] getWords()
    { /* to be implemented in part (c) */ }

    //Constructor and other methods are not shown.
}
```

(a) Write the `Sentence` method `getBlankPositions`, which returns an `ArrayList` of integers that represent the positions in a sentence containing blanks. If there are no blanks in the sentence, `getBlankPositions` should return an empty list.

Some results of calling `getBlankPositions` are shown below.

Sentence	Result of call to getBlankPositions
I love you!	[1, 6]
The cat sat on the mat.	[3, 7, 11, 14, 18]
Why?	[ ]

Complete method getBlankPositions below.

```
/**  @return an ArrayList of integer positions containing a
 *    blank in this sentence. If there are no blanks in the
 *    sentence, returns an empty list.
 */
public List<Integer> getBlankPositions()
```

(b) Write the Sentence method countWords, which returns the number of words in a sentence. Words are sequences of letters or punctuation, separated by a single blank. You may assume that every sentence contains at least one word.

For example:

Sentence	Result returned by countWords
I love you!	3
The cat sat on the mat.	6
Why?	1

Complete method countWords below.

```
/**  @return the number of words in this sentence
 *    Precondition:  Sentence contains at least one word.
 */
public int countWords()
```

(c) Write the Sentence method getWords, which returns an array of words in the sentence. A word is defined as a string of letters and punctuation, and does not contain any blanks. You may assume that a sentence contains at least one word.

Some examples of calling getWords are shown below.

Sentence	Result returned by getWords
The bird flew away.	{The, bird, flew, away.}
Wow!	{Wow!}
Hi! How are you?	{Hi!, How, are, you?}

In writing method getWords, you *must* use methods getBlankPositions and countWords, which were written in parts (a) and (b). You may assume that these methods work correctly, irrespective of what you wrote in parts (a) and (b).

Complete method getWords below.

```
/** @return the array of words in this sentence
 *    Precondition:
 *     - Any two words in the sentence are separated by one blank.
 *     - The sentence contains at least one word.
 *    Postcondition: String[] returned containing the words in
 *              this sentence.
 */
public String[] getWords()
```

GO ON TO THE NEXT PAGE.

3. In this question you will implement two methods for a class `Tournament` that keeps track of the players who have registered for a tournament. The `Tournament` class uses the `Player` class shown below. A `Player` has a name and player number specified when a player is constructed.

```
public class Player
{
    public Player(String name, int playerNumber)
    { /* implementation not shown */ }

    public int getPlayerNumber()
    { /* implementation not shown */ }

    //Private instance variables and other methods are not shown.
}
```

An incomplete declaration for the `Tournament` class is shown below. There are 100 available slots for players in the tournament, and the players are numbered $0, 1, 2, \ldots, 99$.

```
public class Tournament
{
    /** The list of slots in the tournament.
     * Each element corresponds to a slot in the tournament.
     * If slots[i] is null, the slot is not yet taken;
     * otherwise it contains a reference to a Player.
     * For example, slots[i].getPlayerNumber() returns i.
     */
    private Player[] slots;

    /** The list of names of players who wish to participate in
     * the tournament, but cannot because all slots are taken.
     */
    private List<String> waitingList;
```

```
    /** If there are any empty slots (slots with no Player)
     *  assign the player with the specified playerName to an
     *  empty slot. Create and return the new Player.
     *  If there are no available slots, add the player's name
     *  to the end of the waiting list and return null.
     *  @playerName the name of the person requesting a slot
     *  @return the new Player
     */
    public Player requestSlot(String playerName)
    { /* to be implemented in part (a) */ }


    /** Release the slot for player p, thus removing that player
     *  from the tournament. If there are any names in waitingList,
     *  remove the first name and create a Player in the
     *  canceled slot for this person. Return the new Player.
     *  If waitingList is empty, mark the slot specified by p as
     *  empty and return null.
     *  Precondition: p is a valid Player for some slot in
     *                this tournament.
     *  @param p the player who will be removed from the tournament
     *  @return the new Player placed in the canceled slot
     */
    public Player cancelAndReassignSlot(Player p)
    { /* to be implemented in part (b) */ }


    //Constructor and other methods are not shown.
}
```

(a) Write the `Tournament` method `requestSlot`. Method `requestSlot` tries to reserve a slot in the tournament for a given player. If there are any available slots in the tournament, one of them is assigned to the named player, and the newly created `Player` is returned. If there are no available slots, the player's name is added to the end of the waiting list and `null` is returned.

Complete method `requestSlot` below.

```
    /** If there are any empty slots (slots with no Player)
     *  assign the player with the specified playerName to an
     *  empty slot. Create and return the new Player.
     *  If there are no available slots, add the player's name
     *  to the end of the waiting list and return null.
     *  @playerName the name of the person requesting a slot
     *  @return the new Player
     */
    public Player requestSlot(String playerName)
```

(b) Write the `Tournament` method `cancelAndReassignSlot`. This method releases a previous player's slot. If the waiting list for the tournament contains any names, the newly available slot is reassigned to the person at the front of the list. That person's name is removed from the waiting list, and the newly created `Player` is returned. If the waiting list is empty, the newly released slot is marked as empty, and null is returned.

In writing `cancelAndReassignSlot`, you may use any accessible methods in the `Player` and `Tournament` classes. Assume that these methods work as specified.

Information repeated from the beginning of the question

public class Player

public Player(String name, int playerNumber)
public int getPlayerNumber()

public class Tournament

private Player[] slots
private List<String> waitingList
public Player requestSlot(String playerName)
public Player cancelAndReassignSlot(Player p)

Complete method `cancelAndReassignSlot` below.

```
/** Release the slot for player p, thus removing that player
 *  from the tournament. If there are any names in waitingList,
 *  remove the first name and create a Player in the
 *  canceled slot for this person. Return the new Player.
 *  If waitingList is empty, mark the slot specified by p as
 *  empty and return null.
 *  Precondition:  p is a valid Player for some slot in
 *                 this tournament.
 *  @param p the player who will be removed from the tournament
 *  @return the new Player placed in the canceled slot
 */
public Player cancelAndReassignSlot(Player p)
```

4. A chemical solution is said to be *acidic* if it has a pH integer value from 1 to 6, inclusive. The lower the pH, the more acidic the solution.
An experiment has a large number of chemical solutions arranged in a line and a mechanical arm that moves back and forth along the line, so that the acidity of each solution can be altered by adding various chemicals. A chemical solution is specified by the `Solution` interface below.

```
public interface Solution
{
    /** @return an integer value that ranges from 1 (very acidic)
     *  to 14 */
    int getPH();

    /** Set PH to newValue.
     *  @param newValue the new PH value */
    void setPH(int newValue);
}
```

The experiment keeps track of the solutions and the mechanical arm. The figure below represents the solutions and mechanical arm in an experiment. The arm, indicated by the arrow, is currently at index 4 and is facing left. The second row of integers represents the pH values of the solutions.

index	0	1	2	3	4	5	6
pH	7	4	10	5	6	7	13

←

In this experiment, the most acidic solution is at index 1, since its pH value is the lowest.

The state of the mechanical arm includes the index of its location and direction it is facing (to the right or to the left). A mechanical arm is specified by the MechanicalArm interface below.

```
public interface MechanicalArm
{
    /** @return the index of the current location of the
     *  mechanical arm */
    int getCurrentIndex();

    /** @return true if the mechanical arm is facing right
     *  (toward solutions with larger indexes),
     *  false if the mechanical arm is facing left
     *  (toward solutions with smaller indexes)
     */
    boolean isFacingRight();

    /** Changes the current direction of the mechanical arm */
    void changeDirection();

    /** Moves the mechanical arm forward in its current direction
     *  by the number of locations specified.
     *  @param numLocs the number of locations to move
     *  Precondition: numLocs >= 0.
     */
    void moveForward(int numLocs);
}
```

GO ON TO THE NEXT PAGE.

An experiment is represented by the Experiment class shown below.

```
public class Experiment
{
    /** The mechanical arm used to process the solutions */
    private MechanicalArm arm;

    /** The list of solutions */
    private List<Solution> solutions;

    /** Resets the experiment.
     * Postcondition:
     *    - The mechanical arm has a current index of 0.
     *    - It is facing right.
     */
    public void reset()
    { /* to be implemented in part (a) */ }

    /** Finds and returns the index of the most acidic solution.
     * @return index the location of the most acidic solution
     * or -1 if there are no acidic solutions
     * Postcondition:
     *    - The mechanical arm is facing right.
     *    - Its current index is at the most acidic solution, or at
     *       0 if there are no acidic solutions.
     */
    public int mostAcidic()
    { /* to be implemented in part (b) */ }
}
```

(a) Write the Experiment method reset that places the mechanical arm facing right, at index 0.

For example, suppose the experiment contains the solutions with pH values shown. The arrow represents the mechanical arm.

index	0	1	2	3	4	5	6
pH	7	4	10	5	6	7	13

$\leftarrow$

A call to reset will result in

index	0	1	2	3	4	5	6
pH	7	4	10	5	6	7	13

$\rightarrow$

```
Information repeated from the beginning of the question

public interface Solution

int getPH()
void setPH(int newValue)

public interface MechanicalArm

int getCurrentIndex()
boolean isFacingRight()
void changeDirection()
void moveForward(int numLocs)

public class Experiment

private MechanicalArm arm
private List<Solution> solutions
public void reset()
public int mostAcidic()
```

Complete method reset below.

```
/** Resets the experiment.
 *  Postcondition:
 *    - The mechanical arm has a current index of 0.
 *    - It is facing right.
 */
public void reset()
```

(b) Write the Experiment method mostAcidic that returns the index of the most acidic solution and places the mechanical arm facing right at the location of the most acidic solution. A solution is acidic if its pH is less than 7. The lower the pH, the more acidic the solution. If there are no acidic solutions in the experiment, the mostAcidic method should return -1 and place the mechanical arm at index 0, facing right.
For example, suppose the experiment has this state:

index	0	1	2	3	4	5	6
pH	7	4	10	5	6	7	13

←

A call to mostAcidic should return the value 1 and result in the following state for the experiment:

index	0	1	2	3	4	5	6
pH	7	4	10	5	6	7	13

→

GO ON TO THE NEXT PAGE.

If the experiment has this state,

index	0	1	2	3	4	5	6
pH	7	9	8	8	12	13	14

←

a call to mostAcidic should return the value -1 and result in the following state for the experiment:

index	0	1	2	3	4	5	6
pH	7	9	8	8	12	13	14

→

Information repeated from the beginning of the question

```
public interface Solution

int getPH()
void setPH(int newValue)
```

```
public interface MechanicalArm

int getCurrentIndex()
boolean isFacingRight()
void changeDirection()
void moveForward(int numLocs)
```

```
public class Experiment

private MechanicalArm arm
private List<Solution> solutions
public void reset()
public int mostAcidic()
```

Complete method mostAcidic below.

```
/** Finds and returns the index of the most acidic solution.
 *  @return index the location of the most acidic solution
 *  or -1 if there are no acidic solutions
 *  Postcondition:
 *    - The mechanical arm is facing right.
 *    - Its current index is at the most acidic solution, or at
 *      0 if there are no acidic solutions.
 */
public int mostAcidic()
```

END OF EXAMINATION

ANSWER KEY (Section I)

1. D	15. E	29. A
2. B	16. C	30. A
3. C	17. A	31. A
4. A	18. E	32. C
5. B	19. A	33. E
6. E	20. E	34. D
7. B	21. B	35. E
8. C	22. E	36. C
9. B	23. D	37. B
10. A	24. E	38. A
11. C	25. A	39. E
12. B	26. C	40. D
13. A	27. D	
14. A	28. B	

DIAGNOSTIC CHART FOR PRACTICE EXAM

Each multiple-choice question has a complete explanation (p. 47).

The following table relates each question to sections that you should review. For any given question, the topic(s) in the chart represent the concept(s) tested in the question. These topics are explained on the corresponding page(s) in the chart and should provide further insight into answering that question.

Diagnostic Test

ANSWERS EXPLAINED

Section I

1. **(D)** Constructors are never inherited. If a subclass has no constructor, the default constructor for the superclass is generated. If the superclass does not have a default constructor, a compile-time error will occur.

2. **(B)** The programmer is using an object-oriented approach to writing the program and plans to test the simplest classes first. This is bottom-up development. In *top-down* development (choice A), high-level classes are broken down into subsidiary classes. Procedural abstraction (choice C) is the use of helper methods in a class. Information hiding (choice D) is restriction of access to private data and methods in a class. Choice E is wrong because a driver program is one whose sole purpose is to test a given method or class. Implementing the simplest classes first may involve driver programs that test the various methods, but the overall plan is not an example of a driver program.

3. **(C)** 8 bits (1 byte) are required to represent the values from 0 to 255. The base 2 number 11111111 represents $1 + 2 + 4 + 8 + 16 + 32 + 64 + 128 = 255$. Since there are 3 such values in an RGB representation, $(8)(3) = 24$ bits are needed.

4. **(A)** In the constructor, the private instance variables `suit` and `value` must be initialized to the appropriate parameter values. Choice A is the only choice that does this.

5. **(B)** Implementation II invokes the `toString` method of the `Card` class. Implementation I fails because there is no default `toString` method for arrays. Implementation III will cause a `ClassCastException`: You cannot cast a `Card` to a `String`.

6. **(E)** Since the values in `arr` cannot be greater than `Integer.MAX_VALUE`, the test in the `while` loop will be true at least once and will lead to the smallest element being stored in `min`. (If *all* the elements of the array are `Integer.MAX_VALUE`, the code still works.) Similarly, initializing `min` to `arr[0]`, the first element in the array, ensures that all elements in `arr` will be examined and the smallest will be found. Choice I, `Integer.MIN_VALUE`, fails because the test in the loop will always be false! There is no array element that will be less than the smallest possible integer. The method will (incorrectly) return `Integer.MIN_VALUE`.

7. **(B)** The maximum number will be achieved if /* *test* */ is true in each pass through the loop. So the question boils down to: How many times is the loop executed? Try one odd and one even value of n:

$$\text{If } n = 7, \quad i = 0, 2, 4, 6 \qquad \text{Ans} = 4$$
$$\text{If } n = 8, \quad i = 0, 2, 4, 6 \qquad \text{Ans} = 4$$

Notice that choice B is the only expression that works for both $n = 7$ and $n = 8$.

8. **(C)** Here is one of the golden rules of programming: Don't start planning the program until every aspect of the specification is crystal clear. A programmer should never make unilateral decisions about ambiguities in a specification.

9. **(B)** When $x \leq y$, a recursive call is made to `whatIsIt(x-1, y)`. If x decreases at every recursive call, there is no way to reach a successful base case. Thus, the method never terminates and eventually exhausts all available memory.

10. **(A)** The expression !(max != a[i]) is equivalent to max == a[i], so the given expression is equivalent to a[i] == max || max == a[i], which is equivalent to a[i] == max.

11. **(C)** A base-b number can be represented with b characters. Thus, base-2 uses 0,1 for example, and base-10 uses 0, 1,..., 8, 9. A hexadecimal (base-16) number is represented with 16 characters: 0, 1,..., 8, 9, A, B, C, D, E, F, where $A = 10, B = 11, ..., F = 15$. The largest two-place base-2 integer is

$$11 = 1 \times 2^0 + 1 \times 2^1 = 3$$

The largest two-place base-10 integer is

$$99 = 9 \times 10^0 + 9 \times 10^1$$

The largest two-place base-16 integer is

$$FF = F \times 16^0 + F \times 16^1$$

The character F represents 15, so

$$FF = 15 \times 16^0 + 15 \times 16^1 = 255$$

Here's another way to think about this problem: Each hex digit is 4 binary digits (bits), since $16 = 2^4$. Therefore a two-digit hex number is 8 bits. The largest base-10 number that can be represented with 8 bits is $2^8 - 1 = 255$.

12. **(B)** The index range for ArrayList is $0 \leq$ index $\leq$ size()-1. Thus, for methods get, remove, and set, the last in-bounds index is size()-1. The one exception is the add method—to add an element to the end of the list takes an index parameter list.size().

13. **(A)** The array will not be changed by the increment method. Here are the memory slots:

Before the first call, increment(3):

testArray

| | → | 3 | 4 | 5 |

Just after the first call:

testArray

| | → | 3 | 4 | 5 |

n

| 3 |

Just before exiting increment(3):

testArray

| | → | 3 | 4 | 5 |

n

| 4 |

Just after exiting increment(3):

testArray

| | → | 3 | 4 | 5 |

The same analysis applies to the method calls increment(4) and increment(5).

14. **(A)** As in the previous question, the array will not be changed by the increment method. Nor will the local variable element! What *will* be changed by increment is the copy of the parameter during each pass through the loop.

15. **(E)** Subclasses of `Quadrilateral` may also be abstract, in which case they will inherit `perimeter` and/or `area` as abstract methods.

16. **(C)** Segment I starts correctly but fails to initialize the additional private variables of the `Rectangle` class. Segment II is wrong because by using `super` with `theTopLeft` and `theBotRight`, it implies that these values are used in the `Quadrilateral` superclass. This is false—there isn't even a constructor with three arguments in the superclass.

17. **(A)** During execution the appropriate `area` method for each `quad` in `quadList` will be determined (polymorphism or dynamic binding).

18. **(E)** The algorithm has three steps:

    1. Store the object at `i` in `temp`.
    2. Place at location `i` the object at `j`.
    3. Place `temp` at location `j`.

    This has the effect of swapping the objects at `i` and `j`. Notice that choices B and C, while incomplete, are not incorrect. The question, however, asks for the *best* description of the postcondition, which is found in choice E.

19. **(A)** Subtracting 0.5 from a negative real number and then truncating it produces the number correctly rounded to the nearest integer. Note that casting to an `int` truncates a real number. The expression in choice B is correct for rounding a *positive* real number. Choice C won't round correctly. For example, −3.7 will be rounded to −3 instead of −4. Choices D and E don't make sense. Why cast to `double` if you're rounding to the nearest integer?

20. **(E)** The method call `whatsIt(347)` puts on the stack `System.out.print(7)`.
    The method call `whatsIt(34)` puts on the stack `System.out.print(4)`.
    The method call `whatsIt(3)` is a base case and writes out 3.
    Now the stack is popped from the top, and the 3 that was printed is followed by 4, then 7. The result is 347.

21. **(B)** Recall that insertion sort takes each element in turn and (a) finds its insertion point and (b) moves elements to insert that element in its correct place. Thus, if the array is in reverse sorted order, the insertion point will always be at the front of the array, leading to the maximum number of comparisons and data moves— very inefficient. Therefore choices A, C, and E are false.

    Selection sort finds the smallest element in the array and swaps it with `a[0]` and then finds the smallest element in the rest of the array and swaps it with `a[1]`, and so on. Thus, the same number of comparisons and moves will occur, irrespective of the original arrangement of elements in the array. So choice B is true, and choice D is false.

22. **(E)** Method call I fails because `ClassOne` does not have access to the methods of its subclass. Method call II fails because `c2` needs to be cast to `ClassTwo` to be able to access `methodTwo`. Thus, the following would be OK:

    ```
    ((ClassTwo) c2).methodTwo();
    ```

    Method call III works because `ClassTwo` inherits `methodOne` from its superclass, `ClassOne`.

23. **(D)** Notice that in the original code, if n is 1, k is incremented by 1, and if n is 4, k is incremented by 4. This is equivalent to saying "if n is 1 or 4, k is incremented

by n."

24. **(E)** Segment I will throw a `NullPointerException` when `s.equals...` is invoked, because `s` is a null reference. Segment III looks suspect, but when the `startIndex` parameter of the `substring` method equals `s.length()`, the value returned is the empty string. If, however, `startIndex > s.length()`, a `StringIndexOutOfBoundsException` is thrown.

25. **(A)** Since results of calculations with floating-point numbers are not always represented exactly (round-off error), direct tests for equality are not reliable. Instead of the boolean expression `d == c`, a test should be done to check whether the difference of `d` and `c` is within some acceptable tolerance interval (see the Box on comparing floating-point numbers, p. 65).

26. **(C)** If `arr` has elements 2, 3, 5, the values of `value` are

```
2                      //after initialization
2*10 + 3 = 23          //when i = 1
23*10 + 5 = 235        //when i = 2
```

27. **(D)** The point of the binary search algorithm is that the interval containing `key` is repeatedly narrowed down by splitting it in half. For each iteration of the `while` loop, if `key` is in the list, `arr[first]` $\leq$ `key` $\leq$ `arr[last]`. Note that (i) the endpoints of the interval must be included, and (ii) `key` is not necessarily in the list.

28. **(B)**

	first	last	mid	a[mid]
After first iteration	0	13	6	50
After second iteration	7	13	10	220
After third iteration	7	9	8	101
After fourth iteration	9	9	9	205

29. **(A)** The data structure is an array, not an `ArrayList`, so you cannot use the `add` method for inserting elements into the list. This eliminates choices B and D. The expression to return a random integer from 0 to k-1 inclusive is

```
(int) (Math.random() * k)
```

Thus, to get integers from 0 to 100 requires k to be 101, which eliminates choice C. Choice E fails because it gets integers from 1 to 100.

30. **(A)** Suppose `str1` is strawberry and `str2` is cat. Then `insert(str1, str2, 5)` will return the following pieces, concatenated:

```
straw + cat + berry
```

Recall that `s.substring(k, m)` (a method of `String`) returns a substring of `s` starting at position k and ending at position m-1. String `str1` must be split into two parts, `first` and `last`. Then `str2` will be inserted between them. Since `str2` is inserted starting at position 5 (the "b"), `first` = straw, namely `str1.substring(0,pos)`. (Start at 0 and take all the characters up to and including location pos-1, namely 4.) Notice that `last`, the second substring of `str1`, must start at the index for "b", which is pos, the index at which `str2` was inserted. The expression `str1.substring(pos)` returns the substring of `str1` that starts at pos and continues to the end of the string, which was required. Note that you don't need any "special case" tests. In the cases where `str2` is inserted at the front of `str1` (i.e., `pos` is 0) or the back of `str1` (i.e., `pos` is `str1.length()`), the code for the general case works.

31. **(A)** Method `changeMatrix` examines each element and changes it to its absolute value if its row number equals its column number. The only two elements that satisfy the condition `r == c` are `mat[0][0]` and `mat[1][1]`. Thus, `-1` is changed to `1` and `-4` is changed to `4`, resulting in the matrix in choice A.

32. **(C)** Composition is the *has-a* relationship. A `PlayerGroup` *has-a* `Player` (several of them, in fact). Inheritance, (choice D) is the *is-a* relationship, which doesn't apply here. None of the choices A, B, or E apply in this example: An interface is a single class composed of only abstract methods (see p. 144); encapsulation is the bundling together of data fields and operations into a single unit, a class (see p. 93); and `PlayerGroup` and `Player` are clearly dependent on each other since `PlayerGroup` contains several `Player` objects (see p. 212).

33. **(E)** All of these data structures are reasonable. They all represent 20 bingo numbers in a convenient way and provide easy mechanisms for crossing off numbers and recognizing a winning card. Notice that data structure II provides a very quick way of searching for a number on the card. For example, if 48 is called, `bingoCard[48]` is inspected. If it is `true`, then it was one of the 20 original numbers on the card and gets crossed out. If `false`, 48 was not on that player's card. Data structures I and II require a linear search to find any given number that is called. (Note: There is no assumption that the array is sorted, which would allow a more efficient binary search.)

34. **(D)** A `NullPointerException` is thrown whenever an attempt is made to invoke a method with an object that hasn't been created with `new`. Choice A doesn't make sense: To test the `Caller` constructor requires a statement of the form

```
Caller c = new Caller();
```

Choice B is wrong: A missing `return` statement in a method triggers a compile-time error. Choice C doesn't make sense: In the declaration of `numbers`, its default initialization is to `null`. Choice E is bizarre. Hopefully you eliminated it immediately!

35. **(E)** For each element in `a`, `found` is switched to `true` if that element is found anywhere in `b`. Notice that for any element in `a`, if it is not found in `b`, the method returns `false`. Thus, to return `true`, every element in `a` must also be in `b`. Notice that this doesn't necessarily mean that `a` and `b` are permutations of each other. For example, consider the counterexample of `a=[1,1,2,3]` and `b=[1,2,2,3]`. Also, not every element in `b` needs to be in `a`. For example, if `a=[3,3,5]` and `b=[3,5,6]`, the method will return `true`.

36. **(C)** In the example given, `height = 3`, `height/2 = 1`, and `numCols = 3`. Notice that in each pass through the loop, `row` has value 0, while `col` goes from 0 through 2. So here are the assignments:

```
mat[2][0] = mat[0][0]
mat[2][1] = mat[0][1]
mat[2][2] = mat[0][2]
```

From this you should see that row 2 is being replaced by row 0.

37. **(B)** Eliminate choices D and E immediately, since assignment of new values in an `ArrayList` is done with the `set` method, not `get`. Eliminate choice C since you do not know that the `TileBag` class has a swap method. Choice A fails because it replaces the element at position `size` before storing it. Choice B works because the element at position `index` has been saved in `temp`.

38. **(A)** The `size` variable stores the number of unused tiles, which are in the `tiles` list from position `0` to position `size`. A random `int` is selected in this range, giving the index of the `Tile` that will be swapped to the end of the unused part of the `tiles` list. Note that the length of the `tiles` `ArrayList` stays constant. Each execution of `getNewTile` decreases the "unused tiles" part of the list and increases the "already used" part at the end of the list. In this way, both used and unused tiles are stored.

39. **(E)** When `pigeon.act()` is called, the `act` method of `Dove` is called. (This is an example of polymorphism.) The `act` method of `Dove` starts with `super.act()` which goes to the `act` method of `Bird`, the superclass. This prints `fly`, then calls `makeNoise()`. Using polymorphism, the `makeNoise` method in `Dove` is called, which starts with `super.makeNoise()`, which prints `chirp`. Completing the `makeNoise` method in `Dove` prints `coo`. Thus, so far we've printed `fly chirp coo`. But we haven't completed `Dove`'s `act` method, which ends with printing out `waddle`! The rule of thumb is: When `super` is used, find the method in the superclass. But if that method calls a method that's been overridden in the subclass, go back there for the overridden method. You also mustn't forget to check that you've executed any pending lines of code in that superclass method!

40. **(D)** In Implementation 1, the first element assigned is `prod[1]`, and it multiplies `arr[1]` by `prod[0]`, which was initialized to 1. To fix this implementation, you need a statement preceding the loop, which correctly assigns `prod[0]`: `prod[0]=arr[0];`

Section II

1. (a)
```java
public static void reverseArray(int[] arr)
{
    int mid = arr.length/2;
    for (int i = 0; i < mid; i++)
    {
        int temp = arr[i];
        arr[i] = arr[arr.length - i - 1];
        arr[arr.length - i - 1] = temp;
    }
}
```

(b)
```java
public void reverseAllRows()
{
    for (int[] row: mat)
        ArrayUtil.reverseArray (row);
}
```

(c)
```java
public void reverseMatrix()
{
    reverseAllRows();
    int mid = mat.length/2;
    for (int i = 0; i < mid; i++)
    {
        for (int col = 0; col < mat[0].length; col++)
        {
            int temp = mat[i][col];
            mat[i][col] = mat[mat.length - i - 1][col];
            mat[mat.length - i - 1][col] = temp;
        }
    }
}
```

Alternative solution:

```java
public void reverseMatrix()
{
    reverseAllRows();
    int mid = mat.length/2;
    for (int i = 0; i < mid; i++)
    {
        int[] temp = mat[i];
        mat[i] = mat[mat.length - i - 1];
        mat[mat.length - i - 1] = temp;
    }
}
```

NOTE

- Parts (a) and the alternative solution in part (c) use the same algorithm, swapping the first and last elements, then the second and second last, etc., moving toward the middle. If there is an odd number of elements, the middle element does not move. In part (a) the elements are integers. In part (c) they are rows in the matrix.
- In the first solution of part (c), start by reversing all rows. Then for each column, swap the elements in the first and last rows, then the second and second last, and so on, moving toward the middle.
- The alternative solution in part (c) is more elegant. It is not, however, part of the AP subset to replace one row of a matrix with a different array.

2. (a)
```java
public List<Integer> getBlankPositions()
{
    List<Integer> posList = new ArrayList<Integer>();
    for (int i = 0; i < sentence.length(); i++)
    {
        if (sentence.substring(i, i + 1).equals(" "))
            posList.add(i);
    }
    return posList;
}
```

Alternatively (an inferior, unnecessarily complicated solution!),

```java
public List<Integer> getBlankPositions()
{
    List<Integer> posList = new ArrayList<Integer>();
    String s = sentence;
    int diff = 0;
    int index = s.indexOf(" ");
    while (index >= 0)
    {
        posList.add(index + diff);
        diff = sentence.length() - (s.substring(index + 1)).length();
        s = s.substring(index + 1);
        index = s.indexOf(" ");
    }
    return posList;
}
```

(b)
```java
public int countWords()
{
    return getBlankPositions().size() + 1;
}
```

(c)
```java
public String[] getWords()
{
    List<Integer> posList = getBlankPositions();
    int numWords = countWords();
    String[] wordArr = new String[numWords];
    for (int i = 0; i < numWords; i++)
    {
        if (i == 0)
        {
            if (posList.size() != 0)
                wordArr[i] = sentence.substring(0, posList.get(0));
            else
                wordArr[i] = sentence;
        }
        else if (i == posList.size())
            wordArr[i] = sentence.substring(posList.get(i - 1));
        else
            wordArr[i] = sentence.substring(posList.get(i - 1),
                    posList.get(i));
    }
    return wordArr;
}
```

NOTE

- In part (a), it would also work to have the test

```
i < sentence.length() - 1;
```

in the `for` loop. But you don't need the -1 because the last character is a punctuation mark, not a blank.
- In the alternative part (a), you can't just store the positions of `index` as you loop over the sentence. Finding `s.indexOf(" ")` will give a value that is too small, because you are successively taking shorter substrings of `s`. The local variable, `diff`, represents the difference between the length of the original sentence and the length of the current substring. This is what must be added to the current value of `index`, so that you get the position of the blank in the original sentence.
- Part (b) takes advantage of the precondition that there is one and only one blank between words. This means that the number of words will always be the number of blanks plus one.
- In part (c), you have to be careful when you get the first word. If there's only one word in the sentence, there are no blanks, which means `posList` is empty, and you can't use `posList.get(0)` (because that will throw an `IndexOutOfBoundsException`!).
- Also in part (c), the second test deals with getting the last word in the sentence. You have to distinguish between the cases of more than one word in the sentence and exactly one word in the sentence.

3. (a)
```java
public Player requestSlot(String playerName)
{
    for (int i = 0; i < slots.length; i++)
    {
        if (slots[i] == null)
        {
            Player p = new Player(playerName, i);
            slots[i] = p;
            return p;
        }
    }
    waitingList.add(playerName);
    return null;
}
```

(b)
```java
public Player cancelAndReassignSlot(Player p)
{
    int i = p.getPlayerNumber();
    if (waitingList.size() != 0)
    {
        slots[i] = new Player(waitingList.get(0), i);
        waitingList.remove(0);
    }
    else
    {
        slots[i] = null;
    }
    return slots[i];
}
```

NOTE

- In part (a), the last two lines of the method will be executed only if you are still in the method, namely no available slot was found.
- In part (b), the final line will return either a new player, or null if the waiting list was empty.

4. (a)
```
public void reset()
{
    if(arm.isFacingRight())
        arm.changeDirection();
    arm.moveForward(arm.getCurrentIndex());
    arm.changeDirection();
}
```

(b)
```
public int mostAcidic()
{
    reset();
    int minPH = Integer.MAX_VALUE, minIndex = 0;
    int index = 0;
    while (index < solutions.size())
    {
        Solution s = solutions.get(index);
        if (s.getPH() < minPH)
        {
            minPH = s.getPH();
            minIndex = index;
        }
        index++;
    }
    if (minPH >= 7)
        return -1;
    else
    {
        arm.moveForward(minIndex);
        return minIndex;
    }
}
```

NOTE

- In part (b), a for-each loop won't work, because you need to save an index.
- In part (b), notice that resetting the mechanical arm causes the arm to face right.
- In part (b), you could initialize minPH to any integer greater than or equal to 7 for this algorithm to work. You just must be careful not to set it to an "acidic" number, namely 1 to 6.

Introductory Java Language Features

Fifty loops shalt thou make ...
—Exodus 26:5

Chapter Goals

- Packages and classes
- Types and identifiers
- Operators
- Input/output

- Storage of numbers
- Binary and hexadecimal numbers
- Control structures
- Errors and exceptions

The AP Computer Science course includes algorithm analysis, data structures, and the techniques and methods of modern programming, specifically, object-oriented programming. A high-level programming language is used to explore these concepts. Java is the language currently in use on the AP exam.

Java was developed by James Gosling and a team at Sun Microsystems in California; it continues to evolve. The AP exam covers a clearly defined subset of Java language features that are presented throughout this book. The College Board website, *http://www.collegeboard.com/student/testing/ap/subjects.html*, contains a complete listing of this subset.

Java provides basic control structures such as the `if-else` statement, `for` loop, for-each loop, and `while` loop, as well as fundamental built-in data types. But the power of the language lies in the manipulation of user-defined types called objects, many of which can interact in a single program.

PACKAGES AND CLASSES

A typical Java program has user-defined classes whose objects interact with those from Java class libraries. In Java, related classes are grouped into *packages*, many of which are provided with the compiler. You can put your own classes into a package—this facilitates their use in other programs.

The package `java.lang`, which contains many commonly used classes, is automatically provided to all Java programs. To use any other package in a program, an `import` statement must be used. To import all of the classes in a package called `packagename`, use the form

```
import packagename.*;
```

To import a single class called `ClassName` from the package, use

```
import packagename.ClassName;
```

Java has a hierarchy of packages and subpackages. Subpackages are selected using multiple dots:

```
import packagename.subpackagename.ClassName;
```

The `import` statement allows the programmer to use the objects and methods defined in the designated package. By convention Java package names are lowercase. The AP exam does not require knowledge of packages. You will not be expected to write any `import` statements.

A Java program must have at least one class, the one that contains the *main method*. The java files that comprise your program are called *source files*.

A *compiler* converts source code into machine-readable form called *bytecode*.

Here is a typical source file for a Java program.

```
/** Program FirstProg.java
    Start with a comment, giving the program name and a brief
    description of what the program does.
 */
import package1.*;
import package2.subpackage.ClassName;

public class FirstProg  //note that the file name is FirstProg.java
{
    public static type1 method1(parameter list)
    {
        < code for method 1 >
    }
    public static type2 method2(parameter list)
    {
        < code for method 2 >
    }
        ...

    public static void main(String[] args)
    {
        < your code >
    }
}
```

NOTE

1. All Java methods must be contained in a class, and all program statements must be placed inside a method.

2. Typically, the class that contains the main method does not contain many additional methods.

3. The words class, public, static, void, and main are *reserved words*, also called *keywords*.

4. The keyword public signals that the class or method is usable outside of the class, whereas private data members or methods (see Chapter 2) are not.

5. The keyword static is used for methods that will not access any objects of a class, such as the methods in the FirstProg class in the example on the previous page. This is typically true for all methods in a source file that contains no *instance variables* (see Chapter 2). Most methods in Java do operate on objects and are not static. The main method, however, must always be static.

6. The program shown on the previous page is a Java *application*. This is not to be confused with a Java *applet*, a program that runs inside a web browser or applet viewer. Applets are not part of the AP subset.

Javadoc Comments

The Javadoc comments @param, @return, and @throws are part of the AP Java subset. Here is an example.

```
/** Puts obj at location loc in this grid, and returns
 *  the object previously at this location.
 *  Returns null if loc was previously unoccupied.
 *  Precondition: obj is not null, and loc is valid in this grid.
 *  @param loc the location where the object will be placed
 *  @param obj the object to be placed
 *  @return the object previously at the specified location
 *  @throws NullPointerException if the object is null
 */
public E put(Location loc, E obj)
```

This will produce the following Javadoc output:

---

put

public E **put** (Location loc, E obj)

Puts obj at location loc in this grid, and returns
the object previously at this location.
Returns null if loc was previously unoccupied.
Precondition: obj is not null, and loc is valid in this grid.

Parameters:
loc - the location where the object will be placed
obj - the object to be placed

Returns:
the object previously at the specified location

Throws:
NullPointerException - if the object is null

TYPES AND IDENTIFIERS

Identifiers

An *identifier* is a name for a variable, parameter, constant, user-defined method, or user-defined class. In Java an identifier is any sequence of letters, digits, and the underscore character. Identifiers may not begin with a digit. Identifiers are case-sensitive, which means that age and Age are different. Wherever possible identifiers should be concise and self-documenting. A variable called area is more illuminating than one called a.

By convention identifiers for variables and methods are lowercase. Uppercase letters are used to separate these into multiple words, for example getName, findSurfaceArea, preTaxTotal, and so on. Note that a class name starts with a capital letter. Reserved words are entirely lowercase and may not be used as identifiers.

Built-in Types

Every identifier in a Java program has a type associated with it. The *primitive* or *built-in* types that are included in the AP Java subset are

int	An integer. For example, 2, -26, 3000
boolean	A boolean. Just two values, true or false
double	A double precision floating-point number. For example, 2.718, -367189.41, 1.6e4

(Note that primitive type char is not included in the AP Java subset.)

Integer values are stored exactly. Because there's a fixed amount of memory set aside for their storage, however, integers are bounded. If you try to store a value whose magnitude is too big in an int variable, you'll get an *overflow error*. (Java gives you no warning. You just get a wrong result!)

An identifier, for example a *variable*, is introduced into a Java program with a *declaration* that specifies its type. A variable is often initialized in its declaration. Some examples follow:

```
int x;
double y,z;
boolean found;
int count = 1;            //count initialized to 1
double p = 2.3, q = 4.1;  //p and q initialized to 2.3 and 4.1
```

One type can be cast to another compatible type if appropriate. For example,

```
int total, n;
double average;
   ...
average = (double) total/n;   //total cast to double to ensure
                              //real division is used
```

Alternatively,

```
average = total/(double) n;
```

Assigning an int to a double automatically casts the int to double. For example,

```
int num = 5;
double realNum = num;     //num is cast to double
```

Assigning a `double` to an `int` without a cast, however, causes a compile-time error. For example,

```
double x = 6.79;
int intNum = x;       //Error. Need an explicit cast to int
```

Note that casting a floating-point (real) number to an integer simply truncates the number. For example,

```
double cost = 10.95;
int numDollars = (int) cost;    //sets numDollars to 10
```

If your intent was to round `cost` to the nearest dollar, you needed to write

```
int numDollars = (int) (cost + 0.5);  //numDollars has value 11
```

To round a negative number to the nearest integer:

```
double negAmount = -4.8;
int roundNeg = (int) (negAmount - 0.5);   //roundNeg has value -5
```

The strategy of adding or subtracting 0.5 before casting correctly rounds in all cases.

Storage of Numbers

INTEGERS

Integer values in Java are stored exactly, as a string of bits (binary digits). One of the bits stores the sign of the integer, 0 for positive, 1 for negative.

The Java built-in integral type, `byte`, uses one byte (eight bits) of storage.

0	1	1	1	1	1	1	1

The picture represents the largest positive integer that can be stored using type `byte`: $2^7 - 1$.

Type `int` in Java uses four bytes (32 bits). Taking one bit for a sign, the largest possible integer stored is $2^{31} - 1$. In general, an n-bit integer uses $n/8$ bytes of storage, and stores integers from -2^{n-1} to $2^{n-1} - 1$. (Note that the extra value on the negative side comes from not having to store -0.) There are two Java constants that you should know. `Integer.MAX_VALUE` holds the maximum value an `int` can hold, $2^{31} - 1$. `Integer.MIN_VALUE` holds the minimum value an `int` can hold, -2^{31}.

Built-in types in Java are `byte` (one byte), `short` (two bytes), `int` (four bytes), and `long` (eight bytes). Of these, only `int` is in the AP Java subset.

FLOATING-POINT NUMBERS

There are two built-in types in Java that store real numbers: `float`, which uses four bytes, and `double`, which uses eight bytes. A *floating-point number* is stored in two parts: a *mantissa*, which specifies the digits of the number, and an exponent. The JVM (Java Virtual Machine) represents the number using scientific notation:

$$\text{sign} * \text{mantissa} * 2^{\text{exponent}}$$

In this expression, 2 is the *base* or *radix* of the number. In type `double` eleven bits are allocated for the exponent, and (typically) 52 bits for the mantissa. One bit is allocated for the sign. This is a *double-precision* number. Type `float`, which is *single-precision*, is not in the AP Java subset.

When floating-point numbers are converted to binary, most cannot be represented exactly, leading to *round-off error*. These errors are compounded by arithmetic operations. For example,

$$0.1*26 \neq 0.1+0.1+\cdots+0.1 \quad \text{(26 terms)}$$

In Java, no exceptions are thrown for floating-point operations. There are two situations you should be aware of:

- When an operation is performed that gives an undefined result, Java expresses this result as `NaN`, "not a number." Examples of operations that produce `NaN` are: taking the square root of a negative number, and 0.0 divided by 0.0.

- An operation that gives an infinitely large or infinitely small number, like division by zero, produces a result of `Infinity` or `-Infinity` in Java.

Hexadecimal and Octal Numbers

A *hexadecimal number* or *hex number* uses base (radix) 16 and is represented with the symbols 0 – 9 and A – F (occasionally a – f), where A represents 10, and F represents 15. To denote a hex number in Java, the prefix "0x" or "0X" is used, for example, `0xC2A`. On the AP exam, the representation is likely to be with the subscript hex: $C2A_{hex}$. In expanded form, this number means

$$(C)(16^2) + (2)(16^1) + (A)(16^0)$$
$$= (12)(16^2) + (2)(16) + (10)(1)$$
$$= 3114, \text{ or } 3114_{dec}$$

The advantages of hex numbers are their compactness, and the ease of conversion between hex and binary. Notice that any hex digit expands to four bits. For example,

$$5_{hex} = 0101_{bin} \quad \text{and} \quad F_{hex} = 1111_{bin}$$

Thus, $5F_{hex} = 01011111_{bin}$, which is 1011111_{bin}.

Similarly, to convert a binary number to hex, convert in groups of four from right to left. If necessary, pad with zeroes to complete the last group of four. For example,

$$1011101_{bin} = 0101 \quad 1101_{bin}$$
$$= 5 \quad D_{hex}$$
$$= 5D_{hex}$$

An *octal number* uses base 8, and is represented with the symbols 0 – 7. On the AP exam, the representation is likely to be with the subscript oct: 132_{oct}. In expanded form, 132_{oct} means

$$(1)(8^2) + (3)(8^1) + (2)(8^0)$$
$$= (1)(64) + (3)(8) + (2)(1)$$
$$= 64 + 24 + 2$$
$$= 90, \text{ or } 90_{dec}$$

Final Variables

A *final variable* or *user-defined constant*, identified by the keyword `final`, is used to name a quantity whose value will not change. Here are some examples of `final` declarations:

```
final double TAX_RATE = 0.08;
final int CLASS_SIZE = 35;
```

NOTE

1. Constant identifiers are, by convention, capitalized.
2. A `final` variable can be declared without initializing it immediately. For example,

   ```
   final double TAX_RATE;
   if ( < some condition > )
       TAX_RATE = 0.08;
   else
       TAX_RATE = 0.0;
   // TAX_RATE can be given a value just once: its value is final!
   ```

3. A common use for a constant is as an array bound. For example,

   ```
   final int MAXSTUDENTS = 25;
   int[] classList = new int[MAXSTUDENTS];
   ```

4. Using constants makes it easier to revise code. Just a single change in the `final` declaration need be made, rather than having to change every occurrence of a value.

OPERATORS

Arithmetic Operators

Operator	Meaning	Example
+	addition	3 + x
−	subtraction	p − q
*	multiplication	6 * i
/	division	10 / 4 //returns 2, not 2.5!
%	mod (remainder)	11 % 8 //returns 3

NOTE

1. These operators can be applied to types `int` and `double`, even if both types occur in the same expression. For an operation involving a `double` and an `int`, the `int` is promoted to `double`, and the result is a `double`.
2. The mod operator `%`, as in the expression `a % b`, gives the remainder when `a` is divided by `b`. Thus `10 % 3` evaluates to 1, whereas `4.2 % 2.0` evaluates to `0.2`.
3. Integer division `a/b` where both `a` and `b` are of type `int` returns the integer quotient only (i.e., the answer is truncated). Thus, 22/6 gives 3, and 3/4 gives 0. If at least one of the operands is of type `double`, then the operation becomes

regular floating-point division, and there is no truncation. You can control the kind of division that is carried out by explicitly casting (one or both of) the operands from `int` to `double` and vice versa. Thus

```
3.0 / 4          →    0.75
3 / 4.0          →    0.75
(int) 3.0 / 4    →    0
(double) 3 / 4   →    0.75
```

You must, however, be careful:

```
(double) (3 / 4)   →    0.0
```

since the integer division 3/4 is computed first, before casting to `double`.

4. The arithmetic operators follow the normal precedence rules (order of operations):

   (1) parentheses, from the inner ones out (highest precedence)
   (2) `*`, `/`, `%`
   (3) `+`, `-` (lowest precedence)

Here operators on the same line have the same precedence, and, in the absence of parentheses, are invoked from left to right. Thus, the expression `19 % 5 * 3 + 14 / 5` evaluates to `4 * 3 + 2 = 14`. Note that casting has precedence over all of these operators. Thus, in the expression `(double) 3/4`, 3 will be cast to `double` before the division is done.

Relational Operators

Operator	Meaning	Example
`==`	equal to	`if (x == 100)`
`!=`	not equal to	`if (age != 21)`
`>`	greater than	`if (salary > 30000)`
`<`	less than	`if (grade < 65)`
`>=`	greater than or equal to	`if (age >= 16)`
`<=`	less than or equal to	`if (height <= 6)`

NOTE

1. Relational operators are used in *boolean expressions* that evaluate to `true` or `false`.

```
boolean x = (a != b);      //initializes x to true if a != b,
                           // false otherwise
return p == q;   //returns true if p equals q, false otherwise
```

2. If the operands are an `int` and a `double`, the `int` is promoted to a `double` as for arithmetic operators.
3. Relational operators should generally be used only in the comparison of primitive types (i.e., `int`, `double`, or `boolean`). User-defined types are compared using the `equals` and `compareTo` methods (see pp. 145 and 176).
4. Be careful when comparing floating-point values! Since floating-point numbers cannot always be represented exactly in the computer memory, they should not be compared directly using relational operators.

> Do not routinely use `==` to test for equality of floating-point numbers.

Optional topic

Comparing Floating-Point Numbers

Because of round-off errors in floating-point numbers, you can't rely on using the `==` or `!=` operators to compare two `double` values for equality. They may differ in their last significant digit or two because of round-off error. Instead, you should test that the magnitude of the difference between the numbers is less than some number about the size of the machine precision. The machine precision is usually denoted ϵ and is typically about 10^{-16} for double precision (i.e., about 16 decimal digits). So you would like to test something like $|x - y| \leq \epsilon$. But this is no good if x and y are very large. For example, suppose $x = 1234567890.123456$ and $y = 1234567890.123457$. These numbers are essentially equal to machine precision, since they differ only in the 16th significant digit. But $|x - y| = 10^{-6}$, not 10^{-16}. So in general you should check the *relative* difference:

$$\frac{|x - y|}{\max(|x|, |y|)} \leq \epsilon$$

To avoid problems with dividing by zero, code this as

$$|x - y| \leq \epsilon \max(|x|, |y|)$$

An example of code that uses a correct comparison of real numbers can be found in the `Shape` class on p. 146.

Logical Operators

Operator	Meaning	Example
!	NOT	`if (!found)`
&&	AND	`if (x < 3 && y > 4)`
||	OR	`if (age < 2 || height < 4)`

NOTE

1. Logical operators are applied to boolean expressions to form *compound boolean expressions* that evaluate to `true` or `false`.
2. Values of `true` or `false` are assigned according to the truth tables for the logical operators.

&&	T	F		||	T	F		!	
T	T	F		T	T	T		T	F
F	F	F		F	T	F		F	T

For example, F && T evaluates to F, while T || F evaluates to T.

3. *Short-circuit evaluation.* The subexpressions in a compound boolean expression are evaluated from left to right, and evaluation automatically stops as

soon as the value of the entire expression is known. For example, consider a boolean OR expression of the form A || B, where A and B are some boolean expressions. If A is true, then the expression is true irrespective of the value of B. Similarly, if A is false, then A && B evaluates to false irrespective of the second operand. So in each case the second operand is not evaluated. For example,

```
if (numScores != 0 && scoreTotal/numScores > 90)
```

will not cause a run-time ArithmeticException (division-by-zero error) if the value of numScores is 0. This is because numScores != 0 will evaluate to false, causing the entire boolean expression to evaluate to false without having to evaluate the second expression containing the division.

Assignment Operators

Operator	Example	Meaning
=	x = 2	simple assignment
+=	x += 4	x = x + 4
-=	y -= 6	y = y - 6
*=	p *= 5	p = p * 5
/=	n /= 10	n = n / 10
%=	n %= 10	n = n % 10

NOTE

1. All these operators, with the exception of simple assignment, are called *compound assignment operators*.
2. *Chaining* of assignment statements is allowed, with evaluation from right to left.

```
int next, prev, sum;
next = prev = sum = 0;   //initializes sum to 0, then prev to 0
                         //then next to 0
```

Increment and Decrement Operators

Operator	Example	Meaning
++	i++ or ++i	i is incremented by 1
--	k-- or --k	k is decremented by 1

Note that i++ (postfix) and ++i (prefix) both have the net effect of incrementing i by 1, but they are not equivalent. For example, if i currently has the value 5, then System.out.println(i++) will print 5 and then increment i to 6, whereas System.out.println(++i) will first increment i to 6 and then print 6. It's easy to remember: if the ++ is first, you first increment. A similar distinction occurs between k-- and --k. (Note: You do not need to know these distinctions for the AP exam.)

Operator Precedence

highest precedence	→	(1)	`!, ++, --`
		(2)	`*, /, %`
		(3)	`+, -`
		(4)	`<, >, <=, >=`
		(5)	`==, !=`
		(6)	`&&`
		(7)	`||`
lowest precedence	→	(8)	`=, +=, -=, *=, /=, %=`

Here operators on the same line have equal precedence. The evaluation of the operators with equal precedence is from left to right, except for rows (1) and (8) where the order is right to left. It is easy to remember: The only "backward" order is for the unary operators (row 1) and for the various assignment operators (row 8).

Example

What will be output by the following statement?

```
System.out.println(5 + 3 < 6 - 1);
```

Since + and - have precedence over <, 5 + 3 and 6 - 1 will be evaluated before evaluating the boolean expression. Since the value of the expression is false, the statement will output `false`.

INPUT/OUTPUT

Input

Since there are so many ways to provide input to a program, user input is not a part of the AP Java subset. If reading input is a necessary part of a question on the AP exam, it will be indicated something like this:

```
double x = call to a method that reads a floating-point number
```

or

```
double x = IO.readDouble();    //read user input
```

NOTE

The `Scanner` class (since Java 5.0) simplifies both console and file input. It will not, however, be tested on the AP exam.

Output

Testing of output will be restricted to `System.out.print` and `System.out.println`. Formatted output will not be tested.

`System.out` is an object in the `System` class that allows output to be displayed on the screen. The `println` method outputs an item and then goes to a new line. The `print` method outputs an item without going to a new line afterward. An item to be printed can be a string, or a number, or the value of a boolean expression (`true` or `false`). Here are some examples:

```
System.out.print("Hot");
System.out.println("dog");        } prints  Hotdog

System.out.println("Hot");        }           Hot
System.out.println("dog");        } prints    dog

System.out.println(7 + 3);        }  prints  10

System.out.println(7 == 2 + 5);   }  prints  true

int x = 27;
System.out.println(x);            }  prints  27
System.out.println("Value of x is " + x);
                                     prints  Value of x is 27
```

In the last example, the value of x, 27, is converted to the string "27", which is then concatenated to the string "Value of x is ".

To print the "values" of user-defined objects, the toString() method is invoked (see p. 175).

Escape Sequences

An *escape sequence* is a backslash followed by a single character. It is used to print special characters. The three escape sequences that you should know for the AP exam are

Escape Sequence	Meaning
\n	newline
\"	double quote
\\	backslash

Here are some examples:

```
System.out.println("Welcome to\na new line");
```

prints

```
Welcome to
a new line
```

The statement

```
System.out.println("He is known as \"Hothead Harry\".");
```

prints

```
He is known as "Hothead Harry".
```

The statement

```
System.out.println("The file path is d:\\myFiles\\..");
```

prints

```
The file path is d:\myFiles\..
```

CONTROL STRUCTURES

Control structures are the mechanism by which you make the statements of a program run in a nonsequential order. There are two general types: decision making and iteration.

Decision-Making Control Structures

These include the `if`, `if...else`, and `switch` statements. They are all selection control structures that introduce a decision-making ability into a program. Based on the truth value of a boolean expression, the computer will decide which path to follow. The `switch` statement is not part of the AP Java subset.

THE `if` STATEMENT

```
if (boolean expression)
{
    statements
}
```

Here the *statements* will be executed only if the *boolean expression* is true. If it is `false`, control passes immediately to the first statement following the `if` statement.

THE `if...else` STATEMENT

```
if (boolean expression)
{
    statements
}
else
{
    statements
}
```

Here, if the *boolean expression* is `true`, only the *statements* immediately following the test will be executed. If the *boolean expression* is `false`, only the *statements* following the `else` will be executed.

NESTED `if` STATEMENT

If the statement part of an `if` statement is itself an `if` statement, the result is a *nested* `if` *statement*.

Example 1

```
if (boolean expr1)
    if (boolean expr2)
        statement;
```

This is equivalent to

```
if (boolean expr1 && boolean expr2)
    statement;
```

Example 2

Beware the dangling `else`! Suppose you want to read in an integer and print it if it's positive and even. Will the following code do the job?

```java
int n = IO.readInt();          //read user input
if (n > 0)
    if (n % 2 == 0)
        System.out.println(n);
else
    System.out.println(n + " is not positive");
```

A user enters 7 and is surprised to see the output

```
7 is not positive
```

The reason is that `else` always gets matched with the *nearest* unpaired `if`, not the first `if` as the indenting would suggest.

There are two ways to fix the preceding code. The first is to use {} delimiters to group the statements correctly.

```java
int n = IO.readInt();          //read user input
if (n > 0)
{
    if (n % 2 == 0)
        System.out.println(n);
}
else
    System.out.println(n + " is not positive");
```

The second way of fixing the code is to rearrange the statements.

```java
int n = IO.readInt();          //read user input
if (n <= 0)
    System.out.println(n + " is not positive");
else
    if (n % 2 == 0)
        System.out.println(n);
```

EXTENDED `if` STATEMENT

For example,

```java
String grade = IO.readString();          //read user input
if (grade.equals("A"))
    System.out.println("Excellent!");
else if (grade.equals("B"))
    System.out.println("Good");
else if (grade.equals("C") || grade.equals("D"))
    System.out.println("Poor");
else if (grade.equals("F"))
    System.out.println("Egregious!");
else
    System.out.println("Invalid grade");
```

If any of A, B, C, D, or F are entered, an appropriate message will be written, and control will go to the statement immediately following the extended `if` statement. If any other string is entered, the final `else` is invoked, and the message `Invalid grade` will be written.

Iteration

Java has three different control structures that allow the computer to perform iterative tasks: the for loop, while loop, and do...while loop. The do...while loop is not in the AP Java subset.

THE for LOOP

The general form of the for loop is

```
for (initialization; termination condition; update statement)
{
    statements          //body of loop
}
```

The termination condition is tested at the top of the loop; the update statement is performed at the bottom.

Example 1

```
//outputs 1 2 3 4
for (i = 1; i < 5; i++)
    System.out.print(i + " ");
```

Here's how it works. The *loop variable* i is initialized to 1, and the termination condition i < 5 is evaluated. If it is true, the body of the loop is executed, and then the loop variable i is incremented according to the update statement. As soon as the termination condition is false (i.e., i >= 5), control passes to the first statement following the loop.

Example 2

```
//outputs 20 19 18 17 16 15
for (k = 20; k >= 15; k--)
    System.out.print(k + " ");
```

Example 3

```
//outputs 2 4 6 8 10
for (j = 2; j <= 10; j += 2)
    System.out.print(j + " ");
```

NOTE

1. The loop variable should not have its value changed inside the loop body.
2. The initializing and update statements can use any valid constants, variables, or expressions.
3. The scope (see p. 100) of the loop variable can be restricted to the loop body by combining the loop variable declaration with the initialization. For example,

```
for (int i = 0; i < 3; i++)
{
    ...
}
```

4. The following loop is syntactically valid:

```
for (int i = 1; i <= 0; i++)
{
    ...
}
```

The loop body will not be executed at all, since the exiting condition is true before the first execution.

THE FOR-EACH LOOP

This is used to iterate over an array or collection. The general form of the loop is

```
for (SomeType element : collection)
{
    statements
}
```

(Read the top line as "For each `element` of type `SomeType` in `collection`...")

Example

```
//Outputs all elements of arr, one per line.
for (int element : arr)
    System.out.println(element);
```

NOTE

1. The for-each loop cannot be used for replacing or removing elements as you traverse.
2. The loop hides the index variable that is used with arrays.

THE while LOOP

The general form of the while loop is

```
while (boolean test)
{
    statements          //loop body
}
```

The *boolean test* is performed at the beginning of the loop. If `true`, the loop body is executed. Otherwise, control passes to the first statement following the loop. After execution of the loop body, the test is performed again. If `true`, the loop is executed again, and so on.

Example 1

```
int i = 1, mult3 = 3;
while (mult3 < 20)
{
    System.out.print(mult3 + " ");
    i++;
    mult3 *= i;
}                   //outputs 3 6 18
```

NOTE

1. It is possible for the body of a `while` loop never to be executed. This will happen if the test evaluates to `false` the first time.
2. Disaster will strike in the form of an infinite loop if the test can never be false. Don't forget to change the loop variable in the body of the loop in a way that leads to termination!

> The body of a `while` loop must contain a statement that leads to termination.

Example 2

```
int power2 = 1;
while (power2 != 20)
{
    System.out.println(power2);
    power2 *= 2;
}
```

Since power2 will never exactly equal 20, the loop will grind merrily along eventually causing an integer overflow.

Example 3

```
/* Screen out bad data.
 * The loop won't allow execution to continue until a valid
 * integer is entered.
 */
System.out.println("Enter a positive integer from 1 to 100");
int num = IO.readInt();        //read user input
while (num < 1 || num > 100)
{
    System.out.println("Number must be from 1 to 100.");
    System.out.println("Please reenter");
    num = IO.readInt();
}
```

Example 4

```
/* Uses a sentinel to terminate data entered at the keyboard.
 * The sentinel is a value that cannot be part of the data.
 * It signals the end of the list.
 */
final int SENTINEL = -999;
System.out.println("Enter list of positive integers," +
    " end list with " + SENTINEL);
int value = IO.readInt();      //read user input
while (value != SENTINEL)
{
    process the value
    value = IO.readInt();      //read another value
}
```

NESTED LOOPS

You create a *nested loop* when a loop is a statement in the body of another loop.

Example 1

```
for (int k = 1; k <= 3; k++)
{
    for (int i = 1; i <= 4; i++)
        System.out.print("*");
    System.out.println();
}
```

Think:

```
for each of 3 rows
{
        print 4 stars
        go to next line
}
```

Output:

```
****
****
****
```

Example 2

This example has two loops nested in an outer loop.

```
for (int i = 1; i <= 6; i++)
{
    for (int j = 1; j <= i; j++)
        System.out.print("+");
    for (int j = 1; j <= 6 - i; j++)
        System.out.print("*");
    System.out.println();
}
```

Output:

```
+*****
++****
+++***
++++**
+++++*
++++++
```

ERRORS AND EXCEPTIONS

An *exception* is an error condition that occurs during the execution of a Java program. For example, if you divide an integer by zero, an `ArithmeticException` will be thrown. If you use a negative array index, an `ArrayIndexOutOfBoundsException` will be thrown.

An *unchecked exception* is one where you don't provide code to deal with the error. Such exceptions are automatically handled by Java's standard exception-handling methods, which terminate execution. You now need to fix your code!

A *checked exception* is one where you provide code to handle the exception, either a try/catch/finally statement, or an explicit throw new ...Exception clause. These exceptions are not necessarily caused by an error in the code. For example, an unexpected end-of-file could be due to a broken network connection. Checked exceptions are not part of the AP Java subset.

The following exceptions are in the AP Java subset:

Exception	Discussed on page
ArithmeticException	on the previous page
NullPointerException	103
ClassCastException	142
ArrayIndexOutOfBoundsException	233
IndexOutOfBoundsException	244
IllegalArgumentException	this page

See also NoSuchElementException (pp. 247, 248) and IllegalStateException (pp. 247, 249), which refer to iterators, an optional topic.

Java allows you to write code that throws a standard unchecked exception. Here are typical examples:

Example 1

```
if (numScores == 0)
    throw new ArithmeticException("Cannot divide by zero");
else
    findAverageScore();
```

Example 2

```
public void setRadius(int newRadius)
{
    if (newRadius < 0)
        throw new IllegalArgumentException
                ("Radius cannot be negative");
    else
        radius = newRadius;
}
```

NOTE

1. throw and new are both reserved words.
2. The error message is optional: The line in Example 1 could have read

   ```
   throw new ArithmeticException();
   ```

   The message, however, is useful, since it tells the person running the program what went wrong.
3. An IllegalArgumentException is thrown to indicate that a parameter does not satisfy a method's precondition.

Chapter Summary

Be sure that you understand the difference between primitive and user-defined types and between the following types of operators: arithmetic, relational, logical, and assignment. Know which conditions lead to what types of errors.

You should be able to work with numbers—know how to compare them and how to convert between decimal, binary, and hexadecimal numbers. Know how integers and floating-point numbers are stored in memory, and be aware of the conditions that can lead to round-off error.

You should know the `Integer` constants `Integer.MIN_VALUE` and `Integer.MAX_VALUE`.

Be familiar with each of the following control structures: conditional statements, `for` loops, `while` loops, and for-each loops.

Be aware of the AP exam expectations concerning input and output.

MULTIPLE-CHOICE QUESTIONS ON INTRODUCTORY JAVA LANGUAGE CONCEPTS

1. Which of the following pairs of declarations will cause an error message?

```
  I  double x = 14.7;
     int y = x;

 II  double x = 14.7;
     int y = (int) x;

III  int x = 14;
     double y = x;
```

    (A) None
    (B) I only
    (C) II only
    (D) III only
    (E) I and III only

2. What output will be produced by

```
    System.out.print("\\* This is not\n a comment *\\");
```

    (A) * This is not a comment *

    (B) * This is not a comment *\

    (C) * This is not
        a comment *

    (D) * This is not
        a comment *\\

    (E) * This is not
        a comment *\

3. Consider the following code segment

```
    if (n != 0 && x / n > 100)
        statement1;
    else
        statement2;
```

    If n is of type int and has a value of 0 when the segment is executed, what will happen?
    (A) An ArithmeticException will be thrown.
    (B) A syntax error will occur.
    (C) *statement1*, but not *statement2*, will be executed.
    (D) *statement2*, but not *statement1*, will be executed.
    (E) Neither *statement1* nor *statement2* will be executed; control will pass to the first statement following the if statement.

4. Refer to the following code fragment:

```
double answer = 13 / 5;
System.out.println("13 / 5 = " + answer);
```

The output is

```
13 / 5 = 2.0
```

The programmer intends the output to be

```
13 / 5 = 2.6
```

Which of the following replacements for the first line of code will *not* fix the problem?
(A) `double answer = (double) 13 / 5;`
(B) `double answer = 13 / (double) 5;`
(C) `double answer = 13.0 / 5;`
(D) `double answer = 13 / 5.0;`
(E) `double answer = (double) (13 / 5);`

5. What value is stored in `result` if

```
int result = 13 - 3 * 6 / 4 % 3;
```

(A) −5
(B) 0
(C) 13
(D) −1
(E) 12

6. Suppose that addition and subtraction had higher precedence than multiplication and division. Then the expression

```
2 + 3 * 12 / 7 - 4 + 8
```

would evaluate to which of the following?
(A) 11
(B) 12
(C) 5
(D) 9
(E) −4

7. Which is true of the following boolean expression, given that x is a variable of type double?

```
3.0 == x * (3.0 / x)
```

(A) It will always evaluate to false.
(B) It may evaluate to false for some values of x.
(C) It will evaluate to false only when x is zero.
(D) It will evaluate to false only when x is very large or very close to zero.
(E) It will always evaluate to true.

8. Let x be a variable of type `double` that is positive. A program contains the boolean expression (`Math.pow(x,0.5) == Math.sqrt(x)`). Even though $x^{1/2}$ is mathematically equivalent to $\sqrt{x}$, the above expression returns the value `false` in a student's program. Which of the following is the most likely reason?

   (A) `Math.pow` returns an `int`, while `Math.sqrt` returns a `double`.
   (B) x was imprecisely calculated in a previous program statement.
   (C) The computer stores floating-point numbers with 32-bit words.
   (D) There is round-off error in calculating the `pow` and `sqrt` functions.
   (E) There is overflow error in calculating the `pow` function.

9. What will the output be for the following poorly formatted program segment, if the input value for `num` is 22?

```
int num =  call to a method that reads an integer;
if (num > 0)
if (num % 5 == 0)
System.out.println(num);
else System.out.println(num + " is negative");
```

   (A) 22
   (B) 4
   (C) 2 is negative
   (D) 22 is negative
   (E) Nothing will be output.

10. What values are stored in x and y after execution of the following program segment?

```
int x = 30, y = 40;
if (x >= 0)
{
    if (x <= 100)
    {
        y = x * 3;
        if (y < 50)
            x /= 10;
    }
    else
        y = x * 2;
}
else
    y = -x;
```

   (A) x = 30 y = 90
   (B) x = 30 y = -30
   (C) x = 30 y = 60
   (D) x = 3   y = -3
   (E) x = 30 y = 40

11. Which of the following will evaluate to true only if boolean expressions A, B, and C are all false?

    (A) `!A && !(B && !C)`
    (B) `!A || !B || !C`
    (C) `!(A || B || C)`
    (D) `!(A && B && C)`
    (E) `!A || !(B || !C)`

12. Assume that a and b are integers. The boolean expression

    `!(a <= b) && (a * b > 0)`

    will always evaluate to true given that
    (A) `a = b`
    (B) `a > b`
    (C) `a < b`
    (D) `a > b` and `b > 0`
    (E) `a > b` and `b < 0`

13. Given that a, b, and c are integers, consider the boolean expression

    `(a < b) || !((c == a * b) && (c < a))`

    Which of the following will *guarantee* that the expression is true?
    (A) `c < a` is false.
    (B) `c < a` is true.
    (C) `a < b` is false.
    (D) `c == a * b` is true.
    (E) `c == a * b` is true, and `c < a` is true.

14. In the following code segment, you may assume that a, b, and n are all type int.

    ```
    if (a != b && n / (a - b) > 90)
    {
        /* statement 1 */
    }
    else
    {
        /* statement 2 */
    }
    /* statement 3 */
    ```

    What will happen if a == b is false?
    (A) /* *statement 1* */ will be executed.
    (B) /* *statement 2* */ will be executed.
    (C) Either /* *statement 1* */ or /* *statement 2* */ will be executed.
    (D) A compile-time error will occur.
    (E) An exception will be thrown.

15. Given that n and count are both of type int, which statement is true about the following code segments?

```
I for (count = 1; count <= n; count++)
      System.out.println(count);

II count = 1;
   while (count <= n)
   {
       System.out.println(count);
       count++;
   }
```

(A) I and II are exactly equivalent for all input values n.
(B) I and II are exactly equivalent for all input values $n \geq 1$, but differ when $n \leq 0$.
(C) I and II are exactly equivalent only when $n = 0$.
(D) I and II are exactly equivalent only when n is even.
(E) I and II are not equivalent for any input values of n.

16. The following fragment intends that a user will enter a list of positive integers at the keyboard and terminate the list with a sentinel:

```
int value = 0;
final int SENTINEL = -999;
while (value != SENTINEL)
{
    //code to process value
       ...
    value = IO.readInt();      //read user input
}
```

The fragment is not correct. Which is a true statement?
(A) The sentinel gets processed.
(B) The last nonsentinel value entered in the list fails to get processed.
(C) A poor choice of SENTINEL value causes the loop to terminate before all values have been processed.
(D) The code will always process a value that is not on the list.
(E) Entering the SENTINEL value as the first value causes a run-time error.

17. Suppose that base-2 (binary) numbers and base-16 (hexadecimal) numbers can be denoted with subscripts, as shown below:

$$2A_{hex} = 101010_{bin}$$

Which is equal to $3D_{hex}$?
(A) 111101_{bin}
(B) 101111_{bin}
(C) 10011_{bin}
(D) 110100_{bin}
(E) 101101_{bin}

18. A common use of hexadecimal numerals is to specify colors on web pages. Every color has a red, green, and blue component. In decimal notation, these are denoted with an ordered triple (x, y, z), where x, y, and z are the three components, each an int from 0 to 255. For example, a certain shade of red, whose red, green, and blue components are 238, 9, and 63, is represented as $(238, 9, 63)$.

    In hexadecimal, a color is represented in the format #RRGGBB, where RR, GG, and BB are hex values for the red, green, and blue. Using this notation, the color $(238, 9, 63)$ would be coded as #EE093F.

    Which of the following hex codes represents the color $(14, 20, 255)$?
    (A) #1418FE
    (B) #0E20FE
    (C) #0E14FF
    (D) #0FE5FE
    (E) #0D14FF

19. In Java, a variable of type int is represented internally as a 32-bit signed integer. Suppose that one bit stores the sign, and the other 31 bits store the magnitude of the number in base 2. In this scheme, what is the largest value that can be stored as type int?
    (A) 2^{32}
    (B) $2^{32} - 1$
    (C) 2^{31}
    (D) $2^{31} - 1$
    (E) 2^{30}

20. Consider this code segment:

```
int x = 10, y = 0;
while (x > 5)
{
    y = 3;
    while (y < x)
    {
        y *= 2;
        if (y % x == 1)
            y += x;
    }
    x -= 3;
}
System.out.println(x + " " + y);
```

    What will be output after execution of this code segment?
    (A) 1   6
    (B) 7   12
    (C) -3   12
    (D) 4   12
    (E) -3   6

Questions 21 and 22 refer to the following method, checkNumber, which checks the validity of its four-digit integer parameter.

```
/** @param n a 4-digit integer
 *  @return true if n is valid, false otherwise
 */
boolean checkNumber(int n)
{
    int d1,d2,d3,checkDigit,nRemaining,rem;
    //strip off digits
    checkDigit = n % 10;
    nRemaining = n / 10;
    d3 = nRemaining % 10;
    nRemaining /= 10;
    d2 = nRemaining % 10;
    nRemaining /= 10;
    d1 = nRemaining % 10;
    //check validity
    rem = (d1 + d2 + d3) % 7;
    return rem == checkDigit;
}
```

A program invokes method checkNumber with the statement

```
boolean valid = checkNumber(num);
```

21. Which of the following values of num will result in valid having a value of true?
    (A) 6143
    (B) 6144
    (C) 6145
    (D) 6146
    (E) 6147

22. What is the purpose of the local variable nRemaining?
    (A) It is not possible to separate n into digits without the help of a temporary variable.
    (B) nRemaining prevents the parameter num from being altered.
    (C) nRemaining enhances the readability of the algorithm.
    (D) On exiting the method, the value of nRemaining may be reused.
    (E) nRemaining is needed as the left-hand side operand for integer division.

23. What output will be produced by this code segment? (Ignore spacing.)

```
for (int i = 5; i >= 1; i--)
{
    for (int j = i; j >= 1; j--)
        System.out.print(2 * j - 1);
    System.out.println();
}
```

(A) 9 7 5 3 1
    9 7 5 3
    9 7 5
    9 7
    9

(B) 9 7 5 3 1
    7 5 3 1
    5 3 1
    3 1
    1

(C) 9 7 5 3 1
    7 5 3 1 -1
    5 3 1 -1 -3
    3 1 -1 -3 -5
    1 -1 -3 -5 -7

(D) 1
    1 3
    1 3 5
    1 3 5 7
    1 3 5 7 9

(E) 1 3 5 7 9
    1 3 5 7
    1 3 5
    1 3
    1

24. Which of the following program fragments will produce this output? (Ignore spacing.)

```
2 - - - - -
- 4 - - - -
- - 6 - - -
- - - 8 - -
- - - - 10 -
- - - - - 12
```

```
I for (int i = 1; i <= 6; i++)
  {
      for (int k = 1; k <= 6; k++)
          if (k == i)
              System.out.print(2 * k);
          else
              System.out.print("-");
      System.out.println();
  }
```

```
II for (int i = 1; i <= 6; i++)
   {
       for (int k = 1; k <= i - 1; k++)
           System.out.print("-");
       System.out.print(2 * i);
       for (int k = 1; k <= 6 - i; k++)
           System.out.print("-");
       System.out.println();
   }
```

```
III for (int i = 1; i <= 6; i++)
    {
        for (int k = 1; k <= i - 1; k++)
            System.out.print("-");
        System.out.print(2 * i);
        for (int k = i + 1; k <= 6; k++)
            System.out.print("-");
        System.out.println();
    }
```

(A) I only
(B) II only
(C) III only
(D) I and II only
(E) I, II, and III

25. Consider this program segment:

```java
int newNum = 0, temp;
int num = k;              //k is some predefined integer value ≥ 0
while (num > 10)
{
    temp = num % 10;
    num /= 10;
    newNum = newNum * 10 + temp;
}
System.out.print(newNum);
```

Which is a true statement about the segment?

I   If $100 \leq$ num ≤ 1000 initially, the final value of newNum must be in the range $10 \leq$ newNum ≤ 100.

II There is no initial value of num that will cause an infinite while loop.

III If num ≤ 10 initially, newNum will have a final value of 0.

(A) I only
(B) II only
(C) III only
(D) II and III only
(E) I, II, and III

26. Consider the method reverse:

```
/** Precondition:  n > 0.
 *  Postcondition:
 *   - Returns n with its digits reversed.
 *   - Example: If n = 234, method reverse returns 432.
 *  @param n a positive integer
 *  @return n with its digits reversed
 */
int reverse(int n)
{
    int rem, revNum = 0;

    /* code segment */

    return revNum;
}
```

Which of the following replacements for /* *code segment* */ would cause the method to work as intended?

```
I  for (int i = 0; i <= n; i++)
   {
       rem = n % 10;
       revNum = revNum * 10 + rem;
       n /= 10;
   }

II  while (n != 0)
    {
        rem = n % 10;
        revNum = revNum * 10 + rem;
        n /= 10;
    }

III  for (int i = n; i != 0; i /= 10)
     {
         rem = i % 10;
         revNum = revNum * 10 + rem;
     }
```

(A) I only
(B) II only
(C) I and II only
(D) II and III only
(E) I and III only

ANSWER KEY

1. B	10. A	19. D
2. E	11. C	20. D
3. D	12. D	21. B
4. E	13. A	22. C
5. E	14. C	23. B
6. C	15. A	24. E
7. B	16. D	25. D
8. D	17. A	26. D
9. D	18. C	

ANSWERS EXPLAINED

1. **(B)** When x is converted to an integer, as in segment I, information is lost. Java requires that an explicit cast to an int be made, as in segment II. Note that segment II will cause x to be truncated: The value stored in y is 14. By requiring the explicit cast, Java doesn't let you do this accidentally. In segment III y will contain the value 14.0. No explicit cast to a double is required since no information is lost.

2. **(E)** The string argument contains two escape sequences: '\\', which means print a backslash (\), and '\n', which means go to a new line. Choice E is the only choice that does both of these.

3. **(D)** Short-circuit evaluation of the boolean expression will occur. The expression (n != 0) will evaluate to false, which makes the entire boolean expression false. Therefore the expression (x / n > 100) will not be evaluated. Hence no division by zero will occur, causing an ArithmeticException to be thrown. When the boolean expression has a value of false, only the else part of the statement, *statement2*, will be executed.

4. **(E)** For this choice, the integer division 13/5 will be evaluated to 2, which will then be cast to 2.0. The output will be 13/5 = 2.0. The compiler needs a way to recognize that real-valued division is required. All the other options provide a way.

5. **(E)** The operators *, /, and % have equal precedence, all higher than -, and must be performed first, from left to right.

```
    13 - 3 * 6 / 4 % 3
  = '13 - 18 / 4 % 3
  =  13 - 4 % 3
  =  13 - 1
  =  12
```

6. **(C)** The expression must be evaluated as if parenthesized like this:

```
(2 + 3) * 12 / (7 - 4 + 8)
```

This becomes 5 * 12 / 11 = 60 / 11 = 5.

7. **(B)** Although the expression is always algebraically true for nonzero x, the expression may evaluate to false. This could occur because of round-off error in performing the division and multiplication operations. Whether the right-hand side of the expression evaluates to exactly 3.0 depends on the value of x. Note that if x is zero, the expression will be evaluated to `false` because the right-hand side will be assigned a value of `Infinity`.

8. **(D)** Anytime arithmetic operations are done with floating-point numbers, round-off error occurs. The `Math` class methods (see p. 183) such as `pow` and `sqrt` use various approximations to generate their answers to the required accuracy. Since they do different internal arithmetic, however, the round-off will usually not result in exactly the same answers. Note that choice A is not correct because both `Math.pow` and `Math.sqrt` return type `double`. Choice B is wrong because no matter how x was previously calculated, the same x is input to `pow` and `sqrt`. Choice C is wrong since round-off error occurs no matter how many bits are used to represent numbers. Choice E is wrong because if x is representable on the machine (i.e., hasn't overflowed), then its square root, $x^{1/2}$, will not overflow.

9. **(D)** Each `else` gets paired with the nearest unpaired `if`. Thus when the test (22 % 5 == 0) fails, the `else` part indicating that 22 is `negative` will be executed. This is clearly not the intent of the fragment, which can be fixed using delimiters:

```
int num = call to a method that reads an integer;
if (num > 0)
{
    if (num % 5 == 0)
        System.out.println(num);
}
else
    System.out.println(num + " is negative");
```

10. **(A)** Since the first test (x >= 0) is true, the matching `else` part, y = -x, will not be executed. Since (x <= 100) is true, the matching `else` part, y = x * 2, will not be executed. The variable y will be set to x * 3 (i.e., 90) and will now fail the test y < 50. Thus, x will never be altered in this algorithm. Final values are x = 30 and y = 90.

11. **(C)** In order for !(A || B || C) to be true, (A || B || C) must evaluate to false. This will happen only if A, B, and C are *all* false. Choice A evaluates to true when A and B are false and C is true. In choice B, if any *one* of A, B, or C is false, the boolean expression evaluates to true. In choice D, if any one of A, B, or C is false, the boolean expression evaluates to true since we have !(false). All that's required for choice E to evaluate to true is for A to be false. Since true||(any) evaluates to true, both B and C can be either true or false.

12. **(D)** To evaluate to `true`, the expression must reduce to `true && true`. We therefore need !(false) && true. Choice D is the only condition that guarantees this: a > b provides !(false) for the left-hand expression, and a > b and b > 0 implies both a and b positive, which leads to true for the right-hand expression. Choice E, for example, will provide true for the right-hand expression only if a < 0. You have no information about a and can't make assumptions about it.

13. **(A)** If (c < a) is `false`, ((c == a*b) && (c < a)) evaluates to `false` irrespective of the value of c == a*b. In this case, !(c == a*b && c < a) evaluates to `true`. Then (a < b) || `true` evaluates to `true` irrespective of the value of the test (a < b). In all the other choices, the given expression *may* be true. There is not enough information given to guarantee this, however.

14. **(C)** If a == b is false, then a != b is true. Thus, the second piece of the compound test must be evaluated before the value of the whole test is known. Since a == b is false, a - b is not equal to zero. Thus, there is no division by zero, and no exception will be thrown. Also, since the relative values of a, b, and n are unknown, the value of the test n / (a - b) > 90 is unknown, and there is insufficient information to determine whether the compound test is true or false. Thus, either /* *statement 1* */ or /* *statement 2* */ will be executed.

15. **(A)** If $n \geq 1$, both segments will print out the integers from 1 through n. If $n \leq 0$, both segments will fail the test immediately and do nothing.

16. **(D)** The (value != SENTINEL) test occurs before a value has been read from the list. This will cause 0 to be processed, which may cause an error. The code must be fixed by reading the first value before doing the test:

```
final int SENTINEL = -999;
int value = IO.readInt();
while (value != SENTINEL)
{
    //code to process value
    value = IO.readInt();
}
```

17. **(A)** Quick method: Convert each hex digit to binary.

$$
\begin{aligned}
&\quad 3 \qquad\quad D_{hex} \\
&= 0011 \quad 1101 \qquad \text{(where D equals 13 in base 10)} \\
&= 111101_{bin}
\end{aligned}
$$

Slow method: Convert $3D_{hex}$ to base 10.

$$
\begin{aligned}
3D_{hex} &= (3)(16^1) + (D)(16^0) \\
&= 48 + 13 \\
&= 61_{dec}
\end{aligned}
$$

Now convert 61_{dec} to binary. Write 61 as a sum of descending powers of 2:

$$
\begin{aligned}
61 &= 32 + 16 + 8 + 4 + 1 \\
&= 1(2^5) + 1(2^4) + 1(2^3) + 1(2^2) + 0(2^1) + 1(2^0) \\
&= 111101_{bin}
\end{aligned}
$$

18. **(C)** Start by converting each of the three numbers to hexadecimal:

$$
\begin{aligned}
14 &= (0)(16^1) + (14)(16^0) &= 0E \\
20 &= (1)(16^1) + (4)(16^0) &= 14 \\
255 &= (15)(16^1) + (15)(16^0) &= FF
\end{aligned}
$$

Therefore $(14, 20, 255) = \#0E14FF$.

19. (**D**) Think of the integer as having 31 slots for storage. If there were just one slot, the maximum binary number would be $1 = 2^1 - 1$. If there were just two slots, the maximum binary number would be $11 = 2^2 - 1 = 3$. If there were just eight slots, the maximum binary number would be $11111111 = 2^8 - 1$. So for 31 slots, the maximum value is $2^{31} - 1$.

20. (**D**) Here is a trace of the values of x and y during execution. Note that the condition (y % x == 1) is never true in this example.

x	10				7				4
y		3	6	12		3	6	12	

The while loop terminates when x is 4 since the test while (x > 5) fails.

21. (**B**) The algorithm finds the remainder when the sum of the first three digits of n is divided by 7. If this remainder is equal to the fourth digit, checkDigit, the method returns true, otherwise false. Note that (6+1+4) % 7 equals 4. Thus, only choice B is a valid number.

22. (**C**) As n gets broken down into its digits, nRemaining is the part of n that remains after each digit is stripped off. Thus, nRemaining is a self-documenting name that helps describe what is happening. Choice A is false because every digit can be stripped off using some sequence of integer division and mod. Choice B is false because num is passed by value and therefore will not be altered when the method is exited (see p. 104). Eliminate choice D: When the method is exited, all local variables are destroyed. Choice E is nonsense.

23. (**B**) The outer loop produces five rows of output. Each pass through the inner loop goes from i down to 1. Thus five odd numbers starting at 9 are printed in the first row, four odd numbers starting at 7 in the second row, and so on.

24. (**E**) All three algorithms produce the given output. The outer for (int i ...) loop produces six rows, and the inner for (int k ...) loops produce the symbols in each row.

25. (**D**) Statement I is false, since if $100 \le$ num ≤ 109, the body of the while loop will be executed just once. (After this single pass through the loop, the value of num will be 10, and the test if (num > 10) will fail.) With just one pass, newNum will be a one-digit number, equal to temp (which was the original num % 10). Note that statement II is true: There cannot be an infinite loop since num /= 10 guarantees termination of the loop. Statement III is true because if num $\le$ 10, the loop will be skipped, and newNum will keep its original value of 0.

26. (**D**) The algorithm works by stripping off the rightmost digit of n (stored in rem), multiplying the current value of revNum by 10, and adding that rightmost digit. When n has been stripped down to no digits (i.e., n == 0 is true), revNum is complete. Both segments II and III work. Segment I fails to produce the right output whenever the input value n has first digit less than (number of digits − 1). For these cases the output has the first digit of the original number missing from the end of the returned number.

Classes and Objects

Work is the curse of the drinking classes.
—*Oscar Wilde*

Chapter Goals

- Objects and classes
- Encapsulation
- References

- Keywords `public`, `private`, and `static`
- Methods
- Scope of variables

OBJECTS

Every program that you write involves at least one thing that is being created or manipulated by the program. This thing, together with the operations that manipulate it, is called an *object*.

Consider, for example, a program that must test the validity of a four-digit code number that a person will enter to be able to use a photocopy machine. Rules for validity are provided. The object is a four-digit code number. Some of the operations to manipulate the object could be `readNumber`, `getSeparateDigits`, `testValidity`, and `writeNumber`.

Any given program can have several different types of objects. For example, a program that maintains a database of all books in a library has at least two objects:

1. A `Book` object, with operations like `getTitle`, `isOnShelf`, `isFiction`, and `goOutOfPrint`.
2. A `ListOfBooks` object, with operations like `search`, `addBook`, `removeBook`, and `sortByAuthor`.

An object is characterized by its *state* and *behavior*. For example, a book has a state described by its title, author, whether it's on the shelf, and so on. It also has behavior, like going out of print.

Notice that an object is an idea, separate from the concrete details of a programming language. It corresponds to some real-world object that is being represented by the program.

92

All object-oriented programming languages have a way to represent an object as a variable in a program. In Java, a variable that represents an object is called an *object reference*.

CLASSES

A *class* is a software blueprint for implementing objects of a given type. An object is a single *instance* of the class. In a program there will often be several different instances of a given class type.

The current state of a given object is maintained in its *data fields* or *instance variables*, provided by the class. The *methods* of the class provide both the behaviors exhibited by the object and the operations that manipulate the object. Combining an object's data and methods into a single unit called a class is known as *encapsulation*.

Here is the framework for a simple bank account class:

```
public class BankAccount
{
    private String password;
    private double balance;
    public static final double OVERDRAWN_PENALTY = 20.00;

  //constructors
    /** Default constructor.
     *  Constructs bank account with default values. */
    public BankAccount()
    { /* implementation code */ }

    /** Constructs bank account with specified password and balance. */
    public BankAccount(String acctPassword, double acctBalance)
    { /* implementation code */ }

    //accessor
    /** @return balance of this account */
    public double getBalance()
    { /* implementation code */ }

    //mutators
    /** Deposits amount in bank account with given password.
     *  @param acctPassword the password of this bank account
     *  @param amount the amount to be deposited
  */
    public void deposit(String acctPassword, double amount)
    { /* implementation code */ }

    /** Withdraws amount from bank account with given password.
     *  Assesses penalty if balance is less than amount.
     *  @param acctPassword the password of this bank account
     *  @param amount the amount to be withdrawn
     */
    public void withdraw(String acctPassword, double amount)
    { /* implementation code */ }
}
```

PUBLIC, PRIVATE, AND STATIC

The keyword `public` preceding the class declaration signals that the class is usable by all *client programs*. If a class is not public, it can be used only by classes in its own package. In the AP Java subset, all classes are public.

Similarly, *public methods* are accessible to all client programs. Clients, however, are not privy to the class implementation and may not access the private instance variables and private methods of the class. Restriction of access is known as *information hiding*. In Java, this is implemented by using the keyword `private`. *Private methods and variables in a class can be accessed only by methods of that class.* Even though Java allows public instance variables, in the AP Java subset all instance variables are private.

A *static variable* (class variable) contains a value that is shared by all instances of the class. "Static" means that memory allocation happens once.

Typical uses of a static variable are to

- keep track of statistics for objects of the class.

- accumulate a total.

- provide a new identity number for each new object of the class.

For example:

```
public class Employee
{
    private String name;
    private static int employeeCount = 0; //number of employees

    public Employee( < parameter list > )
    {
        < initialization of private instance variables >
        employeeCount++; //increment count of all employees
    }
    ...
}
```

Notice that the static variable was initialized outside the constructor and that its value can be changed.

Static final variables (constants) in a class cannot be changed. They are often declared public (see some examples of `Math` class constants on p. 183). The variable `OVERDRAWN_PENALTY` is an example in the `BankAccount` class. Since the variable is public, it can be used in any client method. The keyword `static` indicates that there is a single value of the variable that applies to the whole class, rather than a new instance for each object of the class. A client method would refer to the variable as `BankAccount.OVERDRAWN_PENALTY`. In its own class it is referred to as simply `OVERDRAWN_PENALTY`.

See p. 97 for static methods.

METHODS

Headers

All method headers, with the exception of constructors (see below) and static methods (p. 97), look like this:

```
public      void     withdraw (String password, double amount)
```

access specifier   return type   method name   parameter list

NOTE

1. The *access specifier* tells which other methods can call this method (see Public, Private, and Static on the previous page).
2. A *return type* of void signals that the method does not return a value.
3. Items in the *parameter list* are separated by commas.

The implementation of the method directly follows the header, enclosed in a {} block.

Types of Methods

CONSTRUCTORS

A *constructor* creates an object of the class. You can recognize a constructor by its name—always the same as the class. Also, a constructor has no return type.

Having several constructors provides different ways of initializing class objects. For example, there are two constructors in the BankAccount class.

1. The *default constructor* has no arguments. It provides reasonable initial values for an object. Here is its implementation:

```
/** Default constructor.
 * Constructs a bank account with default values. */
public BankAccount()
{
    password = "";
    balance = 0.0;
}
```

In a client method, the declaration

```
BankAccount b = new BankAccount();
```

constructs a BankAccount object with a balance of zero and a password equal to the empty string. The new operator returns the address of this newly constructed object. The variable b is assigned the value of this address—we say "b is a *reference* to the object." Picture the setup like this:

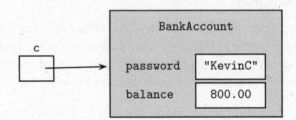

2. The constructor with parameters sets the instance variables of a `BankAccount` object to the values of those parameters.

Here is the implementation:

```
/** Constructor. Constructs a bank account with
 *  specified password and balance. */
public BankAccount(String acctPassword, double acctBalance)
{
    password = acctPassword;
    balance = acctBalance;
}
```

In a client program a declaration that uses this constructor needs matching parameters:

```
BankAccount c = new BankAccount("KevinC", 800.00);
```

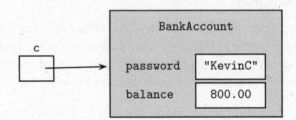

NOTE

`b` and `c` are *object variables* that store the *addresses* of their respective `BankAccount` objects. They do not store the objects themselves (see **References** on p. 101).

ACCESSORS

An *accessor method* accesses a class object without altering the object. An accessor returns some information about the object.

The `BankAccount` class has a single accessor method, `getBalance()`. Here is its implementation:

```
/** @return the  balance of this account */
public double getBalance()
{ return balance; }
```

A client program may use this method as follows:

```
BankAccount b1 = new BankAccount("MattW", 500.00);
BankAccount b2 = new BankAccount("DannyB", 650.50);
if (b1.getBalance() > b2.getBalance())
    ...
```

NOTE

The . *operator* (dot operator) indicates that `getBalance()` is a method of the class to which `b1` and `b2` belong, namely the `BankAccount` class.

MUTATORS

A *mutator method* changes the state of an object by modifying at least one of its instance variables.

Here are the implementations of the `deposit` and `withdraw` methods, each of which alters the value of `balance` in the `BankAccount` class:

```
/** Deposits amount in a bank account with the given password.
 *  @param acctPassword the password of this bank account
 *  @param amount the amount to be deposited
 */
public void deposit(String acctPassword, double amount)
{
    if (!acctPassword.equals(password))
        /* throw an exception */
    else
        balance += amount;
}


/** Withdraws amount from bank account with given password.
 *  Assesses penalty if balance is less than amount.
 *  @param acctPassword the password of this bank account
 *  @param amount the amount to be withdrawn
 */
public void withdraw(String acctPassword, double amount)
{
    if (!acctPassword.equals(password))
        /* throw an exception */
    else
    {
        balance -= amount;        //allows negative balance
        if (balance < 0)
            balance -= OVERDRAWN_PENALTY;
    }
}
```

A mutator method in a client program is invoked in the same way as an accessor: using an object variable with the dot operator. For example, assuming valid `BankAccount` declarations for `b1` and `b2`:

```
b1.withdraw("MattW", 200.00);
b2.deposit("DannyB", 35.68);
```

STATIC METHODS

Static Methods vs. Instance Methods
The methods discussed in the preceding sections—constructors, accessors, and mutators—all operate on individual objects of a class. They are called *instance methods*. A method that performs an operation for the entire class, not its individual objects, is called a *static method* (sometimes called a *class method*).

The implementation of a static method uses the keyword static in its header. There is no implied object in the code (as there is in an instance method). Thus, if the code tries to call an instance method or invoke a private instance variable for this nonexistent object, a syntax error will occur. A static method can, however, use a static variable in its code. For example, in the Employee example on p. 94, you could add a static method that returns the employeeCount:

```
public static int getEmployeeCount()
{ return employeeCount; }
```

Here's an example of a static method that might be used in the BankAccount class. Suppose the class has a static variable intRate, declared as follows:

```
private static double intRate;
```

The static method getInterestRate may be as follows:

```
public static double getInterestRate()
{
    System.out.println("Enter interest rate for bank account");
    System.out.println("Enter in decimal form:");
    intRate = IO.readDouble();           // read user input
    return intRate;
}
```

Since the rate that's read in by this method applies to all bank accounts in the class, not to any particular BankAccount object, it's appropriate that the method should be static.

Recall that an instance method is invoked in a client program by using an object variable followed by the dot operator followed by the method name:

```
BankAccount b = new BankAccount();  //invokes the deposit method for
b.deposit(acctPassword, amount);    //BankAccount object b
```

A static method, by contrast, is invoked by using the *class name* with the dot operator:

```
double interestRate = BankAccount.getInterestRate();
```

Static Methods in a Driver Class

Often a class that contains the main() method is used as a driver program to test other classes. Usually such a class creates no objects of the class. So all the methods in the class must be static. Note that at the start of program execution, no objects exist yet. So the main() method must *always* be static.

For example, here is a program that tests a class for reading integers entered at the keyboard.

```
import java.util.*;
public class GetListTest
{
    /** @return a list of integers from the keyboard */
    public static List<Integer> getList()
    {
        List<Integer> a = new ArrayList<Integer>();
        < code to read integers into a>
        return a;
    }
```

```
    /** Write contents of List a.
     *  @param a the list
     */
    public static void writeList(List<Integer> a)
    {
        System.out.println("List is : " + a);
    }

    public static void main(String[] args)
    {
        List<Integer> list = getList();
        writeList(list);
    }
}
```

NOTE

1. The calls to `writeList(list)` and `getList()` do not need to be preceded by `GetListTest` plus a dot because `main` is not a client program: It is in the same class as `getList` and `writeList`.
2. If you omit the keyword `static` from the `getList` or `writeList` header, you get an error message like the following:

```
    Can't make static reference to method getList()
    in class GetListTest
```

The compiler has recognized that there was no object variable preceding the method call, which means that the methods were static and should have been declared as such.

Method Overloading

Overloaded methods are two or more methods in the same class that have the same name but different parameter lists. For example,

```
public class DoOperations
{
    public int product(int n) { return n * n; }
    public double product(double x) { return x * x; }
    public double product(int x, int y) { return x * y; }
        ...
```

The compiler figures out which method to call by examining the method's *signature*. The signature of a method consists of the method's name and a list of the parameter types. Thus, the signatures of the overloaded `product` methods are

```
product(int)
product(double)
product(int, int)
```

Note that for overloading purposes, the return type of the method is irrelevant. You can't have two methods with identical signatures but different return types. The compiler will complain that the method call is ambiguous.

Having more than one constructor in the same class is an example of overloading. Overloaded constructors provide a choice of ways to initialize objects of the class.

SCOPE

The *scope* of a variable or method is the region in which that variable or method is visible and can be accessed.

The instance variables, static variables, and methods of a class belong to that class's scope, which extends from the opening brace to the closing brace of the class definition. Within the class all instance variables and methods are accessible and can be referred to simply by name (no dot operator!).

A *local variable* is defined inside a method. It can even be defined inside a statement. Its scope extends from the point where it is declared to the end of the block in which its declaration occurs. A *block* is a piece of code enclosed in a {} pair. When a block is exited, the memory for a local variable is automatically recycled.

Local variables take precedence over instance variables with the same name. (Using the same name, however, creates ambiguity for the programmer, leading to errors. You should avoid the practice.)

The this Keyword

An instance method is always called for a particular object. This object is an *implicit parameter* for the method and is referred to with the keyword this. You are expected to know this vocabulary for the exam.

In the implementation of instance methods, all instance variables can be written with the prefix this followed by the dot operator.

Example 1

In the method call obj.doSomething("Mary",num), where obj is some class object and doSomething is a method of that class, "Mary" and num, the parameters in parentheses, are *explicit* parameters, whereas obj is an *implicit* parameter.

Example 2

Here's an example where this is used as a parameter.

```
public class Person
{
    private String name;
    private int age;

    public Person(String aName, int anAge)
    {
        name = aName;
        age = anAge;
    }

    /** @return the String form of this person */
    public String toString()
    { return name + " " + age; }

    public void printPerson()
    { System.out.println(this); }

    //Other variables and methods are not shown.
}
```

Suppose a client class has these lines of code:

```
Person p = new Person("Dan", 10);
p.printPerson();
```

The statement

```
System.out.println(this);
```

in the `printPerson` method means "print the current `Person` object." The output should be: `Dan 10`. Note that `System.out.println` invokes the `toString` method of the `Person` class.

Example 3

The `deposit` method of the `BankAccount` class can refer to `balance` as follows:

```
public void deposit(String acctPassword, double amount)
{
    this.balance += amount;
}
```

The use of `this` is unnecessary in the above example.

Example 4

Consider a rational number class called `Rational`, which has two private instance variables:

```
private int num;          //numerator
private int denom;        //denominator
```

Now consider a constructor for the `Rational` class:

```
public Rational(int num, int denom)
{
    this.num = num;
    this.denom = denom;
}
```

It is definitely *not* a good idea to use the same name for the explicit parameters and the private instance variables. But if you do, you can avoid errors by referring to `this.num` and `this.denom` for the current object that is being constructed. (This particular use of `this` will not be tested on the exam.)

REFERENCES

Reference vs. Primitive Data Types

All of the numerical data types, like `double` and `int`, as well as types `char` and `boolean`, are *primitive* data types. All objects are *reference* data types. The difference lies in the way they are stored.

Consider the statements

```
int num1 = 3;
int num2 = num1;
```

The variables num1 and num2 can be thought of as memory slots, labeled num1 and num2, respectively:

num1   num2

| 3 | | 3 |

If either of the above variables is now changed, the other is not affected. Each has its own memory slot.

Contrast this with the declaration of a reference data type. Recall that an object is created using new:

```
Date d = new Date(2, 17, 1948);
```

This declaration creates a reference variable d that refers to a Date object. The value of d is the address in memory of that object:

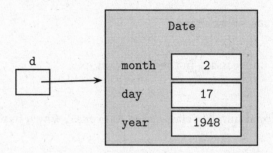

Suppose the following declaration is now made:

```
Date birthday = d;
```

This statement creates the reference variable birthday, which contains the same address as d:

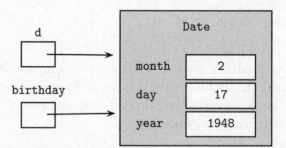

Having two references for the same object is known as *aliasing*. Aliasing can cause unintended problems for the programmer. The statement

```
d.changeDate();
```

will automatically change the object referred to by birthday as well.

What the programmer probably intended was to create a second object called birthday whose attributes exactly matched those of d. This cannot be accomplished without using new. For example,

```
Date birthday = new Date(d.getMonth(), d.getDay(), d.getYear());
```

The statement d.changeDate() will now leave the birthday object unchanged.

The Null Reference

The declaration

```
BankAccount b;
```

defines a reference b that is uninitialized. (To construct the object that b refers to requires the new operator and a BankAccount constructor.) An uninitialized object variable is called a *null reference* or *null pointer*. You can test whether a variable refers to an object or is uninitialized by using the keyword null:

```
if (b == null)
```

If a reference is not null, it can be set to null with the statement

```
b = null;
```

An attempt to invoke an instance method with a null reference may cause your program to terminate with a NullPointerException. For example,

```
public class PersonalFinances
{
    BankAccount b;                        //b is a null reference
    ...
    b.withdraw(acctPassword, amt);        //throws a NullPointerException
    ...                                   //if b not constructed with new
```

NOTE

If you fail to initialize a local variable in a method before you use it, you will get a compile-time error. If you make the same mistake with an instance variable of a class, the compiler provides reasonable default values for primitive variables (0 for numbers, false for booleans), and the code may run without error. However, if you don't initialize *reference* instance variables in a class, as in the above example, the compiler will set them to null. Any method call for an object of the class that tries to access the null reference will cause a run-time error: The program will terminate with a NullPointerException.

> Do not make a method call with an object whose value is null.

Method Parameters

FORMAL VS. ACTUAL PARAMETERS

The header of a method defines the *parameters* of that method. For example, consider the withdraw method of the BankAccount class:

```
public class BankAccount
{   ...
    public void withdraw(String acctPassword, double amount)
        ...
```

This method has two explicit parameters, acctPassword and amount. These are *dummy* or *formal parameters*. Think of them as placeholders for the pair of *actual parameters* or *arguments* that will be supplied by a particular method call in a client program.

For example,

```
BankAccount b = new BankAccount("TimB", 1000);
b.withdraw("TimB", 250);
```

Here "TimB" and 250 are the actual parameters that match up with `acctPassword` and amount for the `withdraw` method.

NOTE

1. The number of arguments in the method call must equal the number of parameters in the method header, and the type of each argument must be compatible with the type of each corresponding parameter.
2. In addition to its explicit parameters, the `withdraw` method has an implicit parameter, `this`, the `BankAccount` from which money will be withdrawn. In the method call

```
b.withdraw("TimB", 250);
```

the actual parameter that matches up with `this` is the object reference `b`.

PASSING PRIMITIVE TYPES AS PARAMETERS

Parameters are *passed by value*. For primitive types this means that when a method is called, a new memory slot is allocated for each parameter. The value of each argument is copied into the newly created memory slot corresponding to each parameter.

During execution of the method, the parameters are local to that method. *Any changes made to the parameters will not affect the values of the arguments in the calling program.* When the method is exited, the local memory slots for the parameters are erased.

Here's an example: What will the output be?

```
public class ParamTest
{
    public static void foo(int x, double y)
    {
        x = 3;
        y = 2.5;
    }

    public static void main(String[] args)
    {
        int a = 7;
        double b = 6.5;
        foo(a, b);
        System.out.println(a + "  " + b);
    }
}
```

The output will be

```
7  6.5
```

The arguments a and b remain unchanged, despite the method call!

This can be understood by picturing the state of the memory slots during execution of the program.

Just before the foo(a, b) method call:

```
       a              b
     ┌─────┐        ┌─────┐
     │  7  │        │ 6.5 │
     └─────┘        └─────┘
```

At the time of the foo(a, b) method call:

```
       a              b
     ┌─────┐        ┌─────┐
     │  7  │        │ 6.5 │
     └─────┘        └─────┘

       x              y
     ┌─────┐        ┌─────┐
     │  7  │        │ 6.5 │
     └─────┘        └─────┘
```

Just before exiting the method: Note that the values of x and y have been changed.

```
       a              b
     ┌─────┐        ┌─────┐
     │  7  │        │ 6.5 │
     └─────┘        └─────┘

       x              y
     ┌─────┐        ┌─────┐
     │  3  │        │ 2.5 │
     └─────┘        └─────┘
```

After exiting the method: Note that the memory slots for x and y have been reclaimed. The values of a and b remain unchanged.

```
       a              b
     ┌─────┐        ┌─────┐
     │  7  │        │ 6.5 │
     └─────┘        └─────┘
```

PASSING OBJECTS AS PARAMETERS

In Java both primitive types and object references are passed by value. When an object's reference is a parameter, the same mechanism of copying into local memory is used. The key difference is that the *address* (reference) is copied, not the values of the individual instance variables. As with primitive types, changes made to the parameters will not change the values of the matching arguments. What this means in practice is that it is not possible for a method to replace an object with another one—you can't change the reference that was passed. It is, however, possible to change the state of the object to which the parameter refers through methods that act on the object.

Example 1

A method that changes the state of an object.

```java
/** Subtracts fee from balance in b if current balance too low. */
public static void chargeFee(BankAccount b, String password,
        double fee)
{
    final double MIN_BALANCE = 10.00;
    if (b.getBalance() < MIN_BALANCE)
        b.withdraw(password, fee);
}

public static void main(String[] args)
{
    final double FEE = 5.00;
    BankAccount andysAccount = new BankAccount("AndyS", 7.00);
    chargeFee(andysAccount, "AndyS", FEE);
        . . .
}
```

Here are the memory slots before the `chargeFee` method call:

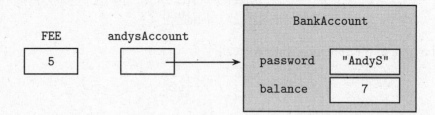

At the time of the `chargeFee` method call, copies of the matching parameters are made:

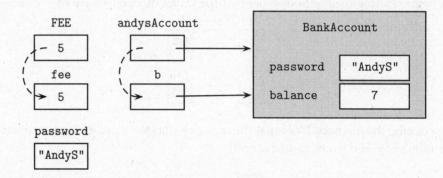

Just before exiting the method: The `balance` field of the `BankAccount` object has been changed.

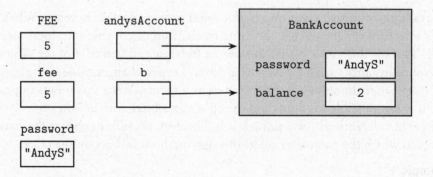

After exiting the method: All parameter memory slots have been erased, but the object remains altered.

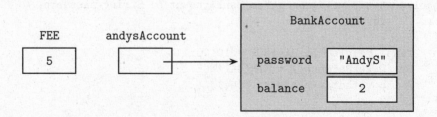

NOTE

The `andysAccount` reference is unchanged throughout the program segment. The object to which it refers, however, has been changed. This is significant. Contrast this with Example 2 below in which an attempt is made to replace the object itself.

Example 2

A chooseBestAccount method attempts—erroneously—to set its betterFund parameter to the BankAccount with the higher balance:

```
public static void chooseBestAccount(BankAccount better,
          BankAccount b1, BankAccount b2)
{
    if (b1.getBalance() > b2.getBalance())
        better = b1;
    else
        better = b2;
}

public static void main(String[] args)
{
    BankAccount briansFund = new BankAccount("BrianL", 10000);
    BankAccount paulsFund = new BankAccount("PaulM", 90000);
    BankAccount betterFund = null;

    chooseBestAccount(betterFund, briansFund, paulsFund);
        ...
}
```

The intent is that betterFund will be a reference to the paulsFund object after execution of the chooseBestAccount statement. A look at the memory slots illustrates why this fails.

Before the chooseBestAccount method call:

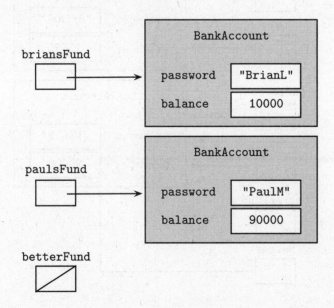

At the time of the chooseBestAccount method call: Copies of the matching references are made.

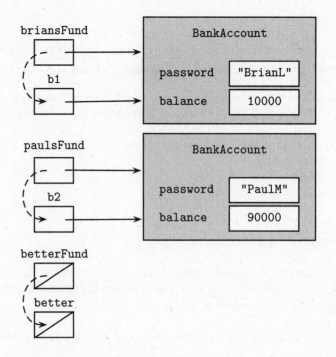

Just before exiting the method: The value of `better` has been changed; `betterFund`, however, remains unchanged.

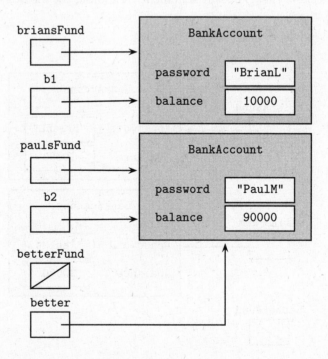

After exiting the method: All parameter slots have been erased.

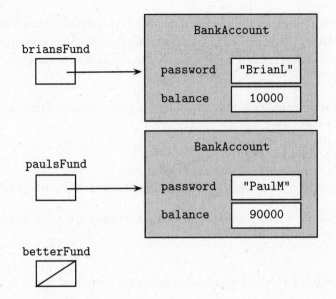

Note that the betterFund reference continues to be null, contrary to the programmer's intent.

The way to fix the problem is to modify the method so that it returns the better account. Returning an object from a method means that you are returning the address of the object.

```
public static BankAccount chooseBestAccount(BankAccount b1,
        BankAccount b2)
{
    BankAccount better;
    if (b1.getBalance() > b2.getBalance())
        better = b1;
    else
        better = b2;
    return better;
}

public static void main(String[] args)
{
    BankAccount briansFund = new BankAccount("BrianL", 10000);
    BankAccount paulsFund = new BankAccount("PaulM", 90000);
    BankAccount betterFund = chooseBestAccount(briansFund, paulsFund);
        ...
}
```

NOTE

The effect of this is to create the betterFund reference, which refers to the same object as paulsFund:

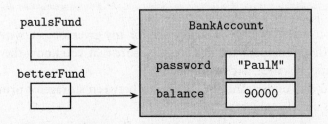

What the method does *not* do is create a new object to which betterFund refers. To do that would require the keyword new and use of a BankAccount constructor. Assuming that a getPassword() accessor has been added to the BankAccount class, the code would look like this:

```
public static BankAccount chooseBestAccount(BankAccount b1,
    BankAccount b2)
{
    BankAccount better;
    if (b1.getBalance() > b2.getBalance())
        better = new BankAccount(b1.getPassword(), b1.getBalance());
    else
        better = new BankAccount(b2.getPassword(), b2.getBalance());
    return better;
}
```

Using this modified method with the same main() method above has the following effect:

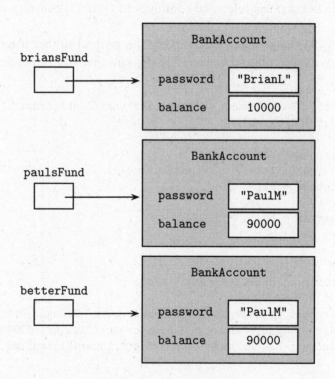

Modifying more than one object in a method can be accomplished using a *wrapper class* (see p. 180).

Chapter Summary

By now you should be able to write code for any given object, with its private data fields and methods encapsulated in a class. Be sure that you know the various types of methods—static, instance, and overloaded.

You should also understand the difference between storage of primitive types and the references used for objects.

MULTIPLE-CHOICE QUESTIONS ON CLASSES AND OBJECTS

Questions 1–3 refer to the Time class declared below:

```java
public class Time
{
    private int hrs;
    private int mins;
    private int secs;

    public Time()
    { /* implementation not shown */ }

    public Time(int h, int m, int s)
    { /* implementation not shown */ }

    /** Resets time to hrs = h, mins = m, secs = s. */
    public void resetTime(int h, int m, int s)
    { /* implementation not shown */ }

    /** Advances time by one second. */
    public void increment()
    { /* implementation not shown */ }

    /** @return true if this time equals t, false otherwise */
    public boolean equals(Time t)
    { /* implementation not shown */ }

    /** @return true if this time is earlier than t, false otherwise */
    public boolean lessThan(Time t)
    { /* implementation not shown */ }

    /** @return a String with the time in the form hrs:mins:secs */
    public String toString()
    { /* implementation not shown */ }
}
```

1. Which of the following is a *false* statement about the methods?
   (A) equals, lessThan, and toString are all accessor methods.
   (B) increment is a mutator method.
   (C) Time() is the default constructor.
   (D) The Time class has three constructors.
   (E) There are no static methods in this class.

2. Which of the following represents correct *implementation code* for the constructor with parameters?

    (A)
```
hrs = 0;
mins = 0;
secs = 0;
```

    (B)
```
hrs = h;
mins = m;
secs = s;
```

    (C) `resetTime(hrs, mins, secs);`

    (D)
```
h = hrs;
m = mins;
s = secs;
```

    (E) `Time = new Time(h, m, s);`

3. A client class has a `display` method that writes the time represented by its parameter:

```
/** Outputs time t in the form hrs:mins:secs.
 *  @param t the time
 */
public void display (Time t)
{
    /* method body */
}
```

Which of the following are correct replacements for /* *method body* */?

    I
```
Time T = new Time(h, m, s);
System.out.println(T);
```

    II `System.out.println(t.hrs + ":" + t.mins + ":" + t.secs);`

    III `System.out.println(t);`

    (A) I only
    (B) II only
    (C) III only
    (D) II and III only
    (E) I, II, and III

4. Which statement about parameters is *false*?
    (A) The scope of parameters is the method in which they are defined.
    (B) Static methods have no implicit parameter `this`.
    (C) Two overloaded methods in the same class must have parameters with different names.
    (D) All parameters in Java are passed by value.
    (E) Two different constructors in a given class can have the same number of parameters.

Questions 5–11 refer to the following Date class declaration:

```
public class Date
{
    private int day;
    private int month;
    private int year;

    public Date()                              //default constructor
    {
        ...
    }

    public Date(int mo, int da, int yr)   //constructor
    {
        ...
    }

    public int month()       //returns month of Date
    {
        ...
    }

    public int day()         //returns day of Date
    {
        ...
    }

    public int year()        //returns year of Date
    {
        ...
    }

    //Returns String representation of Date as "m/d/y", e.g. 4/18/1985.
    public String toString()
    {
        ...
    }
}
```

5. Which of the following correctly constructs a Date object in a client class?

   (A) Date d = new (2, 13, 1947);

   (B) Date d = new Date(2, 13, 1947);

   (C) Date d;
       d = new (2, 13, 1947);

   (D) Date d;
       d = Date(2, 13, 1947);

   (E) Date d = Date(2, 13, 1947);

6. Which of the following will cause an error message?

   ```
    I Date d1 = new Date(8, 2, 1947);
      Date d2 = d1;

   II Date d1 = null;
      Date d2 = d1;

  III Date d = null;
      int x = d.year();
   ```

   (A) I only
   (B) II only
   (C) III only
   (D) II and III only
   (E) I, II, and III

7. A client program creates a `Date` object as follows:

   ```
   Date d = new Date(1, 13, 2002);
   ```

   Which of the following subsequent code segments will cause an error?
   (A) `String s = d.toString();`
   (B) `int x = d.day();`
   (C) `Date e = d;`
   (D) `Date e = new Date(1, 13, 2002);`
   (E) `int y = d.year;`

8. Consider the implementation of a `write()` method that is added to the `Date` class:

   ```
   /** Write the date in the form m/d/y, for example 2/17/1948. */
   public void write()
   {
       /* implementation code */
   }
   ```

   Which of the following could be used as */* implementation code */*?

   ```
    I System.out.println(month + "/" + day + "/" + year);

   II System.out.println(month() + "/" + day() + "/" + year());

  III System.out.println(this);
   ```

   (A) I only
   (B) II only
   (C) III only
   (D) II and III only
   (E) I, II, and III

9. Here is a client program that uses Date objects:

```
public class BirthdayStuff
{
    public static Date findBirthdate()
    {
        /* code to get birthDate */
        return birthDate;
    }

    public static void main(String[] args)
    {
        Date d = findBirthdate();
            ...
    }
}
```

Which of the following is a correct replacement for
/* *code to get* birthDate */?

```
 I  System.out.println("Enter birthdate: mo, day, yr: ");
    int m = IO.readInt();                  //read user input
    int d = IO.readInt();                  //read user input
    int y = IO.readInt();                  //read user input
    Date birthDate = new Date(m, d, y);

 II System.out.println("Enter birthdate: mo, day, yr: ");
    int birthDate.month() = IO.readInt();      //read user input
    int birthDate.day() = IO.readInt();        //read user input
    int birthDate.year() = IO.readInt();       //read user input
    Date birthDate = new Date(birthDate.month(), birthDate.day(),
        birthDate.year());

III System.out.println("Enter birthdate: mo, day, yr: ");
    int birthDate.month = IO.readInt();        //read user input
    int birthDate.day = IO.readInt();          //read user input
    int birthDate.year = IO.readInt();         //read user input
    Date birthDate = new Date(birthDate.month, birthDate.day,
        birthDate.year);
```

(A) I only
(B) II only
(C) III only
(D) I and II only
(E) I and III only

10. A method in a client program for the Date class has this declaration:

    ```
    Date d1 = new Date(mo, da, yr);
    ```

    where mo, da, and yr are previously defined integer variables. The same method now creates a second Date object d2 that is an exact copy of the object d1 refers to. Which of the following code segments will *not* do this correctly?

    I Date d2 = d1;

    II Date d2 = new Date(mo, da, yr);

    III Date d2 = new Date(d1.month(), d1.day(), d1.year());

    (A) I only
    (B) II only
    (C) III only
    (D) II and III only
    (E) I, II, and III

11. The Date class is modified by adding the following mutator method:

    ```
    public void addYears(int n)     //add n years to date
    ```

    Here is part of a poorly coded client program that uses the Date class:

    ```
    public static void addCentury(Date recent, Date old)
    {
        old.addYears(100);
        recent = old;
    }

    public static void main(String[] args)
    {
        Date oldDate = new Date(1, 13, 1900);
        Date recentDate = null;
        addCentury(recentDate, oldDate);
            ...
    }
    ```

    Which will be true after executing this code?
    (A) A NullPointerException is thrown.
    (B) The oldDate object remains unchanged.
    (C) recentDate is a null reference.
    (D) recentDate refers to the same object as oldDate.
    (E) recentDate refers to a separate object whose contents are the same as those of oldDate.

12. Here are the private instance variables for a `Frog` object:

```
public class Frog
{
    private String species;
    private int age;
    private double weight;
    private Position position;      //position (x,y) in pond
    private boolean amAlive;
        ...
```

Which of the following methods in the `Frog` class is the best candidate for being a static method?

(A) `swim`   `//frog swims to new position in pond`

(B) `getPondTemperature`   `//returns temperature of pond`

(C) `eat`   `//frog eats and gains weight`

(D) `getWeight`   `//returns weight of frog`

(E) `die`   `//frog dies with some probability based`
                        `//on frog's age and pond temperature`

13. What output will be produced by this program?

```
public class Mystery
{
    public static void strangeMethod(int x, int y)
    {
        x += y;
        y *= x;
        System.out.println(x + " " + y);
    }

    public static void main(String[] args)
    {
        int a = 6, b = 3;
        strangeMethod(a, b);
        System.out.println(a + " " + b);
    }
}
```

(A) 36
    9

(B) 3 6
    9

(C) 9 27
    9 27

(D) 6 3
    9 27

(E) 9 27
    6 3

Questions 14–17 refer to the following definition of the `Rational` class:

```
public class Rational
{
    private int numerator;
    private int denominator;

    /** default constructor */
    Rational()
    { /* implementation not shown */ }

    /** Constructs a Rational with numerator n and
     *  denominator 1. */
    Rational(int n)
    { /* implementation not shown */ }

    /** Constructs a Rational with specified numerator and
     *  denominator. */
    Rational(int numer, int denom)
    { /* implementation not shown */ }

    /** @return numerator */
    int numerator()
    { /* implementation not shown */ }

    /** @return denominator */
    int denominator()
    { /* implementation not shown */ }

    /** Returns (this + r). Leaves this unchanged.
     *   @return this rational number plus r
     *   @param r a rational number to be added to this Rational
     */
    public Rational plus(Rational r)
    { /* implementation not shown */ }

    //Similarly for times, minus, divide
           ...
    /** Ensures denominator > 0. */
    private void fixSigns()
    { /* implementation not shown */ }

    /** Ensures lowest terms. */
    private void reduce()
    { /* implementation not shown */ }
}
```

14. The method `reduce()` is not a public method because
  (A) methods whose return type is `void` cannot be public.
  (B) methods that change `this` cannot be public.
  (C) the `reduce()` method is not intended for use by clients of the `Rational` class.
  (D) the `reduce()` method is intended for use only by clients of the `Rational` class.
  (E) the `reduce()` method uses only the private data fields of the `Rational` class.

15. The constructors in the `Rational` class allow initialization of `Rational` objects in several different ways. Which of the following will cause an error?
    (A) `Rational r1 = new Rational();`
    (B) `Rational r2 = r1;`
    (C) `Rational r3 = new Rational(2,-3);`
    (D) `Rational r4 = new Rational(3.5);`
    (E) `Rational r5 = new Rational(10);`

16. Here is the implementation code for the `plus` method:

```
/** Returns (this + r). Leaves this unchanged.
 *  @return this rational number plus r
 *  @param r a rational number to be added to this Rational
 */
public Rational plus(Rational r)
{
    fixSigns();
    r.fixSigns();
    int denom = denominator * r.denominator;
    int numer = numerator * r.denominator
                + r.numerator * denominator;
    /* more code */
}
```

    Which of the following is a correct replacement for /* *more code* */?

    (A) `Rational rat(numer, denom);`
        `rat.reduce();`
        `return rat;`

    (B) `return new Rational(numer, denom);`

    (C) `reduce();`
        `Rational rat = new Rational(numer, denom);`
        `return rat;`

    (D) `Rational rat = new Rational(numer, denom);`
        `Rational.reduce();`
        `return rat;`

    (E) `Rational rat = new Rational(numer, denom);`
        `rat.reduce();`
        `return rat;`

17. Assume these declarations:

```
Rational a = new Rational();
Rational r = new Rational(numer, denom);
int n = value;
//numer, denom, and value are valid integer values
```

    Which of the following will cause a compile-time error?
    (A) `r = a.plus(r);`
    (B) `a = r.plus(new Rational(n));`
    (C) `r = r.plus(r);`
    (D) `a = n.plus(r);`
    (E) `r = r.plus(new Rational(n));`

Questions 18–20 refer to the `Temperature` class shown below:

```
public class Temperature
{
    private String scale;   //valid values are "F" or "C"
    private double degrees;

    /** constructor with specified degrees and scale */
    public Temperature(double tempDegrees, String tempScale)
    { /* implementation not shown */ }

    /** Mutator. Converts this Temperature to degrees Fahrenheit.
     * Precondition:  Temperature is a valid temperature
     *                in degrees Celsius.
     * @return this temperature in degrees Fahrenheit
     */
    public Temperature toFahrenheit()
    { /* implementation not shown */ }

    /** Mutator. Converts this Temperature to degrees Celsius.
     * Precondition:  Temperature is a valid temperature
     *                in degrees Fahrenheit.
     * @return this temperature in degrees Celsius
     */
    public Temperature toCelsius()
    { /* implementation not shown */ }

    /** Mutator.
     * @param amt the number of degrees to raise this temperature
     * @return this temperature raised by amt degrees
     */
    public Temperature raise(double amt)
    { /* implementation not shown */ }

    /** Mutator.
     * @param amt the number of degrees to lower this temperature
     * @return this temperature lowered by amt degrees
     */
    public Temperature lower(double amt)
    { /* implementation not shown */ }

    /** @param tempDegrees the number of degrees
     * @param tempScale the temperature scale
     * @return true if tempDegrees is a valid temperature
     * in the given temperature scale, false otherwise
     */
    public static boolean isValidTemp(double tempDegrees,
                                      String tempScale)
    { /* implementation not shown */ }

    //Other methods are not shown.
}
```

18. A client method contains this code segment:

```
Temperature t1 = new Temperature(40, "C");
Temperature t2 = t1;
Temperature t3 = t2.lower(20);
Temperature t4 = t1.toFahrenheit();
```

Which statement is *true* following execution of this segment?
(A) t1, t2, t3, and t4 all represent the identical temperature, in degrees Celsius.
(B) t1, t2, t3, and t4 all represent the identical temperature, in degrees Fahrenheit.
(C) t4 represents a Fahrenheit temperature, while t1, t2, and t3 all represent degrees Celsius.
(D) t1 and t2 refer to the same Temperature object; t3 refers to a Temperature object that is 20 degrees lower than t1 and t2, while t4 refers to an object that is t1 converted to Fahrenheit.
(E) A NullPointerException was thrown.

19. Consider the following code:

```
public class TempTest
{
    public static void main(String[] args)
    {
        System.out.println("Enter temperature scale: ");
        String tempScale = IO.readString();      //read user input
        System.out.println("Enter number of degrees: ");
        double tempDegrees = IO.readDouble();   //read user input
        /* code to construct a valid temperature from user input */
    }
}
```

Which is a correct replacement for */* code to construct... */*?

```
 I Temperature t = new Temperature(tempDegrees, tempScale);
   if (!t.isValidTemp(tempDegrees,tempScale))
       /* error message and exit program */

II if (isValidTemp(tempDegrees,tempScale))
       Temperature t = new Temperature(tempDegrees, tempScale);
   else
       /* error message and exit program */

III if (Temperature.isValidTemp(tempDegrees,tempScale))
       Temperature t = new Temperature(tempDegrees, tempScale);
   else
       /* error message and exit program */
```

(A) I only
(B) II only
(C) III only
(D) I and II only
(E) I and III only

20. The formula to convert degrees Celsius C to Fahrenheit F is

$$F = 1.8C + 32$$

For example, 30° C is equivalent to 86° F.

An `inFahrenheit()` accessor method is added to the `Temperature` class. Here is its implementation:

```
/** Precondition:  The temperature is a valid temperature
 *                 in degrees Celsius.
 * Postcondition:
 *   - An equivalent temperature in degrees Fahrenheit has been
 *     returned.
 *   - Original temperature remains unchanged.
 * @return an equivalent temperature in degrees Fahrenheit
 */
public Temperature inFahrenheit()
{
    Temperature result;
    /* more code */
    return result;
}
```

Which of the following correctly replaces /* *more code* */ so that the postcondition is achieved?

```
 I result = new Temperature(degrees * 1.8 + 32, "F");
```

```
II result = new Temperature(degrees * 1.8, "F");
   result = result.raise(32);
```

```
III degrees *= 1.8;
    this = this.raise(32);
    result = new Temperature(degrees, "F");
```

(A) I only
(B) II only
(C) III only
(D) I and II only
(E) I, II, and III

21. Consider this program:

```
public class CountStuff
{
    public static void doSomething()
    {
        int count = 0;
            ...
        //code to do something - no screen output produced
        count++;
    }

    public static void main(String[] args)
    {
        int count = 0;
        System.out.println("How many iterations?");
        int n = IO.readInt();      //read user input
        for (int  i = 1; i <= n; i++)
        {
            doSomething();
            System.out.println(count);
        }
    }
}
```

If the input value for n is 3, what screen output will this program subsequently produce?

(A) 0
    0
    0

(B) 1
    2
    3

(C) 3
    3
    3

(D) ?
    ?
    ?
    where ? is some undefined value.

(E) No output will be produced.

22. This question refers to the following class:

```
public class IntObject
{
    private int num;

    public IntObject()        //default constructor
    { num = 0; }

    public IntObject(int n)  //constructor
    { num = n; }

    public void increment()  //increment by 1
    { num++; }
}
```

Here is a client program that uses this class:

```
public class IntObjectTest
{
    public static IntObject someMethod(IntObject obj)
    {
        IntObject ans = obj;
        ans.increment();
        return ans;
    }

    public static void main(String[] args)
    {
        IntObject x = new IntObject(2);
        IntObject y = new IntObject(7);
        IntObject a = y;
        x = someMethod(y);
        a = someMethod(x);
    }
}
```

Just before exiting this program, what are the object values of x, y, and a, respectively?

(A) 9, 9, 9
(B) 2, 9, 9
(C) 2, 8, 9
(D) 3, 8, 9
(E) 7, 8, 9

23. Consider the following program:

```
public class Tester
{
    public void someMethod(int a, int b)
    {
        int temp = a;
        a = b;
        b = temp;
    }
}


public class TesterMain
{
    public static void main(String[] args)
    {
        int x = 6, y = 8;
        Tester tester = new Tester();
        tester.someMethod(x, y);
    }
}
```

Just before the end of execution of this program, what are the values of x, y, and temp, respectively?

(A) 6, 8, 6
(B) 8, 6, 6
(C) 6, 8, ?, where ? means undefined
(D) 8, 6, ?, where ? means undefined
(E) 8, 6, 8

ANSWER KEY

1. D	9. A	17. D
2. B	10. A	18. B
3. C	11. C	19. C
4. C	12. B	20. D
5. B	13. E	21. A
6. C	14. C	22. A
7. E	15. D	23. C
8. E	16. E	

ANSWERS EXPLAINED

1. **(D)** There are just two constructors. Constructors are recognizable by having the same name as the class, and no return type.

2. **(B)** Each of the private instance variables should be assigned the value of the matching parameter. Choice B is the only choice that does this. Choice D confuses the order of the assignment statements. Choice A gives the code for the *default* constructor, ignoring the parameters. Choice C would be correct if it were resetTime(h, m, s). As written, it doesn't assign the parameter values h, m, and s to hrs, mins, and secs. Choice E is wrong because the keyword new should be used to create a new object, not to implement the constructor!

3. **(C)** Replacement III will automatically print time t in the required form since a toString method was defined for the Time class. Replacement I is wrong because it doesn't refer to the parameter, t, of the method. Replacement II is wrong because a client program may not access private data of the class.

4. **(C)** The parameter names can be the same—the *signatures* must be different. For example,

   ```
   public void print(int x)      //prints x
   public void print(double x)   //prints x
   ```

   The signatures (method name plus parameter types) here are print(int) and print(double), respectively. The parameter name x is irrelevant. Choice A is true: All local variables and parameters go out of scope (are erased) when the method is exited. Choice B is true: Static methods apply to the whole class. Only instance methods have an implicit this parameter. Choice D is true even for object parameters: Their references are passed by value. Note that choice E is true because it's possible to have two different constructors with different signatures but the same number of parameters (e.g., one for an int argument and one for a double).

5. **(B)** Constructing an object requires the keyword new and a constructor of the Date class. Eliminate choices D and E since they omit new. The class name Date should appear on the right-hand side of the assignment statement, immediately following the keyword new. This eliminates choices A and C.

6. **(C)** Segment III will cause a `NullPointerException` to be thrown since `d` is a null reference. You cannot invoke a method for a null reference. Segment II has the effect of assigning `null` to both `d1` and `d2`—obscure but not incorrect. Segment I creates the object reference `d1` and then declares a second reference `d2` that refers to the same object as `d1`.

7. **(E)** A client program cannot access a private instance variable.

8. **(E)** All are correct. Since `write()` is a `Date` instance method, it is OK to use the private data members in its implementation code. Segment III prints `this`, the current `Date` object. This usage is correct since `write()` is part of the `Date` class. The `toString()` method guarantees that the date will be printed in the required format (see p. 175).

9. **(A)** The idea here is to read in three separate variables for month, day, and year and then to construct the required date using `new` and the `Date` class constructor with three parameters. Code segment II won't work because `month()`, `day()`, and `year()` are accessor methods that access existing values and may not be used to read new values into `bDate`. Segment III is wrong because it tries to access private instance variables from a client program.

10. **(A)** Segment I will not create a second object. It will simply cause `d2` to refer to the *same* object as `d1`, which is not what was required. The keyword `new` *must* be used to create a new object.

11. **(C)** When `recentDate` is declared in `main()`, its value is null. Recall that a method is not able to replace an object reference, so `recentDate` remains null. Note that the intent of the program is to change `recentDate` to refer to the updated `oldDate` object. The code, however, doesn't do this. Choice A is false: No methods are invoked with a null reference. Choice B is false because `addYears()` is a mutator method. Even though a method doesn't change the address of its object parameter, it can change the contents of the object, which is what happens here. Choices D and E are wrong because the `addCentury()` method cannot change the value of its `recentDate` argument.

12. **(B)** The method `getPondTemperature` is the only method that applies to more than one frog. It should therefore be static. All of the other methods relate directly to one particular `Frog` object. So `f.swim()`, `f.die()`, `f.getWeight()`, and `f.eat()` are all reasonable methods for a single instance `f` of a `Frog`. On the other hand, it doesn't make sense to say `f.getPondTemperature()`. It makes more sense to say `Frog.getPondTemperature()`, since the same value will apply to all frogs in the class.

13. **(E)** Here are the memory slots at the start of `strangeMethod(a, b)`:

a   b

| 6 | | 3 |

x   y

| 6 | | 3 |

Before exiting `strangeMethod(a, b)`:

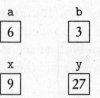

Note that 9 27 is output before exiting. After exiting `strangeMethod(a, b)`, the memory slots are

a   b
6   3

The next step outputs 6 3.

14. **(C)** The `reduce()` method will be used only in the implementation of the instance methods of the `Rational` class.

15. **(D)** None of the constructors in the `Rational` class takes a real-valued parameter. Thus, the real-valued parameter in choice D will need to be converted to an integer. Since in general truncating a real value to an integer involves a loss of precision, it is not done automatically—you have to do it explicitly with a cast. Omitting the cast causes a compile-time error.

16. **(E)** A new `Rational` object must be created using the newly calculated `numer` and `denom`. Then it must be reduced before being returned. Choice A is wrong because it doesn't correctly create the new object. Choice B returns a correctly constructed object, but one that has not been reduced. Choice C reduces the current object, `this`, instead of the new object, `rat`. Choice D is wrong because it invokes `reduce()` for the `Rational` class instead of the specific `rat` object.

17. **(D)** The `plus` method of the `Rational` class can only be invoked by `Rational` objects. Since `n` is an `int`, the statement in choice D will cause an error.

18. **(B)** This is an example of *aliasing*. The keyword `new` is used just once, which means that just one object is constructed. Here are the memory slots after each declaration:

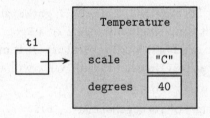

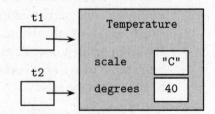

After declaration for `t1`   After declaration for `t2`

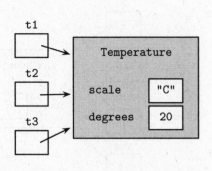

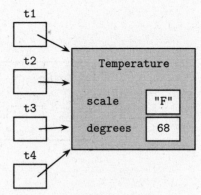

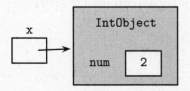

After declaration for t3

After declaration for t4

19. **(C)** Notice that isValidTemp is a static method for the Temperature class, which means that it cannot be invoked with a Temperature object. Thus, segment I is incorrect: t.isValidTemp is wrong. Segment II fails because isValidTemp is not a method of the TempTest class. It therefore must be invoked with its class name, which is what happens (correctly) in segment III: Temperature.isValidTemp.

20. **(D)** A new Temperature object must be constructed to prevent the current Temperature from being changed. Segment I, which applies the conversion formula directly to degrees, is the best way to do this. Segment II, while not the best algorithm, does work. The statement

    ```
    result = result.raise(32);
    ```

    has the effect of raising the result temperature by 32 degrees, and completing the conversion. Segment III fails because

    ```
    degrees *= 1.8;
    ```

    alters the degrees instance variable of the current object, as does

    ```
    this = this.raise(32);
    ```

    To be correct, these operations must be applied to the result object.

21. **(A)** This is a question about the scope of variables. The scope of the count variable that is declared in main() extends up to the closing brace of main(). In doSomething(), count is a local variable. After the method call in the for loop, the local variable count goes out of scope, and the value that's being printed is the value of the count in main(), which is unchanged from 0.

22. **(A)** Here are the memory slots before the first someMethod call:

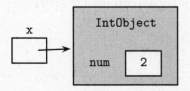

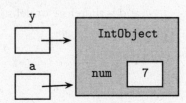

Just before exiting x = someMethod(y):

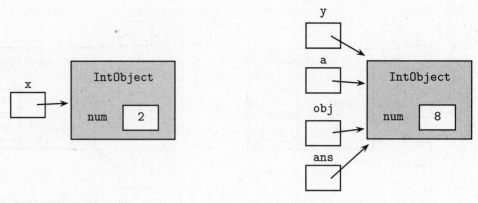

After exiting

```
x = someMethod(y);
```

x has been reassigned, so the object with num = 2 has been recycled:

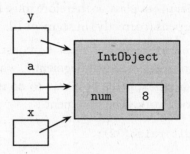

After exiting a = someMethod(x):

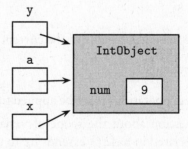

23. **(C)** Recall that when primitive types are passed as parameters, copies are made of the actual arguments. All manipulations in the method are performed on the copies, and the arguments remain unchanged. Thus x and y retain their values of 6 and 8. The local variable `temp` goes out of scope as soon as `someMethod` is exited and is therefore undefined just before the end of execution of the program.

Inheritance and Polymorphism

Say not you know another entirely,
till you have divided an inheritance with him.
—*Johann Kaspar Lavatar,* Aphorisms on Man

Chapter Goals

- Superclasses and subclasses
- Inheritance hierarchy
- Polymorphism
- Type compatibility
- Abstract classes
- Interfaces

INHERITANCE

Superclass and Subclass

Inheritance defines a relationship between objects that share characteristics. Specifically it is the mechanism whereby a new class, called a *subclass*, is created from an existing class, called a *superclass*, by absorbing its state and behavior and augmenting these with features unique to the new class. We say that the subclass *inherits* characteristics of its superclass.

Don't get confused by the names: a subclass is bigger than a superclass—it contains more data and more methods!

Inheritance provides an effective mechanism for code reuse. Suppose the code for a superclass has been tested and debugged. Since a subclass object shares features of a superclass object, the only new code required is for the additional characteristics of the subclass.

Inheritance Hierarchy

A subclass can itself be a superclass for another subclass, leading to an *inheritance hierarchy* of classes.

For example, consider the relationship between these objects: `Person`, `Employee`, `Student`, `GradStudent`, and `UnderGrad`.

131

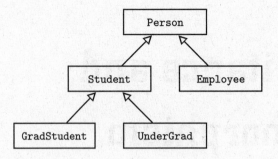

For any of these classes, an arrow points to its superclass. The arrow designates an inheritance relationship between classes, or, informally, an *is-a* relationship. Thus, an Employee *is-a* Person; a Student *is-a* Person; a GradStudent *is-a* Student; an UnderGrad *is-a* Student. Notice that the opposite is not necessarily true: A Person may not be a Student, nor is a Student necessarily an UnderGrad.

Note that the *is-a* relationship is transitive: If a GradStudent *is-a* Student and a Student *is-a* Person, then a GradStudent *is-a* Person.

Every subclass inherits the public or protected variables and methods of its superclass (see p. 135). Subclasses may have additional methods and instance variables that are not in the superclass. A subclass may redefine a method it inherits. For example, GradStudent and UnderGrad may use different algorithms for computing the course grade, and need to change a computeGrade method inherited from Student. This is called *method overriding*. If part of the original method implementation from the superclass is retained, we refer to the rewrite as *partial overriding* (see p. 135).

Implementing Subclasses

THE extends KEYWORD

The inheritance relationship between a subclass and a superclass is specified in the declaration of the subclass, using the keyword extends. The general format looks like this:

```
public class Superclass
{
    //private instance variables
    //other data members
    //constructors
    //public methods
    //private methods
}

public class Subclass extends Superclass
{
    //additional private instance variables
    //additional data members
    //constructors  (Not inherited!)
    //additional public methods
    //inherited public methods whose implementation is overridden
    //additional private methods
}
```

For example, consider the following inheritance hierarchy:

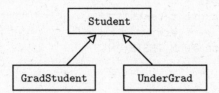

The implementation of the classes may look something like this (discussion follows the code):

```java
public class Student
{
    //data members
    public final static int NUM_TESTS = 3;
    private String name;
    private int[] tests;
    private String grade;

    //constructor
    public Student()
    {
        name = "";
        tests = new int[NUM_TESTS];
        grade = "";
    }

    //constructor
    public Student(String studName, int[] studTests, String studGrade)
    {
        name = studName;
        tests = studTests;
        grade = studGrade;
    }

    public String getName()
    { return name; }

    public String getGrade()
    { return grade; }

    public void setGrade(String newGrade)
    { grade = newGrade; }

    public void computeGrade()
    {
        if (name.equals(""))
            grade = "No grade";
        else if (getTestAverage() >= 65)
            grade = "Pass";
        else
            grade = "Fail";
    }
```

```
        public double getTestAverage()
        {
            double total = 0;
            for (int score : tests)
                total += score;
            return total/NUM_TESTS;
        }
    }

public class UnderGrad extends Student
{
    public UnderGrad()    //default constructor
    { super(); }

    //constructor
    public UnderGrad(String studName, int[] studTests, String studGrade)
    { super(studName, studTests, studGrade); }

    public void computeGrade()
    {
        if (getTestAverage() >= 70)
            setGrade("Pass");
        else
            setGrade("Fail");
    }
}

public class GradStudent extends Student
{
    private int gradID;

    public GradStudent()       //default constructor
    {
        super();
        gradID = 0;
    }

    //constructor
    public GradStudent(String studName, int[] studTests,
            String studGrade, int gradStudID)
    {
        super(studName, studTests, studGrade);
        gradID = gradStudID;
    }

    public int getID()
    { return gradID; }

    public void computeGrade()
    {
        //invokes computeGrade in Student superclass
        super.computeGrade();
        if (getTestAverage() >= 90)
            setGrade("Pass with distinction");
    }
}
```

INHERITING INSTANCE METHODS AND VARIABLES

The semantics of talking about inheritance is tricky. Subclasses do not inherit the private instance variables or private methods of their superclasses. However, objects of subclasses contain memory for those private instance variables, even though they can't directly access them. A subclass inherits all the public and protected data members of its parent.

In the `Student` example, the `UnderGrad` and `GradStudent` subclasses inherit all of the methods of the `Student` superclass. Notice, however, that the `Student` instance variables `name`, `tests`, and `grade` are private and are therefore not inherited or directly accessible to the methods in the `UnderGrad` and `GradStudent` subclasses. A subclass can, however, directly invoke the public accessor and mutator methods of the super-class. Thus, both `UnderGrad` and `GradStudent` use `getTestAverage`. Additionally, both `UnderGrad` and `GradStudent` use `setGrade` to access indirectly—and modify—`grade`.

If, instead of `private`, the access specifier for the instance variables in `Student` were `public` or `protected`, then the subclasses could directly access these variables. The keyword `protected` is not part of the AP Java subset.

Classes on the same level in a hierarchy diagram do not inherit anything from each other (for example, `UnderGrad` and `GradStudent`). All they have in common is the identical code they inherit from their superclass.

METHOD OVERRIDING AND THE super KEYWORD

Any public method in a superclass can be overridden in a subclass by defining a method with the same return type and signature (name and parameter types). For example, the `computeGrade` method in the `UnderGrad` subclass overrides the `computeGrade` method in the `Student` superclass.

Sometimes the code for overriding a method includes a call to the superclass method. This is called *partial overriding*. Typically this occurs when the subclass method wants to do what the superclass does, plus something extra. This is achieved by using the keyword super in the implementation. The `computeGrade` method in the `GradStudent` subclass partially overrides the matching method in the `Student` class. The statement

```
super.computeGrade();
```

signals that the `computeGrade` method in the superclass should be invoked here. The additional test

```
if (getTestAverage() >= 90)
    ...
```

allows a `GradStudent` to have a grade `Pass with distinction`. Note that this option is open to `GradStudents` only.

NOTE

Private methods cannot be overridden.

CONSTRUCTORS AND super

Constructors are never inherited! If no constructor is written for a subclass, the superclass default constructor with no parameters is generated. If the superclass does

Be sure to provide at least one constructor when you write a subclass. Constructors are never inherited from the superclass.

not have a default (zero-parameter) constructor, but only a constructor with parameters, a compiler error will occur. If there is a default constructor in the superclass, inherited data members will be initialized as for the superclass. Additional instance variables in the subclass will get a default initialization—0 for primitive types and `null` for reference types.

A subclass constructor can be implemented with a call to the `super` method, which invokes the superclass constructor. For example, the default constructor in the `UnderGrad` class is identical to that of the `Student` class. This is implemented with the statement

```
super();
```

The second constructor in the `UnderGrad` class is called with parameters that match those in the constructor of the `Student` superclass.

```
public UnderGrad(String studName, int[] studTests, String studGrade)
{ super(studName, studTests, studGrade); }
```

For each constructor, the call to super has the effect of initializing the instance variables `name`, `tests`, and `grade` exactly as they are initialized in the `Student` class.

Contrast this with the constructors in `GradStudent`. In each case, the instance variables `name`, `tests`, and `grade` are initialized as for the `Student` class. Then the new instance variable, `gradID`, must be explicitly initialized.

```
public GradStudent()
{
    super();
    gradID = 0;
}

public GradStudent(String studName, int[] studTests,
         String studGrade, int gradStudID)
{
    super(studName, studTests, studGrade);
    gradID = gradStudID;
}
```

NOTE

1. If super is used in the implementation of a subclass constructor, it *must* be used in the first line of the constructor body.
2. If no constructor is provided in a subclass, the compiler provides the following default constructor:

```
public SubClass()
{
    super();       //calls default constructor of superclass
}
```

> ### Rules for Subclasses
>
> - A subclass can add new private instance variables.
> - A subclass can add new public, private, or static methods.
> - A subclass can override inherited methods.
> - A subclass may not redefine a public method as private.
> - A subclass may not override static methods of the superclass.
> - A subclass should define its own constructors.
> - A subclass cannot directly access the private members of its superclass. It must use accessor or mutator methods.

Declaring Subclass Objects

When a superclass object is declared in a client program, that reference can refer not only to an object of the superclass, but also to objects of any of its subclasses. Thus, each of the following is legal:

```
Student s = new Student();
Student g = new GradStudent();
Student u = new UnderGrad();
```

This works because a `GradStudent` *is-a* `Student`, and an `UnderGrad` *is-a* `Student`.

Note that since a `Student` is not necessarily a `GradStudent` nor an `UnderGrad`, the following declarations are *not* valid:

```
GradStudent g = new Student();
UnderGrad u = new Student();
```

Consider these valid declarations:

```
Student s = new Student("Brian Lorenzen", new int[] {90,94,99},
        "none");
Student u = new UnderGrad("Tim Broder", new int[] {90,90,100},
        "none");
Student g = new GradStudent("Kevin Cristella",
        new int[] {85,70,90}, "none", 1234);
```

Suppose you make the method call

```
s.setGrade("Pass");
```

The appropriate method in `Student` is found and the new grade assigned. The method calls

```
g.setGrade("Pass");
```

and

```
u.setGrade("Pass");
```

achieve the same effect on g and u since `GradStudent` and `UnderGrad` both inherit the `setGrade` method from `Student`. The following method calls, however, won't work:

```
int studentNum = s.getID();
int underGradNum = u.getID();
```

Neither `Student` s nor `UnderGrad` u inherit the `getID` method from the `GradStudent` class: A superclass does not inherit from a subclass.

Now consider the following valid method calls:

```
s.computeGrade();
g.computeGrade();
u.computeGrade();
```

Since s, g, and u have all been declared to be of type `Student`, will the appropriate method be executed in each case? That is the topic of the next section, *polymorphism*.

NOTE

The initializer list syntax used in constructing the array parameters—for example, `new int[] {90,90,100}`— will not be tested on the AP exam.

POLYMORPHISM

A method that has been overridden in at least one subclass is said to be *polymorphic*. An example is `computeGrade`, which is redefined for both `GradStudent` and `UnderGrad`.

Polymorphism is the mechanism of selecting the appropriate method for a particular object in a class hierarchy. The correct method is chosen because, in Java, method calls are always determined by the type of the *actual object*, not the type of the object reference. For example, even though s, g, and u are all declared as type `Student`, `s.computeGrade()`, `g.computeGrade()`, and `u.computeGrade()` will all perform the correct operations for their particular instances. In Java, the selection of the correct method occurs *during the run of the program*.

Dynamic Binding (Late Binding)

Making a run-time decision about which instance method to call is known as *dynamic binding* or *late binding*. Contrast this with selecting the correct method when methods are *overloaded* (see p. 99) rather than overridden. The compiler selects the correct overloaded method at compile time by comparing the methods' signatures. This is known as *static binding*, or *early binding*. In polymorphism, the actual method that will be called is not determined by the compiler. Think of it this way: The compiler determines *if* a method can be called (i.e., is it legal?), while the run-time environment determines *how* it will be called (i.e., which overridden form should be used?).

Example 1

```
Student s = null;
Student u = new UnderGrad("Tim Broder", new int[] {90,90,100},
        "none");
Student g = new GradStudent("Kevin Cristella",
        new int[] {85,70,90}, "none", 1234);
System.out.print("Enter student status: ");
System.out.println("Grad (G), Undergrad (U), Neither (N)");
String str = IO.readString();        //read user input
if (str.equals("G"))
    s = g;
else if (str.equals("U"))
    s = u;
else
    s = new Student();
s.computeGrade();
```

When this code fragment is run, the computeGrade method used will depend on the type of the actual object s refers to, which in turn depends on the user input.

Example 2

```java
public class StudentTest
{
    public static void computeAllGrades(Student[] studentList)
    {
        for (Student s : studentList)
            if (s != null)
                s.computeGrade();
    }

    public static void main(String[] args)
    {
        Student[] stu = new Student[5];
        stu[0] = new Student("Brian Lorenzen",
                    new int[] {90,94,99}, "none");
        stu[1] = new UnderGrad("Tim Broder",
                    new int[] {90,90,100}, "none");
        stu[2] = new GradStudent("Kevin Cristella",
                    new int[] {85,70,90}, "none", 1234);
        computeAllGrades(stu);
    }
}
```

Here an array of five Student references is created, all of them initially null. Three of these references, stu[0], stu[1], and stu[2], are then assigned to actual objects. The computeAllGrades method steps through the array invoking for each of the objects the appropriate computeGrade method, using dynamic binding in each case. The null test in computeAllGrades is necessary because some of the array references could be null.

> Polymorphism applies only to overridden methods in subclasses.

Using super in a Subclass

A subclass can call a method in its superclass by using super. Suppose that the superclass method then calls another method that has been overridden in the subclass. By polymorphism, the method that is executed is the one in the subclass. The computer keeps track and executes any pending statements in either method.

Example

```java
public class Dancer
{
    public void act()
    {
        System.out.print (" spin");
        doTrick();
    }

    public void doTrick()
    {
        System.out.print (" float");
    }
}
```

```
public class Acrobat extends Dancer
{
    public void act()
    {
        super.act();
        System.out.print (" flip");
    }

    public void doTrick()
    {
        System.out.print (" somersault");
    }
}
```

Suppose the following declaration appears in a class other than Dancer or Acrobat:

```
Dancer a = new Acrobat();
```

What is printed as a result of the call a.act()?

When a.act() is called, the act method of Acrobat is executed. This is an example of polymorphism. The first line, super.act(), goes to the act method of Dancer, the superclass. This prints spin, then calls doTrick(). Again, using polymorphism, the doTrick method in Acrobat is called, printing somersault. Now, completing the act method of Acrobat, flip is printed. So what all got printed?

```
spin somersault flip
```

NOTE

Even though there are no constructors in either the Dancer or Acrobat classes, the declaration

```
Dancer a = new Acrobat();
```

compiles without error. This is because Dancer, while not having an explicit super-class, has an implicit superclass, Object, and gets its default (no-argument) constructor slotted into its code. Similarly the Acrobat class gets this constructor slotted into its code.

The statement Dancer a = new Acrobat(); will not compile, however, if the Dancer class has at least one constructor with parameters but no default constructor.

TYPE COMPATIBILITY

Downcasting

Consider the statements

```
Student s = new GradStudent();
GradStudent g = new GradStudent();
int x = s.getID();              //compile-time error
int y = g.getID();              //legal
```

Both s and g represent GradStudent objects, so why does s.getID() cause an error? The reason is that s is of type Student, and the Student class doesn't have a getID method. At compile time, only nonprivate methods of the Student class can appear to the right of the dot operator when applied to s. Don't confuse this with polymorphism: getID is not a polymorphic method. It occurs in just the GradStudent class and can therefore be called only by a GradStudent object.

The error shown above can be fixed by casting s to the correct type:

```
int x = ((GradStudent) s).getID();
```

Since s (of type Student) is actually representing a GradStudent object, such a cast can be carried out. Casting a superclass to a subclass type is called a *downcast*.

NOTE

1. The outer parentheses are necessary:

```
int x = (GradStudent) s.getID();
```

will still cause an error, despite the cast. This is because the dot operator has higher precedence than casting, so s.getID() is invoked before s is cast to GradStudent.

2. The statement

```
int y = g.getID();
```

compiles without problem because g is declared to be of type GradStudent, and this is the class that contains getID. No cast is required.

Type Rules for Polymorphic Method Calls

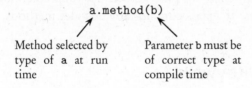

Method selected by type of a at run time

Parameter b must be of correct type at compile time

- For a declaration like

```
Superclass a = new Subclass();
```

the type of a at compile time is Superclass; at run time it is Subclass.

- At compile time, method must be found in the class of a, that is, in Superclass. (This is true whether the method is polymorphic or not.) If method cannot be found in the class of a, you need to do an explicit cast on a to its actual type.

- For a polymorphic method, at run time the actual type of a is determined—Subclass in this example—and method is selected from Subclass. This could be an inherited method if there is no overriding method.

- The type of parameter b is checked at compile time. You may need to do an explicit cast to the subclass type to make this correct.

The `ClassCastException`

The `ClassCastException` is a run-time exception thrown to signal an attempt to cast an object to a class of which it is not an instance.

```
Student u = new UnderGrad();
System.out.println((String) u);     //ClassCastException
                                //u is not an instance of String
int x = ((GradStudent) u).getID(); //ClassCastException
                            //u is not an instance of GradStudent
```

ABSTRACT CLASSES

Abstract Class

An *abstract class* is a superclass that represents an abstract concept, and therefore should not be instantiated. For example, a maze program could have several different maze components—paths, walls, entrances, and exits. All of these share certain features (e.g., location, and a way of displaying). They can therefore all be declared as subclasses of the abstract class `MazeComponent`. The program will create path objects, wall objects, and so on, but no instances of `MazeComponent`.

An abstract class may contain *abstract methods*. An abstract method has no implementation code, just a header. The rationale for an abstract method is that there is no good default code for the method. Every subclass will need to override this method, so why bother with a meaningless implementation in the superclass? The method appears in the abstract class as a placeholder. The implementation for the method occurs in the subclasses. If a class contains any abstract methods, it *must* be declared an abstract class.

The abstract Keyword

An abstract class is declared with the keyword `abstract` in the header:

```
public abstract class AbstractClass
{   ...
```

The keyword `extends` is used as before to declare a subclass:

```
public class SubClass extends AbstractClass
{   ...
```

If a subclass of an abstract class does not provide implementation code for all the abstract methods of its superclass, it too becomes an abstract class and must be declared as such to avoid a compile-time error:

```
public abstract class SubClass extends AbstractClass
{   ...
```

Here is an example of an abstract class, with two concrete (nonabstract) subclasses.

```java
public abstract class Shape
{
    private String name;

    //constructor
    public Shape(String shapeName)
    { name = shapeName; }

    public String getName()
    { return name; }

    public abstract double area();
    public abstract double perimeter();

    public double semiPerimeter()
    { return perimeter() / 2; }
}

public class Circle extends Shape
{
    private double radius;

    //constructor
    public Circle(double circleRadius, String circleName)
    {
        super(circleName);
        radius = circleRadius;
    }

    public double perimeter()
    { return 2 * Math.PI * radius; }

    public double area()
    { return Math.PI * radius * radius; }
}

public class Square extends Shape
{
    private double side;

    //constructor
    public Square(double squareSide, String squareName)
    {
        super(squareName);
        side = squareSide;
    }

    public double perimeter()
    { return 4 * side; }

    public double area()
    { return side * side; }
}
```

NOTE

1. It is meaningless to define `perimeter` and `area` methods for `Shape`—thus, these are declared as abstract methods.

2. An abstract class can have both instance variables and concrete (nonabstract) methods. See, for example, `name`, `getName`, and `semiPerimeter` in the `Shape` class.

3. Abstract methods are declared with the keyword `abstract`. There is no method body. The header is terminated with a semicolon.

4. A concrete (non-abstract) subclass of an abstract superclass must provide implementation code for all abstract methods of the superclass. Therefore both the `Circle` and `Square` classes implement both the `perimeter` and `area` methods.

5. It is possible for an abstract class to have no abstract methods. (An abstract subclass of an abstract superclass inherits the abstract methods without explicitly declaring them.)

6. An abstract class may or may not have constructors.

7. No instances can be created for an abstract class:

```
Shape a = new Shape("blob");  //Illegal.
                    //Can't create instance of abstract class.
Shape c = new Circle(1.5, "small circle");  //legal
```

8. Polymorphism works with abstract classes as it does with concrete classes:

```
Shape circ = new Circle(10, "circle");
Shape sq = new Square(9.4, "square");
Shape s = null;
System.out.println("Which shape?");
String str = IO.readString();        //read user input
if (str.equals("circle"))
    s = circ;
else
    s = sq;
System.out.println("Area of " + s.getName() + " is "
        + s.area());
```

INTERFACES

Interface

An *interface* is a collection of related methods, either abstract (headers only) or default (implementation provided in the interface). Default methods are new in Java 8, and will not be tested on the AP exam. Non-default (i.e., abstract) methods will be tested on the exam and are discussed below.

Students may be required to design, create, or modify classes that implement interfaces with abstract methods.

The non-default methods are both public and abstract—no need to explicitly include these keywords. As such, they provide a framework of behavior for any class.

The classes that implement a given interface may represent objects that are vastly different. They all, however, have in common a capability or feature expressed in the methods of the interface. An interface called `FlyingObject`, for example, may have the methods `fly` and `isFlying`. Some classes that implement `FlyingObject` could be `Bird`,

Airplane, Missile, Butterfly, and Witch. A class called Turtle would be unlikely to implement FlyingObject because turtles don't fly.

An interface called Computable may have just three methods: add, subtract, and multiply. Classes that implement Computable could be Fraction, Matrix, LongInteger, and ComplexNumber. It would not be meaningful, however, for a TelevisionSet to implement Computable—what does it mean, for example, to multiply two TelevisionSet objects?

A class that implements an interface can define any number of methods. In particular, it contracts to provide implementations for *all* the non-default (i.e., abstract) methods declared in the interface. If it fails to implement any of the methods, the class must be declared abstract.

> A nonabstract class that implements an interface must implement every abstract method of the interface.

Defining an Interface

An interface is declared with the interface keyword. For example,

```
public interface FlyingObject
{
    void fly();          //method that simulates flight of object
    boolean isFlying();  //true if object is in flight,
                         //false otherwise
}
```

The implements Keyword

Interfaces are implemented using the implements keyword. For example,

```
public class Bird implements FlyingObject
{
    ...
```

This declaration means that two of the methods in the Bird class must be fly and isFlying. Note that any subclass of Bird will automatically implement the interface FlyingObject, since fly and isFlying will be inherited by the subclass.

A class that extends a superclass can also *directly* implement an interface. For example,

```
public class Mosquito extends Insect implements FlyingObject
{
    ...
```

NOTE

1. The extends clause must precede the implements clause.
2. A class can have just one superclass, but it can implement any number of interfaces:

```
public class SubClass extends SuperClass
        implements Interface1, Interface2, ...
```

The Comparable Interface

Starting in 2015, this will not be tested on the AP exam. Students will, however, be required to use compareTo for comparison of strings (p. 178).

The standard java.lang package contains the Comparable interface, which provides a useful method for comparing objects.

Optional topic

(continued)

Classes written for objects that need to be compared should implement Comparable.

```
public interface Comparable
{
    int compareTo(Object obj);
}
```

Any class that implements Comparable must provide a compareTo method. This method compares the implicit object (this) with the parameter object (obj) and returns a negative integer, zero, or a positive integer depending on whether the implicit object is less than, equal to, or greater than the parameter. If the two objects being compared are not type compatible, a ClassCastException is thrown by the method.

Example

The abstract Shape class defined previously (p. 143) is modified to implement the Comparable interface:

```
public abstract class Shape implements Comparable
{
    private String name;

    //constructor
    public Shape(String shapeName)
    { name = shapeName; }

    public String getName()
    { return name; }

    public abstract double area();
    public abstract double perimeter();

    public double semiPerimeter()
    { return perimeter() / 2; }

    public int compareTo(Object obj)
    {
        final double EPSILON = 1.0e-15;    //slightly bigger than
                                           //machine precision
        Shape rhs = (Shape) obj;
        double diff = area() - rhs.area();
        if (Math.abs(diff) <= EPSILON * Math.abs(area()))
            return 0;  //area of this shape equals area of obj
        else if (diff < 0)
            return -1; //area of this shape less than area of obj
        else
            return 1;  //area of this shape greater than area of obj
    }
}
```

NOTE

1. The Circle, Square, and other subclasses of Shape will all automatically implement Comparable and inherit the compareTo method.
2. It is tempting to use a simpler test for equality of areas, namely

```
        if (diff == 0)
            return 0;
```

(continued)

But recall that real numbers can have round-off errors in their storage (Box p. 65). This means that the simple test may return false even though the two areas are essentially equal. A more robust test is implemented in the code given, namely to test if the relative error in `diff` is small enough to be considered zero.

3. The `Object` class is a universal superclass (see p. 174). This means that the `compareTo` method can take as a parameter any object reference that implements `Comparable`.

4. One of the first steps of a `compareTo` method must cast the `Object` argument to the class type, in this case `Shape`. If this is not done, the compiler won't find the `area` method—remember, an `Object` is not necessarily a `Shape`.

5. The algorithm one chooses in `compareTo` should in general be consistent with the `equals` method (see p. 176): Whenever `object1.equals(object2)` returns true, `object1.compareTo(object2)` returns 0.

Here is a program that finds the larger of two `Comparable` objects.

```
public class FindMaxTest
{
    /** Return the larger of two objects a and b. */
    public static Comparable max(Comparable a, Comparable b)
    {
        if (a.compareTo(b) > 0) //if a > b ...
            return a;
        else
            return b;
    }

    /** Test max on two Shape objects. */
    public static void main(String[] args)
    {
        Shape s1 = new Circle(3.0, "circle");
        Shape s2 = new Square(4.5, "square");
        System.out.println("Area of " + s1.getName() + " is " +
                s1.area());
        System.out.println("Area of " + s2.getName() + " is " +
                s2.area());
        Shape s3 = (Shape) max(s1, s2);
        System.out.println("The larger shape is the " +
                s3.getName());
    }
}
```

Here is the output:

```
Area of circle is 28.27
Area of square is 20.25
The larger shape is the circle
```

NOTE

1. The `max` method takes parameters of type `Comparable`. Since `s1` *is-a* `Comparable` object and `s2` *is-a* `Comparable` object, no casting is necessary in the method call.

2. The `max` method can be called with any two `Comparable` objects, for example, two `String` objects or two `Integer` objects (see Chapter 4).

3. The objects must be type compatible (i.e., it must make sense to compare them). For example, in the program shown, if s1 *is-a* Shape and s2 *is-a* String, the compareTo method will throw a ClassCastException at the line

   ```
   Shape rhs = (Shape) obj;
   ```

4. The cast is needed in the line

   ```
   Shape s3 = (Shape) max(s1, s2);
   ```

   since max(s1, s2) returns a Comparable.

5. A primitive type is not an object and therefore cannot be passed as Comparable. You can, however, use a wrapper class and in this way convert a primitive type to a Comparable (see p. 180).

ABSTRACT CLASS VS. INTERFACE

Consider writing a program that simulates a game of Battleships. The program may have a Ship class with subclasses Submarine, Cruiser, Destroyer, and so on. The various ships will be placed in a two-dimensional grid that represents a part of the ocean.

An abstract class Ship is a good design choice. There will not be any instances of Ship objects because the specific features of the subclasses must be known in order to place these ships in the grid. A Grid interface that manipulates objects in a two-dimensional setting suggests itself for the two-dimensional grid.

Notice that the abstract Ship class is specific to the Battleships application, whereas the Grid interface is not. You could use the Grid interface in any program that has a two-dimensional grid.

Interface vs. Abstract Class

- Use an abstract class for an object that is application-specific but incomplete without its subclasses.

- Consider using an interface when its methods are suitable for your program but could be equally applicable in a variety of programs.

- An interface typically doesn't provide implementations for any of its methods, whereas an abstract class does. (In Java 8, implementation of default methods is allowed in interfaces.)

- An interface cannot contain instance variables, whereas an abstract class can.

- It is not possible to create an instance of an interface object or an abstract class object.

Chapter Summary

You should be able to write your own subclasses, given any superclass, and also design, create, or modify a class that implements an interface.

Be sure you understand the use of the keyword super, both in writing constructors and calling methods of the superclass.

You should understand what polymorphism is: Recall that it only operates when methods have been overridden in at least one subclass. You should also be able to explain the difference between the following concepts:

- An abstract class and an interface.

- An overloaded method and an overridden method.

- Dynamic binding (late binding) and static binding (early binding).

MULTIPLE-CHOICE QUESTIONS ON INHERITANCE AND POLYMORPHISM

Questions 1–10 refer to the BankAccount, SavingsAccount, and CheckingAccount classes defined below:

```java
public class BankAccount
{
    private double balance;

    public BankAccount()
    { balance = 0; }

    public BankAccount(double acctBalance)
    { balance = acctBalance; }

    public void deposit(double amount)
    { balance += amount; }

    public void withdraw(double amount)
    { balance -= amount; }

    public double getBalance()
    { return balance; }
}

public class SavingsAccount extends BankAccount
{
    private double interestRate;

    public SavingsAccount()
    { /* implementation not shown */ }

    public SavingsAccount(double acctBalance, double rate)
    { /* implementation not shown */ }

    public void addInterest()    //Add interest to balance
    { /* implementation not shown */ }
}

public class CheckingAccount extends BankAccount
{
    private static final double FEE = 2.0;
    private static final double MIN_BALANCE = 50.0;

    public CheckingAccount(double acctBalance)
    { /* implementation not shown */ }

    /** FEE of $2 deducted if withdrawal leaves balance less
     *  than MIN_BALANCE. Allows for negative balance. */
    public void withdraw(double amount)
    { /* implementation not shown */ }
}
```

1. Of the methods shown, how many different nonconstructor methods can be invoked by a `SavingsAccount` object?
    (A) 1
    (B) 2
    (C) 3
    (D) 4
    (E) 5

2. Which of the following correctly implements the default constructor of the `SavingsAccount` class?

    I   `interestRate = 0;`
        `super();`

    II `super();`
        `interestRate = 0;`

    III `super();`

    (A) II only
    (B) I and II only
    (C) II and III only
    (D) III only
    (E) I, II, and III

3. Which is a correct implementation of the constructor with parameters in the `SavingsAccount` class?

    (A) `balance = acctBalance;`
        `interestRate = rate;`

    (B) `getBalance() =  acctBalance;`
        `interestRate = rate;`

    (C) `super();`
        `interestRate = rate;`

    (D) `super(acctBalance);`
        `interestRate = rate;`

    (E) `super(acctBalance, rate);`

4. Which is a correct implementation of the `CheckingAccount` constructor?

    I   `super(acctBalance);`

    II `super();`
        `deposit(acctBalance);`

    III `deposit(acctBalance);`

    (A) I only
    (B) II only
    (C) III only
    (D) II and III only
    (E) I, II, and III

5. Which is correct implementation code for the `withdraw` method in the `CheckingAccount` class?

   (A) ```
       super.withdraw(amount);
       if (balance < MIN_BALANCE)
           super.withdraw(FEE);
       ```

   (B) ```
       withdraw(amount);
       if (balance < MIN_BALANCE)
           withdraw(FEE);
       ```

   (C) ```
       super.withdraw(amount);
       if (getBalance() < MIN_BALANCE)
           super.withdraw(FEE);
       ```

   (D) ```
       withdraw(amount);
       if (getBalance() < MIN_BALANCE)
           withdraw(FEE);
       ```

   (E) ```
       balance -= amount;
       if (balance < MIN_BALANCE)
           balance -= FEE;
       ```

6. Redefining the `withdraw` method in the `CheckingAccount` class is an example of
   (A) method overloading.
   (B) method overriding.
   (C) downcasting.
   (D) dynamic binding (late binding).
   (E) static binding (early binding).

Use the following for Questions 7–9.

A program to test the `BankAccount`, `SavingsAccount`, and `CheckingAccount` classes has these declarations:

```
BankAccount b = new BankAccount(1400);
BankAccount s = new SavingsAccount(1000, 0.04);
BankAccount c = new CheckingAccount(500);
```

7. Which method call will cause an error?
   (A) `b.deposit(200);`
   (B) `s.withdraw(500);`
   (C) `c.withdraw(500);`
   (D) `s.deposit(10000);`
   (E) `s.addInterest();`

8. In order to test polymorphism, which method must be used in the program?
   (A) Either a `SavingsAccount` constructor or a `CheckingAccount` constructor
   (B) `addInterest`
   (C) `deposit`
   (D) `withdraw`
   (E) `getBalance`
```

9. Which of the following will *not* cause a `ClassCastException` to be thrown?
   (A) `((SavingsAccount) b).addInterest();`
   (B) `((CheckingAccount) b).withdraw(200);`
   (C) `((CheckingAccount) c).deposit(800);`
   (D) `((CheckingAccount) s).withdraw(150);`
   (E) `((SavingsAccount) c).addInterest();`

10. A new method is added to the `BankAccount` class.

```
/** Transfer amount from this BankAccount to another BankAccount.
 * Precondition: balance > amount
 * @param another a different BankAccount object
 * @param amount the amount to be transferred
 */
public void transfer(BankAccount another, double amount)
{
    withdraw(amount);
    another.deposit(amount);
}
```

A program has these declarations:

```
BankAccount b = new BankAccount(650);
SavingsAccount timsSavings = new SavingsAccount(1500, 0.03);
CheckingAccount daynasChecking = new CheckingAccount(2000);
```

Which of the following will transfer money from one account to another without error?

I `b.transfer(timsSavings, 50);`

II `timsSavings.transfer(daynasChecking, 30);`

III `daynasChecking.transfer(b, 55);`

(A) I only
(B) II only
(C) III only
(D) I, II, and III
(E) None

11. Consider these class declarations:

```
public class Person
{
    ...
}

public class Teacher extends Person
{
    ...
}
```

Which is a true statement?

I Teacher inherits the constructors of Person.
II Teacher can add new methods and private instance variables.
III Teacher can override existing private methods of Person.

(A) I only
(B) II only
(C) III only
(D) I and II only
(E) II and III only

12. Which statement about abstract classes and interfaces is *false*?
  (A) An interface cannot implement any non-default instance methods, whereas an abstract class can.
  (B) A class can implement many interfaces but can have only one superclass.
  (C) An unlimited number of unrelated classes can implement the same interface.
  (D) It is not possible to construct either an abstract class object or an interface object.
  (E) All of the methods in both an abstract class and an interface are public.

13. Consider the following hierarchy of classes:

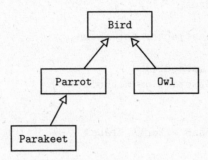

A program is written to print data about various birds:

```
public class BirdStuff
{
    public static void printName(Bird b)
    { /* implementation not shown */ }

    public static void printBirdCall(Parrot p)
    { /* implementation not shown */ }

    //several more Bird methods

    public static void main(String[] args)
    {
        Bird bird1 = new Bird();
        Bird bird2 = new Parrot();
        Parrot parrot1 = new Parrot();
        Parrot parrot2 = new Parakeet();
        /* more code */
    }
}
```

Assuming that none of the given classes is abstract and all have default constructors, which of the following segments of /* *more code* */ will *not* cause an error?

(A) `printName(parrot2);`
    `printBirdCall((Parrot) bird2);`

(B) `printName((Parrot) bird1);`
    `printBirdCall(bird2);`

(C) `printName(bird2);`
    `printBirdCall(bird2);`

(D) `printName((Parakeet) parrot1);`
    `printBirdCall(parrot2);`

(E) `printName((Owl) parrot2);`
    `printBirdCall((Parakeet) parrot2);`

Refer to the classes below for Questions 14 and 15.

```
public class ClassA
{
    //default constructor not shown ...

    public void method1()
    { /* implementation of method1 */ }
}

public class ClassB extends ClassA
{
    //default constructor not shown ...

    public void method1()
    { /* different implementation from method1 in ClassA*/ }


    public void method2()
    { /* implementation of method2 */ }
}
```

14. The `method1` method in `ClassB` is an example of
    (A) method overloading.
    (B) method overriding.
    (C) polymorphism.
    (D) information hiding.
    (E) procedural abstraction.

15. Consider the following declarations in a client class.

    ```
    ClassA ob1 = new ClassA();
    ClassA ob2 = new ClassB();
    ```

    Which of the following method calls will cause an error?

     I `ob1.method2();`

     II `ob2.method2();`

     III `((ClassB) ob1).method2();`

    (A) I only
    (B) II only
    (C) III only
    (D) I and III only
    (E) I, II, and III

Use the declarations below for Questions 16–18.

```
public abstract class Solid
{
    private String name;

    //constructor
    public Solid(String solidName)
    { name = solidName; }

    public String getName()
    { return name; }

    public abstract double volume();
}

public class Sphere extends Solid
{
    private double radius;

    //constructor
    public Sphere(String sphereName, double sphereRadius)
    {
        super(sphereName);
        radius = sphereRadius;
    }

    public double volume()
    { return (4.0/3.0) * Math.PI * radius * radius * radius; }
}

public class RectangularPrism extends Solid
{
    private double length;
    private double width;
    private double height;

    //constructor
    public RectangularPrism(String prismName, double l, double w,
            double h)
    {
        super(prismName);
        length = l;
        width = w;
        height = h;
    }

    public double volume()
    { return length * width * height; }
}
```

16. A program that tests these classes has the following declarations and assignments:

```
Solid s1, s2, s3, s4;
s1 = new Solid("blob");
s2 = new Sphere("sphere", 3.8);
s3 = new RectangularPrism("box", 2, 4, 6.5);
s4 = null;
```

How many of the above lines of code are incorrect?
(A) 0
(B) 1
(C) 2
(D) 3
(E) 4

17. Which is *false*?
    (A) If a program has several objects declared as type `Solid`, the decision about which `volume` method to call will be resolved at run time.
    (B) If the `Solid` class were modified to provide a default implementation for the `volume` method, it would no longer need to be an abstract class.
    (C) If the `Sphere` and `RectangularPrism` classes failed to provide an implementation for the `volume` method, they would need to be declared as abstract classes.
    (D) The fact that there is no reasonable default implementation for the `volume` method in the `Solid` class suggests that it should be an abstract method.
    (E) Since `Solid` is abstract and its subclasses are nonabstract, polymorphism no longer applies when these classes are used in a program.

18. Here is a program that prints the volume of a solid:

```
public class SolidMain
{
    /** Output volume of Solid s. */
    public static void printVolume(Solid s)
    {
        System.out.println("Volume = " + s.volume() +
                " cubic units");
    }

    public static void main(String[] args)
    {
        Solid sol;
        Solid sph = new Sphere("sphere", 4);
        Solid rec = new RectangularPrism("box", 3, 6, 9);
        int flipCoin = (int) (Math.random() * 2);   //0 or 1
        if (flipCoin == 0)
            sol = sph;
        else
            sol = rec;
        printVolume(sol);
    }
}
```

Which is a true statement about this program?
(A) It will output the volume of the sphere or box, as intended.
(B) It will output the volume of the default Solid s, which is neither a sphere nor a box.
(C) A ClassCastException will be thrown.
(D) A compile-time error will occur because there is no implementation code for volume in the Solid class.
(E) A run-time error will occur because of parameter type mismatch in the method call printVolume(sol).

19. Consider the `Computable` interface below for performing simple calculator operations:

```
public interface Computable
{
    /** Return this Object + y. */
    Object add(Object y);

    /** Return this Object - y. */
    Object subtract(Object y);

    /** Return this Object * y. */
    Object multiply(Object y);
}
```

Which of the following is the *least* suitable class for implementing `Computable`?

(A) `LargeInteger`   //integers with 100 digits or more

(B) `Fraction`   //implemented with numerator and
                  //denominator of type int

(C) `IrrationalNumber` //nonrepeating, nonterminating decimal

(D) `Length`   //implemented with different units, such
                //as inches, centimeters, etc.

(E) `BankAccount`   //implemented with balance

Refer to the `Player` interface shown below for Questions 20–23.

```
public interface Player
{
    /** Return an integer that represents a move in a game. */
    int getMove();

    /** Display the status of the game for this Player after
     *  implementing the next move. */
    void updateDisplay();
}
```

20. `HumanPlayer` is a class that implements the `Player` interface. Another class, `SmartPlayer`, is a subclass of `HumanPlayer`. Which statement is *false*?
    (A) `SmartPlayer` automatically implements the `Player` interface.
    (B) `HumanPlayer` must contain implementations of both the `updateDisplay` and `getMove` methods, or be declared as abstract.
    (C) It is not possible to declare a reference of type `Player`.
    (D) The `SmartPlayer` class can override the methods `updateDisplay` and `getMove` of the `HumanPlayer` class.
    (E) A method in a client program can have `Player` as a parameter type.

21. A programmer plans to write programs that simulate various games. In each case he will have several classes, each representing a different kind of competitor in the game, such as ExpertPlayer, ComputerPlayer, RecklessPlayer, CheatingPlayer, Beginner, IntermediatePlayer, and so on. It may or may not be suitable for these classes to implement the Player interface, depending on the particular game being simulated. In the games described below, which is the *least* suitable for having the competitor classes implement the given Player interface?

(A) High-Low Guessing Game: The computer thinks of a number and the competitor who guesses it with the least number of guesses wins. After each guess, the computer tells whether its number is higher or lower than the guess.

(B) Chips: Start with a pile of chips. Each player in turn removes some number of chips. The winner is the one who removes the final chip. The first player may remove any number of chips, but not all of them. Each subsequent player must remove at least one chip and at most twice the number removed by the preceding player.

(C) Chess: Played on a square board of 64 squares of alternating colors. There are just two players, called White and Black, the colors of their respective pieces. The players each have a set of pieces on the board that can move according to a set of rules. The players alternate moves, where a move consists of moving any one piece to another square. If that square is occupied by an opponent's piece, the piece is captured and removed from the board.

(D) Tic-Tac-Toe: Two players alternate placing "X" or "O" on a 3 × 3 grid. The first player to get three in a row, where a row can be vertical, horizontal, or diagonal, wins.

(E) Battleships: There are two players, each with a 10 × 10 grid hidden from his opponent. Various "ships" are placed on the grid. A move consists of calling out a grid location, trying to "hit" an opponent's ship. Players alternate moves. The first player to sink his opponent's fleet wins.

Consider these declarations for Questions 22 and 23:

```
public class HumanPlayer implements Player
{
    private String name;

    //Constructors not shown ...

    //Code to implement getMove and updateDisplay not shown ...

    public String getName()
    { /* implementation not shown */ }
}

public class ExpertPlayer extends HumanPlayer
{
    private int rating;

    //Constructors not shown ...

    public int compareTo(ExpertPlayer expert)
    { /* implementation not shown */ }
}
```

22. Which code segment in a client program will cause an error?

```
 I  Player p1 = new HumanPlayer();
    Player p2 = new ExpertPlayer();
    int x1 = p1.getMove();
    int x2 = p2.getMove();

 II int x;
    Player c1 = new ExpertPlayer(/* correct parameter list */);
    Player c2 = new ExpertPlayer(/* correct parameter list */);
    if (c1.compareTo(c2) < 0)
        x = c1.getMove();
    else
        x = c2.getMove();

III int x;
    HumanPlayer h1 = new HumanPlayer(/* correct parameter list */);
    HumanPlayer h2 = new HumanPlayer(/* correct parameter list */);
    if (h1.compareTo(h2) < 0)
        x = h1.getMove();
    else
        x = h2.getMove();
```

(A) II only
(B) III only
(C) II and III only
(D) I, II, and III
(E) None

23. Which of the following is correct implementation code for the `compareTo` method in the `ExpertPlayer` class?

```
 I if (rating == expert.rating)
        return 0;
    else if (rating < expert.rating)
        return -1;
    else
        return 1;
```

```
 II return rating - expert.rating;
```

```
 III if (getName().equals(expert.getName()))
        return 0;
    else if (getName().compareTo(expert.getName()) < 0)
        return -1;
    else
        return 1;
```

(A) I only
(B) II only
(C) III only
(D) I and II only
(E) I, II, and III

24. Which of the following classes is the least suitable candidate for containing a compareTo method?

(A)
```
public class Point
{
      private double x;
      private double y;

      //various methods follow
          ...
}
```

(B)
```
public class Name
{
      private String firstName;
      private String lastName;

      //various methods follow
          ...
}
```

(C)
```
public class Car
{
      private int modelNumber;
      private int year;
      private double price;

      //various methods follow
          ...
}
```

(D)
```
public class Student
{
      private String name;
      private double gpa;

      //various methods follow
          ...
}
```

(E)
```
public class Employee
{
      private String name;
      private int hireDate;
      private double salary;

      //various methods follow
          ...
}
```

25. A programmer has the task of maintaining a database of students of a large university. There are two types of students, undergraduates and graduate students. About a third of the graduate students are doctoral candidates.

    All of the students have the same personal information stored, like name, address, and phone number, and also student information like courses taken and grades. Each student's GPA is computed, but differently for undergraduates and graduates. The doctoral candidates have information about their dissertations and faculty advisors.

    The programmer will write a Java program to handle all the student information. Which of the following is the best design, in terms of programmer efficiency and code reusability? Note: { ... } denotes class code.

    (A) ```
    public interface Student { ...}
    public class Undergraduate implements Student { ... }
    public class Graduate implements Student { ... }
    public class DocStudent extends Graduate { ... }
    ```

    (B) ```
    public abstract class Student { ...}
    public class Undergraduate extends Student { ... }
    public class Graduate extends Student { ... }
    public class DocStudent extends Graduate { ... }
    ```

    (C) ```
    public class Student { ...}
    public class Undergraduate extends Student { ... }
    public class Graduate extends Student { ... }
    public class DocStudent extends Graduate { ... }
    ```

    (D) ```
    public abstract class Student { ...}
    public class Undergraduate extends Student { ... }
    public class Graduate extends Student { ... }
    public class DocStudent extends Student { ... }
    ```

    (E) ```
    public interface PersonalInformation { ... }
    public class Student implements PersonalInformation { ...}
    public class Undergraduate extends Student { ... }
    public abstract class Graduate extends Student { ... }
    public class DocStudent extends Graduate { ... }
    ```
    ```

26. Consider the Orderable interface and the partial implementation of the Temperature class defined below:

```
public interface Orderable
{
    /** Returns -1, 0, or 1 depending on whether the implicit
     *  object is less than, equal to, or greater than other.
     */
    int compareTo (Object other);
}


public class Temperature implements Orderable
{
    private String scale;
    private double degrees;

    //default constructor
    public Temperature ()
    { /* implementation not shown */ }

    //constructor
    public Temperature(String tempScale, double tempDegrees)
    { /* implementation not shown */ }

    public int compareTo(Object obj)
    { /* implementation not shown */ }

    public String toString()
    { /* implementation not shown */ }

    //Other methods are not shown.
}
```

Here is a program that finds the lowest of three temperatures:

```
public class TemperatureMain
{
    /** Find smaller of objects a and b. */
    public static Orderable min(Orderable a, Orderable b)
    {
        if (a.compareTo(b) < 0)
            return a;
        else
            return b;
    }

    /** Find smallest of objects a, b, and c. */
    public static Orderable minThree(Orderable a,
            Orderable b, Orderable c)
    {
        return min(min(a, b), c);
    }

    public static void main(String[] args)
    {
        /* code to test minThree method */
    }
}
```

Which are correct replacements for /* *code to test* minThree *method* */?

```
 I Temperature t1 = new Temperature("C", 85);
   Temperature t2 = new Temperature("F", 45);
   Temperature t3 = new Temperature("F", 120);
   System.out.println("The lowest temperature is " +
           minThree(t1, t2, t3));

II Orderable c1 = new Temperature("C", 85);
   Orderable c2 = new Temperature("F", 45);
   Orderable c3 = new Temperature("F", 120);
   System.out.println("The lowest temperature is " +
           minThree(c1, c2, c3));

III Orderable c1 = new Orderable("C", 85);
    Orderable c2 = new Orderable("F", 45);
    Orderable c3 = new Orderable("F", 120);
    System.out.println("The lowest temperature is " +
            minThree(c1, c2, c3));
```

(A) II only
(B) I and II only
(C) II and III only
(D) I and III only
(E) I, II, and III

27. A certain interface provided by a Java package contains just a single method:

```
public interface SomeName
{
    int method1(Object o);
}
```

A programmer adds some functionality to this interface by adding another abstract method to it, method2:

```
public interface SomeName
{
    int method1(Object ob1);
    void method2(Object ob2);
}
```

As a result of this addition, which of the following is true?

(A) A ClassCastException will occur if ob1 and ob2 are not compatible.

(B) All classes that implement the original SomeName interface will need to be rewritten because they no longer implement SomeName.

(C) A class that implements the original SomeName interface will need to modify its declaration as follows:

```
public class ClassName implements SomeName extends method2
{   ...
```

(D) SomeName will need to be changed to an abstract class and provide implementation code for method2, so that the original and upgraded versions of SomeName are compatible.

(E) Any new class that implements the upgraded version of SomeName will not compile.

ANSWER KEY

1. D	10. D	19. E
2. C	11. B	20. C
3. D	12. E	21. C
4. E	13. A	22. C
5. C	14. B	23. E
6. B	15. E	24. A
7. E	16. B	25. B
8. D	17. E	26. B
9. C	18. A	27. B

ANSWERS EXPLAINED

1. **(D)** The methods are deposit, withdraw, and getBalance, all inherited from the BankAccount class, plus addInterest, which was defined just for the class SavingsAccount.

2. **(C)** Implementation I fails because super() *must* be the first line of the implementation whenever it is used in a constructor. Implementation III may appear to be incorrect because it doesn't initialize interestRate. Since interestRate, however, is a primitive type—double—the compiler will provide a default initialization of 0, which was required.

3. **(D)** First, the statement super(acctBalance) initializes the inherited private variable balance as for the BankAccount superclass. Then the statement interestRate = rate initializes interestRate, which belongs uniquely to the SavingsAccount class. Choice E fails because interestRate does not belong to the BankAccount class and therefore cannot be initialized by a super method. Choice A is wrong because the SavingsAccount class cannot directly access the private instance variables of its superclass. Choice B assigns a value to an accessor method, which is meaningless. Choice C is incorrect because super() invokes the *default* constructor of the superclass. This will cause balance of the SavingsAccount object to be initialized to 0, rather than acctBalance, the parameter value.

4. **(E)** The constructor must initialize the inherited instance variable balance to the value of the acctBalance parameter. All three segments achieve this. Implementation I does it by invoking super(acctBalance), the constructor in the superclass. Implementation II first initializes balance to 0 by invoking the *default* constructor of the superclass. Then it calls the inherited deposit method of the superclass to add acctBalance to the account. Implementation III works because super() is automatically called as the first line of the constructor code if there is no explicit call to super.

5. **(C)** First the withdraw method of the BankAccount superclass is used to withdraw amount. A prefix of super must be used to invoke this method, which eliminates

choices B and D. Then the balance must be tested using the accessor method getBalance, which is inherited. You can't test balance directly since it is private to the BankAccount class. This eliminates choices A and E, and provides another reason for eliminating choice B.

6. **(B)** When a superclass method is redefined in a subclass, the process is called *method overriding*. Which method to call is determined at run time. This is called *dynamic binding* (p. 138). *Method overloading* is two or more methods with different signatures in the same class (p. 99). The compiler recognizes at compile time which method to call. This is *early binding*. The process of *downcasting* is unrelated to these principles (p. 140).

7. **(E)** The addInterest method is defined only in the SavingsAccount class. It therefore cannot be invoked by a BankAccount object. The error can be fixed by casting s to the correct type:

```
((SavingsAccount) s).addInterest();
```

The other method calls do not cause a problem because withdraw and deposit are both methods of the BankAccount class.

8. **(D)** The withdraw method is the only method that has one implementation in the superclass and a *different* implementation in a subclass. Polymorphism is the mechanism of selecting the correct method from the different possibilities in the class hierarchy. Notice that the deposit method, for example, is available to objects of all three bank account classes, but it's the *same* code in all three cases. So polymorphism isn't tested.

9. **(C)** You will get a ClassCastException whenever you try to cast an object to a class of which it is not an instance. Choice C is the only statement that doesn't attempt to do this. Look at the other choices: In choice A, b is not an instance of SavingsAccount. In choice B, b is not an instance of CheckingAccount. In choice D, s is not an instance of CheckingAccount. In choice E, c is not an instance of SavingsAccount.

10. **(D)** It is OK to use timsSavings and daynasChecking as parameters since each of these *is-a* BankAccount object. It is also OK for timsSavings and daynasChecking to call the transfer method (statements II and III), since they inherit this method from the BankAccount superclass.

11. **(B)** Statement I is false: A subclass must specify its own constructors. Otherwise the default constructor of the superclass will automatically be invoked. Note that statement III is false: Private instance methods cannot be overridden.

12. **(E)** All of the methods in an interface are by default public (the public keyword isn't needed). An abstract class can have both private and public methods. Note that choice A would be false if it simply stated "An interface cannot implement any methods, whereas an abstract class can." Java 8 allows an interface to implement default methods.

13. **(A)** There are two quick tests you can do to find the answer to this question:

(1) Test the *is-a* relationship, namely the parameter for printName *is-a* Bird? and the parameter for printBirdCall *is-a* Parrot?
(2) A reference cannot be cast to something it's not an instance of.

Choice A passes both of these tests: parrot2 *is-a* Bird, and (Parrot) bird2 *is-a* `Parrot`. Also `bird2` is an instance of a `Parrot` (as you can see by looking at the right-hand side of the assignment), so the casting is correct. In choice B, `printBirdCall(bird2)` is wrong because `bird2` *is-a* `Bird` and the `printBirdCall` method is expecting a `Parrot`. Therefore `bird2` must be downcast to a `Parrot`. Also, the method call `printName((Parrot) bird1)` fails because `bird1` is an instance of a `Bird` and therefore cannot be cast to a `Parrot`. In choice C, `printName(bird2)` is correct: `bird2` *is-a* `Bird`. However, `printBirdCall(bird2)` fails as already discussed. In choice D, `(Parakeet) parrot1` is an incorrect cast: `parrot1` is an instance of a `Parrot`. Note that `printBirdCall(parrot2)` is OK since `parrot2` *is-a* `Parrot`. In choice E, `(Owl) parrot2` is an incorrect cast: `parrot2` is an instance of `Parakeet`. Note that `printBirdCall((Parakeet) parrot2)` is correct: A `Parakeet` *is-a* `Parrot`, and `parrot2` is an instance of a `Parakeet`.

14. **(B)** Method overriding occurs whenever a method in a superclass is redefined in a subclass. Method overloading is a method in the same class that has the same name but different parameter types. Polymorphism is when the correct overridden method is called for a particular subclass object during run time. Information hiding is the use of `private` to restrict access. Procedural abstraction is the use of helper methods.

15. **(E)** All will cause an error!
    I: An object of a superclass does not have access to a new method of its subclass.
    II: `ob2` is declared to be of type `ClassA`, so a compile-time error will occur with a message indicating that there is no `method2` in `ClassA`. Casting `ob2` to `ClassB` would correct the problem.
    III: A `ClassCastException` will be thrown, since `ob1` is of type `ClassA`, and therefore cannot be cast to `ClassB`.

16. **(B)** The only incorrect line is `s1 = new Solid("blob")`: You can't create an instance of an abstract class. Abstract class references can, however, refer to objects of concrete (nonabstract) subclasses. Thus, the assignments for `s2` and `s3` are OK. Note that an abstract class reference can also be null, so the final assignment, though redundant, is correct.

17. **(E)** The point of having an abstract method is to postpone until run time the decision about which subclass version to call. This is what polymorphism is—calling the appropriate method at run time based on the type of the object.

18. **(A)** This is an example of polymorphism: The correct `volume` method is selected at run time. The parameter expected for `printVolume` is a `Solid` reference, which is what it gets in `main()`. The reference `sol` will refer either to a `Sphere` or a `RectangularPrism` object depending on the outcome of the coin flip. Since a `Sphere` is a `Solid` and a `RectangularPrism` is a `Solid`, there will be no type mismatch when these are the actual parameters in the `printVolume` method. (Note: The `Math.random` method is discussed in Chapter 4.)

19. **(E)** Each of choices A though D represent `Computable` objects: It makes sense to add, subtract, or multiply two large integers, two fractions, two irrational numbers, and two lengths. (One can multiply lengths to get an area, for example.) While it may make sense under certain circumstances to add or subtract two bank accounts, it does not make sense to multiply them!

20. **(C)** You can *declare a reference* of type `Player`. What you cannot do is *construct an object* of type `Player`. The following declarations are therefore legal:

```
SmartPlayer s = new SmartPlayer();
Player p1 = s;
Player p2 = new HumanPlayer();
```

21. **(C)** Remember, to implement the `Player` interface a class must provide implementations for `getMove` and `updateDisplay`. The `updateDisplay` method is suitable for all five games described. The `getMove` method returns a single integer, which works well for the High-Low game of choice A and the Chips game of choice B. In Tic-Tac-Toe (choice D) and Battleships (choice E) a move consists of giving a grid location. This can be provided by a single integer if the grid locations are numbered in a unique way. It's not ideal, but certainly doable. In the Chess game, however, it's neither easy nor intuitive to describe a move with a single integer. The player needs to specify both the grid location he is moving the piece to *and* which piece he is moving. The `getMove` method would need to be altered in a way that changes its return type. This makes the `Player` interface unsuitable.

22. **(C)** Segments II and III have errors in the `compareTo` calls. References `c1` and `c2` are of type `Player`, which doesn't have a `compareTo` method, and references `h1` and `h2` are of type `HumanPlayer`, which also doesn't have a `compareTo` method. Note that Segment II can be fixed by downcasting `c1` and `c2` to `ExpertPlayer`:

    ```
    if (((ExpertPlayer) c1).compareTo((ExpertPlayer) c2) < 0)
    ```

    A cast won't work in Segment III, because you can't cast a `HumanPlayer` to an `ExpertPlayer`. In Segments I, II, and III, the `getMove` calls are all correct, because `p1`, `p2`, `c1`, and `c2` are all of type `Player` which has a `getMove` method; and `h1` and `h2` are of type `HumanPlayer` which implements `Player` and therefore has a `getMove` method.

23. **(E)** All implementations are correct. This is *not* a question about whether it is better to compare `ExpertPlayer`s based on their ratings or their names! One might need an alphabetized list of players, or one might need a list according to ranking. In practice, the program specification will instruct the programmer which to use. Note that segment II is correct because `compareTo` doesn't need to return 1 or −1. Any positive or negative integer is OK. Note also that in segments I and II it is OK to use `expert.rating`, since `expert` is of type `ExpertPlayer`, the current class being written. Normally, a parameter of some class type cannot access the private instance variables of another class.

24. **(A)** While it is certainly possible to write a `compareTo` method for a `Point` class, there's no good intuitive way to compare points. Two points (x_1, y_1) and (x_2, y_2) are equal if and only if $x_1 = x_2$ and $y_1 = y_2$. But if points P_1 and P_2 are not equal, what will determine if $P_1 < P_2$ or $P_1 > P_2$? You could try using the distance from the origin. Define $P_1 > P_2$ if and only if $OP_1 > OP_2$, and $P_1 < P_2$ if and only if $OP_1 < OP_2$, where O is $(0,0)$. This definition means that points (a, b) and (b, a) are equal, which violates the definition of equals! The problem is that there is no way to map the two-dimensional set of points to a one-dimensional distance function and still be consistent with the definition of equals. The objects in each of the other classes can be compared without a problem. In choice B, two `Name` objects can be ordered alphabetically. In choice C, two `Car` objects can be ordered by year or by price. In choice D, two `Student` objects can be ordered by name or GPA. In choice E, two `Employee` objects can be ordered by name or seniority (date of hire).

25. **(B)** Here is the hierarchy of classes:

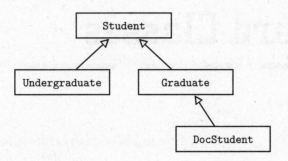

Eliminate choice D which fails to make `DocStudent` a subclass of `Graduate`. This is a poor design choice since a `DocStudent` *is-a* `Graduate`. Making `Student` an abstract class is desirable since the methods that are common to all students can go in there with implementations provided. The method to calculate the GPA, which differs among student types, will be declared in `Student` as an abstract method. Then unique implementations will be provided in both the `Graduate` and `Undergraduate` classes. Choice A is a poor design because making `Student` an interface means that all of its methods will need to be implemented in both the `Undergraduate` and `Graduate` classes. Many of these methods will have the same implementations. As far as possible, you want to arrange for classes to inherit common methods and to avoid repeated code. Choice C is slightly inferior to choice B because you are told that all students are either graduates or under-graduates. Having the `Student` class abstract guarantees that you won't create an instance of a `Student` (who is neither a graduate nor an undergraduate). Choice E has a major design flaw: making `Graduate` an abstract class means that you can't create any instances of `Graduate` objects. Disaster! If the keyword `abstract` is removed from choice E, it becomes a fine design, as good as that in choice B. Once `Student` has implemented all the common `PersonalInformation` methods, these are inherited by each of the subclasses.

26. **(B)** Segment III is wrong because you can't construct an interface object. Segments I and II both work because the `minThree` method is expecting three parameters, each of which is an `Orderable`. Since `Temperature` implements `Orderable`, each of the `Temperature` objects is an `Orderable` and can be used as a parameter in this method. Note that the program assumes that the `compareTo` method is able to compare `Temperature` objects with different scales. This is an internal detail that would be dealt with in the `compareTo` method, and hidden from the client. When a class implements `Orderable` there is an assumption that the `compareTo` method will be implemented in a reasonable way.

27. **(B)** Classes that implement an interface must provide implementation code for all non-default (i.e., abstract) methods in the interface. Adding `method2` to the `SomeName` interface means that all of those classes need to be rewritten with implementation code for `method2`. (This is not good—it violates the sacred principle of code reusability, and programmers relying on the interface will squeal.) Choices A, C, and D are all meaningless garbage. Choice E *may* be true if there is some other error in the new class. Otherwise, as long as the new class provides implementation code for both `method1` and `method2`, the class will compile.

Some Standard Classes

> *Anyone who considers arithmetical methods of producing random digits is, of course, in a state of sin.*
> —*John von Neumann (1951)*

Chapter Goals

- The `Object` class
- The `String` class
- Wrapper classes
- The `Math` class
- Random numbers

THE `Object` CLASS

The Universal Superclass

Think of `Object` as the superclass of the universe. Every class automatically extends `Object`, which means that `Object` is a direct or indirect superclass of every other class. In a class hierarchy tree, `Object` is at the top:

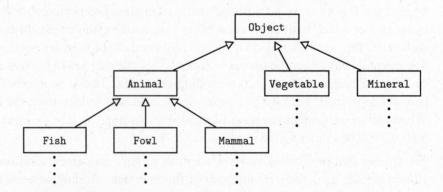

Methods in `Object`

There are many methods in `Object`, all of them inherited by every other class. Since `Object` is not an abstract class, all of its methods have implementations. The expectation is that these methods will be overridden in any class where the default implementation is not suitable. The methods of `Object` in the AP Java subset are `toString` and `equals`.

THE `toString` METHOD

```
public String toString()
```

This method returns a version of your object in `String` form.

When you attempt to print an object, the inherited default `toString` method is invoked, and what you will see is the class name followed by an @ followed by a meaningless number (the address in memory of the object). For example,

```
SavingsAccount s = new SavingsAccount(500);
System.out.println(s);
```

produces something like

```
SavingsAccount@fea485c4
```

To have more meaningful output, you need to override the `toString` method for your own classes. Even if your final program doesn't need to output any objects, you should define a `toString` method for each class to help in debugging.

Example 1

```
public class OrderedPair
{
    private double x;
    private double y;

    //constructors and other methods ...

    /** @return this OrderedPair in String form */
    public String toString()
    {
        return "(" + x + "," + y + ")";
    }
}
```

Now the statements

```
OrderedPair p = new OrderedPair(7,10);
System.out.println(p);
```

will invoke the overridden `toString` method and produce output that looks like an ordered pair:

```
(7,10)
```

Example 2

For a `BankAccount` class the overridden `toString` method may look something like this:

```
/** @return this  BankAccount in String form */
public String toString()
{
    return "Bank Account: balance = $" + balance;
}
```

The statements

```
BankAccount b = new BankAccount(600);
System.out.println(b);
```

will produce output that looks like this:

```
Bank Account: balance = $600
```

NOTE

1. The + sign is a concatenation operator for strings (see p. 178).
2. Array objects are unusual in that they do not have a toString method. To print the elements of an array, the array must be traversed and each element must explicitly be printed.

THE equals METHOD

```
public boolean equals(Object other)
```

All classes inherit this method from the Object class. It returns true if this object and other are the same object, false otherwise. Being the same object means referencing the same memory slot. For example,

```
Date d1 = new Date("January", 14, 2001);
Date d2 = d1;
Date d3 = new Date("January", 14, 2001);
```

Do not use == to test objects for equality. Use the equals method.

The test if (d1.equals(d2)) returns true, but the test if (d1==d3) returns false, since d1 and d3 do not refer to the same object. Often, as in this example, you may want two objects to be considered equal if their *contents* are the same. In that case, you have to override the equals method in your class to achieve this. Some of the standard classes described later in this chapter have overridden equals in this way. You will not be required to write code that overrides equals on the AP exam.

NOTE

1. The default implementation of equals is equivalent to the == relation for objects: In the Date example above, the test if (d1 == d2) returns true; the test if (d1 == d3) returns false.
2. The operators <, >, and so on, are not overloaded in Java. To compare objects, one must use either the equals method or define a compareTo method for the class.

Optional topic

THE hashCode METHOD

Every class inherits the hashCode method from Object. The value returned by hashCode is an integer produced by some formula that maps your object to an address in a hash table. A given object must always produce the same hash code. Also, two objects that are equal should produce the same hash code; that is, if obj1.equals(obj2) is true, then obj1 and obj2 should have the same hash code. Note that the opposite is not necessarily true. Hash codes do not have to be unique—two objects with the same hash code are not necessarily equal.

To maintain the condition that obj1.equals(obj2) is true implies that obj1 and obj2 have the same hash code, overriding equals means that you should override hashCode at the same time. You will not be required to do this on the AP exam.

You should, however, understand that every object is associated with an integer value called its hash code, and that objects that are equal have the same hash code.

(continued)

THE String CLASS

String Objects

An object of type String is a sequence of characters. All *string literals*, such as "yikes!", are implemented as instances of this class. A string literal consists of zero or more characters, including escape sequences, surrounded by double quotes. (The quotes are not part of the String object.) Thus, each of the following is a valid string literal:

```
""                  //empty string
"2468"
"I must\n go home"
```

String objects are *immutable*, which means that there are no methods to change them after they've been constructed. You can, however, always create a new String that is a mutated form of an existing String.

Constructing String Objects

A String object is unusual in that it can be initialized like a primitive type:

```
String s = "abc";
```

This is equivalent to

```
String s = new String("abc");
```

in the sense that in both cases s is a reference to a String object with contents "abc" (see Box on p. 179).

It is possible to reassign a String reference:

```
String s = "John";
s = "Harry";
```

This is equivalent to

```
String s = new String("John");
s = new String("Harry");
```

Notice that this is consistent with the immutable feature of String objects. "John" has not been changed; he has merely been discarded! The fickle reference s now refers to a new String, "Harry". It is also OK to reassign s as follows:

```
s = s + " Windsor";
```

s now refers to the object "Harry Windsor".
Here are other ways to initialize String objects:

```
String s1 = null;        //s1 is a null reference
String s2 = new String(); //s2 is an empty character sequence

String state = "Alaska";
String dessert = "baked " + state;  //dessert has value "baked Alaska"
```

The Concatenation Operator

The `dessert` declaration above uses the *concatenation operator*, +, which operates on `String` objects. Given two `String` operands `lhs` and `rhs`, `lhs + rhs` produces a single `String` consisting of `lhs` followed by `rhs`. If either `lhs` or `rhs` is an object other than a `String`, the `toString` method of the object is invoked, and `lhs` and `rhs` are concatenated as before. If one of the operands is a `String` and the other is a primitive type, then the non-`String` operand is converted to a `String`, and concatenation occurs as before. If neither `lhs` nor `rhs` is a `String` object, an error occurs. Here are some examples:

```
int five = 5;
String state = "Hawaii-";
String tvShow = state + five + "-0";  //tvShow has value
                                      //"Hawaii-5-0"
int x = 3, y = 4;
String sum = x + y;         //error: can't assign int 7 to String
```

Suppose a `Date` class has a `toString` method that outputs dates that look like this: 2/17/1948.

```
Date d1 = new Date(8, 2, 1947);
Date d2 = new Date(2, 17, 1948);
String s = "My birthday is " + d2;  //s has value
                                    //"My birthday is 2/17/1948"
String s2 = d1 + d2;    //error: + not defined for objects
String s3 = d1.toString() + d2.toString();  //s3 has value
                                    //8/2/19472/17/1948
```

Comparison of `String` Objects

There are two ways to compare `String` objects:

1. Use the `equals` method that is inherited from the `Object` class and overridden to do the correct thing:

   ```
   if (string1.equals(string2)) ...
   ```

   This returns `true` if `string1` and `string2` are identical strings, `false` otherwise.

2. Use the `compareTo` method. The `String` class has a `compareTo` method:

   ```
   int compareTo(String otherString)
   ```

   It compares strings in dictionary (lexicographical) order:

   - If `string1.compareTo(string2) < 0`, then `string1` precedes `string2` in the dictionary.
   - If `string1.compareTo(string2) > 0`, then `string1` follows `string2` in the dictionary.
   - If `string1.compareTo(string2) == 0`, then `string1` and `string2` are identical. (This test is an alternative to `string1.equals(string2)`.)

Be aware that Java is case-sensitive. Thus, if `s1` is "cat" and `s2` is "Cat", `s1.equals(s2)` will return `false`.

Characters are compared according to their position in the ASCII chart. All you need to know is that all digits precede all capital letters, which precede all lowercase letters. Thus "5" comes before "R", which comes before "a". Two strings are compared as follows: Start at the left end of each string and do a character-by-character comparison until you reach the first character in which the strings differ, the kth character, say. If the kth character of s1 comes before the kth character of s2, then s1 will come before s2, and vice versa. If the strings have identical characters, except that s1 terminates before s2, then s1 comes before s2. Here are some examples:

```
String s1 = "HOT", s2 = "HOTEL", s3 = "dog";
if (s1.compareTo(s2) < 0))     //true, s1 terminates first
   ...
if (s1.compareTo(s3) > 0))     //false, "H" comes before "d"
```

Don't Use == to Test Strings!

The expression if(string1 == string2) tests whether string1 and string2 are the same reference. It does not test the actual strings. Using == to compare strings may lead to unexpected results.

Example 1

```
String s = "oh no!";
String t = "oh no!";
if (s == t) ...
```

The test returns true even though it appears that s and t are different references. The reason is that for efficiency Java makes only one String object for equivalent string literals. This is safe in that a String cannot be altered.

Example 2

```
String s = "oh no!";
String t = new String("oh no!");
if (s == t) ...
```

The test returns false because use of new creates a new object, and s and t *are* different references in this example!

The moral of the story? Use equals not == to test strings. It always does the right thing.

Other String Methods

The Java String class provides many methods, only a small number of which are in the AP Java subset. In addition to the constructors, comparison methods, and concatenation operator + discussed so far, you should know the following methods:

```
int length()
```

Returns the length of this string.

```
String substring(int startIndex)
```

Returns a new string that is a substring of this string. The substring starts with the character at startIndex and extends to the end of the string. The first character is at index zero. The method throws an IndexOutOfBoundsException if startIndex is negative or larger than the length of the string. Note that if you're using Java 7 or above, you will see the error StringIndexOutOfBoundsException. However, the AP Java subset lists only IndexOutOfBoundsException, which is what they will use on the AP exam.

```
String substring(int startIndex, int endIndex)
```

Returns a new string that is a substring of this string. The substring starts at index startIndex and extends to the character at endIndex-1. (Think of it this way: startIndex is the first character that you want; endIndex is the first character that you *don't* want.) The method throws a StringIndexOutOfBoundsException if startIndex is negative, or endIndex is larger than the length of the string, or startIndex is larger than endIndex.

```
int indexOf(String str)
```

Returns the index of the first occurrence of str within this string. If str is not a substring of this string, -1 is returned. The method throws a NullPointerException if str is null.

Here are some examples:

```
"unhappy".substring(2)        //returns "happy"
"cold".substring(4)           //returns "" (empty string)
"cold".substring(5)           //StringIndexOutOfBoundsException
"strawberry".substring(5,7)   //returns "be"
"crayfish".substring(4,8)     //returns "fish"
"crayfish".substring(4,9)     //StringIndexOutOfBoundsException
"crayfish".substring(5,4)     //StringIndexOutOfBoundsException

String s = "funnyfarm";
int x = s.indexOf("farm");    //x has value 5
x = s.indexOf("farmer");      //x has value -1
int y = s.length();           //y has value 9
```

WRAPPER CLASSES

A *wrapper class* takes either an existing object or a value of primitive type, "wraps" or "boxes" it in an object, and provides a new set of methods for that type. The point of a wrapper class is to provide extended capabilities for the boxed quantity:

- It can be used in generic Java methods that require objects as parameters.

- It can be used in Java container classes that require the items be objects (see p. 242).

In each case, the wrapper class allows

1. Construction of an object from a single value (wrapping or boxing the primitive in a wrapper object).
2. Retrieval of the primitive value (unwrapping or unboxing from the wrapper object).

Java provides a wrapper class for each of its primitive types. The two that you should know for the AP exam are the `Integer` and `Double` classes.

The `Integer` Class

The `Integer` class wraps a value of type `int` in an object. An object of type `Integer` contains just one instance variable whose type is `int`.

Here are the `Integer` methods you should know for the AP exam:

```
Integer(int value)
```

Constructs an `Integer` object from an `int`. (Boxing.)

```
int compareTo(Integer other)
```

Returns `0` if the value of this `Integer` is equal to the value of `other`, a negative integer if it is less than the value of `other`, and a positive integer if it is greater than the value of `other`.

```
int intValue()
```

Returns the value of this `Integer` as an `int`. (Unboxing.)

```
boolean equals(Object obj)
```

Returns `true` if and only if this `Integer` has the same `int` value as `obj`.

NOTE

1. This method overrides `equals` in class `Object`.
2. This method throws a `ClassCastException` if `obj` is not an `Integer`.

```
String toString()
```

Returns a `String` representing the value of this `Integer`.

Here are some examples to illustrate the `Integer` methods:

```
Integer intObj = new Integer(6);  //boxes 6 in Integer object
int j = intObj.intValue();        //unboxes 6 from Integer object

System.out.println("Integer value is " + intObj);
//calls toString() for intObj
//output is
//Integer value is 6
```

```
Object object = new Integer(5);   //Integer is a subclass of Object

Integer intObj2 = new Integer(3);
int k = intObj2.intValue();
if (intObj.equals(intObj2))        //OK, evaluates to false
    ...
if (intObj.intValue() == intObj2.intValue())
    ...                //OK, since comparing primitive types

if (k.equals(j))       //error, k and j not objects
    ...
if ((intObj.intValue()).compareTo(intObj2.intValue()) < 0)
    ...                //error, can't use compareTo on primitive types

if (intObj.compareTo(object) < 0)  //Error. Parameter needs Integer cast
if (intObj.compareTo((Integer) object) < 0)  //OK
    ...
if (object.compareTo(intObj) < 0)  //error, no compareTo in Object
    ...
if (((Integer) object).compareTo(intObj) < 0)  //OK
    ...
```

The Double Class

The Double class wraps a value of type double in an object. An object of type Double contains just one instance variable whose type is double.

The methods you should know for the AP exam are analogous to those for type Integer.

```
Double(double value)
```

Constructs a Double object from a double. (Boxing.)

```
double doubleValue()
```

Returns the value of this Double as a double. (Unboxing.)

```
int compareTo(Double other)
```

Returns 0 if the value of this Double is equal to the value of other, a negative integer if it is less than the value of other, and a positive integer if it is greater than the value of other.

```
boolean equals(Object obj)
```

This method overrides equals in class Object and throws a ClassCastException if obj is not a Double. Otherwise it returns true if and only if this Double has the same double value as obj.

```
String toString()
```

Returns a String representing the value of this Double.

Here are some examples:

```
Double dObj = new Double(2.5);     //boxes 2.5 in Double object
double d = dObj.doubleValue();     //unboxes 2.5 from Double object

Object object = new Double(7.3);   //Double is a subclass of Object
Object intObj = new Integer(4);
if (dObj.compareTo(object) > 0) //Error. Parameter needs cast to Double
if (dObj.compareTo((Double) object) > 0)     //OK
    ...
if (dObj.compareTo(intObj) > 0)    //ClassCastException
    ...                            //can't compare Integer to Double
```

Remember: `Integer`, `Double`, and `String` all have a `compareTo` method.

NOTE

1. `Integer` and `Double` objects are immutable: There are no mutator methods in the classes.
2. See p. 242 for a discussion of auto-boxing and -unboxing. This useful feature will *not* be tested on the AP exam.

THE Math CLASS

This class implements standard mathematical functions such as absolute value, square root, trigonometric functions, the log function, the power function, and so on. It also contains mathematical constants such as π and e.

Here are the functions you should know for the AP exam:

`static int abs(int x)`

Returns the absolute value of integer x.

`static double abs(double x)`

Returns the absolute value of real number x.

`static double pow(double base, double exp)`

Returns base^{exp}. Assumes base > 0, or base = 0 and exp > 0, or base < 0 and exp is an integer.

`static double sqrt(double x)`

Returns $\sqrt{x}$, $x \geq 0$.

`static double random()`

Returns a random number r, where $0.0 \leq r < 1.0$. (See the next section, Random Numbers.)

All of the functions and constants are implemented as static methods and variables, which means that there are no instances of Math objects. The methods are invoked using the class name, Math, followed by the dot operator.

Here are some examples of mathematical formulas and the equivalent Java statements.

1. The relationship between the radius and area of a circle:

$$r = \sqrt{A/\pi}$$

In code:

```
radius = Math.sqrt(area / Math.PI);
```

2. The amount of money A in an account after ten years, given an original deposit of P and an interest rate of 5% compounded annually, is

$$A = P(1.05)^{10}$$

In code:

```
a = p * Math.pow(1.05, 10);
```

3. The distance D between two points $P(x_P, y)$ and $Q(x_Q, y)$ on the same horizontal line is

$$D = |x_P - x_Q|$$

In code:

```
d = Math.abs(xp - xq);
```

NOTE

The static import construct allows you to use the static members of a class without the class name prefix. For example, the statement

```
import static java.lang.Math.*;
```

allows use of all `Math` methods and constants without the `Math` prefix. Thus, the statement in formula 1 above could be written

```
radius = sqrt(area / PI);
```

Static imports are not part of the AP subset.

Random Numbers

RANDOM REALS

The statement

```
double r = Math.random();
```

produces a random real number in the range 0.0 to 1.0, where 0.0 is included and 1.0 is not.

This range can be scaled and shifted. On the AP exam you will be expected to write algebraic expressions involving `Math.random()` that represent linear transformations of the original interval $0.0 \leq x < 1.0$.

Example 1

Produce a random real value x in the range $0.0 \le x < 6.0$.

```
double x = 6 * Math.random();
```

Example 2

Produce a random real value x in the range $2.0 \le x < 3.0$.

```
double x = Math.random() + 2;
```

Example 3

Produce a random real value x in the range $4.0 \le x < 6.0$.

```
double x = 2 * Math.random() + 4;
```

In general, to produce a random real value in the range `lowValue` $\le x <$ `highValue`:

```
double x = (highValue - lowValue) * Math.random() + lowValue;
```

RANDOM INTEGERS

Using a cast to `int`, a scaling factor, and a shifting value, `Math.random()` can be used to produce random integers in any range.

Example 1

Produce a random integer, from 0 to 99.

```
int num = (int) (Math.random() * 100);
```

In general, the expression

```
(int) (Math.random() * k)
```

produces a random `int` in the range $0, 1, \dots, k-1$, where k is called the scaling factor. Note that the cast to `int` truncates the real number `Math.random() * k`.

Example 2

Produce a random integer, from 1 to 100.

```
int num = (int) (Math.random() * 100) + 1;
```

In general, if k is a scaling factor, and p is a shifting value, the statement

```
int n = (int) (Math.random() * k) + p;
```

produces a random integer n in the range $p, p+1, \dots, p+(k-1)$.

Example 3

Produce a random integer from 5 to 24.

```
int num = (int) (Math.random() * 20) + 5;
```

Note that there are 20 possible integers from 5 to 24, inclusive.

NOTE

There is further discussion of strings and random numbers, plus additional questions, in Chapter 9 (The AP Computer Science Labs).

Chapter Summary

All students should know about overriding the `equals` and `toString` methods of the `Object` class and should be familiar with the `Integer` and `Double` wrapper classes.

Know the AP subset methods of the `Math` class, especially the use of `Math.random()` for generating random integers. Know the `String` methods `substring` and `indexOf` like the back of your hand, including knowing where exceptions are thrown in the `String` methods.

MULTIPLE-CHOICE QUESTIONS ON STANDARD CLASSES

1. Here is a program segment to find the quantity base^{exp}. Both base and exp are entered at the keyboard.

```
System.out.println("Enter base and exponent: ");
double base = IO.readDouble();   //read user input
double exp = IO.readDouble();    //read user input
/* code to find power, which equals base^exp */
System.out.print(base + " raised to the power " + exp);
System.out.println(" equals " + power);
```

Which is a correct replacement for
/* *code to find* power, *which equals* base^{exp} */?

```
 I  double power;
    Math m = new Math();
    power = m.pow(base, exp);

 II double power;
    power = Math.pow(base, exp);

III int power;
    power = Math.pow(base, exp);
```

(A) I only
(B) II only
(C) III only
(D) I and II only
(E) I and III only

2. Consider the `squareRoot` method defined below:

```
/** @param d a real number such that d >= 0
 *  Postcondition: Returns a Double whose value is the square
 *                 root of the value represented by d.
 */
public Double squareRoot(Double d)
{
    /* implementation code */
}
```

Which /* *implementation code* */ satisfies the postcondition?

```
I  double x = d.doubleValue();
   x = Math.sqrt(x);
   return new Double(x);

II  return new Double(Math.sqrt(d.doubleValue()));

III  return Double(Math.sqrt(d.doubleValue()));
```

(A) I only
(B) I and II only
(C) I and III only
(D) II and III only
(E) I, II, and III

3. Here are some examples of negative numbers rounded to the nearest integer.

Negative real number	Rounded to nearest integer
−3.5	−4
−8.97	−9
−5.0	−5
−2.487	−2
−0.2	0

Refer to the declaration

```
double d = -4.67;
```

Which of the following correctly rounds d to the nearest integer?

(A) `int rounded = Math.abs(d);`

(B) `int rounded = (int) (Math.random() * d);`

(C) `int rounded = (int) (d - 0.5);`

(D) `int rounded = (int) (d + 0.5);`

(E) `int rounded = Math.abs((int) (d - 0.5));`

4. A program is to simulate plant life under harsh conditions. In the program, plants die randomly according to some probability. Here is part of a `Plant` class defined in the program.

```
public class Plant
{
    /** probability that plant dies, a real number between 0 and 1 */
    private double probDeath;

    public Plant(double plantProbDeath, < other parameters >)
    {
        probDeath = plantProbDeath;
        < initialization of other instance variables >
    }

    /** Plant lives or dies. */
    public void liveOrDie()
    {
        /* statement to generate random number */
        if (/* test to determine if plant dies */)
            < code to implement plant's death >
        else
            < code to make plant continue living >
    }

    //Other variables and methods are not shown.
}
```

Which of the following are correct replacements for
(1) /* *statement to generate random number* */ and
(2) /* *test to determine if plant dies* */?

(A)   (1) `double x = Math.random();`
       (2) `x == probDeath`

(B)   (1) `double x = (int) (Math.random());`
       (2) `x > probDeath`

(C)   (1) `double x = Math.random();`
       (2) `x < probDeath`

(D)   (1) `int x = (int) (Math.random() * 100);`
       (2) `x < (int) probDeath`

(E)   (1) `int x = (int) (Math.random() * 100) + 1;`
       (2) `x == (int) probDeath`

5. A program simulates fifty slips of paper, numbered 1 through 50, placed in a bowl for a raffle drawing. Which of the following statements stores in `winner` a random integer from 1 to 50?
(A) `int winner = (int) (Math.random() * 50) + 1;`
(B) `int winner = (int) (Math.random() * 50);`
(C) `int winner = (int) (Math.random() * 51);`
(D) `int winner = (int) (Math.random() * 51) + 1;`
(E) `int winner = (int) (1 + Math.random() * 49);`

6. Consider the code segment

```
Integer i = new Integer(20);
/* more code */
```

Which of the following replacements for /* *more code* */ correctly sets i to have an integer value of 25?

   I `i = new Integer(25);`

   II `i.intValue() = 25;`

   III `Integer j = new Integer(25);`
           `i = j;`

(A) I only
(B) II only
(C) III only
(D) I and III only
(E) II and III only

7. Consider these declarations:

```
Integer intOb = new Integer(3);
Object ob = new Integer(4);
Double doubOb = new Double(3.0);
```

Which of the following will *not* cause an error?
(A) `if ((Integer) ob.compareTo(intOb) < 0) ...`
(B) `if (ob.compareTo(intOb) < 0) ...`
(C) `if (intOb.compareTo(doubOb) < 0) ...`
(D) `if (intOb.compareTo(ob) < 0) ...`
(E) `if (intOb.compareTo((Integer) ob) < 0) ...`

8. Refer to these declarations:

```
Integer k = new Integer(8);
Integer m = new Integer(4);
```

Which test will *not* generate an error?

   I `if (k.intValue() == m.intValue())...`

   II `if ((k.intValue()).equals(m.intValue()))...`

   III `if ((k.toString()).equals(m.toString()))...`

(A) I only
(B) II only
(C) III only
(D) I and III only
(E) I, II, and III

9. Consider the code fragment

   ```
   Object intObj = new Integer(9);
   System.out.println((String) intObj);
   ```

   What will be output as a result of running the fragment?
   (A) No output. A `ClassCastException` will be thrown.
   (B) No output. An `ArithmeticException` will be thrown.
   (C) 9
   (D) "9"
   (E) nine

10. Consider these declarations:

    ```
    String s1 = "crab";
    String s2 = new String("crab");
    String s3 = s1;
    ```

    Which expression involving these strings evaluates to true?

     I `s1 == s2`

    II `s1.equals(s2)`

    III `s3.equals(s2)`

    (A) I only
    (B) II only
    (C) II and III only
    (D) I and II only
    (E) I, II, and III

11. Suppose that `strA = "TOMATO"`, `strB = "tomato"`, and `strC = "tom"`. Given that `"A"` comes before `"a"` in dictionary order, which is true?
    (A) `strA.compareTo(strB) < 0 && strB.compareTo(strC) < 0`
    (B) `strB.compareTo(strA) < 0 || strC.compareTo(strA) < 0`
    (C) `strC.compareTo(strA) < 0 && strA.compareTo(strB) < 0`
    (D) `!(strA.equals(strB)) && strC.compareTo(strB) < 0`
    (E) `!(strA.equals(strB)) && strC.compareTo(strA) < 0`

12. This question refers to the following declaration:

    ```
    String line = "Some more silly stuff on strings!";
    //the words are separated by a single space
    ```

    What string will `str` refer to after execution of the following?

    ```
    int x = line.indexOf("m");
    String str = line.substring(10, 15) + line.substring(25, 25 + x);
    ```

    (A) "sillyst"
    (B) "sillystr"
    (C) "silly st"
    (D) "silly str"
    (E) "sillystrin"

13. A program has a `String` variable `fullName` that stores a first name, followed by a space, followed by a last name. There are no spaces in either the first or last names. Here are some examples of `fullName` values: `"Anthony Coppola"`, `"Jimmy Carroll"`, and `"Tom DeWire"`. Consider this code segment that extracts the last name from a `fullName` variable, and stores it in `lastName` with no surrounding blanks:

    ```
    int k = fullName.indexOf(" ");     //find index of blank
    String lastName = /* expression */
    ```

    Which is a correct replacement for /* *expression* */?

    I `fullName.substring(k);`

    II `fullName.substring(k + 1);`

    III `fullName.substring(k + 1, fullName.length());`

    (A) I only
    (B) II only
    (C) III only
    (D) II and III only
    (E) I and III only

14. One of the rules for converting English to Pig Latin states: If a word begins with a consonant, move the consonant to the end of the word and add "ay". Thus "dog" becomes "ogday," and "crisp" becomes "rispcay". Suppose `s` is a `String` containing an English word that begins with a consonant. Which of the following creates the correct corresponding word in Pig Latin? Assume the declarations

    ```
    String ayString = "ay";
    String pigString;
    ```

    (A) `pigString = s.substring(0, s.length()) + s.substring(0,1)`
            `+ ayString;`

    (B) `pigString = s.substring(1, s.length()) + s.substring(0,0)`
            `+ ayString;`

    (C) `pigString = s.substring(0, s.length()-1) + s.substring(0,1)`
            `+ ayString;`

    (D) `pigString = s.substring(1, s.length()-1) + s.substring(0,0)`
            `+ ayString;`

    (E) `pigString = s.substring(1, s.length()) + s.substring(0,1)`
            `+ ayString;`

15. This question refers to the getString method shown below:

```
public static String getString(String s1, String s2)
{
    int index = s1.indexOf(s2);
    return s1.substring(index, index + s2.length());
}
```

Which is true about getString? It may return a string that

  I Is equal to s2.
  II Has no characters in common with s2.
  III Is equal to s1.

(A) I and III only
(B) II and III only
(C) I and II only
(D) I, II, and III
(E) None is true.

16. Consider this method:

```
public static String doSomething(String s)
{
    final String BLANK = " ";    //BLANK contains a single space
    String str = "";             //empty string
    String temp;
    for (int i = 0; i < s.length(); i++)
    {
        temp = s.substring(i, i + 1);
        if (!(temp.equals(BLANK)))
            str += temp;
    }
    return str;
}
```

Which of the following is the most precise description of what doSomething does?
(A) It returns s unchanged.
(B) It returns s with all its blanks removed.
(C) It returns a String that is equivalent to s with all its blanks removed.
(D) It returns a String that is an exact copy of s.
(E) It returns a String that contains s.length() blanks.

Questions 17 and 18 refer to the classes `Position` and `PositionTest` below.

```java
public class Position
{
    /** row and col are both >= 0 except in the default
     *  constructor where they are initialized to -1.
     */
    private int row, col;

    public Position()           //constructor
    {
        row = -1;
        col = -1;
    }

    public Position(int r, int c)        //constructor
    {
        row = r;
        col = c;
    }

    /** @return row of Position */
    public int getRow()
    { return row; }

    /** @return column of Position */
    public int getCol()
    { return col; }

    /** @return Position north of (up from) this position */
    public Position north()
    { return new Position(row - 1, col); }

    //Similar methods south, east, and west
            . . .

    /** Compares this Position to another Position object.
     *  @param p a Position object
     *  @return -1 (less than), 0 (equals), or 1 (greater than)
     */
    public int compareTo(Position p)
    {
        if (this.getRow() < p.getRow() || this.getRow() == p.getRow()
            && this.getCol() < p.getCol())
                return -1;
        if (this.getRow() > p.getRow() || this.getRow() == p.getRow()
            && this.getCol() > p.getCol())
                return 1;
        return 0;                //row and col both equal
    }

    /** @return string form of Position */
    public String toString()
    { return "(" + row + "," + col + ")"; }
}
```

```
public class PositionTest
{
    public static void main(String[] args)
    {
        Position p1 = new Position(2, 3);
        Position p2 = new Position(4, 1);
        Position p3 = new Position(2, 3);

        //tests to compare positions
            ...
    }
}
```

17. Which is true about the value of p1.compareTo(p2)?
   (A) It equals true.
   (B) It equals false.
   (C) It equals 0.
   (D) It equals 1.
   (E) It equals -1.

18. Which boolean expression about p1 and p3 is true?

      I p1 == p3

     II p1.equals(p3)

    III p1.compareTo(p3) == 0

   (A) I only
   (B) II only
   (C) III only
   (D) II and III only
   (E) I, II, and III

Questions 19 and 20 deal with the problem of swapping two integer values. Three methods are proposed to solve the problem, using primitive int types, Integer objects, and IntPair objects, where IntPair is defined as follows:

```
public class IntPair
{
    private int firstValue;
    private int secondValue;

    public IntPair(int first, int second)
    {
        firstValue = first;
        secondValue = second;
    }

    public int getFirst()
    { return firstValue; }

    public int getSecond()
    { return secondValue; }

    public void setFirst(int a)
    { firstValue = a; }

    public void setSecond(int b)
    { secondValue = b;}
}
```

19. Here are three different swap methods, each intended for use in a client program.

    ```
    I public static void swap(int a, int b)
      {
          int temp = a;
          a = b;
          b = temp;
      }
    ```

    ```
    II public static void swap(Integer obj_a, Integer obj_b)
       {
           Integer temp = new Integer(obj_a.intValue());
           obj_a = obj_b;
           obj_b = temp;
       }
    ```

    ```
    III public static void swap(IntPair pair)
        {
            int temp = pair.getFirst();
            pair.setFirst(pair.getSecond());
            pair.setSecond(temp);
        }
    ```

    When correctly used in a client program with appropriate parameters, which method will swap two integers, as intended?
    (A) I only
    (B) II only
    (C) III only
    (D) II and III only
    (E) I, II, and III

20. Consider the following program that uses the `IntPair` class:

```
public class TestSwap
{
    public static void swap(IntPair pair)
    {
        int temp = pair.getFirst();
        pair.setFirst(pair.getSecond());
        pair.setSecond(temp);
    }

    public static void main(String[] args)
    {
        int x = 8, y = 6;
        /* code to swap x and y */
    }
}
```

Which is a correct replacement for /* *code to swap* x *and* y */?

```
 I  IntPair iPair = new IntPair(x, y);
    swap(x, y);
    x = iPair.getFirst();
    y = iPair.getSecond();

 II IntPair iPair = new IntPair(x, y);
    swap(iPair);
    x = iPair.getFirst();
    y = iPair.getSecond();

III IntPair iPair = new IntPair(x, y);
    swap(iPair);
    x = iPair.setFirst();
    y = iPair.setSecond();
```

(A) I only
(B) II only
(C) III only
(D) II and III only
(E) None is correct.

Refer to the Name class below for Questions 21 and 22.

```java
public class Name
{
    private String firstName;
    private String lastName;

    public Name(String first, String last)  //constructor
    {
        firstName = first;
        lastName = last;
    }

    public String toString()
    { return firstName + " " + lastName; }

    public boolean equals(Object obj)
    {
        Name n = (Name) obj;
        return n.firstName.equals(firstName) &&
                n.lastName.equals(lastName);
    }

    public int hashCode()
    { /* implementation not shown */ }

    public int compareTo(Name n)
    {
        /* more code */
    }
}
```

21. The `compareTo` method implements the standard name-ordering algorithm where last names take precedence over first names. Lexicographic or dictionary ordering of `Strings` is used. For example, the name Scott Dentes comes before Nick Elser, and Adam Cooper comes before Sara Cooper.

    Which of the following is a correct replacement for */* more code */*?

    ```
    I  int lastComp = lastName.compareTo(n.lastName);
       if (lastComp != 0)
           return lastComp;
       else
           return firstName.compareTo(n.firstName);

    II if (lastName.equals(n.lastName))
           return firstName.compareTo(n.firstName);
       else
           return 0;

    III if (!(lastName.equals(n.lastName)))
            return firstName.compareTo(n.firstName);
        else
            return lastName.compareTo(n.lastName);
    ```

    (A) I only
    (B) II only
    (C) III only
    (D) I and II only
    (E) I, II, and III

22. Which statement about the `Name` class is *false*?
    (A) `Name` objects are immutable.
    (B) It is possible for the methods in `Name` to throw a `NullPointerException`.
    (C) If `n1` and `n2` are `Name` objects in a client class, then the expressions `n1.equals(n2)` and `n1.compareTo(n2) == 0` must have the same value.
    (D) The `compareTo` method throws a run-time exception if the parameter is null.
    (E) Since the `Name` class has a `compareTo` method, it *must* provide an implementation for an `equals` method.

ANSWER KEY

1. **B**	9. **A**	17. **E**
2. **B**	10. **C**	18. **C**
3. **C**	11. **D**	19. **C**
4. **C**	12. **A**	20. **B**
5. **A**	13. **D**	21. **A**
6. **D**	14. **E**	22. **E**
7. **E**	15. **A**	
8. **D**	16. **C**	

ANSWERS EXPLAINED

1. **(B)** All the `Math` class methods are static methods, which means you can't use a `Math` object that calls the method. The method is invoked using the class name, `Math`, followed by the dot operator. Thus segment II is correct, and segment I is incorrect. Segment III will cause an error: Since the parameters of `pow` are of type `double`, the result should be stored in a `double`.

2. **(B)** The `Math.sqrt` method must be invoked on a primitive type `double`, which is the reason `d.doubleValue()` is used. (Note that auto-unboxing would apply if you failed to use `d.doubleValue()`, and used just `d` instead.) Segment III fails because you can't use the `Double` constructor to create a new object without using the keyword `new`.

3. **(C)** The value −4.67 must be rounded to −5. Subtracting 0.5 gives a value of −5.17. Casting to `int` truncates the number (chops off the decimal part) and leaves a value of −5. None of the other choices produces −5. Choice A gives the absolute value of d: 4.67. Choice B is an incorrect use of `Random`. The parameter for `nextInt` should be an integer n, $n \geq 2$. The method then returns a random int k, where $0 \leq k < n$. Choice D is the way to round a *positive* real number to the nearest integer. In the actual case it produces −4. Choice E gives the absolute value of −5, namely 5.

4. **(C)** The statement `double x = Math.random();` generates a random `double` in the range $0 \leq x < 1$. Suppose `probDeath` is 0.67, or 67%. Assuming that random doubles are uniformly distributed in the interval, one can expect that 67% of the time x will be in the range $0 \leq x < 0.67$. You can therefore simulate the probability of death by testing if x is between 0 and 0.67, that is, if $x < 0.67$. Thus, `x < probDeath` is the desired condition for plant death, eliminating choices A and B. Choices D and E fail because `(int) probDeath` truncates `probDeath` to 0. The test `x < 0` will always be false, and the test `x == 0` will only be true if the random number generator returned exactly 0, an extremely unlikely occurrence! Neither of these choices correctly simulates the probability of death.

5. **(A)** The expression

```
(int) (Math.random() * 50);
```

returns an `int` from 0 to 49. Therefore, adding 1 shifts the range to be 1 to 50, which was required.

6. **(D)** The `Integer` class has no methods that can change the contents of `i`. However, `i` can be reassigned so that it refers to another object. This happens in both segments I and III. Segment II is wrong because `intValue` is an *accessor*—it cannot be used to change the value of object `i`.

7. **(E)** Choice D fails because you can't compare an `Integer` to an `Object`. You need to cast `ob` to `Integer`, as is done in choice E, the correct answer. Choice D will give the error message

   ```
   compareTo(java.lang.Integer) in java.lang.Integer cannot
   be applied to (java.lang.Object)
   ```

   Choice C will cause a `ClassCastException` since the calling and parameter objects are incompatible types. The `compareTo` method will try erroneously to cast its parameter to the type of the object calling the method. Choice A *almost* works: It fails because the dot operator has higher precedence than casting, which means that `ob.compareTo` is parsed before `ob` is cast to `Integer`, generating a message that the `compareTo` method is not in class `Object`. Choice A can be fixed with an extra pair of parentheses:

   ```
   if (((Integer) ob).compareTo(intOb) < 0) ...
   ```

   Choice B causes the same error message as choice A: no `compareTo` method in class `Object`.

8. **(D)** Test I is correct because it's OK to compare primitive types (in this case `int` values) using `==`. Test III works because `k.toString()` and `m.toString()` are `String`s, which should be compared with `equals`. Test II is wrong because you can't invoke a method (in this case `equals`) on an `int`.

9. **(A)** An `Integer` cannot be cast to a `String`. Don't confuse this with

   ```
   System.out.println(intObj.toString());    //outputs 9
   ```

   Note that if the first line of the code fragment were

   ```
   Integer intObj = new Integer(9);
   ```

   then the error would be detected at compile time.

10. **(C)** Here are the memory slots:

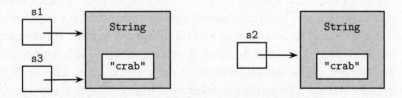

   Statements II and III are true because the contents of `s1` and `s2` are the same, and the contents of `s3` and `s2` are the same. Statement I is false because `s1` and `s2` are not the same reference. Note that the expression `s1 == s3` would be true since `s1` and `s3` *are* the same reference.

11. **(D)** Note that `"TOMATO"` precedes both `"tomato"` and `"tom"`, since `"T"` precedes `"t"`. Also, `"tom"` precedes `"tomato"` since the length of `"tom"` is less than the length of `"tomato"`. Therefore each of the following is true:

```
strA.compareTo(strB) < 0
strA.compareTo(strC) < 0
strC.compareTo(strB) < 0
```

So

> Choice A is T and F which evaluates to F
> Choice B is F or F which evaluates to F
> Choice C is F and T which evaluates to F
> Choice D is T and T which evaluates to T
> Choice E is T and F which evaluates to F

12. **(A)** `x` contains the index of the first occurrence of `"m"` in `line`, namely 2. (Remember that `"S"` is at index 0.) The method call `line.substring(10,15)` returns `"silly"`, the substring starting at index 10 and extending though index 14. The method call `line.substring(25,27)` returns `"st"` (don't include the character at index 27!). The concatenation operator, `+`, joins these.

13. **(D)** The first character of the last name starts at the first character after the space. Thus, `startIndex` for `substring` must be `k+1`. This eliminates expression I. Expression II takes all the characters from position `k+1` to the end of the `fullName` string, which is correct. Expression III takes all the characters from position `k+1` to position `fullName.length()-1`, which is also correct.

14. **(E)** Suppose `s` contains `"cat"`. You want `pigString = "at" + "c" + "ay"`. Now the string `"at"` is the substring of `s` starting at position 1 and ending at position `s.length()-1`. The correct substring call for this piece of the word is `s.substring(1,s.length())`, which eliminates choices A, C, and D. (Recall that the first parameter is the starting position, and the second parameter is one position past the last index of the substring.) The first letter of the word—`"c"` in the example—starts at position 0 and ends at position 0. The correct expression is `s.substring(0,1)`, which eliminates choice B.

15. **(A)** Statement I is true whenever `s2` occurs in `s1`. For example, if strings `s1 = "catastrophe"` and `s2 = "cat"`, then `getString` returns `"cat"`. Statement II will never happen. If `s2` is not contained in `s1`, the `indexOf` call will return `-1`. Using a negative integer as the first parameter of `substring` will cause a `StringIndexOutOfBoundsException`. Statement III will be true whenever `s1` equals `s2`.

16. **(C)** The `String temp` represents a single-character substring of `s`. The method examines each character in `s` and, if it is a nonblank, appends it to `str`, which is initially empty. Each assignment `str += temp` assigns a new reference to `str`. Thus, `str` ends up as a copy of `s` but without the blanks. A reference to the final `str` object is returned. Choice A is correct in that `s` is left unchanged, but it is not the *best* characterization of what the method does. Choice B is not precise because an object parameter is never modified: Changes, if any, are performed on a copy. Choices D and E are wrong because the method removes blanks.

17. **(E)** The `compareTo` method returns an `int`, so eliminate choices A and B. In the implementation of `compareTo`, the code segment that applies to the particular example is

```
if (this.getRow() < p.getRow() || ...
    return -1;
```

Since 2 < 4, the value –1 is returned.

18. **(C)** Expression III is true: The `compareTo` method is implemented to return `0` if two `Position` objects have the same row and column. Expression I is false because `object1 == object2` returns `true` only if `object1` and `object2` are the *same reference*. Expression II is tricky. One would like `p1` and `p3` to be equal since they have the same row and column values. This is not going to happen automatically, however. The `equals` method must explicitly be overridden for the `Position` class. If this hasn't been done, the default `equals` method, which is inherited from class `Object`, will return true only if `p1` and `p3` are the same reference, which is not true.

19. **(C)** Recall that primitive types and object references are passed by value. This means that copies are made of the actual arguments. Any changes that are made are made to the *copies*. The actual parameters remain unchanged. Thus, in methods I and II, the parameters will retain their original values and remain unswapped.

    To illustrate, for example, why method II fails, consider this piece of code that tests it:

```
public static void main(String[] args)
{
    int x = 8, y = 6;
    Integer xObject = new Integer(x);
    Integer yObject = new Integer(y);
    swap(xObject, yObject);
    x = xObject.intValue();    //surprise! still has value 8
    y = yObject.intValue();    //surprise! still has value 6
        ...
}
```

Here are the memory slots before `swap` is called:

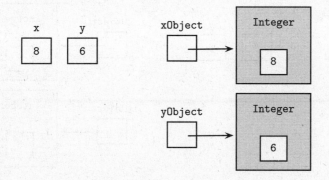

Here they are when `swap` is invoked:

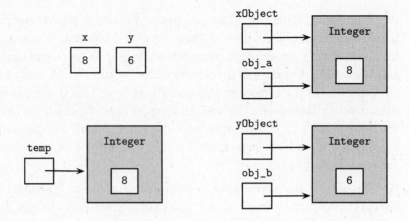

Just before exiting the swap method:

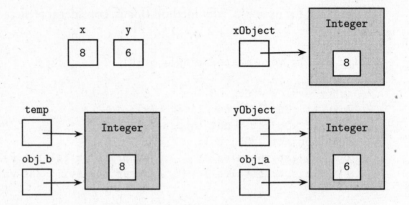

After exiting, xObject and yObject have retained their original values:

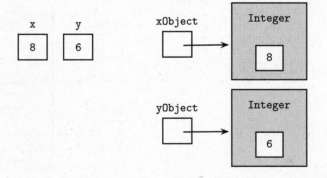

The reason method III works is that instead of the object references being changed, the object *contents* are changed. Thus, after exiting the method, the IntPair reference is as it was, but the first and second values have been interchanged. (See explanation to next question for diagrams of the memory slots.) In this question, IntPair is used as a wrapper class for a pair of integers whose values need to be swapped.

20. **(B)** The swap method has just a single IntPair parameter, which eliminates segment I. Segment III fails because setFirst and setSecond are used incorrectly. These are mutator methods that change an IntPair object. What is desired is to return the (newly swapped) first and second values of the pair: Accessor methods

`getFirst` and `getSecond` do the trick. To see why this `swap` method works, look at the memory slots.

Before the `swap` method is called:

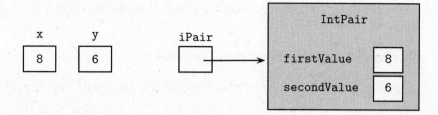

Just after the `swap` method is called:

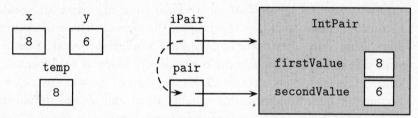

Just before exiting the `swap` method:

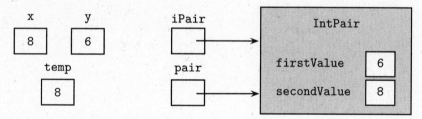

Just after exiting the `swap` method:

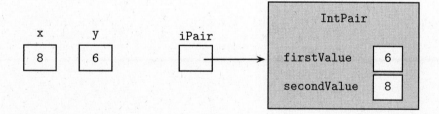

After the statements:

```
x = iPair.getFirst();
y = iPair.getSecond();
```

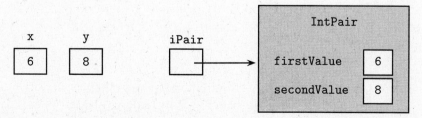

Notice that x and y have been swapped!

21. **(A)** The first statement of segment I compares last names. If these are different, the method returns the `int` value `lastComp`, which is negative if `lastName` precedes `n.lastName`, positive otherwise. If last names are the same, the method returns the `int` result of comparing first names. Segments II and III use incorrect algorithms for comparing names. Segment II would be correct if the `else` part were

    ```
    return lastName.compareTo(n.lastName);
    ```

    Segment III would be correct if the two `return` statements were interchanged.

22. **(E)** It is *wise* to have an `equals` method that is compatible with the `compareTo` method, namely, `n1.equals(n2)` and `n1.compareTo(n2)==0` have the same value if `n1` and `n2` are `Name` objects. However, nothing in the Java language *mandates* that if a class has a `compareTo` method, it must also have an `equals` method. Choice A is true. You know this because the `Name` class has no mutator methods. Thus, `Name` objects can never be changed. Choice B is true: If a `Name` is initialized with null references, each of the methods will throw a `NullPointerException`. Choice C is true: If `n1.equals(n2)` is true, then `n1.compareTo(n2) == 0` is true, because both are conditions for equality of `n1` and `n2` and should therefore be consistent. Choice D is true: If the parameter is null, the `compareTo` method will throw a `NullPointerException`.

Program Design and Analysis

Weeks of coding can save you hours of planning.
—Anonymous

Chapter Goals

- Program development, including design and testing
- Object-oriented program design
- Relationships between classes
- Program analysis
- Efficiency

Students of introductory computer science typically see themselves as programmers. They no sooner have a new programming project in their heads than they're at the computer, typing madly to get some code up and running. (Is this you?)

To succeed as a programmer, however, you have to combine the practical skills of a software engineer with the analytical mindset of a computer scientist. A software engineer oversees the life cycle of software development: initiation of the project, analysis of the specification, and design of the program, as well as implementation, testing, and maintenance of the final product. A computer scientist (among other things!) analyzes the implementation, correctness, and efficiency of algorithms. All these topics are tested on the APCS exam.

THE SOFTWARE DEVELOPMENT LIFE CYCLE

The Waterfall Model

The waterfall model of software development came about in the 1960s in order to bring structure and efficiency into the process of creating large programs.

Each step in the process flows into the next: The picture resembles a waterfall.

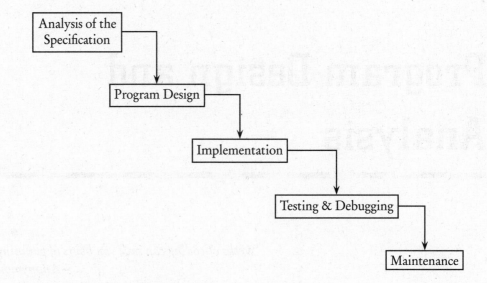

Program Specification

The *specification* is a written description of the project. Typically it is based on a customer's requirements. The first step in writing a program is to analyze the specification, make sure you understand it, and clarify with the customer anything that is unclear.

Program Design

Even for a small-scale program a good design can save programming time and enhance the reliability of the final program. The design is a fairly detailed plan for solving the problem outlined in the specification. It should include all objects that will be used in the solution, the data structures that will implement them, plus a detailed list of the tasks to be performed by the program.

A good design provides a fairly detailed overall plan at a glance, without including the minutiae of Java code.

Program Implementation

Program implementation is the coding phase. Design and implementation are discussed in more detail on p. 210.

Testing and Debugging

TEST DATA

Not every possible input value can be tested, so a programmer should be diligent in selecting a representative set of *test data*. Typical values in each part of a domain of the program should be selected, as well as endpoint values and out-of-range values. If only positive input is required, your test data should include a negative value just to check that your program handles it appropriately.

Example

A program must be written to insert a value into its correct position in this sorted list:

     2   5   9

Test data should include

- A value less than 2
- A value between 2 and 5
- A value between 5 and 9
- A value greater than 9
- 2, 5, and 9
- A negative value

TYPES OF ERRORS (BUGS)

- A *compile-time error* occurs during compilation of the program. The compiler is unable to translate the program into bytecode and prints an appropriate error message. A *syntax error* is a compile-time error caused by violating the rules of the programming language. Some examples are omitting semicolons or braces, using undeclared identifiers, using keywords inappropriately, having parameters that don't match in type and number, and invoking a method for an object whose class definition doesn't contain that method.

- A *run-time error* occurs during execution of the program. The Java run-time environment *throws an exception*, which means that it stops execution and prints an error message. Typical causes of run-time errors include attempting to divide an integer by zero, using an array index that is out of bounds, attempting to open a file that cannot be found, and so on. An error that causes a program to run forever ("infinite loop") can also be regarded as a run-time error. (See also Errors and Exceptions, p. 74.)

- An *intent* or *logic error* is one that fails to carry out the specification of the program. The program compiles and runs but does not do the job. These are sometimes the hardest types of errors to fix.

ROBUSTNESS

Always assume that any user of your program is not as smart as you are. You must therefore aim to write a *robust* program, namely one that

- Won't give inaccurate answers for some input data.
- Won't crash if the input data are invalid.
- Won't allow execution to proceed if invalid data are entered.

Examples of bad input data include out-of-range numbers, characters instead of numerical data, and a response of "maybe" when "yes" or "no" was asked for.

Note that bad input data that invalidates a computation won't be detected by Java. Your program should include code that catches the error, allows the error to be fixed, and allows program execution to resume.

Program Maintenance

Program maintenance involves upgrading the code as circumstances change. New features may be added. New programmers may come on board. To make their task easier, the original program must have clear and precise documentation.

OBJECT-ORIENTED PROGRAM DESIGN

Object-oriented programming has been the dominant programming methodology since the mid 1990s. It uses an approach that blurs the lines of the waterfall model. Analysis of the problem, development of the design, and pieces of the implementation all overlap and influence one another.

Here are the steps in object-oriented design:

- Identify classes to be written.
- Identify behaviors (i.e., methods) for each class.
- Determine the relationships between classes.
- Write the interface (public method headers) for each class.
- Implement the methods.

Identifying Classes

Identify the objects in the program by picking out the nouns in the program specification. Ignore pronouns and nouns that refer to the user. Select those nouns that seem suitable as classes, the "big-picture" nouns that describe the major objects in the application. Some of the other nouns may end up as attributes of the classes.

Many applications have similar object types: a low-level basic component; a collection of low-level components; a controlling object that puts everything together; and a display object that could be a GUI (graphical user interface) but doesn't have to be.

Example 1

Write a program that maintains an inventory of stock items for a small store.

Nouns to consider: inventory, item, store.

Basic Object:	`StockItem`
Collection:	`Inventory` (a list of `StockItems`)
Controller:	`Store` (has an `Inventory`, uses a `StoreDisplay`)
Display:	`StoreDisplay` (could be a GUI)

Example 2

Write a program that simulates a game of bingo. There should be at least two players, each of whom has a bingo card, and a caller who calls the numbers.

Nouns to consider: game, players, bingo card, caller.

Basic Objects:	`BingoCard`, `Caller`
Collection:	`Players` (each has a `BingoCard`)
Controller:	`GameMaster` (sets up the `Players` and `Caller`)
Display:	`BingoDisplay` (shows each player's card and displays winners, etc.)

Example 3

Write a program that creates random bridge deals and displays them in a specified format. (The specification defines a "deal" as consisting of four hands. It also describes a deck of cards, and shows how each card should be displayed.)

Nouns to consider: deal, hand, format, deck, card.

Basic Object:	Card
Collection:	Deck (has an array of Cards)
	Hand (has an array of Cards)
	Deal (has an array of Hands)
	Dealer (has a Deck, or several Decks)
Controller:	Formatter (has a Deal and a TableDisplay)
Display:	TableDisplay (could be a GUI)

Identifying Behaviors

Find all verbs in the program description that help lead to the solution of the programming task. These are likely behaviors that will probably become the methods of the classes. Now decide which methods belong in which classes. Recall that the process of bundling a group of methods and data fields into a class is called *encapsulation*.

Think carefully about who should do what. Do not ask a basic object to perform operations for the group. For example, a StockItem should keep track of its own details (price, description, how many on the shelf, etc.) but should not be required to search for another item. A Card should know its value and suit but should not be responsible for keeping track of how many cards are left in a deck. A Caller in a bingo game should be responsible for keeping track of the numbers called so far and for producing the next number but not for checking whether a player has bingo: That is the job of an individual player (element of Players) and his BingoCard.

You will also need to decide which data fields each class will need and which data structures should store them. For example, if an object represents a list of items, consider an array or ArrayList as the data structure.

Determining Relationships Between Classes

INHERITANCE RELATIONSHIPS

Look for classes with common behaviors. This will help identify *inheritance relationships*. Recall the *is-a* relationship—if object1 *is-a* object2, then object2 is a candidate for a superclass.

COMPOSITION RELATIONSHIPS

Composition relationships are defined by the *has-a* relationship. For example, a Nurse *has-a* Uniform. Typically, if two classes have a composition relationship, one of them contains an instance variable whose type is the other class.

Note that a wrapper class always implements a *has-a* relationship with any objects that it wraps.

UML Diagrams

An excellent way to keep track of the relationships between classes and show the inheritance hierarchy in your programs is with a UML (Unified Modeling Language) diagram. This is a standard graphical scheme used by object-oriented programmers. Although it is not part of the AP subset, on the AP exam you may be expected to interpret simple UML diagrams and inheritance hierarchies.

Here is a simplified version of the UML rules:

- Represent classes with rectangles.

- Use angle brackets with the word "abstract" or "interface" to indicate either an abstract class or interface.

- Show the *is-a* relationship between classes with an open up-arrow.

- Show the *is-a* relationship that involves an interface with an open, dotted up-arrow.

- Show the *has-a* relationship with a down arrow or sideways arrow (indicates composition).

Example

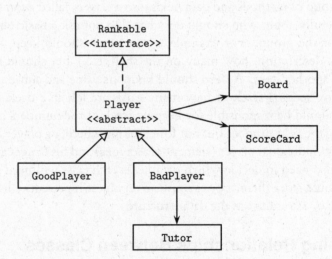

From this diagram you can see at a glance that `GoodPlayer` and `BadPlayer` are subclasses of an abstract class `Player`, and that each `Player` implements the `Rankable` interface. Every `Player` has a `Board` and a `ScoreCard`, while only the `BadPlayer` has a `Tutor`.

Implementing Classes

BOTTOM-UP DEVELOPMENT

For each method in a class, list all of the other classes needed to implement that particular method. These classes are called *collaborators*. A class that has no collaborators is *independent*.

To implement the classes, often an incremental, *bottom-up* approach is used. This means that independent classes are fully implemented and tested before being incorporated into the overall project. Typically, these are the basic objects of the program, like `StockItem`, `Card`, and `BingoCard`. Unrelated classes in a programming project can be implemented by different programmers.

Note that a class can be tested using a dummy `Tester` class that will be discarded when the methods of the class are working. Constructors, then methods, should be added, and tested, one at a time. A *driver class* that contains a `main` method can be used to test the program as you go. The purpose of the driver is to test the class fully before incorporating it as an object in a new class.

When each of the independent classes is working, classes that depend on just one other class are implemented and tested, and so on. This may lead to a working, bare bones version of the project. New features and enhancements can be added later.

Design flaws can be corrected at each stage of development. Remember, a design is never set in stone: It simply guides the implementation.

TOP-DOWN DEVELOPMENT

In a top-down design, the programmer starts with an overview of the program, selecting the highest-level controlling object and the tasks needed. During development of the program, subsidiary classes may be added to simplify existing classes.

Implementing Methods

PROCEDURAL ABSTRACTION

A good programmer avoids chunks of repeated code wherever possible. To this end, if several methods in a class require the same task, like a search or a swap, you should use *helper methods*. The `reduce` method in the `Rational` class on p. 118 is an example of such a method. Also, wherever possible you should enhance the readability of your code by using helper methods to break long methods into smaller tasks. The use of helper methods within a class is known as *procedural abstraction* and is an example of top-down development within a class. This process of breaking a long method into a sequence of smaller tasks is sometimes called *stepwise refinement*.

INFORMATION HIDING

Instance variables and helper methods are generally declared as `private`, which prevents client classes from accessing them. This strategy is called *information hiding*.

STUB METHOD

Sometimes it makes more sense in the development of a class to test a calling method before testing a method it invokes. A *stub* is a dummy method that stands in for a method until the actual method has been written and tested. A stub typically has an output statement to show that it was called in the correct place, or it may return some reasonable values if necessary.

ALGORITHM

An *algorithm* is a precise step-by-step procedure that solves a problem or achieves a goal. Don't write any code for an algorithm in a method until the steps are completely clear to you.

Example 1

A program must test the validity of a four-digit code number that a person will enter to be able to use a photocopy machine. The number is valid if the fourth digit equals the remainder when the sum of the first three digits is divided by seven.

Classes in the program may include an IDNumber, the four-digit code; Display, which would handle input and output; and IDMain, the driver for the program. The data structure used to implement an IDNumber could be an instance variable of type int, or an instance variable of type String, or four instance variables of type int—one per digit, and so on.

A top-down design for the program that tests the validity of the number is reflected in the steps of the main method of IDMain:

Create Display
Read in IDNumber
Check validity
Print message

Each method in this design is tested before the next method is added to main. If the display will be handled in a GUI (graphical user interface), stepwise refinement of the design might look like this:

Create Display
    Construct a Display
    Create window panels
    Set up text fields
    Add panels and fields to window

Read in IDNumber
    Prompt and read

Check validity of IDNumber
    Check input
        Check characters
        Check range
    Separate into digits
    Check validity property

Print message
    Write number
    State if valid

NOTE

1. The IDNumber class, which contains the four-digit code, is responsible for the following operations:
       Split value into separate digits
       Check condition for validity
   The Display class, which contains objects to read and display, must also contain an IDNumber object. It is responsible for the following operations:
       Set up display
       Read in code number
       Display validity message
   Creating these two classes with their data fields (instance variables) and operations (methods) is an example of encapsulation.

2. The `Display` method `readCodeNumber` needs private helper methods to check the input: `checkCharacters` and `checkRange`. This is an example of procedural abstraction (use of helper methods) and information hiding (making them private).

3. Initially the programmer had just an `IDNumber` class and a driver class. The `Display` class was added as a refinement, when it was realized that handling the input and message display was separate from checking the validity of the `IDNumber`. This is an example of top-down development (adding an auxiliary class to clarify the code).

4. The `IDNumber` class contains no data fields that are objects. It is therefore an independent class. The `Display` class, which contains an `IDNumber` data member, has a composition relationship with `IDNumber` (`Display` *has-a* `IDNumber`).

5. When testing the final program, the programmer should be sure to include each of the following as a user-entered code number: a valid four-digit number, an invalid four-digit number, an n-digit number, where $n \neq 4$, and a "number" that contains a nondigit character. A robust program should be able to deal with all these cases.

Example 2

A program must create a teacher's grade book. The program should maintain a class list of students for any number of classes in the teacher's schedule. A menu should be provided that allows the teacher to

- Create a new class of students.
- Enter a set of scores for any class.
- Correct any data that's been entered.
- Display the record of any student.
- Calculate the final average and grade for all students in a class.
- Print a class list, with or without grades.
- Add a student, delete a student, or transfer a student to another class.
- Save all the data in a file.

IDENTIFYING CLASSES

Use the nouns in the specification as a starting point for identifying classes in the program. The nouns are: program, teacher, grade book, class list, class, student, schedule, menu, set of scores, data, record, average, grade, and file.

Use nouns in the specification to identify possible classes.

Eliminate each of the following:

program	(Always eliminate "program" when used in this context.)
teacher	(Eliminate, because he or she is the user.)
schedule	(This will be reflected in the name of the external file for each class, e.g., `apcs_period3.dat`.)
data, record	(These are synonymous with student name, scores, grades, etc., and will be covered by these features.)
class	(This is synonymous with class list.)

The following seem to be excellent candidates for classes: GradeBook, ClassList, Student, and FileHandler. Other possibilities are Menu, ScoreList, and a GUI_Display.

On further thought: Basic independent objects are Student, Menu, Score, and FileHandler. Group objects are ClassList (collection of students), ScoreList (collection of scores), and AllClasses (collection of ClassLists). The controlling class is the GradeBook. A Display class is essential for many of the grade book operations, like showing a class list or displaying information for a single student.

RELATIONSHIPS BETWEEN CLASSES

There are no inheritance relationships. There are many composition relationships between objects, however. The GradeBook *has-a* Menu, the ClassList *has-a* Student (several, in fact!), a Student *has-a* name, average, grade, list_of_scores, etc. The programmer must decide whether to code these attributes as classes or data fields.

IDENTIFYING BEHAVIORS

Use verbs in the specification to identify possible methods.

Use the verbs in the specification to identify required operations in the program. The verbs are: maintain <list>, provide <menu>, allow <user>, create <list>, enter <scores>, correct <data>, display <record>, calculate <average>, calculate <grade>, print <list>, add <student>, delete <student>, transfer <student>, and save <data>.

You must make some design decisions about which class is responsible for which behavior. For example, will a ClassList display the record of a single Student, or will a Student display his or her own record? Who will enter scores—the GradeBook, a ClassList, or a Student? Is it desirable for a Student to enter scores of other Students? Probably not!

DECISIONS

Here are some preliminary decisions. The GradeBook will provideMenu. The menu selection will send execution to the relevant object.

The ClassList will maintain an updated list of each class. It will have these public methods: addStudent, deleteStudent, transferStudent, createNewClass, printClassList, printScores, and updateList. A good candidate for a helper method in this class is search for a given student.

Each Student will have complete personal and grade information. Public methods will include setName, getName, enterScore, correctData, findAverage, getAverage, getGrade, and displayRecord.

Saving and retrieving information is crucial to this program. The FileHandler will take care of openFileForReading, openFileForWriting, closeFiles, loadClass, and saveClass. The FileHandler class should be written and tested right at the beginning, using a small dummy class list.

Score, ScoreList, and Student are easy classes to implement. When these are working, the programmer can go on to ClassList. Finally the Display GUI class, which will have the GradeBook, can be developed. This is an example of bottom-up development.

Example 3

A program simulates a game of Battleships, which is a game between two players, each of whom has a grid where ships are placed. Each player has five ships:

```
battleship o o o o o
cruiser    o o o o
submarine  o o o
destroyer  o o
frigate    o
```

The grids of the players' fleets may look like this. Any two adjacent squares that are taken must belong to the same ship, i.e., different ships shouldn't "touch."

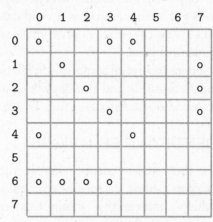

Each player's grid is hidden from the other player. Players alternate "shooting" at each other's ships by calling out a position, a row and column number. A player must make an honest response, "hit" or "miss." If it's a hit, a player gets another turn. If the whole ship has been hit, the owner must say something like, "You sank my cruiser." Each player must keep track of hits and misses. The first player to sink his opponent's fleet is the winner.

IDENTIFYING CLASSES

The nouns in the specification are program, game, players, grid, ship, battleship, cruiser, submarine, destroyer, frigate, square, position, opponent, row, column, turn, hits, misses, fleet, winner.

Eliminate each of the following:

program	Always eliminate.
row, col	These are parts of a given position or square, more suitable as instance variables for a position or square object.
hits, misses	These are simply marked positions and probably don't need their own class.
turn	Taking a turn is an action and will be described by a method rather than a class.
opponent	This is another word for player.

The following seem to be good candidates for classes: `Player`, `Grid`, `Position`, `Ship`, `Battleship`, `Cruiser`, `Submarine`, `Destroyer`, and `Frigate`. Additionally, it seems there should be a `GameManager` and `Display`.

RELATIONSHIP BETWEEN CLASSES

This program provides two examples of inheritance relationships. Each of the five ships *is-a* Ship, and shares common features, like isHit, isSunk, and array of positions. However, each has a unique name, length, and position in the grid. This means that Ship is a good candidate for an abstract class with abstract methods like getLength, getName, and getPositions, which depend on the kind of ship.

The second inheritance relationship is between the grids. There are two types of grids for each player: his own FleetGrid (the current state of his own ships) and his opponent's HitGrid, which keeps track of his hits and misses. Each of these grids *is-a* Grid. A grid is a candidate for an interface, with a list of methods like getAdjacentNeighbors, getRightNeighbor, etc. Each of FleetGrid and HitGrid would implement Grid.

There are several composition relationships in this program. A Player *has-a* HitGrid and a FleetGrid and also has five ships. The GameManager has each of the two Player objects and also *has-a* Display. The Display has each of the grids.

IDENTIFYING BEHAVIORS

Use the verbs to identify key methods in the program: simulate <game>, place <ships>, shoot <at position>, call out <position>, respond <hit or miss>, sink <ship>, inform that <ship was sunk>, keep track of <hits or misses>, sink <opponent's fleet>, win <game>.

You need to decide who will do what. There's no definitive way of implementing the program, but it seems clear that the GameManager should run the game and declare the winner. Should the GameManager also be in charge of announcing if a ship is sunk? It makes sense because the game manager can see both players' grids. Each player should keep track of his calls, so that he can make an intelligent next call and also respond "hit" or "miss." Will each player have a display? Or will the Display have both players? You have to set it up so that a player can't see his opponent's FleetGrid, but he can see his own and also a grid showing the state of the calls he has made. Should each player have a list of his ships, so he can keep track of the state of his fleet? And what about each ship in the fleet? Should a ship have a list of its positions, and should it keep track of if it's hit or sunk?

Saving and retrieving updated information is crucial to this program. It seems a bit overwhelming. Where should you start? The Ship classes are low-level classes, independent of the players and grids. Start with these and test that you can get accurate information about each ship. In your driver program create an ArrayList<Ship>. Have a loop that prints information about each ship. Polymorphism will take care of getting the correct information about each ship.

Now try the Grid classes. This is a complicated program where each small piece should be coded and tested with simple output. For example, a Grid can be displayed with a two-dimensional array of 0's and 1's to show the positions of ships. Other symbols can be used to show what's been hit and what's been sunk.

When everything is working with the grids, you could add a Display class that has Grid variables and a display method.

Try a Player. Give him a list of ships, two grids and a Display.

Then create a GameManager. Give her two Player variables and be sure she has a playGame method.

The program development shown above is an example of bottom-up development.

Vocabulary Summary

Know these terms for the AP exam:

Vocabulary	Meaning
software development	Writing a program
object-oriented program	Uses interacting objects
program specification	Description of a task
program design	A written plan, an overview of the solution
program implementation	The code
test data	Input to test the program
program maintenance	Keeping the program working and up to date
top-down development	Implement main classes first, subsidiary classes later
independent class	Doesn't use other classes of the program in its code
bottom-up development	Implement lowest level, independent classes first
driver class	Used to test other classes; contains `main` method
inheritance relationship	*is-a* relationship between classes
composition relationship	*has-a* relationship between classes
inheritance hierarchy	Inheritance relationship shown in a tree-like diagram
UML diagram	Tree-like representation of relationship between classes
data structure	Java construct for storing a data field (e.g., array)
encapsulation	Combining data fields and methods in a class
information hiding	Using `private` to restrict access
stepwise refinement	Breaking methods into smaller methods
procedural abstraction	Using helper methods
algorithm	Step-by-step process that solves a problem
stub method	Dummy method called by another method being tested
debugging	Fixing errors
robust program	Screens out bad input
compile-time error	Usually a syntax error; prevents program from compiling
syntax error	Bad language usage (e.g., missing brace)
run-time error	Occurs during execution (e.g., `int` division by 0)
exception	Run-time error thrown by Java method
logic error	Program runs but does the wrong thing

PROGRAM ANALYSIS

Program Correctness

Testing that a program works does not prove that the program is correct. After all, you can hardly expect to test programs for every conceivable set of input data. Computer scientists have developed mathematical techniques to prove correctness in certain cases, but these are beyond the scope of the APCS course. Nevertheless, you are expected to be able to make assertions about the state of a program at various points during its execution.

Assertions

An *assertion* is a precise statement about a program at any given point. The idea is that if an assertion is proved to be true, then the program is working correctly at that point.

An informal step on the way to writing correct algorithms is to be able to make different kinds of assertions about your code.

PRECONDITION

The *precondition* for any piece of code, whether it is a method, loop, or block, is a statement of what is true immediately before execution of that code.

POSTCONDITION

The *postcondition* for a piece of code is a statement of what is true immediately after execution of that code.

Efficiency

An efficient algorithm is one that is economical in the use of

- CPU time. This refers to the number of machine operations required to carry out the algorithm (arithmetic operations, comparisons, data movements, etc.).
- Memory. This refers to the number and complexity of the variables used.

Some factors that affect run-time efficiency include unnecessary tests, excessive movement of data elements, and redundant computations, especially in loops.

Always aim for early detection of output conditions: Your sorting algorithm should halt when the list is sorted; your search should stop if the key element has been found.

In discussing efficiency of an algorithm, we refer to the *best case*, *worst case*, and *average case*. The best case is a configuration of the data that causes the algorithm to run in the least possible amount of time. The worst case is a configuration that leads to the greatest possible run time. Typical configurations (i.e., not specially chosen data) give the average case. It is possible that best, worst, and average cases don't differ much in their run times.

For example, suppose that a list of distinct random numbers must be searched for a given key value. The algorithm used is a sequential search starting at the beginning of the list. In the best case, the key will be found in the first position examined. In the worst case, it will be in the last position or not in the list at all. On average, the key will be somewhere in the middle of the list.

Chapter Summary

There's a lot of vocabulary that you are expected to know in this chapter. Learn the words!

Never make assumptions about a program specification, and always write a design before starting to write code. Even if you don't do this for your own programs, these are the answers you will be expected to give on the AP exam. You are certain to get questions about program design. Know the procedures and terminology involved in developing an object-oriented program.

Be sure you understand what is meant by best case, worst case, and average case for an algorithm. There will be questions about efficiency on the AP exam.

By now you should know what a precondition and postcondition are.

MULTIPLE-CHOICE QUESTIONS ON PROGRAM DESIGN AND ANALYSIS

1. A program that reads in a five-digit identification number is to be written. The specification does not state whether zero can be entered as a first digit. The programmer should
   (A) write the code to accept zero as a first digit since zero is a valid digit.
   (B) write the code to reject zero as a first digit since five-digit integers do not start with zero.
   (C) eliminate zero as a possibility for any of the digits.
   (D) treat the identification number as a four-digit number if the user enters a number starting with zero.
   (E) check with the writer of the specification whether zero is acceptable as a first digit.

2. Refer to the following three program descriptions:

   I Test whether there exists at least one three-digit integer whose value equals the sum of the squares of its digits.
   II Read in a three-digit code number and check if it is valid according to some given formula.
   III Passwords consist of three digits and three capital letters in any order. Read in a password, and check if there are any repeated characters.

   For which of the preceding program descriptions would a `ThreeDigitNumber` class be suitable?
   (A) I only
   (B) II only
   (C) III only
   (D) I and II only
   (E) I, II, and III

3. Top-down programming is illustrated by which of the following?
   (A) Writing a program from top to bottom in Java
   (B) Writing an essay describing how the program will work, without including any Java code
   (C) Using driver programs to test all methods in the order that they're called in the program
   (D) Writing and testing the lowest level methods first and then combining them to form appropriate abstract operations
   (E) Writing the program in terms of the operations to be performed and then refining these operations by adding more detail

4. Which of the following should influence your choice of a particular algorithm?

    I The run time of the algorithm
    II The memory requirements of the algorithm
    III The ease with which the logic of the algorithm can be understood

    (A) I only
    (B) III only
    (C) I and III only
    (D) I and II only
    (E) I, II, and III

5. A list of numbers is stored in a sorted array. It is required that the list be maintained in sorted order. This requirement leads to inefficient execution for which of the following processes?

    I Summing the five smallest numbers in the list
    II Finding the maximum value in the list
    III Inserting and deleting numbers

    (A) I only
    (B) III only
    (C) II and III only
    (D) I and III only
    (E) I, II, and III

6. Which of the following is *not* necessarily a feature of a robust program?
    (A) Does not allow execution to proceed with invalid data
    (B) Uses algorithms that give correct answers for extreme data values
    (C) Will run on any computer without modification
    (D) Will not allow division by zero
    (E) Will anticipate the types of errors that users of the program may make

7. A certain freight company charges its customers for shipping overseas according to this scale:

    $80 per ton for a weight of 10 tons or less
    $40 per ton for each additional ton over 10 tons but
        not exceeding 25 tons
    $30 per ton for each additional ton over 25 tons

For example, to ship a weight of 12 tons will cost $10(80) + 2(40) = \$880$. To ship 26 tons will cost $10(80) + 15(40) + 1(30) = \$1430$.

    A method takes as parameter an integer that represents a valid shipping weight and outputs the charge for the shipment. Which of the following is the smallest set of input values for shipping weights that will adequately test this method?
    (A) 10, 25
    (B) 5, 15, 30
    (C) 5, 10, 15, 25, 30
    (D) 0, 5, 10, 15, 25, 30
    (E) 5, 10, 15, 20, 25, 30

8. A code segment calculates the mean of values stored in integers n1, n2, n3, and n4 and stores the result in `average`, which is of type `double`. What kind of error is caused with this statement?

    ```
    double average = n1 + n2 + n3 + n4 / (double) 4;
    ```

    (A) Logic
    (B) Run-time
    (C) Overflow
    (D) Syntax
    (E) Type mismatch

9. A program evaluates binary arithmetic expressions that are read from an input file. All of the operands are integers, and the only operators are +, -, *, and /. In writing the program, the programmer forgot to include a test that checks whether the right-hand operand in a division expression equals zero. When will this oversight be detected by the computer?
    (A) At compile time
    (B) While editing the program
    (C) As soon as the data from the input file is read
    (D) During evaluation of the expressions
    (E) When at least one incorrect value for the expressions is output

10. Which best describes the precondition of a method? It is an assertion that
    (A) describes precisely the conditions that must be true at the time the method is called.
    (B) initializes the parameters of the method.
    (C) describes the effect of the method on its postcondition.
    (D) explains what the method does.
    (E) states what the initial values of the local variables in the method must be.

11. Consider the following code fragment:

```
/** Precondition: a1, a2, a3 contain 3 distinct integers.
 *  Postcondition: max contains the largest of a1, a2, a3.
 */
//first set max equal to larger of a1 and a2
if (a1 > a2)
    max = a1;
else
    max = a2;
//set max equal to larger of max and a3
if (max < a3)
    max = a3;
```

For this algorithm, which of the following initial setups for a1, a2, and a3 will cause

(1) the least number of computer operations (best case) and

(2) the greatest number of computer operations (worst case)?

(A)   (1) largest value in a1 or a2   (2) largest value in a3
(B)   (1) largest value in a2 or a3   (2) largest value in a1
(C)   (1) smallest value in a1   (2) largest value in a2
(D)   (1) largest value in a2   (2) smallest value in a3
(E)   (1) smallest value in a1 or a2   (2) largest value in a3

12. Refer to the following code segment.

```
/** Compute the mean of integers 1 .. N.
 *  N is an integer >= 1 and has been initialized.
 */
int k = 1;
double mean, sum = 1.0;
while (k < N)
{
    /* loop body */
}
mean = sum / N;
```

What is the precondition for the while loop?
(A) k ≥ N, sum = 1.0
(B) sum = 1 + 2 + 3 + ... + k
(C) k < N, sum = 1.0
(D) N ≥ 1, k = 1, sum = 1.0
(E) mean = sum / N

13. The sequence of Fibonacci numbers is 1, 1, 2, 3, 5, 8, 13, 21, ... The first two
Fibonacci numbers are each 1. Each subsequent number is obtained by adding
the previous two. Consider this method:

```
/** Precondition:  n >= 1.
 *  Postcondition: The nth Fibonacci number has been returned.
 */
public static int fib(int n)
{
    int prev = 1, next = 1, sum = 1;
    for (int i = 3; i <= n; i++)
    {
        /* assertion */
        sum = next + prev;
        prev = next;
        next = sum;
    }
    return sum;
}
```

Which of the following is a correct /* *assertion* */ about the loop variable i?
(A) $1 \leq$ i $\leq$ n
(B) $0 \leq$ i $\leq$ n
(C) $3 \leq$ i $\leq$ n
(D) $3 <$ i $\leq$ n
(E) $3 <$ i $<$ n+1

14. Refer to the following method.

```
/** Precondition:  a and b are initialized integers.
 */
public static int mystery(int a, int b)
{
    int total = 0, count = 1;
    while (count <= b)
    {
        total += a;
        count++;
    }
    return total;
}
```

What is the postcondition for method mystery?
(A) total $= a + b$
(B) total $= a^b$
(C) total $= b^a$
(D) total $= a * b$
(E) total $= a/b$

15. A program is to be written that prints an invoice for a small store. A copy of the invoice will be given to the customer and will display

    - A list of items purchased.
    - The quantity, unit price, and total price for each item.
    - The amount due.

    Three candidate classes for this program are `Invoice`, `Item`, and `ItemList`, where an `Item` is a single item purchased and `ItemList` is the list of all items purchased. Which class is a reasonable choice to be responsible for the `amountDue` method, which returns the amount the customer must pay?

       I `Item`

      II `ItemList`

     III `Invoice`

    (A) I only
    (B) III only
    (C) I and II only
    (D) II and III only
    (E) I, II, and III

16. Which is a *false* statement about classes in object-oriented program design?
    (A) If a class `C1` has an instance variable whose type is another class, `C2`, then `C1` *has-a* `C2`.
    (B) If a class `C1` is associated with another class, `C2`, then `C1` depends on `C2` for its implementation.
    (C) If classes `C1` and `C2` are related such that `C1` *is-a* `C2`, then `C2` *has-a* `C1`.
    (D) If class `C1` is independent, then none of its methods will have parameters that are objects of other classes.
    (E) Classes that have common methods do not necessarily define an inheritance relationship.

17. A Java program maintains a large database of vehicles and parts for a car dealership. Some of the classes in the program are `Vehicle`, `Car`, `Truck`, `Tire`, `Circle`, `SteeringWheel`, and `AirBag`. The declarations below show the relationships between classes. Which is a poor choice?

    (A)
    ```java
    public class Vehicle
    {   ...
        private Tire[] tires;
        private SteeringWheel sw;
        ...
    }
    ```

    (B)
    ```java
    public class Tire extends Circle
    {   ...
        //inherits methods that compute circumference
        //and center point
    }
    ```

    (C)
    ```java
    public class Car extends Vehicle
    {   ...
        //inherits private Tire[] tires from Vehicle class
        //inherits private SteeringWheel sw from Vehicle class
        ...
    }
    ```

    (D)
    ```java
    public class Tire
    {   ...
        private String rating;      //speed rating of tire
        private Circle boundary;
    }
    ```

    (E)
    ```java
    public class SteeringWheel
    {   ...
        private AirBag ab;  //AirBag is stored in SteeringWheel
        private Circle boundary;
    }
    ```

18. A Java programmer has completed a preliminary design for a large program. The programmer has developed a list of classes, determined the methods for each class, established the relationships between classes, and written an outline for each class. Which class(es) should be implemented first?
    (A) Any superclasses
    (B) Any subclasses
    (C) All collaborator classes (classes that will be used to implement other classes)
    (D) The class that represents the dominant object in the program
    (E) All independent classes (classes that have no references to other classes)

Use the program description below for Questions 19–21.

A program is to be written that simulates bumper cars in a video game. The cars move on a square grid and are located on grid points (x, y), where x and y are integers between -20 and 20. A bumper car moves in a random direction, either left, right, up, or down. If it reaches a boundary (i.e., x or y is ± 20), then it reverses direction. If it is about to collide with another bumper car, it reverses direction. Your program should be able to add bumper cars and run the simulation. One step of the simulation allows each car in the grid to move. After a bumper car has reversed direction twice, its turn is over and the next car gets to move.

19. To identify classes in the program, the nouns in the specification are listed:

    program, bumper car, grid, grid point, integer, direction, boundary, simulation

    How many nouns in the list should immediately be discarded because they are unsuitable as classes for the program?
    (A) 0
    (B) 1
    (C) 2
    (D) 3
    (E) 4

A programmer decides to include the following classes in the program. Refer to them for Questions 20 and 21.

- `Simulation` will run the simulation.

- `Display` will show the state of the game.

- `BumperCar` will know its identification number, position in the grid, and current direction when moving.

- `GridPoint` will be a position in the grid. It will be represented by two integer fields, `x_coord` and `y_coord`.

- `Grid` will keep track of all bumper cars in the game, the number of cars, and their positions in the grid. It will update the grid each time a car moves. It will be implemented with a two-dimensional array of `BumperCar`.

20. Which operation should not be the responsibility of the `GridPoint` class?

    (A) `isEmpty`   returns false if grid point contains a `BumperCar`, true otherwise

    (B) `atBoundary` returns true if x or y coordinate $= \pm 20$, false otherwise

    (C) `left`   if not at left boundary, change grid point to 1 unit left of current point

    (D) `up`   if not at top of grid, change grid point to 1 unit above current point

    (E) `get_x`   return x-coordinate of this point

21. Which method is not suitable for the `BumperCar` class?

    (A) `public boolean atBoundary()`
          `//Returns true if BumperCar at boundary, false otherwise.`

    (B) `public void selectRandomDirection()`
          `//Select random direction (up, down, left, or right)`
          `// at start of turn.`

    (C) `public void reverseDirection()`
          `//Move to grid position that is in direction opposite to`
          `// current direction.`

    (D) `public void move()`
          `//Take turn to move. Stop move after two changes`
          `// of direction.`

    (E) `public void update()`
          `//Modify Grid to reflect new position after each stage`
          `// of move.`

ANSWER KEY

1. E	8. A	15. D
2. D	9. D	16. C
3. E	10. A	17. B
4. E	11. A	18. E
5. B	12. D	19. C
6. C	13. C	20. A
7. C	14. D	21. E

ANSWERS EXPLAINED

1. **(E)** A programmer should never make unilateral decisions about a program specification. When in doubt, check with the person who wrote the specification.

2. **(D)** In I and II a three-digit number is the object being manipulated. For III, however, the object is a six-character string, which suggests a class other than a `ThreeDigitNumber`.

3. **(E)** Top-down programming consists of listing the methods for the main object and then using stepwise refinement to break each method into a list of subtasks. Eliminate choices A, C, and D: Top-down programming refers to the design and planning stage and does not involve any actual writing of code. Choice B is closer to the mark, but "top-down" implies a list of operations, not an essay describing the methods.

4. **(E)** All three considerations are valid when choosing an algorithm. III is especially important if your code will be part of a larger project created by several programmers. Yet even if you are the sole writer of a piece of software, be aware that your code may one day need to be modified by others.

5. **(B)** A process that causes excessive data movement is inefficient. Inserting an element into its correct (sorted) position involves moving elements to create a slot for this element. In the worst case, the new element must be inserted into the first slot, which involves moving every element up one slot. Similarly, deleting an element involves moving elements down a slot to close the "gap." In the worst case, where the first element is deleted, all elements in the array will need to be moved. Summing the five smallest elements in the list means summing the first five elements. This requires no testing of elements and no excessive data movement, so it is efficient. Finding the maximum value in a sorted list is very fast—just select the element at the appropriate end of the list.

6. **(C)** "Robustness" implies the ability to handle all data input by the user and to give correct answers even for extreme values of data. A program that is not robust may well run on another computer without modification, and a robust program may need modification before it can run on another computer.

7. **(C)** Eliminate choice D because 0 is an invalid weight, and you may infer from the method description that invalid data have already been screened out. Eliminate

choice E because it tests two values in the range 10–25. (This is not wrong, but choice C is better.) Eliminate choice A since it tests only the endpoint values. Eliminate B because it tests *no* endpoint values.

8. **(A)** The statement is syntactically correct, but as written it will not find the mean of the integers. The bug is therefore an intent or logic error. To execute as intended, the statement needs parentheses:

```
double average = (n1 + n2 + n3 + n4) / (double) 4;
```

9. **(D)** The error that occurs is a run-time error caused by an attempt to divide by zero (`ArithmeticException`). Don't be fooled by choice C. Simply reading an expression 8/0 from the input file won't cause the error. Note that if the operands were of type `double`, the correct answer would be E. In this case, dividing by zero does not cause an exception; it gives an answer of `Infinity`. Only on inspecting the output would it be clear that something was wrong.

10. **(A)** A precondition does not concern itself with the action of the method, the local variables, the algorithm, or the postcondition. Nor does it initialize the parameters. It simply asserts what must be true directly before execution of the method.

11. **(A)** The best case causes the fewest computer operations, and the worst case leads to the maximum number of operations. In the given algorithm, the initial test `if (a1 > a2)` and the assignment to `max` will occur irrespective of which value is the largest. The second test, `if (max < a3)`, will also always occur. The final statement, `max = a3`, will occur only if the largest value is in `a3`; thus, this represents the worst case. So the best case must have the biggest value in `a1` or `a2`.

12. **(D)** The precondition is an assertion about the variables in the loop just before the loop is executed. Variables `N`, `k`, and `sum` have all been initialized to the values shown in choice D. Choice C is wrong because `k` may equal `N`. Choice A is wrong because `k` may be less than `N`. Choice E is wrong because `mean` is not defined until the loop has been exited. Choice B is wrong because it omits the assertions about `N` and `k`.

13. **(C)** Eliminate choices A and B, since `i` is initialized to 3 in the `for` loop. Choices D and E are wrong because `i` is equal to 3 the first time through the loop.

14. **(D)** `a` is being added to `total` `b` times, which means that at the end of execution `total = a*b`.

15. **(D)** It makes sense for an `Item` to be responsible for its name, unit price, quantity, and total price. It is *not* reasonable for it to be responsible for other `Item`s. Since an `ItemList`, however, will contain information for all the `Item`s purchased, it is reasonable to have it also compute the total `amountDue`. It makes just as much sense to give an `Invoice` the responsibility for displaying information for the items purchased, as well as providing a final total, `amountDue`.

16. **(C)** The *is-a* relationship defines inheritance, while the *has-a* relationship defines association. These types of relationship are mutually exclusive. For example, a graduate student *is-a* student. It doesn't make sense to say a student *has-a* graduate student!

17. **(B)** Even though it's convenient for a `Tire` object to inherit `Circle` methods, an inheritance relationship between a `Tire` and a `Circle` is incorrect: It is false to say

that a Tire *is-a* Circle. A Tire is a car part, while a Circle is a geometric shape. Notice that there is an *association* relationship between a Tire and a Circle: A Tire *has-a* Circle as its boundary.

18. **(E)** Independent classes do not have relationships with other classes and can therefore be more easily coded and tested.

19. **(C)** The word "program" is never included when it's used in this context. The word "integer" describes the type of coordinates x and y and has no further use in the specification. While words like "direction," "boundary," and "simulation" may later be removed from consideration as classes, it is not unreasonable to keep them as candidates while you ponder the design.

20. **(A)** A GridPoint object knows only its x and y coordinates. It has no information about whether a BumperCar is at that point. Notice that operations in all of the other choices depend on the x and y coordinates of a GridPoint object. An isEmpty method should be the responsibility of the Grid class that keeps track of the status of each position in the grid.

21. **(E)** A BumperCar is responsible for itself—keeping track of its own position, selecting an initial direction, making a move, and reversing direction. It is not, however, responsible for maintaining and updating the grid. That should be done by the Grid class.

Arrays and Array Lists

Should array indices start at 0 or 1?
My compromise of 0.5 was rejected,
without, I thought, proper consideration.
—S. Kelly-Bootle

Chapter Goals

- One-dimensional arrays
- The `ArrayList<E>` class
- Two-dimensional arrays
- The `List<E>` interface

ONE-DIMENSIONAL ARRAYS

An array is a data structure used to implement a list object, where the elements in the list are of the same type; for example, a class list of 25 test scores, a membership list of 100 names, or a store inventory of 500 items.

For an array of N elements in Java, index values ("subscripts") go from 0 to $N-1$. Individual elements are accessed as follows: If arr is the name of the array, the elements are `arr[0]`, `arr[1]`, ..., `arr[N-1]`. If a negative subscript is used, or a subscript k where $k \geq N$, an `ArrayIndexOutOfBoundsException` is thrown.

Initialization

In Java, an array is an object; therefore, the keyword `new` must be used in its creation. The size of an array remains fixed once it has been created. As with `String` objects, however, an array reference may be reassigned to a new array of a different size.

Example

All of the following are equivalent. Each creates an array of 25 `double` values and assigns the reference data to this array.

1. `double[] data = new double[25];`

2. `double data[] = new double[25];`

3. `double[] data;`
   `data = new double[25];`

A subsequent statement like

```
data = new double[40];
```

reassigns `data` to a new array of length 40. The memory allocated for the previous `data` array is recycled by Java's automatic garbage collection system.

When arrays are declared, the elements are automatically initialized to zero for the primitive numeric data types (`int` and `double`), to `false` for boolean variables, or to `null` for object references.

It is possible to declare several arrays in a single statement. For example,

```
int[] intList1, intList2;    //declares intList1 and intList2 to
                             //contain int values
int[] arr1 = new int[15], arr2 = new int[30];  //reserves 15 slots
                                              //for arr1, 30 for arr2
```

INITIALIZER LIST

Small arrays whose values are known can be declared with an *initializer list*. For example, instead of writing

```
int[] coins = new int[4];
coins[0] = 1;
coins[1] = 5;
coins[2] = 10;
coins[3] = 25;
```

you can write

```
int[] coins = {1, 5, 10, 25};
```

This construction is the one case where `new` is not required to create an array.

Length of Array

A Java array has a final public instance variable (i.e., a constant), `length`, which can be accessed when you need the number of elements in the array. For example,

```
String[] names = new String[25];
< code to initialize names >

//loop to process all names in array
for (int i = 0; i < names.length; i++)
    < process names >
```

NOTE

1. The array subscripts go from 0 to `names.length-1`; therefore, the test on `i` in the `for` loop must be strictly less than `names.length`.
2. `length` is not a method and therefore is not followed by parentheses. Contrast this with `String` objects, where `length` *is* a method and *must* be followed by parentheses. For example,

```
String s = "Confusing syntax!";
int size = s.length();    //assigns 17 to size
```

Traversing an Array

Use a for-each loop whenever you need access to every element in an array without replacing or removing any elements. Use a `for` loop in all other cases: to access the index of any element, to replace or remove elements, or to access just some of the elements.

> Do not use a for-each loop to remove or replace elements of an array.

Note that if you have an array of objects (not primitive types), you can use the for-each loop and mutator methods of the object to modify the fields of any instance (see the `shuffleAll` method on p. 239).

Example 1

```
/** @return the number of even integers in array arr of integers */
public static int countEven(int[] arr)
{
    int count = 0;
    for (int num : arr)
        if ( num % 2 == 0)    //num is even
            count++;
    return count;
}
```

Example 2

```
/** Change each even-indexed element in array arr to 0.
 *  Precondition:  arr contains integers.
 *  Postcondition: arr[0], arr[2], arr[4], ... have value 0.
 */
public static void changeEven(int[] arr)
{
    for (int i = 0; i < arr.length; i += 2)
        arr[i] = 0;
}
```

Arrays as Parameters

Since arrays are treated as objects, passing an array as a parameter means passing its object reference. No copy is made of the array. *Thus, the elements of the actual array can be accessed—and modified.*

Example 1

Array elements accessed but not modified:

```
/** @return index of smallest element in array arr of integers */
public static int findMin (int[] arr)
{
    int min = arr[0];
    int minIndex = 0;
    for (int i = 1; i < arr.length; i++)
        if (arr[i] < min)     //found a smaller element
        {
            min = arr[i];
            minIndex = i;
        }
    return minIndex;
}
```

To call this method (in the same class that it's defined):

```
int[] array;
< code to initialize array >
int min = findMin(array);
```

Example 2

Array elements modified:

```
/** Add 3 to each element of array b. */
public static void changeArray(int[] b)
{
    for (int i = 0; i < b.length; i++)
        b[i] += 3;
}
```

To call this method (in the same class):

```
int[] list = {1, 2, 3, 4};
changeArray(list);
System.out.print("The changed list is ");
for (int num : list)
    System.out.print(num + " ");
```

The output produced is

```
The changed list is 4 5 6 7
```

> When an array is passed as a parameter, it is possible to alter the contents of the array.

Look at the memory slots to see how this happens:

Before the method call: At the start of the method call:

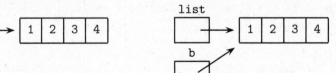

Just before exiting the method: After exiting the method:

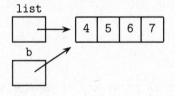
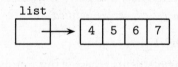

Example 3

Contrast the `changeArray` method with the following attempt to modify one array element:

```
/** Add 3 to an element. */
public static void changeElement(int n)
{ n += 3; }
```

Here is some code that invokes this method:

```
int[] list = {1, 2, 3, 4};
System.out.print("Original array: ");
for (int num : list)
    System.out.print(num + " ");
changeElement(list[0]);
System.out.print("\nModified array: ");
for (int num : list)
    System.out.print(num + " ");
```

Contrary to the programmer's expectation, the output is

```
Original array: 1 2 3 4
Modified array: 1 2 3 4
```

A look at the memory slots shows why the list remains unchanged.

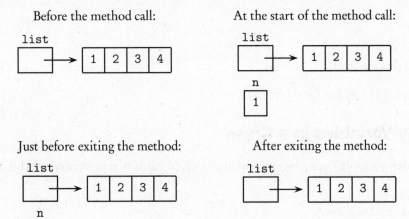

The point of this is that primitive types—including single array elements of type int or double—are passed by value. A copy is made of the actual parameter, and the copy is erased on exiting the method.

Example 4

```
/** Swap arr[i] and arr[j] in array arr. */
public static void swap(int[] arr, int i, int j)
{
    int temp = arr[i];
    arr[i] = arr[j];
    arr[j] = temp;
}
```

To call the swap method:

```
int[] list = {1, 2, 3, 4};
swap(list, 0, 3);
System.out.print("The changed list is: ");
for (int num : list)
    System.out.print(num + " ");
```

The output shows that the program worked as intended:

```
The changed list is: 4 2 3 1
```

Example 5

```
/** @return array containing NUM_ELEMENTS integers read from the keyboard
 *  Precondition:  Array undefined.
 *  Postcondition: Array contains NUM_ELEMENTS integers read from
 *                 the keyboard.
 */
public int[] getIntegers()
{
    int[] arr = new int[NUM_ELEMENTS];
    for (int i = 0; i < arr.length; i++)
    {
        System.out.println("Enter integer: ");
        arr[i] = IO.readInt();              //read user input
    }
    return arr;
}
```

To call this method:

```
int[] list = getIntegers();
```

Array Variables in a Class

Consider a simple Deck class in which a deck of cards is represented by the integers 0 to 51.

```
public class Deck
{
    private int[] deck;
    public static final int NUMCARDS = 52;

    /** constructor */
    public Deck()
    {
        deck = new int[NUMCARDS];
        for (int i = 0; i < NUMCARDS; i++)
            deck[i] = i;
    }

    /** Write contents of Deck. */
    public void writeDeck()
    {
        for (int card : deck)
            System.out.print(card + " ");
        System.out.println();
        System.out.println();
    }

    /** Swap arr[i] and arr[j] in array arr. */
    private void swap(int[] arr, int i, int j)
    {
        int temp = arr[i];
        arr[i] = arr[j];
        arr[j] = temp;
    }
```

```
/** Shuffle Deck: Generate a random permutation by picking a
 *    random card from those remaining and putting it in the
 *    next slot, starting from the right.
 */
public void shuffle()
{
    int index;
    for (int i = NUMCARDS - 1; i > 0; i--)
    {
        //generate an int from 0 to i
        index = (int) (Math.random() * (i + 1));
        swap(deck, i, index);
    }
}
```

Here is a simple driver class that tests the Deck class:

```
public class DeckMain
{
    public static void main(String args[])
    {
        Deck d = new Deck();
        d.shuffle();
        d.writeDeck();
    }
}
```

NOTE

There is no evidence of the array that holds the deck of cards—deck is a private instance
variable and is therefore invisible to clients of the Deck class.

Array of Class Objects

Suppose a large card tournament needs to keep track of many decks. The code to do
this could be implemented with an array of Deck:

```
public class ManyDecks
{
    private Deck[] allDecks;
    public static final int NUMDECKS = 500;

    /** constructor */
    public ManyDecks()
    {
        allDecks = new Deck[NUMDECKS];
        for (int i = 0; i < NUMDECKS; i++)
            allDecks[i] = new Deck();
    }

    /** Shuffle the Decks. */
    public void shuffleAll()
    {
        for (Deck d : allDecks)
            d.shuffle();
    }
```

```
/** Write contents of all the Decks. */
public void printDecks()
{
    for (Deck d : allDecks)
        d.writeDeck();
}
}
```

NOTE

1. The statement

```
allDecks = new Deck[NUMDECKS];
```

creates an array, `allDecks`, of 500 `Deck` objects. The default initialization for these `Deck` objects is null. In order to initialize them with actual decks, the `Deck` constructor must be called for each array element. This is achieved with the `for` loop of the `ManyDecks` constructor.

2. In the `shuffleAll` method, it's OK to use a for-each loop to modify each deck in the array with the mutator method `shuffle`.

Analyzing Array Algorithms

Example 1

Discuss the efficiency of the `countNegs` method below. What are the best and worst case configurations of the data?

```
/** Precondition:  arr[0],...,arr[arr.length-1] contain integers.
 * @return the number of negative values in arr
 */
public static int countNegs(int[] arr)
{
    int count = 0;
    for (int num : arr)
        if (num < 0)
            count++;
    return count;
}
```

Solution:
This algorithm sequentially examines each element in the array. In the best case, there are no negative elements, and `count++` is never executed. In the worst case, all the elements are negative, and `count++` is executed in each pass of the `for` loop.

Example 2

The code fragment below inserts a value, num, into its correct position in a sorted array of integers. Discuss the efficiency of the algorithm.

```
/** Precondition:
 *    - arr[0],...,arr[n-1] contain integers sorted in increasing order.
 *    - n < arr.length.
 *  Postcondition: num has been inserted in its correct position.
 */
{
    //find insertion point
    int i = 0;
    while (i < n && num > arr[i])
        i++;
    //if necessary, move elements arr[i]...arr[n-1] up 1 slot
    for (int j = n; j >= i + 1; j--)
        arr[j] = arr[j-1];
    //insert num in i-th slot and update n
    arr[i] = num;
    n++;
}
```

Solution:

In the best case, num is greater than all the elements in the array: Because it gets inserted at the end of the list, no elements must be moved to create a slot for it. The worst case has num less than all the elements in the array. In this case, num must be inserted in the first slot, arr[0], and every element in the array must be moved up one position to create a slot.

This algorithm illustrates a disadvantage of arrays: Insertion and deletion of an element in an ordered list is inefficient, since, in the worst case, it may involve moving all the elements in the list.

ARRAY LISTS

An ArrayList provides an alternative way of storing a list of objects and has the following advantages over an array:

- An ArrayList shrinks and grows as needed in a program, whereas an array has a fixed length that is set when the array is created.

- In an ArrayList list, the last slot is always list.size()-1, whereas in a partially filled array, you, the programmer, must keep track of the last slot currently in use.

- For an ArrayList, you can do insertion or deletion with just a single statement. Any shifting of elements is handled automatically. In an array, however, insertion or deletion requires you to write the code that shifts the elements.

The Collections API

The ArrayList class is in the Collections API (Application Programming Interface), which is a library provided by Java. Most of the API is in java.util. This library gives the programmer access to prepackaged data structures and the methods to manipulate them. The implementations of these *container classes* are invisible and should not be of concern to the programmer. The code works. And it is reusable.

All of the collections classes, including ArrayList, have the following features in common:

- They are designed to be both memory and run-time efficient.
- They provide methods for insertion and removal of items (i.e., they can grow and shrink).
- They provide for iteration over the entire collection.

The Collections Hierarchy

Inheritance is a defining feature of the Collections API. The interfaces that are used to manipulate the collections specify the operations that must be defined for any container class that implements that interface.

The diagram below shows that the `ArrayList` class implements the `List` interface.

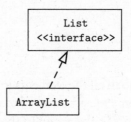

Collections and Generics

The collections classes are generic, with type parameters. Thus, `List<E>` and `ArrayList<E>` contain elements of type E.

When a generic class is declared, the type parameter is replaced by an actual object type. For example,

```
private ArrayList<Clown> clowns;
```

NOTE

1. The `clowns` list must contain only `Clown` objects. An attempt to add an `Acrobat` to the list, for example, will cause a compile-time error.
2. Since the type of objects in a generic class is restricted, the elements can be accessed without casting.
3. All of the type information in a program with generic classes is examined at compile time. After compilation the type information is erased. This feature of generic classes is known as *erasure*. During execution of the program, any attempt at incorrect casting will lead to a `ClassCastException`.

Auto-Boxing and -Unboxing

There are no primitive types in collections classes. An `ArrayList` must contain *objects*, not types like `double` and `int`. Numbers must therefore be boxed—placed in wrapper classes like `Integer` and `Double`—before insertion into an `ArrayList`.

Auto-boxing is the automatic wrapping of primitive types in their wrapper classes.

To retrieve the numerical value of an `Integer` (or `Double`) stored in an `ArrayList`, the `intValue()` (or `doubleValue()`) method must be invoked (unwrapping). *Auto-unboxing* is the automatic conversion of a wrapper class to its corresponding primitive type. This means that you don't need to explicitly call the `intValue()` or doubleValue() methods. Be aware that if a program tries to auto-unbox null, the method will throw a NullPointerException.

Note that while auto-boxing and -unboxing cut down on code clutter, these operations must still be performed behind the scenes, leading to decreased run-time efficiency. It is much more efficient to assign and access primitive types in an array than an ArrayList. You should therefore consider using an array for a program that manipulates sequences of numbers and does not need to use objects.

NOTE

Auto-boxing and -unboxing is a feature in Java 5.0 and later versions and will not be tested on the AP exam. It is OK, however, to use this convenient feature in code that you write in the free-response questions.

THE List<E> INTERFACE

A class that implements the List<E> interface—ArrayList<E>, for example—is a list of elements of type E. In a list, duplicate elements are allowed. The elements of the list are indexed, with 0 being the index of the first element.

A list allows you to

- Access an element at any position in the list using its integer index.
- Insert an element anywhere in the list.
- Iterate over all elements using ListIterator or Iterator (not in the AP subset).

The Methods of List<E>

Here are the methods you should know.

```
boolean add(E obj)
```

Appends obj to the end of the list. Always returns true. If the specified element is not of type E, throws a ClassCastException.

```
int size()
```

Returns the number of elements in the list.

```
E get(int index)
```

Returns the element at the specified index in the list.

```
E set(int index, E element)
```

Replaces item at specified index in the list with specified element. Returns the element that was previously at index. Throws a ClassCastException if the specified element is not of type E.

```
void add(int index, E element)
```

Inserts `element` at specified `index`. Elements from position `index` and higher have 1 added to their indices. Size of list is incremented by 1.

```
E remove(int index)
```

Removes and returns the element at the specified `index`. Elements to the right of position `index` have 1 subtracted from their indices. Size of list is decreased by 1.

Optional topic

```
Iterator<E> iterator()
```

Returns an iterator over the elements in the list, in proper sequence, starting at the first element.

The ArrayList<E> Class

This is an array implementation of the `List<E>` interface. The main difference between an array and an `ArrayList` is that an `ArrayList` is resizable during run time, whereas an array has a fixed size at construction.

Shifting of elements, if any, caused by insertion or deletion, is handled automatically by `ArrayList`. Operations to insert or delete at the end of the list are very efficient. Be aware, however, that at some point there will be a resizing; but, on average, over time, an insertion at the end of the list is a single, quick operation. In general, insertion or deletion in the middle of an `ArrayList` requires elements to be shifted to accommodate a new element (`add`), or to close a "hole" (`remove`).

THE METHODS OF ArrayList<E>

In addition to the two `add` methods, and `size`, `get`, `set`, and `remove`, you must know the following constructor.

```
ArrayList()
```

Constructs an empty list.

NOTE

Each method above that has an index parameter—`add`, `get`, `remove`, and `set`—throws an `IndexOutOfBoundsException` if index is out of range. For `get`, `remove`, and `set`, index is out of range if

```
index < 0 || index >= size()
```

For `add`, however, it is OK to add an element at the end of the list. Therefore index is out of range if

```
index < 0 || index > size()
```

Using `ArrayList<E>`

Example 1

```
//Create an ArrayList containing 0 1 4 9.
List<Integer> list = new ArrayList<Integer>(); //An ArrayList is-a List
for (int i = 0; i < 4; i++)
    list.add(i * i);   //example of auto-boxing
                       //i*i wrapped in an Integer before insertion
Integer intOb = list.get(2); //assigns Integer with value 4 to intOb.
                             //Leaves list unchanged.
int n = list.get(3);   //example of auto-unboxing
                       //Integer is retrieved and converted to int
                       //n contains 9
Integer x = list.set(3, 5);   //list is 0 1 4 5
                              //x contains Integer with value 9
x = list.remove(2);           //list is 0 1 5
                              //x contains Integer with value 4
list.add(1, 7);               //list is 0 7 1 5
list.add(2, 8);               //list is 0 7 8 1 5
```

Example 2

```
//Traversing an ArrayList of Integer.
//Print the elements of list, one per line.
for (Integer num : list)
    System.out.println(num);
```

Example 3

```
/** Precondition:  List list is an ArrayList that contains Integer
 *                 values sorted in increasing order.
 *  Postcondition: value inserted in its correct position in list.
 */
public static void insert(List<Integer> list, Integer value)
{
    int index = 0;
    //find insertion point
    while (index < list.size() &&
            value.compareTo(list.get(index)) > 0)
        index++;
    //insert value
    list.add(index, value);
}
```

NOTE

Suppose `value` is larger than all the elements in `list`. Then the insert method will throw an `IndexOutOfBoundsException` if the first part of the test is omitted, namely `index < list.size()`.

Example 4
```java
/** @return an ArrayList of random integers from 0 to 100 */
public static List<Integer> getRandomIntList()
{
    List<Integer> list = new ArrayList<Integer>();
    System.out.print("How many integers? ");
    int length = IO.readInt();      //read user input
    for (int i = 0; i < length; i++)
    {
        int newNum = (int) (Math.random() * 101);
        list.add(new Integer(newNum));
    }
    return list;
}
```

NOTE

1. The variable `list` is declared to be of type `List<Integer>` (the interface) but is instantiated as type `ArrayList<Integer>` (the implementation).
2. The `add` method in `getRandomIntList` is the `List` method that appends its parameter to the end of the list.

Example 5
```java
/** Swap two values in list, indexed at i and j. */
public static void swap(List<E> list, int i, int j)
{
    E temp = list.get(i);
    list.set(i, list.get(j));
    list.set(j, temp);
}
```

Example 6
```java
/** Print all negatives in list a.
 * Precondition: a contains Integer values.
 */
public static void printNegs(List<Integer> a)
{
    System.out.println("The negative values in the list are: ");
    for (Integer i : a)
        if (i.intValue() < 0)
            System.out.println(i);
}
```

Example 7
```java
/** Change every even-indexed element of strList to the empty string.
 * Precondition: strList contains String values.
 */
public static void changeEvenToEmpty(List<String> strList)
{
    boolean even = true;
    int index = 0;
    while (index < strList.size())
    {
        if (even)
            strList.set(index, "");
        index++;
        even = !even;
    }
}
```

COLLECTIONS AND ITERATORS

Definition of an Iterator

An *iterator* is an object whose sole purpose is to traverse a collection, one element at a time. During iteration, the iterator object maintains a current position in the collection, and is the controlling object in manipulating the elements of the collection.

The `Iterator<E>` Interface

The package `java.util` provides a generic interface, `Iterator<E>`, whose methods are `hasNext`, `next`, and `remove`. The Java Collections API allows iteration over each of its collections classes.

THE METHODS OF `Iterator<E>`

```
boolean hasNext()
```

Returns `true` if there's at least one more element to be examined, `false` otherwise.

```
E next()
```

Returns the next element in the iteration. If no elements remain, the method throws a `NoSuchElementException`.

```
void remove()
```

Deletes from the collection the last element that was returned by `next`. This method can be called only once per call to `next`. It throws an `IllegalStateException` if the `next` method has not yet been called, or if the `remove` method has already been called after the last call to `next`.

Using a Generic Iterator

To iterate over a parameterized collection, you must use a parameterized iterator whose parameter is the same type.

Example 1

```
List<String> list = new ArrayList<String>();
< code to initialize list with strings>
//Print strings in list, one per line.
Iterator<String> itr = list.iterator();
while (itr.hasNext())
    System.out.println(itr.next());
```

NOTE

1. Only classes that allow iteration can use the for-each loop. This is because the loop operates by using an iterator. Thus, the loop in the above example is equivalent to

(continued)

```
        for (String str : list)    //no iterator in sight!
            System.out.println(str);
```

2. Recall, however, that a for-each loop cannot be used to remove elements from the list. The easiest way to "remove all occurrences of . . ." from an `ArrayList` is to use an iterator.

Example 2

```
/** Remove all 2-character strings from strList.
 * Precondition: strList initialized with String objects.
 */
public static void removeTwos(List<String> strList)
{
    Iterator<String> itr = strList.iterator();
    while (itr.hasNext())
        if (itr.next().length() == 2)
            itr.remove();
}
```

Example 3

```
/** Assume a list of integer strings.
 * Remove all occurrences of "6" from the list.
 */
Iterator<String> itr = list.iterator();
while (itr.hasNext())
{
    String num = itr.next();
    if (num.equals("6"))
    {
        itr.remove();
        System.out.println(list);
    }
}
```

If the original list is 2 6 6 3 5 6 the output will be

```
[2, 6, 3, 5, 6]
[2, 3, 5, 6]
[2, 3, 5]
```

Example 4

```
/** Illustrate NoSuchElementException. */
Iterator<SomeType> itr = list.iterator();
while (true)
    System.out.println(itr.next());
```

The list elements will be printed, one per line. Then an attempt will be made to move past the end of the list, causing a `NoSuchElementException` to be thrown. The loop can be corrected by replacing true with `itr.hasNext()`.

(continued)

Example 5

```
/** Illustrate IllegalStateException. */
Iterator<SomeType> itr = list.iterator();
SomeType ob = itr.next();
itr.remove();
itr.remove();
```

Every remove call must be preceded by a next. The second `itr.remove()` statement will therefore cause an `IllegalStateException` to be thrown.

NOTE

In a given program, the declaration

```
Iterator<SomeType> itr = list.iterator();
```

must be made every time you need to initialize the iterator to the beginning of the list.

Example 6

```
/** Remove all negatives from intList.
 * Precondition: intList contains Integer objects.
 */
public static void removeNegs(List<Integer> intList)
{
    Iterator<Integer> itr = intList.iterator();
    while (itr.hasNext())
        if (itr.next().intValue() < 0)
            itr.remove();
}
```

NOTE

1. In Example 6 on p. 246 a for-each loop is used because each element is accessed without changing the list. An iterator operates unseen in the background. Contrast this with Example 6 above, where the list is changed by removing elements. Here you cannot use a for-each loop.
2. To test for a negative value, you could use

   ```
   if (itr.next() < 0)
   ```

   because of auto-unboxing.
3. Use a for-each loop for accessing and modifying objects in a list. Use an iterator for removal of objects.

> Every call to remove must be preceded by next.

TWO-DIMENSIONAL ARRAYS

A two-dimensional array (matrix) is often the data structure of choice for objects like board games, tables of values, theater seats, and mazes.

Look at the following 3 × 4 matrix:

$$2 \quad 6 \quad 8 \quad 7$$
$$1 \quad 5 \quad 4 \quad 0$$
$$9 \quad 3 \quad 2 \quad 8$$

If mat is the matrix variable, the row subscripts go from 0 to 2 and the column subscripts go from 0 to 3. The element mat[1][2] is 4, whereas mat[0][2] and mat[2][3] are both 8. As with one-dimensional arrays, if the subscripts are out of range, an ArrayIndexOutOfBoundsException is thrown.

Declarations

Each of the following declares a two-dimensional array:

```
int[][] table;      //table can reference a 2-D array of integers
                    //table is currently a null reference
double[][] matrix = new double[3][4];  //matrix references a 3 × 4
                                       //array of real numbers.
                                       //Each element has value 0.0
String[][] strs = new String[2][5]; //strs references a 2 × 5
                                       //array of String objects.
                                       //Each element is null
```

An *initializer list* can be used to specify a two-dimensional array:

```
int[][] mat = { {3, 4, 5},      //row 0
                {6, 7, 8} };     //row 1
```

This defines a 2 × 3 *rectangular* array (i.e., one in which each row has the same number of elements).

The initializer list is a list of lists in which each inside list represents a row of the matrix.

Matrix as Array of Row Arrays

A matrix is implemented as an array of rows, where each row is a one-dimensional array of elements. Suppose mat is the 3 × 4 matrix

```
2 6 8 7
1 5 4 0
9 3 2 8
```

Then mat is an array of three arrays:

mat[0]	contains	{2, 6, 8, 7}
mat[1]	contains	{1, 5, 4, 0}
mat[2]	contains	{9, 3, 2, 8}

The quantity mat.length represents the number of rows. In this case it equals 3 because there are three row-arrays in mat. For any given row k, where $0 \leq k < $ mat.length, the quantity mat[k].length represents the number of elements in that row, namely the number of columns. (Java allows a variable number of elements in each row. Since these "jagged arrays" are not part of the AP Java subset, you can assume that mat[k].length is the same for all rows k of the matrix, i.e., that the matrix is rectangular.)

Processing a Two-Dimensional Array

There are three common ways to traverse a two-dimensional array:

- row-column (for accessing elements, modifying elements that are class objects, or replacing elements)
- for-each loop (for accessing elements or modifying elements that are class objects, but no replacement)
- row-by-row array processing (for accessing, modifying, or replacement)

Example 1

Find the sum of all elements in a matrix mat. Here is a row-column traversal.

```
/** Precondition: mat is initialized with integer values. */
int sum = 0;
for (int r = 0; r < mat.length; r++)
    for (int c = 0; c < mat[r].length; c++)
        sum += mat[r][c];
```

NOTE

1. mat[r][c] represents the rth row and the cth column.
2. Rows are numbered from 0 to mat.length-1, and columns are numbered from 0 to mat[r].length-1. Any index that is outside these bounds will generate an ArrayIndexOutOfBoundsException.

Since elements are not being replaced, nested for-each loops can be used instead:

```
for (int[] row : mat)        //for each row array in mat
    for (int element : row)  //for each element in this row
        sum += element;
```

NOTE

Starting in 2015, you will need to know how to use a nested for-each traversal. You will also need to know how to process a matrix as shown below, using the third type of traversal, row-by-row array processing. This traversal assumes access to a method that processes an array. So, continuing with the example to find the sum of all elements in mat: In the class where mat is defined, suppose you have the method sumArray.

```
/** @return the sum of integers in arr */
public int sumArray(int[] arr)
{ /* implementation not shown */ }
```

You could use this method to sum all the elements in mat as follows:

```
int sum = 0;
for (int row = 0; row < mat.length; row++) //for each row in mat,
    sum += sumArray(mat[row]);             //add that row's total to sum
```

Note how, since mat[row] is an array of int for $0 \le row < mat.length$, you can use the sumArray method for each row in mat.

Example 2

Add 10 to each element in row 2 of matrix mat.

```
for (int c = 0; c < mat[2].length; c++)
    mat[2][c] += 10;
```

NOTE

1. In the for loop, you can use c < mat[k].length, where $0 \leq k < mat.length$, since each row has the same number of elements.
2. You cannot use a for-each loop here because elements are being replaced.
3. You can, however, use row-by-row array processing. Suppose you have method addTen shown below.

```
/** Add 10 to each int in arr */
public void addTen(int[] arr)
{
    for (int i = 0; i < arr.length; i++)
        arr[i] += 10;
}
```

You could add 10 to each element in row 2 with the single statement

```
addTen(mat[2]);
```

You could also add 10 to every element in mat:

```
for (int row = 0; row < mat.length; row++)
    addTen(mat[row]);
```

Example 3

Suppose Card objects have a mutator method changeValue:

```
public void changeValue(int newValue)
{ value = newValue; }
```

Now consider the declaration

```
Card[][] cardMatrix;
```

Suppose cardMatrix is initialized with Card objects. A piece of code that traverses the cardMatrix and changes the value of each Card to v is

```
for (Card[] row : cardMatrix)   //for each row array in cardMatrix,
    for (Card c : row)          //for each Card in that row,
        c.changeValue(v);       //change the value of that card
```

Alternatively:

```
for (int row = 0; row < cardMatrix.length; row++)
    for (int col = 0; col < cardMatrix[0].length; col++)
        cardMatrix[row][col].changeValue(v);
```

NOTE

The use of the nested for-each loop is OK. Modifying the objects in the matrix with a mutator method is fine. What you can't do is *replace* the Card objects with new Cards.

Example 4

The major and minor diagonals of a square matrix are shown below:

Major diagonal

Minor diagonal

You can process the diagonals as follows:

```
int[][] mat = new int[SIZE][SIZE];  //SIZE is a constant int value
for (int i = 0; i < SIZE; i++)
    Process mat[i][i];               //major diagonal
        OR
    Process mat[i][SIZE - i - 1];   //minor diagonal
```

Two-Dimensional Array as Parameter

Example 1

Here is a method that counts the number of negative values in a matrix.

```
/** Precondition: mat is initialized with integers.
 *  @return count of negative values in mat
 */
public static int countNegs (int[][] mat)
{
    int count = 0;
    for (int[] row : mat)
        for (int num : row)
            if (num < 0)
                count++;
    return count;
}
```

A method in the same class can invoke this method with a statement such as

```
int negs = countNegs(mat);
```

Example 2

Reading elements into a matrix:

```
/** Precondition: Number of rows and columns known.
 *  @return matrix containing rows × cols integers
 *  read from the keyboard
 */
public static int[][] getMatrix(int rows, int cols)
{
    int[][] mat = new int[rows][cols];   //initialize slots
    System.out.println("Enter matrix, one row per line:");
    System.out.println();

    //read user input and fill slots
    for (int r = 0; r < rows; r++)
        for (int c = 0; c < cols; c++)
            mat[r][c] = IO.readInt();   //read user input
    return mat;
}
```

To call this method:

```
//prompt for number of rows and columns
int rows = IO.readInt();      //read user input
int cols = IO.readInt();      //read user input
int[][] mat = getMatrix(rows, cols);
```

NOTE

You cannot use a for-each loop in `getMatrix` because elements in `mat` are being replaced. (Their current value is the initialized value of `0`. The new value is the input value from the keyboard.)

There is further discussion of arrays and matrices, plus additional questions, in Chapter 9 (The AP Computer Science Labs).

Chapter Summary

Manipulation of one-dimensional arrays, two-dimensional arrays, and array lists should be second nature to you by now. Know the Java subset methods for the `List<E>` class. You must also know when these methods throw an `IndexOutOfBoundsException` and when an `ArrayIndexOutOfBoundsException` can occur.

When traversing an `ArrayList`:

- Use a for-each loop to access each element without changing it, or to modify each object in the list using a mutator method.

- Use an `Iterator` to remove elements. (This is not in the AP subset, but it is the easiest way to remove elements from an `ArrayList`.)

A matrix is an array of row arrays. The number of rows is `mat.length`. The number of columns is `mat[0].length`.

When traversing a matrix:

- Use a row-column traversal to access, modify, or replace elements.

- Use a nested for loop to access or modify elements, but not replace them.

- Know how to do row-by-row array processing if you have an appropriate method that takes an array parameter.

MULTIPLE-CHOICE QUESTIONS ON ARRAYS AND ARRAY LISTS

1. Which of the following correctly initializes an array `arr` to contain four elements each with value 0?

    ```
    I  int[] arr = {0, 0, 0, 0};

    II  int[] arr = new int[4];

    III int[] arr = new int[4];
        for (int i = 0; i < arr.length; i++)
            arr[i] = 0;
    ```

    (A) I only
    (B) III only
    (C) I and III only
    (D) II and III only
    (E) I, II, and III

2. The following program segment is intended to find the index of the first negative integer in `arr[0]...arr[N-1]`, where `arr` is an array of N integers.

    ```
    int i = 0;
    while (arr[i] >= 0)
    {
        i++;
    }
    location = i;
    ```

    This segment will work as intended
    (A) always.
    (B) never.
    (C) whenever arr contains at least one negative integer.
    (D) whenever arr contains at least one nonnegative integer.
    (E) whenever arr contains no negative integers.

3. Refer to the following code segment. You may assume that `arr` is an array of `int` values.

    ```
    int sum = arr[0], i = 0;
    while (i < arr.length)
    {
        i++;
        sum += arr[i];
    }
    ```

    Which of the following will be the result of executing the segment?
    (A) Sum of `arr[0]`, `arr[1]`, ..., `arr[arr.length-1]` will be stored in `sum`.
    (B) Sum of `arr[1]`, `arr[2]`, ..., `arr[arr.length-1]` will be stored in `sum`.
    (C) Sum of `arr[0]`, `arr[1]`, ..., `arr[arr.length]` will be stored in `sum`.
    (D) An infinite loop will occur.
    (E) A run-time error will occur.

4. Refer to the following code segment. You may assume that array `arr1` contains elements `arr1[0]`, `arr1[1]`,..., `arr1[N-1]`, where N = `arr1.length`.

```
int count = 0;
for (int i = 0; i < N; i++)
    if (arr1[i] != 0)
    {
        arr1[count] = arr1[i];
        count++;
    }
int[] arr2 = new int[count];
for (int i = 0; i < count; i++)
    arr2[i] = arr1[i];
```

If array `arr1` initially contains the elements 0, 6, 0, 4, 0, 0, 2 in this order, what will `arr2` contain after execution of the code segment?
(A) 6, 4, 2
(B) 0, 0, 0, 0, 6, 4, 2
(C) 6, 4, 2, 4, 0, 0, 2
(D) 0, 6, 0, 4, 0, 0, 2
(E) 6, 4, 2, 0, 0, 0, 0

5. Consider this program segment:

```
for (int i = 2; i <= k; i++)
    if (arr[i] < someValue)
        System.out.print("SMALL");
```

What is the maximum number of times that SMALL can be printed?
(A) 0
(B) 1
(C) k - 1
(D) k - 2
(E) k

6. What will be output from the following code segment, assuming it is in the same class as the doSomething method?

```
int[] arr = {1, 2, 3, 4};
doSomething(arr);
System.out.print(arr[1] + " ");
System.out.print(arr[3]);
    ...
public void doSomething(int[] list)
{
    int[] b = list;
    for (int i = 0; i < b.length; i++)
        b[i] = i;
}
```

(A) 0 0
(B) 2 4
(C) 1 3
(D) 0 2
(E) 0 3

7. Consider writing a program that reads the lines of any text file into a sequential list of lines. Which of the following is a good reason to implement the list with an ArrayList of String objects rather than an array of String objects?
   (A) The get and set methods of ArrayList are more convenient than the [] notation for arrays.
   (B) The size method of ArrayList provides instant access to the length of the list.
   (C) An ArrayList can contain objects of any type, which leads to greater generality.
   (D) If any particular text file is unexpectedly long, the ArrayList will automatically be resized. The array, by contrast, may go out of bounds.
   (E) The String methods are easier to use with an ArrayList than with an array.

8. Consider writing a program that produces statistics for long lists of numerical data. Which of the following is the best reason to implement each list with an array of int (or double), rather than an ArrayList of Integer (or Double) objects?
   (A) An array of primitive number types is more efficient to manipulate than an ArrayList of wrapper objects that contain numbers.
   (B) Insertion of new elements into a list is easier to code for an array than for an ArrayList.
   (C) Removal of elements from a list is easier to code for an array than for an ArrayList.
   (D) Accessing individual elements in the middle of a list is easier for an array than for an ArrayList.
   (E) Accessing all the elements is more efficient in an array than in an ArrayList.

Refer to the following classes for Questions 9–12.

```
public class Address
{
    private String name;
    private String street;
    private String city;
    private String state;
    private String zip;

    //constructors
        ...

    //accessors
    public String getName()
    { return name; }
    public String getStreet()
    { return street; }
    public String getCity()
    { return city; }
    public String getState()
    { return state; }
    public String getZip()
    { return zip; }
}

public class Student
{
    private int idNum;
    private double gpa;
    private Address address;

    //constructors
        ...

    //accessors
    public Address getAddress()
    { return address; }
    public int getIdNum()
    { return idNum; }
    public double getGpa()
    { return gpa; }
}
```

9. A client method has this declaration, followed by code to initialize the list:

```
Address[] list = new Address[100];
```

Here is a code segment to generate a list of *names only*.

```
for (Address a : list)
    /* line of code */
```

Which is a correct /* *line of code* */?
(A) System.out.println(Address[i].getName());
(B) System.out.println(list[i].getName());
(C) System.out.println(a[i].getName());
(D) System.out.println(a.getName());
(E) System.out.println(list.getName());

10. The following code segment is to print out a list of addresses:

```
for (Address addr : list)
{
    /* more code */
}
```

Which is a correct replacement for /* *more code* */?

```
 I  System.out.println(list[i].getName());
    System.out.println(list[i].getStreet());
    System.out.print(list[i].getCity() + ", ");
    System.out.print(list[i].getState() + " ");
    System.out.println(list[i].getZip());

II  System.out.println(addr.getName());
    System.out.println(addr.getStreet());
    System.out.print(addr.getCity() + ", ");
    System.out.print(addr.getState() + " ");
    System.out.println(addr.getZip());

III System.out.println(addr);
```

(A) I only
(B) II only
(C) III only
(D) I and II only
(E) I, II, and III

11. A client method has this declaration:

```
Student[] allStudents = new Student[NUM_STUDS];  //NUM_STUDS is
                                                 //an int constant
```

Here is a code segment to generate a list of Student names only. (You may assume that allStudents has been initialized.)

```
for (Student student : allStudents)
    /* code to print list of names */
```

Which is a correct replacement for */* code to print list of names */*?

(A) `System.out.println(allStudents.getName());`

(B) `System.out.println(student.getName());`

(C) `System.out.println(student.getAddress().getName());`

(D) `System.out.println(allStudents.getAddress().getName());`

(E) `System.out.println(student[i].getAddress().getName());`

12. Here is a method that locates the Student with the highest idNum:

```
/** Precondition: Array stuArr of Student is initialized.
 *  @return Student with highest idNum
 */
public static Student locate(Student[] stuArr)
{
    /* method body */
}
```

Which of the following could replace /* *method body* */ so that the method works as intended?

```
I  int max = stuArr[0].getIdNum();
   for (Student student : stuArr)
       if (student.getIdNum() > max)
       {
           max = student.getIdNum();
           return student;
       }
   return stuArr[0];
```

```
II Student highestSoFar = stuArr[0];
   int max = stuArr[0].getIdNum();
   for (Student student : stuArr)
       if(student.getIdNum() > max)
       {
           max = student.getIdNum();
           highestSoFar = student;
       }
   return highestSoFar;
```

```
III int maxPos = 0;
    for(int i = 1; i < stuArr.length; i++)
        if(stuArr[i].getIdNum() > stuArr[maxPos].getIdNum())
            maxPos = i;
    return stuArr[maxPos];
```

(A) I only
(B) II only
(C) III only
(D) I and III only
(E) II and III only

Questions 13–15 refer to the `Ticket` and `Transaction` classes below.

```java
public class Ticket
{
    private String row;
    private int seat;
    private double price;

    //constructor
    public Ticket(String aRow, int aSeat, double aPrice)
    {
        row = aRow;
        seat = aSeat;
        price = aPrice;
    }

    //accessors getRow(), getSeat(), and getPrice()
    ...
}

public class Transaction
{
    private int numTickets;
    private Ticket[] tickList;

    //constructor
    public Transaction(int numTicks)
    {
        numTickets = numTicks;
        tickList = new Ticket[numTicks];
        String theRow;
        int theSeat;
        double thePrice;
        for (int i = 0; i < numTicks; i++)
        {
            < read user input for theRow, theSeat, and thePrice >
                ...

            /* more code */
        }
    }

    /** @return total amount paid for this transaction */
    public double totalPaid()
    {
        double total = 0.0;
        /* code to calculate amount */
        return total;
    }
}
```

13. Which of the following correctly replaces /* *more code* */ in the Transaction constructor to initialize the tickList array?

    (A) `tickList[i] = new Ticket(getRow(), getSeat(), getPrice());`

    (B) `tickList[i] = new Ticket(theRow, theSeat, thePrice);`

    (C) `tickList[i] = new tickList(getRow(), getSeat(), getPrice());`

    (D) `tickList[i] = new tickList(theRow, theSeat, thePrice);`

    (E) `tickList[i] = new tickList(numTicks);`

14. Which represents correct /* *code to calculate amount* */ in the totalPaid method?

    (A)
    ```
    for (Ticket t : tickList)
        total += t.price;
    ```

    (B)
    ```
    for (Ticket t : tickList)
        total += tickList.getPrice();
    ```

    (C)
    ```
    for (Ticket t : tickList)
        total += t.getPrice();
    ```

    (D)
    ```
    Transaction T;
    for (Ticket t : T)
        total += t.getPrice();
    ```

    (E)
    ```
    Transaction T;
    for (Ticket t : T)
        total += t.price;
    ```

15. Suppose it is necessary to keep a list of all ticket transactions. Assuming that there are NUMSALES transactions, a suitable declaration would be

    (A) `Transaction[] listOfSales = new Transaction[NUMSALES];`

    (B) `Transaction[] listOfSales = new Ticket[NUMSALES];`

    (C) `Ticket[] listOfSales = new Transaction[NUMSALES];`

    (D) `Ticket[] listOfSales = new Ticket[NUMSALES];`

    (E) `Transaction[] Ticket = new listOfSales[NUMSALES];`

16. The following code fragment is intended to find the smallest value in
    `arr[0]...arr[n-1]`.

```
/** Precondition:
 *   - arr is an array, arr.length = n.
 *   - arr[0]...arr[n-1] initialized with integers.
 *  Postcondition: min = smallest value in arr[0]...arr[n-1].
 */
int min = arr[0];
int i = 1;
while (i < n)
{
    i++;
    if (arr[i] < min)
        min = arr[i];
}
```

This code is incorrect. For the segment to work as intended, which of the following modifications could be made?

I Change the line

```
int i = 1;
```

to

```
int i = 0;
```

Make no other changes.

II Change the body of the `while` loop to

```
{
    if (arr[i] < min)
        min = arr[i];
    i++;
}
```

Make no other changes.

III Change the test for the `while` loop as follows:

```
while (i <= n)
```

Make no other changes.

(A) I only
(B) II only
(C) III only
(D) I and II only
(E) I, II, and III

17. Refer to method `match` below:

```
/** @param v an array of int sorted in increasing order
 *  @param w an array of int sorted in increasing order
 *  @param N the number of elements in array v
 *  @param M the number of elements in array w
 *  @return true if there is an integer k that occurs
 *  in both arrays; otherwise returns false
 *  Precondition:
 *    v[0]..v[N-1] and w[0]..w[M-1] initialized with integers.
 *    v[0] < v[1] < .. < v[N-1] and w[0] < w[1] < .. < w[M-1].
 */
public static boolean match(int[] v, int[] w, int N, int M)
{
    int vIndex = 0, wIndex = 0;
    while (vIndex < N && wIndex < M)
    {
        if (v[vIndex] == w[wIndex])
            return true;
        else if (v[vIndex] < w[wIndex])
            vIndex++;
        else
            wIndex++;
    }
    return false;
}
```

Assuming that the method has not been exited, which assertion is true at the end of every execution of the `while` loop?

(A) `v[0]..v[vIndex-1]` and `w[0]..w[wIndex-1]` contain no common value, `vIndex` $\leq$ `N` and `wIndex` $\leq$ `M`.

(B) `v[0]..v[vIndex]` and `w[0]..w[wIndex]` contain no common value, `vIndex` $\leq$ `N` and `wIndex` $\leq$ `M`.

(C) `v[0]..v[vIndex-1]` and `w[0]..w[wIndex-1]` contain no common value, `vIndex` $\leq$ `N-1` and `wIndex` $\leq$ `M-1`.

(D) `v[0]..v[vIndex]` and `w[0]..w[wIndex]` contain no common value, `vIndex` $\leq$ `N-1` and `wIndex` $\leq$ `M-1`.

(E) `v[0]..v[N-1]` and `w[0]..w[M-1]` contain no common value, `vIndex` $\leq$ `N` and `wIndex` $\leq$ `M`.

18. Consider this class:

```
public class Book
{
    private String title;
    private String author;
    private boolean checkoutStatus;

    public Book(String bookTitle, String bookAuthor)
    {
        title = bookTitle;
        author = bookAuthor;
        checkoutStatus = false;
    }

    /** Change checkout status. */
    public void changeStatus()
    { checkoutStatus = !checkoutStatus; }

    //Other methods are not shown.
}
```

A client program has this declaration:

```
Book[] bookList = new Book[SOME_NUMBER];
```

Suppose bookList is initialized so that each Book in the list has a title, author, and checkout status. The following piece of code is written, whose intent is to change the checkout status of each book in bookList.

```
for (Book b : bookList)
    b.changeStatus();
```

Which is *true* about this code?
(A) The bookList array will remain unchanged after execution.
(B) Each book in the bookList array will have its checkout status changed, as intended.
(C) A NullPointerException may occur.
(D) A run-time error will occur because it is not possible to modify objects using the for-each loop.
(E) A logic error will occur because it is not possible to modify objects in an array without accessing the indexes of the objects.

Consider this class for Questions 19 and 20:

```
public class BingoCard
{
    private int[] card;

    /** Default constructor: Creates BingoCard with
     *   20 random digits in the range 1 - 90.
     */
    public BingoCard()
    { /* implementation not shown */ }

    /* Display BingoCard. */
    public void display()
    { /* implementation not shown */ }
        ...
}
```

A program that simulates a bingo game declares an array of BingoCard. The array has NUMPLAYERS elements, where each element represents the card of a different player. Here is a code segment that creates all the bingo cards in the game:

```
/* declare array of BingoCard */
/* construct each BingoCard */
```

19. Which of the following is a correct replacement for

    /* *declare array of* BingoCard */?

    (A) int[] BingoCard = new BingoCard[NUMPLAYERS];

    (B) BingoCard[] players = new int[NUMPLAYERS];

    (C) BingoCard[] players = new BingoCard[20];

    (D) BingoCard[] players = new BingoCard[NUMPLAYERS];

    (E) int[] players = new BingoCard[NUMPLAYERS];

20. Assuming that players has been declared as an array of BingoCard, which of the following is a correct replacement for

    /* *construct each* BingoCard */

    I for (BingoCard card : players)
           card = new BingoCard();

    II for (BingoCard card : players)
           players[card] = new BingoCard();

    III for (int i = 0; i < players.length; i++)
           players[i] = new BingoCard();

    (A) I only
    (B) II only
    (C) III only
    (D) I and III only
    (E) I, II, and III

21. Which declaration will cause an error?

    I `List<String> stringList = new ArrayList<String>();`

    II `List<int> intList = new ArrayList<int>();`

    III `ArrayList<String> compList = new ArrayList<String>();`

    (A) I only
    (B) II only
    (C) III only
    (D) I and III only
    (E) II and III only

22. Consider these declarations:

    ```
    List<String> strList = new ArrayList<String>();
    String ch = " ";
    Integer intOb = new Integer(5);
    ```

    Which statement will cause an error?
    (A) `strList.add(ch);`
    (B) `strList.add(new String("handy andy"));`
    (C) `strList.add(intOb.toString());`
    (D) `strList.add(ch + 8);`
    (E) `strList.add(intOb + 8);`

23. Let `list` be an `ArrayList<Integer>` containing these elements:

    ```
    2 5 7 6 0 1
    ```

    Which of the following statements would *not* cause an error to occur? Assume that each statement applies to the given list, independent of the other statements.
    (A) `Object ob = list.get(6);`
    (B) `Integer intOb = list.add(3.4);`
    (C) `list.add(6, 9);`
    (D) `Object x = list.remove(6);`
    (E) `Object y = list.set(6, 8);`

24. Refer to method `insert` below:

```
/** @param list an ArrayList of String objects
 *  @param element a String object
 *  Precondition:  list contains String values sorted
 *                 in decreasing order.
 *  Postcondition: element inserted in its correct position in list.
 */
public void insert(List<String> list, String element)
{
    int index = 0;
    while (element.compareTo(list.get(index)) < 0)
        index++;
    list.add(index, element);
}
```

Assuming that the type of `element` is compatible with the objects in the list, which is a *true* statement about the `insert` method?
(A) It works as intended for all values of `element`.
(B) It fails for all values of `element`.
(C) It fails if `element` is greater than the first item in `list` and works in all other cases.
(D) It fails if `element` is smaller than the last item in `list` and works in all other cases.
(E) It fails if `element` is either greater than the first item or smaller than the last item in `list` and works in all other cases.

25. Consider the following code segment, applied to `list`, an `ArrayList` of `Integer` values.

```
int len = list.size();
for (int i = 0; i < len; i++)
{
    list.add(i + 1, new Integer(i));
    Object x = list.set(i, new Integer(i + 2));
}
```

If `list` is initially 6 1 8, what will it be following execution of the code segment?
(A) 2 3 4 2 1 8
(B) 2 3 4 6 2 2 0 1 8
(C) 2 3 4 0 1 2
(D) 2 3 4 6 1 8
(E) 2 3 3 2

Questions 26 and 27 are based on the `Coin` and `Purse` classes given below:

```
/* A simple coin class */
public class Coin
{
    private double value;
    private String name;

    //constructor
    public Coin(double coinValue, String coinName)
    {
        value = coinValue;
        name = coinName;
    }

    /** @return the value of this coin */
    public double getValue()
    { return value; }

    /** @return the name of this coin */
    public String getName()
    { return name; }

    /** @param obj a Coin object
     *  @return true if this coin equals obj; otherwise false
     */
    public boolean equals(Object obj)
    { return name.equals(((Coin) obj).name); }

    //Other methods are not shown.
}


/* A purse holds a collection of coins */
public class Purse
{
    private List<Coin> coins;

    /** Creates an empty purse. */
    public Purse()
    { coins = new ArrayList<Coin>(); }

    /** Adds aCoin to the purse.
     *  @param aCoin the coin to be added to the purse
     */
    public void add(Coin aCoin)
    { coins.add(aCoin); }

    /** @return the total value of coins in purse */
    public double getTotal()
    { /* implementation not shown */}

}
```

26. Here is the getTotal method from the Purse class:

```
/** @return the total value of coins in purse */
public double getTotal()
{
    double total = 0;
    /* more code */
    return total;
}
```

Which of the following is a correct replacement for /* *more code* */?

(A)
```
for (Coin c : coins)
{
    c = coins.get(i);
    total += c.getValue();
}
```

(B)
```
for (Coin c : coins)
{
    Coin value = c.getValue();
    total += value;
}
```

(C)
```
for (Coin c : coins)
{
    Coin c = coins.get(i);
    total += c.getValue();
}
```

(D)
```
for (Coin c : coins)
{
    total += coins.getValue();
}
```

(E)
```
for (Coin c : coins)
{
    total += c.getValue();
}
```

27. Two coins are said to *match* each other if they have the same name or the same value. You may assume that coins with the same name have the same value and coins with the same value have the same name. A boolean method find is added to the Purse class:

```
/** @return true if the purse has a coin that matches aCoin,
 *  false otherwise
 */
public boolean find(Coin aCoin)
{
    for (Coin c : coins)
    {
        /* code to find match */
    }
    return false;
}
```

Which is a correct replacement for /* *code to find match* */?

```
I   if (c.equals(aCoin))
        return true;

II  if ((c.getName()).equals(aCoin.getName()))
        return true;

III if ((c.getValue()).equals(aCoin.getValue()))
        return true;
```

(A) I only
(B) II only
(C) III only
(D) I and II only
(E) I, II, and III

28. Which of the following initializes an 8 × 10 matrix with integer values that are perfect squares? (0 is a perfect square.)

```
I    int[][] mat = new int[8][10];

II   int[][] mat = new int[8][10];
     for (int r = 0; r < mat.length; r++)
         for (int c = 0; c < mat[r].length; c++)
             mat[r][c] = r * r;

III  int[][] mat = new int[8][10];
     for (int c = 0; c < mat[r].length; c++)
         for (int r = 0; r < mat.length; r++)
             mat[r][c] = c * c;
```

(A) I only
(B) II only
(C) III only
(D) I and II only
(E) I, II, and III

29. Consider a class that has this private instance variable:

    ```
    private int[][] mat;
    ```

    The class has the following method, alter.

    ```
    public void alter(int c)
    {
        for (int i = 0; i < mat.length; i++)
            for (int j = c + 1; j < mat[0].length; j++)
                mat[i][j-1] = mat[i][j];
    }
    ```

    If a 3 × 4 matrix mat is

    ```
    1 3 5 7
    2 4 6 8
    3 5 7 9
    ```

    then alter(1) will change mat to

    (A) 1 5 7 7
         2 6 8 8
         3 7 9 9

    (B) 1 5 7
         2 6 8
         3 7 9

    (C) 1 3 5 7
         3 5 7 9

    (D) 1 3 5 7
         3 5 7 9
         3 5 7 9

    (E) 1 7 7 7
         2 8 8 8
         3 9 9 9

30. Consider the following method that will alter the matrix mat:

```
/** @param mat the initialized matrix
 *  @param row the row number
 */
public static void matStuff(int[][] mat, int row)
{
    int numCols = mat[0].length;
    for (int col = 0; col < numCols; col++)
        mat[row][col] = row;
}
```

Suppose mat is originally

```
1  4  9  0
2  7  8  6
5  1  4  3
```

After the method call matStuff(mat,2), matrix mat will be

(A)
```
1  4  9  0
2  7  8  6
2  2  2  2
```

(B)
```
1  4  9  0
2  2  2  2
5  1  4  3
```

(C)
```
2  2  2  2
2  2  2  2
2  2  2  2
```

(D)
```
1  4  2  0
2  7  2  6
5  1  2  3
```

(E)
```
1  2  9  0
2  2  8  6
5  2  4  3
```

31. Assume that a square matrix mat is defined by

    ```
    int[][] mat = new int[SIZE][SIZE];
    //SIZE is an integer constant >= 2
    ```

    What does the following code segment do?

    ```
    for (int i = 0; i < SIZE - 1; i++)
        for (int j = 0; j < SIZE - i - 1; j++)
            swap(mat, i, j, SIZE - j - 1, SIZE - i - 1);
    ```

    You may assume the existence of this swap method:

    ```
    /** Interchange mat[a][b] and mat[c][d]. */
    public void swap(int[][] mat, int a, int b, int c, int d)
    ```

    (A) Reflects mat through its major diagonal. For example,

    $$
    \begin{matrix} 2 & 6 \\ 4 & 3 \end{matrix} \longrightarrow \begin{matrix} 2 & 4 \\ 6 & 3 \end{matrix}
    $$

    (B) Reflects mat through its minor diagonal. For example,

    $$
    \begin{matrix} 2 & 6 \\ 4 & 3 \end{matrix} \longrightarrow \begin{matrix} 3 & 6 \\ 4 & 2 \end{matrix}
    $$

    (C) Reflects mat through a horizontal line of symmetry. For example,

    $$
    \begin{matrix} 2 & 6 \\ 4 & 3 \end{matrix} \longrightarrow \begin{matrix} 4 & 3 \\ 2 & 6 \end{matrix}
    $$

    (D) Reflects mat through a vertical line of symmetry. For example,

    $$
    \begin{matrix} 2 & 6 \\ 4 & 3 \end{matrix} \longrightarrow \begin{matrix} 6 & 2 \\ 3 & 4 \end{matrix}
    $$

    (E) Leaves mat unchanged.

32. Consider a class `MatrixStuff` that has a private instance variable:

    ```
    private int[][] mat;
    ```

    Refer to method `alter` below that occurs in the `MatrixStuff` class. (The lines are numbered for reference.)

    ```
    Line 1: /** @param mat the matrix initialized with integers
    Line 2:  *   @param c the column to be removed
    Line 3:  *   Postcondition:
    Line 4:  *    - Column c has been removed.
    Line 5:  *    - The last column is filled with zeros.
    Line 6:  */
    Line 7: public void alter(int[][] mat, int c)
    Line 8: {
    Line 9:     for (int i = 0; i < mat.length; i++)
    Line 10:        for (int j = c; j < mat[0].length; j++)
    Line 11:            mat[i][j] = mat[i][j+1];
    Line 12:     //code to insert zeros in rightmost column
    Line 13:        ...
    Line 14: }
    ```

    The intent of the method `alter` is to remove column c. Thus, if the input matrix mat is

    ```
    2  6  8  9
    1  5  4  3
    0  7  3  2
    ```

    the method call `alter(mat, 1)` should change mat to

    ```
    2  8  9  0
    1  4  3  0
    0  3  2  0
    ```

    The method does not work as intended. Which of the following changes will correct the problem?

    I Change line 10 to

    ```
    for (int j = c; j < mat[0].length - 1; j++)
    ```

    and make no other changes.

    II Change lines 10 and 11 to

    ```
    for (int j = c + 1; j < mat[0].length; j++)
        mat[i][j-1] = mat[i][j];
    ```

    and make no other changes.

    III Change lines 10 and 11 to

    ```
    for (int j = mat[0].length - 1; j > c; j--)
        mat[i][j-1] = mat[i][j];
    ```

    and make no other changes.

    (A) I only
    (B) II only
    (C) III only
    (D) I and II only
    (E) I, II, and III

33. This question refers to the following method:

```
public static boolean isThere(String[][] mat, int row, int col,
    String symbol)
{
    boolean yes;
    int i, count = 0;
    for (i = 0; i < SIZE; i++)
        if (mat[i][col].equals(symbol))
            count++;
    yes = (count == SIZE);
    count = 0;
    for (i = 0; i < SIZE; i++)
        if (mat[row][i].equals(symbol))
            count++;
    return (yes || count == SIZE);
}
```

Now consider this code segment:

```
public final int SIZE = 8;
String[][] mat = new String[SIZE][SIZE];
```

Which of the following conditions on a matrix mat of the type declared in the code segment will by itself guarantee that

```
isThere(mat, 2, 2, "$")
```

will have the value true when evaluated?

   I The element in row 2 and column 2 is "$"
  II All elements in both diagonals are "$"
 III All elements in column 2 are "$"

(A) I only
(B) III only
(C) I and II only
(D) I and III only
(E) II and III only

34. The method `changeNegs` below should replace every occurrence of a negative integer in its matrix parameter with 0.

```
/** @param mat the matrix
 *  Precondition: mat is initialized with integers.
 *  Postcondition: All negative values in mat replaced with 0.
 */
public static void changeNegs(int[][] mat)
{
    /* code */
}
```

Which is correct replacement for /* *code* */?

```
 I  for (int r = 0; r < mat.length; r++)
        for (int c = 0; c < mat[r].length; c++)
            if (mat[r][c] < 0)
                mat[r][c] = 0;
```

```
 II  for (int c = 0; c < mat[0].length; c++)
         for (int r = 0; r < mat.length; r++)
             if (mat[r][c] < 0)
                 mat[r][c] = 0;
```

```
 III  for (int[] row : mat)
          for (int element : row)
              if (element < 0)
                  element = 0;
```

(A) I only
(B) II only
(C) III only
(D) I and II only
(E) I, II, and III

35. A two-dimensional array of `double`, `rainfall`, will be used to represent the daily rainfall for a given year. In this scheme, `rainfall[month][day]` represents the amount of rain on the given day and month. For example,

    `rainfall[1][15]`   is the amount of rain on Jan. 15
    `rainfall[12][25]` is the amount of rain on Dec. 25

The array can be declared as follows:

```
double[][] rainfall = new double[13][32];
```

This creates 13 rows indexed from 0 to 12 and 32 columns indexed from 0 to 31, all initialized to `0.0`. Row 0 and column 0 will be ignored. Column 31 in row 4 will be ignored, since April 31 is not a valid day. In years that are not leap years, columns 29, 30, and 31 in row 2 will be ignored since Feb. 29, 30, and 31 are not valid days.

Consider the method `averageRainfall` below:

```
/** Precondition:
 *    - rainfall is initialized with values representing amounts
 *      of rain on all valid days.
 *    - Invalid days are initialized to 0.0.
 *    - Feb 29 is not a valid day.
 *  Postcondition: Returns average rainfall for the year.
 */
public double averageRainfall(double rainfall[][])
{
    double total = 0.0;
    /* more code */
}
```

Which of the following is a correct replacement for /* *more code* */ so that the postcondition for the method is satisfied?

```
 I for (int month = 1; month < rainfall.length; month++)
       for (int day = 1; day < rainfall[month].length; day++)
           total += rainfall[month][day];
   return total / (13 * 32);

 II for (int month = 1; month < rainfall.length; month++)
        for (int day = 1; day < rainfall[month].length; day++)
            total += rainfall[month][day];
    return total / 365;

III for (double[] month : rainfall)
        for (double rainAmt : month)
            total += rainAmt;
    return total / 365;
```

(A) None
(B) I only
(C) II only
(D) III only
(E) II and III only

36. This question is based on the Point class below:

```
public class Point
{
    /** The coordinates. */
    private int x;
    private int y;

    public Point (int xValue, int yValue)
    {
        x = xValue;
        y = yValue;
    }

    /** @return the x-coordinate of this point */
    public int getx()
    { return x; }

    /** @return the y-coordinate of this point */
    public int gety()
    { return y; }

    /** Set x and y to new_x and new_y. */
    public void setPoint(int new_x, int new_y)
    {
        x = new_x;
        y = new_y;
    }

    //Other methods are not shown.
}
```

The method changeNegs below takes a matrix of Point objects as parameter and replaces every Point that has as least one negative coordinate with the Point (0,0).

```
/** @param pointMat the matrix of points
 *  Precondition:  pointMat is initialized with Point objects.
 *  Postcondition: Every point with at least one negative coordinate
 *                 has been changed to have both coordinates
 *                 equal to zero.
 */
public static void changeNegs (Point [][] pointMat)
{
    /* code */
}
```

Which is a correct replacement for /* *code* */?

```
I  for (int r = 0; r < pointMat.length; r++)
       for (int c = 0; c < pointMat[r].length; c++)
           if (pointMat[r][c].getx() < 0
               || pointMat[r][c].gety() < 0)
                   pointMat[r][c].setPoint(0, 0);

II  for (int c = 0; c < pointMat[0].length; c++)
       for (int r = 0; r < pointMat.length; r++)
           if (pointMat[r][c].getx() < 0
               || pointMat[r][c].gety() < 0)
                   pointMat[r][c].setPoint(0, 0);

III  for (Point[] row : pointMat)
        for (Point p : row)
            if (p.getx() < 0 || p.gety() < 0)
                    p.setPoint(0, 0);
```

(A) I only
(B) II only
(C) III only
(D) I and II only
(E) I, II, and III

37. A simple Tic-Tac-Toe board is a 3 × 3 array filled with either X's, O's, or blanks. Here is a class for a game of Tic-Tac-Toe:

```java
public class TicTacToe
{
    private String[][] board;
    private static final int ROWS = 3;
    private static final int COLS = 3;

    /** Construct an empty board. */
    public TicTacToe()
    {
        board = new String[ROWS][COLS];
        for (int r = 0; r < ROWS; r++)
            for (int c = 0; c < COLS; c++)
                board[r][c] = " ";
    }

    /** @param r the row number
     *  @param c the column number
     *  @param symbol the symbol to be placed on board[r][c]
     *  Precondition: The square board[r][c] is empty.
     *  Postcondition: symbol placed in that square.
     */
    public void makeMove(int r, int c, String symbol)
    {
        board[r][c] = symbol;
    }

    /** Creates a string representation of the board, e.g.
     *      |o  |
     *      |xx |
     *      |  o|
     * @return the string representation of board
     */
    public String toString()
    {
        String s = "";      //empty string
        /* more code */
        return s;
    }
}
```

Which segment represents a correct replacement for */* more code */* for the toString method?

```java
(A) for (int r = 0; r < ROWS; r++)
    {
        for (int c = 0; c < COLS; c++)
        {
            s = s + "|";
            s = s + board[r][c];
            s = s + "|\n";
        }
    }
```

```
(B) for (int r = 0; r < ROWS; r++)
    {
        s = s + "|";
        for (int c = 0; c < COLS; c++)
        {
            s = s + board[r][c];
            s = s + "|\n";
        }
    }

(C) for (int r = 0; r < ROWS; r++)
    {
        s = s + "|";
        for (int c = 0; c < COLS; c++)
            s = s + board[r][c];
    }
    s = s + "|\n";

(D) for (int r = 0; r < ROWS; r++)
        s = s + "|";
    for (int c = 0; c < COLS; c++)
    {
        s = s + board[r][c];
        s = s + "|\n";
    }

(E) for (int r = 0; r < ROWS; r++)
    {
        s = s + "|";
        for (int c = 0; c < COLS; c++)
            s = s + board[r][c];
        s = s + "|\n";
    }
```

ANSWER KEY

1. E	14. C	27. D
2. C	15. A	28. D
3. E	16. B	29. A
4. A	17. A	30. A
5. C	18. B	31. B
6. C	19. D	32. D
7. D	20. C	33. B
8. A	21. B	34. D
9. D	22. E	35. E
10. B	23. C	36. E
11. C	24. D	37. E
12. E	25. A	
13. B	26. E	

ANSWERS EXPLAINED

1. **(E)** Segment I is an initializer list which is equivalent to

```
int[] arr = new int[4];
arr[0] = 0;
arr[1] = 0;
arr[2] = 0;
arr[3] = 0;
```

Segment II creates four slots for integers, which by default are initialized to 0. The `for` loop in segment III is therefore unnecessary. It is not, however, incorrect.

2. **(C)** If arr contains no negative integers, the value of i will eventually exceed N-1, and arr[i] will cause an `ArrayIndexOutOfBoundsException` to be thrown.

3. **(E)** The intent is to sum elements arr[0], arr[1], ..., arr[arr.length-1]. Notice, however, that when i has the value arr.length-1, it is incremented to arr.length in the loop, so the statement sum += arr[i] uses arr[arr.length], which is out of range.

4. **(A)** The code segment has the effect of removing all occurrences of 0 from array arr1. The algorithm copies the nonzero elements to the front of arr1. Then it transfers them to array arr2.

5. **(C)** If arr[i] < someValue for all i from 2 to k, SMALL will be printed on each iteration of the for loop. Since there are k - 1 iterations, the maximum number of times that SMALL can be printed is k - 1.

6. **(C)** Array arr is changed by doSomething. Here are the memory slots:

Just before doSomething is called:

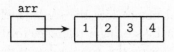

Just after doSomething is called,
but before the for loop is executed:

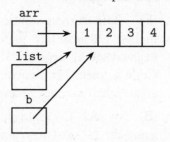

Just before exiting doSomething:

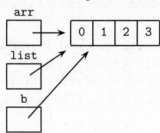

Just after exiting doSomething:

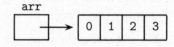

7. **(D)** Arrays are of fixed length and do not shrink or grow if the size of the data set varies. An `ArrayList` automatically resizes the list. Choice A is false: The `[]` notation is compact and easy to use. Choice B is not a valid reason because an array `arr` also provides instant access to its length with the quantity `arr.length`. Choice C is invalid because an array can also contain objects. Also, generality is beside the point in the given program: The list *must* hold `String` objects. Choice E is false: Whether a `String` object is `arr[i]` or `list.get(i)`, the `String` methods are equally easy to invoke.

8. **(A)** In order for numerical elements to be added to an `ArrayList`, each element must be wrapped in a wrapper class before insertion into the list. Then, to retrieve a numerical value from the `ArrayList`, the element must be unboxed using the `intValue` or `doubleValue` methods. Even though these operations can be taken care of with auto-boxing and -unboxing, there are efficiency costs. In an array, you simply use the `[]` notation for assignment (as in `arr[i] = num`) or retrieval (`value = arr[i]`). Note that choices B and C are false statements: Both insertion and deletion for an array involve writing code to shift elements. An `ArrayList` automatically takes care of this through its `add` and `remove` methods. Choice D is a poor reason for choosing an array. While the get and set methods of `ArrayList` might be slightly more awkward than using the `[]` notation, both mechanisms work pretty easily. Choice E is false: Efficiency of access is roughly the same.

9. **(D)** For each `Address` object a in `list`, access the name of the object with `a.getName()`.

10. **(B)** Since the `Address` class does not have a `toString` method, each data field must explicitly be printed. Segment III would work if there *were* a `toString` method for the class (but there isn't, so it doesn't!). Segment I fails because of incorrect use of the for-each loop: The array index should not be accessed.

11. **(C)** Each `Student` name must be accessed through the `Address` class accessor `getName()`. The expression `student.getAddress()` accesses the entire address of

that student. The name field is then accessed using the getName() accessor of the Address class.

12. **(E)** Both correct solutions are careful not to lose the student who has the highest idNum so far. Segment II does it by storing a reference to the student, highestSoFar. Segment III does it by storing the array index of that student. Code segment I is incorrect because it returns the first student whose idNum is greater than max, not necessarily the student with the highest idNum in the list.

13. **(B)** For each i, tickList[i] is a new Ticket object that must be constructed using the Ticket constructor. Therefore eliminate choices C, D, and E. Choice A is wrong because getRow(), getSeat(), and getPrice() are accessors for values *that already exist* for some Ticket object. Note also the absence of the dot member construct.

14. **(C)** To access the price for each Ticket in the tickList array, the getPrice() accessor in the Ticket class must be used, since price is private to that class. This eliminates choices A and E. Choice B uses the array name incorrectly. Choices D and E incorrectly declare a Transaction object. (The method applies to an existing Transaction object.)

15. **(A)** An array of type Transaction is required. This eliminates choices C and D. Additionally, choices B and D incorrectly use type Ticket on the right-hand side. Choice E puts the identifier listOfSales in the wrong place.

16. **(B)** There are two problems with the segment as given:

    1. arr[1] is not tested.
    2. When i has a value of n-1, incrementing i will lead to an out-of-range error for the if(arr[i] < min) test.

    Modification II corrects both these errors. The change suggested in III corrects neither of these errors. The change in I corrects (1) but not (2).

17. **(A)** Notice that either vIndex or wIndex is incremented at the end of the loop. This means that, when the loop is exited, the current values of v[vIndex] and w[wIndex] have not been compared. Therefore, you can only make an assertion for values v[0]..v[vIndex-1] and w[0]..w[wIndex-1]. Also, notice that if there is no common value in the arrays, the exiting condition for the while loop will be that the end of one of the arrays has been reached, namely vIndex equals N or wIndex equals M.

18. **(B)** Objects in an array can be changed in a for-each loop by using mutator methods of the objects' class. The changeStatus method, a mutator in the Book class, will work as intended in the given code. Choice C would be true if it were not given that each Book in bookList was initialized. If any given b had a value of null, then a NullPointerException would be thrown.

19. **(D)** The declaration must start with the type of value in the array, namely BingoCard. This eliminates choices A and E. Eliminate choice B: The type on the right of the assignment should be BingoCard. Choice C is wrong because the number of slots in the array should be NUMPLAYERS, not 20.

20. **(C)** Segment III is the only segment that works, since the for-each loop cannot be used to replace elements in an array. After the declaration

```
BingoCard[] players = new BingoCard[NUMPLAYERS];
```

each element in the `players` array is `null`. The intent in the given code is to replace each null reference with a newly constructed `BingoCard`.

21. **(B)** The type parameter in a generic `ArrayList` must be a class type, not a primitive. Declaration II would be correct if it were

    ```
    List<Integer> intList = new ArrayList<Integer>();
    ```

22. **(E)** All elements added to `strList` must be of type `String`. Each choice satisfies this except choice E. Note that in choice D, the expression `ch + 8` becomes a `String` since `ch` is a `String` (just one of the operands needs to be a `String` to convert the whole expression to a `String`). In choice E, neither `intOb` nor `8` is a `String`.

23. **(C)** The effect of choice C is to adjust the size of the list to 7 and to add the `Integer 9` to the last slot (i.e., the slot with index 6). Choices A, D, and E will all cause an `IndexOutOfBoundsException` because there is no slot with index 6: the last slot has index 5. Choice B will cause a compile-time error, since it is attempting to add an element of type `Double` to a list of type `Integer`.

24. **(D)** If `element` is smaller than the last item in the list, it will be compared with every item in the list. Eventually `index` will be incremented to a value that is out of bounds. To avoid this error, the test in the `while` loop should be

    ```
    while(index < list.size() &&
            element.compareTo(list.get(index)) < 0)
    ```

    Notice that if `element` is greater than or equal to at least one item in `list`, the test as given in the problem will eventually be false, preventing an out-of-range error.

25. **(A)** Recall that `add(index, obj)` shifts all elements, starting at `index`, one unit to the right, then inserts `obj` at position `index`. The `set(index, obj)` method replaces the element in position `index` with `obj`. So here is the state of `list` after each change:

    ```
    i = 0     6 0 1 8
              2 0 1 8
    i = 1     2 0 1 1 8
              2 3 1 1 8
    i = 2     2 3 1 2 1 8
              2 3 4 2 1 8
    ```

26. **(E)** The value of each `Coin c` in coins must be accessed with `c.getValue()`. This eliminates choice D. Eliminate choices A and B: The loop accesses each `Coin` in the `coins ArrayList`, which means that there should not be any statements attempting to get the next `Coin`. Choice B would be correct if the first statement in the loop body were

    ```
    double value = c.getValue();
    ```

27. **(D)** Code segment III is wrong because the `equals` method is defined for objects only. Since `getValue` returns a `double`, the quantities `c.getValue()` and `aCoin.getValue()` must be compared either using `==`, or as described in the box on p. 65 (better).

28. **(D)** Segment II is the straightforward solution. Segment I is correct because it initializes all slots of the matrix to 0, a perfect square. (By default, all arrays of `int` or `double` are initialized to 0.) Segment III fails because `r` is undefined in the condition `c < mat[r].length`. In order to do a column-by-column traversal, you need to get the number of columns in each row. The outer `for` loop could be

```
for (int c = 0; c < mat[0].length; c++)
```

Now segment III works. Note that since the array is rectangular, you can use any index k in the conditional c < mat[k].length, provided that k satisfies the condition 0 ≤ k < mat.length (the number of rows).

29. **(A)** Method `alter` shifts all the columns, starting at column c+1, one column to the left. Also, it does it in a way that overwrites column c. Here are the replacements for the method call `alter(1)`:

```
mat[0][1] = mat[0][2]
mat[0][2] = mat[0][3]
mat[1][1] = mat[1][2]
mat[1][2] = mat[1][3]
mat[2][1] = mat[2][2]
mat[2][2] = mat[2][3]
```

30. **(A)** `matStuff` processes the row selected by the row parameter, 2 in the method call. The row value, 2, overwrites each element in row 2. Don't make the mistake of selecting choice B—the row labels are 0, 1, 2.

31. **(B)** Hand execute this for a 2 × 2 matrix. i goes from 0 to 0, j goes from 0 to 0, so the only interchange is swap `mat[0][0]` with `mat[1][1]`, which suggests choice B. Check with a 3 × 3 matrix:

```
i = 0   j = 0   swap mat[0][0] with mat[2][2]
        j = 1   swap mat[0][1] with mat[1][2]
i = 1   j = 0   swap mat[1][0] with mat[2][1]
```

The elements to be interchanged are shown paired in the following figure. The result will be a reflection through the minor diagonal.

32. **(D)** The method as given will throw an `ArrayIndexOutOfBoundsException`. For the matrix in the example, `mat[0].length` is 4. The call `mat.alter(1)` gives c a value of 1. Thus, in the inner `for` loop, j goes from 1 to 3. When j is 3, the line `mat[i][j] = mat[i][j+1]` becomes `mat[i][3] = mat[i][4]`. Since columns go from 0 to 3, `mat[i][4]` is out of range. The changes in segments I and II both fix this problem. In each case, the correct replacements are made for each row i: `mat[i][1] = mat[i][2]` and `mat[i][2] = mat[i][3]`. Segment III makes the following incorrect replacements as j goes from 3 to 2: `mat[i][2] = mat[i][3]` and `mat[i][1] = mat[i][2]`. This will cause both columns 1 and 2 to be overwritten. Before inserting zeros in the last column, `mat` will be

```
2  9  9  9
1  3  3  3
0  2  2  2
```

This does not achieve the intended postcondition of the method.

33. **(B)** For the method call `isThere(mat, 2, 2, "$")`, the code counts how many times "$" appears in row 2 and how many times in column 2. The method returns true only if `count == SIZE` for either the row or column pass (i.e., the

whole of row 2 or the whole of column 2 contains the symbol "$"). This eliminates choices I and II.

34. **(D)** Segment I is a row-by-row traversal; segment II is a column-by-column traversal. Each achieves the correct postcondition. Segment III traverses the matrix but does not alter it. All that is changed is the local variable `element`. You cannot use this kind of loop to replace elements in an array.

35. **(E)** Since there are 365 valid days in a year, the divisor in calculating the average must be 365. It may appear that segments II and III are incorrect because they include rainfall for invalid days in `total`. Since these values are initialized to `0.0`, however, including them in the total won't affect the final result.

36. **(E)** This is similar to the previous question, but in this case segment III is also correct. This is because instead of *replacing* a matrix element, you are *modifying* it using a mutator method.

37. **(E)** There are three things that must be done in each row:

- Add an opening boundary line:

```
s = s + "|";
```

- Add the symbol in each square:

```
for (int c = 0; c < COLS; c++)
    s = s + board[r][c];
```

- Add a closing boundary line and go to the next line:

```
s = s + "|\n";
```

All of these statements must therefore be enclosed in the outer `for` loop, that is,

```
for (int r = ...)
```

Recursion

recursion *n. See* recursion.
—*Eric S. Raymond,* The New Hacker's Dictionary *(1991)*

Chapter Goals

- Understanding recursion
- Recursive methods
- Recursion in two-dimensional grids
- Recursive helper methods
- Analysis of recursive algorithms
- Tracing recursive algorithms

In the multiple-choice section of the AP exam, you will be asked to understand and trace recursive methods. You will not, however, be asked to come up with code for recursive methods in the free-response part of the exam.

RECURSIVE METHODS

A *recursive method* is a method that calls itself. For example, here is a program that calls a recursive method stackWords.

```java
public class WordPlay
{
    public static void stackWords()
    {
        String word = IO.readString();     //read user input
        if (word.equals("."))
            System.out.println();
        else
            stackWords();
        System.out.println(word);
    }

    public static void main(String args[])
    {
        System.out.println("Enter list of words, one per line.");
        System.out.println("Final word should be a period (.)");
        stackWords();
    }
}
```

Here is the output if you enter

```
hold
my
hand
.
```

You get

```
.
hand
my
hold
```

The program reads in a list of words terminated with a period, and prints the list in reverse order, starting with the period. How does this happen?

Each time the recursive call to stackWords() is made, execution goes back to the start of a new method call. The computer must remember to complete all the pending calls to the method. It does this by stacking the statements that must still be executed as follows: The first time stackWords() is called, the word "hold" is read and tested for being a period. No it's not, so stackWords() is called again. The statement to output "hold" (which has not yet been executed) goes on a stack, and execution goes to the start of the method. The word "my" is read. No, it's not a period, so the command to output "my" goes on the stack. And so on. The stack looks something like this before the recursive call in which the period is read:

```
|
| System.out.println("hand");
|   System.out.println("my");
| System.out.println("hold");
```

Imagine that these statements are stacked like plates. In the final stackWords() call, word has the value ".". Yes, it *is* a period, so the stackWords() line is skipped, the period is printed on the screen, and the method call terminates. The computer now completes each of the previous method calls in turn by "popping" the statements off the top of the stack. It prints "hand", then "my", then "hold", and execution of method stackWords() is complete.[1]

NOTE

1. Each time stackWords() is called, a new local variable word is created.
2. The first time the method actually terminates, the program returns to complete the most recently invoked previous call. That's why the words get reversed in this example.

GENERAL FORM OF SIMPLE RECURSIVE METHODS

Every recursive method has two distinct parts:

- A base case or termination condition that causes the method to end.
- A nonbase case whose actions move the algorithm toward the base case and termination.

---

[1] Actually, the computer stacks the pending statements in a recursive method call more efficiently than the way described. But *conceptually* this is how it is done.

Here is the framework for a simple recursive method that has no specific return type.

```
public void recursiveMeth( ... )
{
    if (base case)
        < Perform some action >
    else
    {
        < Perform some other action >
        recursiveMeth( ... );    //recursive method call
    }
}
```

The base case typically occurs for the simplest case of the problem, such as when an integer has a value of 0 or 1. Other examples of base cases are when some key is found, or an end-of-file is reached. A recursive algorithm can have more than one base case.

In the else or nonbase case of the framework shown, the code fragment *< Perform some other action >* and the method call recursiveMeth can sometimes be interchanged without altering the net effect of the algorithm. Be careful though, because what *does* change is the order of executing statements. This can sometimes be disastrous. (See the eraseBlob example on p. 299.)

Example 1

```
public void drawLine(int n)
{
    if (n == 0)
        System.out.println("That's all, folks!");
    else
    {
        for (int i = 1; i <= n; i++)
            System.out.print("*");
        System.out.println();
        drawLine(n - 1);
    }
}
```

The method call drawLine(3) produces this output:

```
***
**
*
That's all, folks!
```

NOTE

1. A method that has no pending statements following the recursive call is an example of *tail recursion*. Method drawLine is such a case, but stackWords is not.
2. The base case in the drawLine example is n == 0. Notice that each subsequent call, drawLine(n - 1), makes progress toward termination of the method. If your method has no base case, or if you never reach the base case, you will create *infinite recursion*. This is a catastrophic error that will cause your computer eventually to run out of memory and give you heart-stopping messages like java.lang.StackOverflowError ... .

Example 2

```
//Illustrates infinite recursion.
public void catastrophe(int n)
{
    System.out.println(n);
    catastrophe(n);
}
```

Try running the case `catastrophe(1)` if you have lots of time to waste!

A recursive method must have a base case.

WRITING RECURSIVE METHODS

To come up with a recursive algorithm, you have to be able to frame a process *recursively* (i.e., in terms of a simpler case of itself). This is different from framing it *iteratively*, which repeats a process until a final condition is met. A good strategy for writing recursive methods is to first state the algorithm recursively in words.

Optional topic

Example 1

Write a method that returns *n*! (*n* factorial).

n! defined iteratively	*n*! defined recursively
0! = 1	0! = 1
1! = 1	1! = (1)(0!)
2! = (2)(1)	2! = (2)(1!)
3! = (3)(2)(1)	3! = (3)(2!)
…	…

The general recursive definition for *n*! is

$$n! = \begin{cases} 1 & n = 0 \\ n(n-1)! & n > 0 \end{cases}$$

The definition seems to be circular until you realize that if 0! is defined, all higher factorials are defined. Code for the recursive method follows directly from the recursive definition:

```
/** Compute n! recursively.
 *  @param n a nonnegative integer
 *  @return n!
 */
public static int factorial(int n)
{
    if (n == 0)      //base case
        return 1;
    else
        return n * factorial(n - 1);
}
```

Example 2

Write a recursive method `revDigs` that outputs its integer parameter with the digits reversed. For example,

(continued)

```
revDigs(147)   outputs   741
revDigs(4)     outputs   4
```

First, describe the process recursively: Output the rightmost digit. Then, if there are still digits left in the remaining number n/10, reverse its digits. Repeat this until n/10 is 0. Here is the method:

```java
/** @param n a nonnegative integer
 *  @return n with its digits reversed
 */
public static void revDigs(int n)
{
    System.out.print(n % 10);  //rightmost digit
    if (n / 10 != 0)                   //base case
        revDigs(n / 10);
}
```

NOTE

On the AP exam, you are expected to "understand and evaluate" recursive methods. This means that you would not be asked to come up with the code for methods such as factorial and revDigs (as shown above). You could, however, be asked to identify output for any given call to factorial or revDigs.

ANALYSIS OF RECURSIVE METHODS

Recall the Fibonacci sequence 1, 1, 2, 3, 5, 8, 13, ... The nth Fibonacci number equals the sum of the previous two numbers if $n \geq 3$. Recursively,

$$\text{Fib}(n) = \begin{cases} 1, & n = 1, 2 \\ \text{Fib}(n-1) + \text{Fib}(n-2), & n \geq 3 \end{cases}$$

Here is the method:

```java
/** @param n a positive integer
 *  @return the nth Fibonacci number
 */
public static int fib(int n)
{
    if (n == 1 || n == 2)
        return 1;
    else
        return fib(n - 1) + fib(n - 2);
}
```

Notice that there are two recursive calls in the last line of the method. So to find Fib(5), for example, takes eight recursive calls to fib!

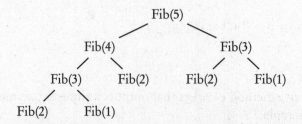

In general, each call to `fib` makes two more calls, which is the tipoff for an exponential algorithm (i.e., one that is *very* inefficient). This is *much* slower than the run time of the corresponding iterative algorithm (see Chapter 5, Question 13).

You may ask: Since every recursive algorithm can be written iteratively, when should programmers use recursion? Bear in mind that recursive algorithms can incur extra run time and memory. Their major plus is elegance and simplicity of code.

General Rules for Recursion

1. Avoid recursion for algorithms that involve large local arrays—too many recursive calls can cause memory overflow.
2. Use recursion when it significantly simplifies code.
3. Avoid recursion for simple iterative methods like factorial, Fibonacci, and the linear search on the next page.
4. Recursion is especially useful for

   - Branching processes like traversing trees or directories.
   - Divide-and-conquer algorithms like mergesort and binary search.

SORTING ALGORITHMS THAT USE RECURSION

Mergesort and quicksort are discussed in Chapter 8.

RECURSIVE HELPER METHODS

A common technique in designing recursive algorithms is to have a public nonrecursive driver method that calls a private *recursive helper method* to carry out the task. The main reasons for doing this are

- To hide the implementation details of the recursion from the user.
- To enhance the efficiency of the program.

Optional topic

Example 1

Consider the simple example of recursively finding the sum of the first *n* positive integers.

```java
/** @param n a positive integer
 *  @return 1 + 2 + 3 + ... + n
 */
public static int sum(int n)
{
    if (n == 1)
        return 1;
    else
        return n + sum(n - 1);
}
```

(continued)

Notice that you get infinite recursion if $n \le 0$. Suppose you want to include a test for $n > 0$ before you execute the algorithm. Placing this test in the recursive method is inefficient because if n is initially positive, it will remain positive in subsequent recursive calls. You can avoid this problem by using a driver method called getSum, which does the test on *n just once*. The recursive method sum becomes a private helper method.

```java
public class FindSum
{
    /** Private recursive helper method.
     *  @param n a positive integer
     *  @return 1 + 2 + 3 + ... + n
     */
    private static int sum(int n)
    {
        if (n == 1)
            return 1;
        else
            return n + sum(n - 1);
    }


    /* Driver method */
    public static int getSum(int n)
    {
        if (n > 0)
            return sum(n);
        else
        {
            throw new IllegalArgumentException
                    ("Error: n must be positive");
        }
    }
}
```

NOTE

This is a trivial method used to illustrate a private recursive helper method. In practice, you would never use recursion to find a simple sum!

Example 2

Consider a recursive solution to the problem of doing a sequential search for a key in an array of strings. If the key is found, the method returns true, otherwise it returns false.

The solution can be stated recursively as follows:

- If the key is in a[0], then the key is found.

- If not, recursively search the array starting at a[1].

- If you are past the end of the array, then the key wasn't found.

Here is a straightforward (but inefficient) implementation:

(continued)

```
public class Searcher
{
    /** Recursively search array a for key.
     * @param a the array of String objects
     * @param key a String object
     * @return true if a[k] equals key for 0 <= k < a.length;
     * false otherwise
     */
    public boolean search(String[] a, String key)
    {
        if (a.length == 0)   //base case. key not found
            return false;
        else if (a[0].compareTo(key) == 0) //base case
            return true;                      //key found
        else
        {
            String[] shorter = new String[a.length-1];
            for (int i = 0; i < shorter.length; i++)
                shorter[i] = a[i+1];
            return search(shorter, key);
        }
    }

    public static void main(String[] args)
    {
        String[] list = {"Mary", "Joe", "Lee", "Jake"};
        Searcher s = new Searcher();
        System.out.println("Enter key: Mary, Joe, Lee or Jake.");
        String key = IO.readString();  //read user input
        boolean result = s.search(list, key);
        if (!result)
            System.out.println(key + " was not found.");
        else
            System.out.println(key + " was found.");
    }
}
```

Notice how horribly inefficient the search method is: For each recursive call, a new array shorter has to be created! It is much better to use a parameter, startIndex, to keep track of where you are in the array. Replace the search method above with the following one, which calls the private helper method recurSearch:

```
/** Driver method. Searches array a for key.
 * Precondition: a contains at least one element.
 * @param a the array of String objects
 * @param key a String object
 * @return true if a[k] equals key for 0 <= k < a.length;
 * false otherwise
 */
public boolean search(String[] a, String key)
{
    return recurSearch(a, 0, key);
}
```

(continued)

```
/** Recursively search array a for key, starting at startIndex.
 *  Precondition:
 *   - a contains at least one element.
 *   - 0 <= startIndex <= a.length.
 *  @return true if a[k] equals key for 0 <= k < a.length;
 *  false otherwise
 */
private boolean recurSearch(String[] a, int startIndex,
    String key)
{
    if(startIndex == a.length)   //base case. key not found
        return false;
    else if(a[startIndex].compareTo(key) == 0) //base case
        return true;                            //key found
    else
        return recurSearch(a, startIndex+1, key);
}
```

NOTE

Use a recursive helper method to hide private coding details from a client.

1. Using the parameter `startIndex` avoids having to create a new array object for each recursive call. Making `startIndex` a parameter of a helper method hides implementation details from the user.
2. The helper method is private because it is called only by `search` within the `Searcher` class.
3. It's easy to modify the `search` method to return the index in the array where the key is found: Make the return type `int` and return `startIndex` if the key is found, `-1` (say) if it isn't.

RECURSION IN TWO-DIMENSIONAL GRIDS

Here is a commonly used technique: using recursion to traverse a two-dimensional array. The problem comes in several different guises, for example,

1. A game board from which you must remove pieces.
2. A maze with walls and paths from which you must try to escape.
3. White "containers" enclosed by black "walls" into which you must "pour paint."

In each case, you will be given a starting position (row, col) and instructions on what to do. The recursive solution typically involves these steps:

> *Check that the starting position is not out of range:*
> > *If (starting position satisfies some requirement)*
> > > *Perform some action to solve problem*
> > > *RecursiveCall(row + 1, col)*
> > > *RecursiveCall(row − 1, col)*
> > > *RecursiveCall(row, col + 1)*
> > > *RecursiveCall(row, col − 1)*

Example

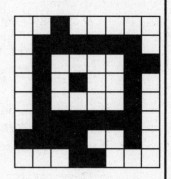

On the right is an image represented as a square grid of black and white cells. Two cells in an image are part of the same "blob" if each is black and there is a sequence of moves from one cell to the other, where each move is either horizontal or vertical to an adjacent black cell. For example, the diagram represents an image that contains two blobs, one of them consisting of a single cell.

Assuming the following Image class declaration, you are to write the body of the eraseBlob method, using a recursive algorithm.

```java
public class Image
{
    private final int BLACK = 1;
    private final int WHITE = 0;
    private int[][] image;    //square grid
    private int size;         //number of rows and columns

    public Image()    //constructor
    { /* implementation not shown */ }

    public void display()    //displays Image
    { /* implementation not shown */ }

    /** Precondition:  Image is defined with either BLACK or WHITE cells.
     *  Postcondition: If 0 <= row < size, 0 <= col < size, and
     *                 image[row][col] is BLACK, set all cells in the
     *                 same blob to WHITE. Otherwise image is unchanged.
     *  @param row the given row
     *  @param col the given column
     */
    public void eraseBlob(int row, int col)
    /* your code goes here */
}
```

Solution:

```java
public void eraseBlob(int row, int col)
{
    if (row >= 0 && row < size && col >= 0 && col < size)
        if (image[row][col] == BLACK)
        {
            image[row][col] = WHITE;
            eraseBlob(row - 1, col);
            eraseBlob(row + 1, col);
            eraseBlob(row, col - 1);
            eraseBlob(row, col + 1);
        }
}
```

NOTE

1. The ordering of the four recursive calls is irrelevant.

2. The test

```
if (image[row][col] == BLACK)
```

can be included as the last piece of the test in the first line:

```
if (row >= 0 && ...
```

If `row` or `col` is out of range, the test will short-circuit, avoiding the dreaded `ArrayIndexOutOfBoundsException`.

3. If you put the statement

```
image[row][col] = WHITE;
```

after the four recursive calls, you get infinite recursion if your blob has more than one cell. This is because, when you visit an adjacent cell, one of its recursive calls visits the original cell. If this cell is still `BLACK`, yet more recursive calls are generated, *ad infinitum*.

A final thought: Recursive algorithms can be tricky. Try to state the solution recursively *in words* before you launch into code. Oh, and don't forget the base case!

Sample Free-Response Question 1

Here is a sample free-response question that uses recursion in a two-dimensional array. See if you can answer it before looking at the solution.

A *color grid* is defined as a two-dimensional array whose elements are character strings having values "b" (blue), "r" (red), "g" (green), or "y" (yellow). The elements are called pixels because they represent pixel locations on a computer screen. For example,

```
                              y g r
    b b g r                   b y g
    g r g r     r r r r       g r b
                              b b g
```

A *connected region* for any pixel is the set of all pixels of the same color that can be reached through a direct path along horizontal or vertical moves starting at that pixel. A connected region can consist of just a single pixel or the entire color grid. For example, if the two-dimensional array is called `pixels`, the connected region for `pixels[1][0]` is as shown here for three different arrays.

```
                    y g r b
    b b g r          g g y g        b b
    g r g r          b g r g        b b
```

The class `ColorGrid`, whose declaration is shown below, is used for storing, displaying, and changing the colors in a color grid.

(continued)

```
public class ColorGrid
{
    private String[][] pixels;
    private int rows;
    private int cols;

    /** Creates numRows × numCols ColorGrid from String s.
     *  @param s the string containing colors of the ColorGrid
     *  @param numRows the number of rows in the ColorGrid
     *  @param numCols the number of columns in the ColorGrid
     */
    public ColorGrid(String s, int numRows, int numCols)
    { /* to be implemented in part (a) */ }

    /** Precondition:
     *    - pixels[row][col] is oldColor, one of "r", "b","g", or "y".
     *    - newColor is one of "r","b","g", or "y".
     *  Postcondition:
     *    - If 0 <= row < rows and 0 <= col < cols, paints the
     *       connected region of pixels[row][col] the newColor.
     *    - Does nothing if oldColor is the same as newColor.
     *  @param row the given row
     *  @param col the given column
     *  @param newColor the new color for painting
     *  @param oldColor the current color of pixels[row][col]
     */
    public void paintRegion(int row, int col, String newColor,
        String oldColor)
    { /* to be implemented in part (b) */ }

    //Other methods are not shown.
}
```

(a) Write the implementation code for the `ColorGrid` constructor. The constructor should initialize the `pixels` matrix of the `ColorGrid` as follows: The dimensions of `pixels` are numRows × numCols. String s contains numRows × numCols characters, where each character is one of the colors of the grid—"r", "g", "b", or "y". The characters are contained in s row by row from top to bottom and left to right. For example, given that numRows is 3, and numCols is 4, if s is "brrygrggyyyr", pixels should be initialized to be

```
b r r y
g r g g
y y y r
```

Complete the constructor below:

```
/** Creates numRows × numCols ColorGrid from String s.
 *  @param s the string containing colors of the ColorGrid
 *  @param numRows the number of rows in the ColorGrid
 *  @param numCols the number of columns in the ColorGrid
 */
public ColorGrid(String s, int numRows, int numCols)
```

(continued)

(b) Write the implementation of the `paintRegion` method as started below. **Note: You must write a recursive solution.** The `paintRegion` paints the connected region of the given pixel, specified by `row` and `col`, a different color specified by the `newColor` parameter. If `newColor` is the same as `oldColor`, the color of the given pixel, `paintRegion` does nothing. To visualize what `paintRegion` does, imagine that the different colors surrounding the connected region of a given pixel form a boundary. When paint is poured onto the given pixel, the new color will fill the connected region up to the boundary.

For example, the effect of the method call `c.paintRegion(2, 3, "b", "r")` on the `ColorGrid` c is shown here. (The starting pixel is shown in a frame, and its connected region is shaded.)

	before						after				
r	r	b	g	y	y		r	r	b	g	y	y
b	r	b	y	r	r		b	r	b	y	b	b
g	g	r	r	r	b		g	g	b	b	b	b
y	r	r	y	r	b		y	b	b	y	b	b

Complete the method `paintRegion` below. **Note: Only a recursive solution will be accepted.**

```
/** Precondition:
 *    - pixels[row][col] is oldColor, one of "r", "b","g", or "y".
 *    - newColor is one of "r","b","g", or "y".
 *  Postcondition:
 *    - If 0 <= row < rows and 0 <= col < cols, paints the
 *      connected region of pixels[row][col] the newColor.
 *    - Does nothing if oldColor is the same as newColor.
 *  @param row the given row
 *  @param col the given column
 *  @param newColor the new color for painting
 *  @param oldColor the current color of pixels[row][col]
 */
public void paintRegion(int row, int col, String newColor,
    String oldColor)
```

Solution

```
(a) public ColorGrid(String s, int numRows, int numCols)
    {
        rows = numRows;
        cols = numCols;
        pixels = new String[numRows][numCols];
        int stringIndex = 0;
        for (int r = 0; r < numRows; r++)
            for (int c = 0; c < numCols; c++)
            {
                pixels[r][c] = s.substring(stringIndex,
                    stringIndex + 1);
                stringIndex++;
            }
    }
```

(continued)

```
(b) public void paintRegion(int row, int col, String newColor,
        String oldColor)
    {
        if (row >= 0 && row < rows && col >= 0 && col < cols)
            if (!pixels[row][col].equals(newColor) &&
                pixels[row][col].equals(oldColor))
            {
                pixels[row][col] = newColor;
                paintRegion(row + 1, col, newColor, oldColor);
                paintRegion(row - 1, col, newColor, oldColor);
                paintRegion(row, col + 1, newColor, oldColor);
                paintRegion(row, col - 1, newColor, oldColor);
            }
    }
```

NOTE

- In part (a), you don't need to test if stringIndex is in range: The precondition states that the number of characters in s is numRows × numCols.
- In part (b), each recursive call must test whether row and col are in the correct range for the pixels array; otherwise, your algorithm may sail right off the edge!
- Don't forget to test if newColor is different from that of the starting pixel. Method paintRegion does nothing if the colors are the same.
- Also, don't forget to test if the current pixel is oldColor—you don't want to overwrite *all* the colors, just the connected region of oldColor!
- The color-change assignment pixels[row][col] = newColor must precede the recursive calls to avoid infinite recursion.

Sample Free-Response Question 2

Here is another sample free-response question that uses recursion.

This question refers to the Sentence class below. Note: A *word* is a string of consecutive nonblank (and nonwhitespace) characters. For example, the sentence

"Hello there!" she said.

consists of the four words

```
"Hello     there!"     she     said.
```

(continued)

```
public class Sentence
{
    private String sentence;
    private int numWords;

    /** Constructor. Creates sentence from String str.
     *                Finds the number of words in sentence.
     * Precondition: Words in str separated by exactly one blank.
     * @param str the string containing a sentence
     */
    public Sentence(String str)
    { /* to be implemented in part (a) */ }

    public int getNumWords()
    { return numWords; }

    public String getSentence()
    { return sentence; }

    /** @param s the specified string
     * @return a copy of String s with all blanks removed
     * Postcondition: Returned string contains just one word.
     */
    private static String removeBlanks(String s)
    { /* implementation not shown */ }

    /** @param s the specified string
     * @return a copy of String s with all letters in lowercase
     * Postcondition: Number of words in returned string equals
     *                number of words in s.
     */
    private static String lowerCase(String s)
    { /* implementation not shown */ }

    /** @param s the specified string
     * @return a copy of String s with all punctuation removed
     * Postcondition: Number of words in returned string equals
     *                number of words in s.
     */
    private static String removePunctuation(String s)
    { /* implementation not shown */ }
}
```

(a) Complete the Sentence constructor as started below. The constructor assigns str to sentence. You should write the subsequent code that assigns a value to numWords, the number of words in sentence.

Complete the constructor below:

(continued)

```
/** Constructor. Creates sentence from String str.
 *                Finds the number of words in sentence.
 * Precondition: Words in str separated by exactly one blank.
 * @param str the string containing a sentence
 */
public Sentence(String str)
{
    sentence = str;
```

(b) Consider the problem of testing whether a string is a palindrome. A *palindrome* reads the same from left to right and right to left, ignoring spaces, punctuation, and capitalization. For example,

> A Santa lived as a devil at NASA.
> Flo, gin is a sin! I golf.
> Eva, can I stab bats in a cave?

A public method isPalindrome is added to the Sentence class. Here is the method and its implementation:

```
/** @return true if sentence is a palindrome, false otherwise
 */
public boolean isPalindrome()
{
    String temp = removeBlanks(sentence);
    temp = removePunctuation(temp);
    temp = lowerCase(temp);
    return isPalindrome(temp, 0, temp.length() - 1);
}
```

The overloaded isPalindrome method contained in the code is a private recursive helper method, also added to the Sentence class. You are to write the implementation of this method. It takes a "purified" string as a parameter, namely one that has been stripped of blanks and punctuation and is all lowercase letters. It also takes as parameters the first and last index of the string. It returns true if this "purified" string is a palindrome, false otherwise.

A recursive algorithm for testing if a string is a palindrome is as follows:

- If the string has length 0 or 1, it's a palindrome.
- Remove the first and last letters.
- If those two letters are the same, and the remaining string is a palindrome, then the original string is a palindrome. Otherwise it's not.

Complete the isPalindrome method below:

```
/** Private recursive helper method that tests whether a substring
 * of string s is a palindrome.
 * @param s the given string
 * @param start the index of the first character of the substring
 * @param end the index of the last character of the substring
 * @return true if the substring is a palindrome, false otherwise
 * Precondition: s contains no spaces, punctuation, or capitals.
 */
private static boolean isPalindrome(String s, int start, int end)
```

(continued)

Solution

```
(a) public Sentence(String str)
    {
        sentence = str;
        numWords = 1;
        int k = str.indexOf(" ");
        while (k != -1)   //while there are still blanks in str
        {
            numWords++;
            str = str.substring(k + 1); //substring after blank
            k = str.indexOf(" ");        //get index of next blank
        }
    }

(b) private static boolean isPalindrome(String s, int start,
            int end)
    {
        if (start >= end)  //substring has length 0 or 1
            return true;
        else
        {
            String first = s.substring(start, start + 1);
            String last = s.substring(end, end + 1);
            if (first.equals(last))
                return isPalindrome(s, start + 1, end - 1);
            else
                return false;
        }
    }
```

NOTE

- In part (a), for every occurrence of a blank in `sentence`, `numWords` must be incremented. (Be sure to initialize `numWords` to 1!)
- In part (a), the code locates all the blanks in `sentence` by replacing `str` with the substring that consists of the piece of `str` directly following the most recently located blank.
- Recall that `indexOf` returns −1 if its `String` parameter does not occur as a substring in its `String` calling object.
- In part (b), the `start` and `end` indexes move toward each other with each subsequent recursive call. This shortens the string to be tested in each call. When `start` and `end` meet, the base case has been reached.
- Notice the private static methods in the `Sentence` class, including the helper method you were asked to write. They are static because they are not invoked by a `Sentence` object (no dot member construct). The only use of these methods is to help achieve the postconditions of other methods in the class.

Chapter Summary

On the AP exam you will be expected to calculate the results of recursive method calls. Recursion becomes second nature when you practice a lot of examples. For the more difficult questions, untangle the statements with either repeated method calls (like that shown in the solution to Question 5 on p. 319), or box diagrams (as shown in the solution to Question 12 on p. 320).

You should understand that recursive algorithms can be *very* inefficient.

MULTIPLE-CHOICE QUESTIONS ON RECURSION

1. Which of the following statements about recursion are true?

    I Every recursive algorithm can be written iteratively.
    II Tail recursion is always used in "divide-and-conquer" algorithms.
    III In a recursive definition, a process is defined in terms of a simpler case of itself.

    (A) I only
    (B) III only
    (C) I and II only
    (D) I and III only
    (E) II and III only

2. Which of the following, when used as the /* *body* */ of method sum, will enable that method to compute $1 + 2 + \cdots + n$ correctly for any $n > 0$?

    ```
    /** @param n a positive integer
     *  @return 1 + 2 + ... + n
     */
    public int sum(int n)
    {
        /* body */
    }
    ```

    ```
    I  return n + sum(n - 1);
    ```

    ```
    II  if (n == 1)
            return 1;
        else
            return n + sum(n - 1);
    ```

    ```
    III  if (n == 1)
             return 1;
         else
             return sum(n) + sum(n - 1);
    ```

    (A) I only
    (B) II only
    (C) III only
    (D) I and II only
    (E) I, II, and III

3. Refer to the method `stringRecur`:

```
public void stringRecur(String s)
{
    if (s.length() < 15)
        System.out.println(s);
    stringRecur(s + "*");
}
```

When will method `stringRecur` terminate without error?
(A) Only when the length of the input string is less than 15
(B) Only when the length of the input string is greater than or equal to 15
(C) Only when an empty string is input
(D) For all string inputs
(E) For no string inputs

4. Refer to method `strRecur`:

```
public void strRecur(String s)
{
    if (s.length() < 15)
    {
        System.out.println(s);
        strRecur(s + "*");
    }
}
```

When will method `strRecur` terminate without error?
(A) Only when the length of the input string is less than 15
(B) Only when the length of the input string is greater than or equal to 15
(C) Only when an empty string is input
(D) For all string inputs
(E) For no string inputs

Questions 5 and 6 refer to method `result`:

```
public int result(int n)
{
    if (n == 1)
        return 2;
    else
        return 2 * result(n - 1);
}
```

5. What value does `result(5)` return?
(A) 64
(B) 32
(C) 16
(D) 8
(E) 2

6. If $n > 0$, how many times will `result` be called to evaluate `result(n)` (including the initial call)?
    (A) 2
    (B) 2^n
    (C) n
    (D) $2n$
    (E) n^2

7. Refer to method `mystery`:

    ```
    public int mystery(int n, int a, int d)
    {
        if (n == 1)
            return a;
        else
            return d + mystery(n - 1, a, d);
    }
    ```

    What value is returned by the call `mystery(3, 2, 6)`?
    (A) 20
    (B) 14
    (C) 10
    (D) 8
    (E) 2

8. Refer to method `f`:

    ```
    public int f(int k, int n)
    {
        if (n == k)
            return k;
        else
            if (n > k)
                return f(k, n - k);
            else
                return f(k - n, n);
    }
    ```

    What value is returned by the call `f(6, 8)`?
    (A) 8
    (B) 4
    (C) 3
    (D) 2
    (E) 1

9. What does method recur do?

```
/** @param x an array of n integers
 *  @param n a positive integer
 */
public int recur(int[] x, int n)
{
    int t;
    if (n == 1)
        return x[0];
    else
    {
        t = recur(x, n - 1);
        if (x[n-1] > t)
            return x[n-1];
        else
            return t;
    }
}
```

(A) It finds the largest value in x and leaves x unchanged.
(B) It finds the smallest value in x and leaves x unchanged.
(C) It sorts x in ascending order and returns the largest value in x.
(D) It sorts x in descending order and returns the largest value in x.
(E) It returns x[0] or x[n-1], whichever is larger.

10. Which best describes what the printString method below does?

```
public void printString(String s)
{
    if (s.length() > 0)
    {
        printString(s.substring(1));
        System.out.print(s.substring(0, 1));
    }
}
```

(A) It prints string s.
(B) It prints string s in reverse order.
(C) It prints only the first character of string s.
(D) It prints only the first two characters of string s.
(E) It prints only the last character of string s.

11. Refer to the method power:

```
/** @param base a nonzero real number
 *  @param expo an integer
 *  @return base raised to the expo power
 */
public double power(double base, int expo)
{
    if (expo == 0)
        return 1;
    else if (expo > 0)
        return base * power(base, expo - 1);
    else
        return /* code */;
}
```

Which /* *code* */ correctly completes method power?
(Recall that $a^{-n} = 1/a^n$, $a \neq 0$; for example, $2^{-3} = 1/2^3 = 1/8$.)
(A) `(1 / base) * power(base, expo + 1)`
(B) `(1 / base) * power(base, expo - 1)`
(C) `base * power(base, expo + 1)`
(D) `base * power(base, expo - 1)`
(E) `(1 / base) * power(base, expo)`

12. Consider the following method:

```
public void doSomething(int n)
{
    if (n > 0)
    {
        doSomething(n - 1);
        System.out.print(n);
        doSomething(n - 1);
    }
}
```

What would be output following the call `doSomething(3)`?
(A) 3211211
(B) 1121213
(C) 1213121
(D) 1211213
(E) 1123211

13. A user enters several positive integers at the keyboard and terminates the list with a sentinel (-999). A writeEven method reads those integers and outputs the even integers only, in the reverse order that they are read. Thus, if the user enters

```
3 5 14 6 1 8 -999
```

the output for the writeEven method will be

```
8 6 14
```

Assume that the user enters at least one positive integer and terminates the list with −999. Here is the method:

```
/** Postcondition: All even integers in the list are output in
 *                  reverse order.
 */
public static void writeEven()
{
    int num = IO.readInt();     //read user input
    if (num != -999)
    {
        /* code */
    }
}
```

Which /* *code* */ satisfies the postcondition of method writeEven?

```
  I if (num % 2 == 0)
        System.out.print(num + " ");
     writeEven();
```

```
 II if (num % 2 == 0)
        writeEven();
     System.out.print(num + " ");
```

```
III writeEven();
     if (num % 2 == 0)
        System.out.print(num + " ");
```

(A) I only
(B) II only
(C) III only
(D) I and II only
(E) I, II, and III

14. Refer to the following recursive method.

```
public int mystery(int n)
{
    if (n < 0)
        return 2;
    else
        return mystery(n - 1) + mystery(n - 3);
}
```

What value is returned by the call mystery(3)?

(A) 12

(B) 10

(C) 8

(D) 6

(E) 4

Questions 15 and 16 refer to method t:

```
/** @param n a positive integer */
public int t(int n)
{
    if (n == 1 || n == 2)
        return 2 * n;
    else
        return t(n - 1) - t(n - 2);
}
```

15. What will be returned by t(5)?
    (A) 4
    (B) 2
    (C) 0
    (D) −2
    (E) −4

16. For the method call t(6), how many calls to t will be made, including the original call?
    (A) 6
    (B) 7
    (C) 11
    (D) 15
    (E) 25

17. This question refers to methods f1 and f2 that are in the same class:

```
    public int f1(int a, int b)
    {
        if (a == b)
            return b;
        else
            return a + f2(a - 1, b);
    }

    public int f2(int p, int q)
    {
        if (p < q)
            return p + q;
        else
            return p + f1(p - 2, q);
    }
```

What value will be returned by a call to f1(5, 3)?
    (A) 5
    (B) 6
    (C) 7
    (D) 12
    (E) 15

18. Consider method `foo`:

```
public int foo(int x)
{
    if (x == 1 || x == 3)
        return x;
    else
        return x * foo(x - 1);
}
```

Assuming no possibility of integer overflow, what will be the value of z after execution of the following statement?

```
int z = foo(foo(3) + foo(4));
```

(A) (15!)/(2!)
(B) 3!+4!
(C) (7!)!
(D) (3!+4!)!
(E) 15

Questions 19 and 20 refer to the `IntFormatter` class below.

```
public class IntFormatter
{
    /** Write 3 digits adjacent to each other.
     *  @param n a nonnegative integer
     */
    public static void writeThreeDigits(int n)
    {
        System.out.print(n / 100);
        System.out.print((n / 10) % 10);
        System.out.print(n % 10);
    }

    /** Insert commas in n, every 3 digits starting at the right.
     *  @param n a nonnegative integer
     */
    public static void writeWithCommas(int n)
    {
        if (n < 1000)
            System.out.print(n);
        else
        {
            writeThreeDigits(n % 1000);
            System.out.print(",");
            writeWithCommas(n / 1000);
        }
    }
}
```

19. The method `writeWithCommas` is supposed to print its nonnegative `int` argument with commas properly inserted (every three digits, starting at the right). For example, the integer 27048621 should be printed as 27,048,621. Method `writeWithCommas` does not always work as intended, however. Assuming no integer overflow, which of the following integer arguments will *not* be printed correctly?
    (A) 896
    (B) 251462251
    (C) 365051
    (D) 278278
    (E) 4

20. Which change in the code of the given methods will cause method `writeWithCommas` to work as intended?
    (A) Interchange the lines `System.out.print(n / 100)` and `System.out.print(n % 10)` in method `writeThreeDigits`.
    (B) Interchange the lines `writeThreeDigits(n % 1000)` and `writeWithCommas(n / 1000)` in method `writeWithCommas`.
    (C) Change the test in `writeWithCommas` to `if (n > 1000)`.
    (D) In the method `writeWithCommas`, change the line `writeThreeDigits(n % 1000)` to `writeThreeDigits(n / 1000)`.
    (E) In the method `writeWithCommas`, change the recursive call `writeWithCommas(n / 1000)` to `writeWithCommas(n % 1000)`.

21. Consider the following method:

```
public static void sketch(int x1, int y1, int x2, int y2, int n)
{
    if (n <= 0)
        drawLine(x1, y1, x2, y2);
    else
    {
        int xm = (x1 + x2 + y1 - y2) / 2;
        int ym = (y1 + y2 + x2 - x1) / 2;
        sketch(x1, y1, xm, ym, n - 1);
        sketch(xm, ym, x2, y2, n - 1);
    }
}
```

Assume that the screen looks like a Cartesian coordinate system with the origin at the center, and that `drawLine` connects (x1,y1) to (x2,y2). Assume also that x1, y1, x2, and y2 are never too large or too small to cause errors. Which picture best represents the sketch drawn by the method call

```
sketch(a, 0, -a, 0, 2)
```

where a is a positive integer?

(A)

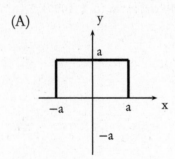

(B)

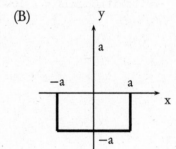

(C)

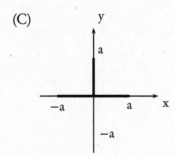

(D)

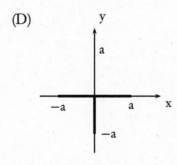

(E)

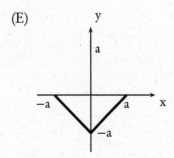

ANSWER KEY

1. D	8. D	15. E
2. B	9. A	16. D
3. E	10. B	17. E
4. D	11. A	18. A
5. B	12. C	19. C
6. C	13. C	20. B
7. B	14. A	21. B

ANSWERS EXPLAINED

1. **(D)** Tail recursion is when the recursive call of a method is made as the last executable step of the method. Divide-and-conquer algorithms like those used in mergesort or quicksort have recursive calls *before* the last step. Thus, statement II is false.

2. **(B)** Code segment I is wrong because there is no base case. Code segment III is wrong because, besides anything else, `sum(n)` prevents the method from terminating—the base case `n == 1` will not be reached.

3. **(E)** When `stringRecur` is invoked, it calls itself irrespective of the length of s. Since there is no action that leads to termination, the method will not terminate until the computer runs out of memory (run-time error).

4. **(D)** The base case is `s.length()` $\geq$ 15. Since s gets longer on each method call, the method will eventually terminate. If the original length of s is $\geq$ 15, the method will terminate without output on the first call.

5. **(B)** Letting R denote the method `result`, we have

$$
\begin{aligned}
R(5) &= 2 * R(4) \\
&= 2 * (2 * (R(3))) \\
&= \cdots \\
&= 2 * (2 * (2 * (2 * R(1)))) \\
&= 2^5 \\
&= 32
\end{aligned}
$$

6. **(C)** For `result(n)` there will be $(n-1)$ recursive calls before `result(1)`, the base case, is reached. Adding the initial call gives a total of n method calls.

7. **(B)** This method returns the nth term of an arithmetic sequence with first term a and common difference d. Letting M denote method `mystery`, we have

$$
\begin{aligned}
M(3,2,6) &= 6 + M(2,2,6) \\
&= 6 + (6 + M(1,2,6)) \quad \text{(base case)} \\
&= 6 + 6 + 2 \\
&= 14
\end{aligned}
$$

8. **(D)** Here are the recursive calls that are made, in order: $f(6,8) \rightarrow f(6,2) \rightarrow f(4,2) \rightarrow f(2,2)$, base case. Thus, 2 is returned.

9. **(A)** If there is only one element in x, then recur returns that element. Having the recursive call at the beginning of the else part of the algorithm causes the if part for each method call to be stacked until t eventually gets assigned to x[0]. The pending if statements are then executed, and t is compared to each element in x. The largest value in x is returned.

10. **(B)** Since the recursive call is made directly following the base case, the System.out.print... statements are stacked up. If printString("cat") is called, here is the sequence of recursive calls and pending statements on the stack:

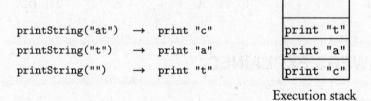

Execution stack

When printString(""), the base case, is called, the print statements are then popped off the stack in reverse order, which means that the characters of the string will be printed in reverse order.

11. **(A)** The required code is for a negative expo. For example, power(2, -3) should return $2^{-3} = 1/8$. Notice that

$$2^{-3} = \tfrac{1}{2}\left(2^{-2}\right)$$
$$2^{-2} = \tfrac{1}{2}\left(2^{-1}\right)$$
$$2^{-1} = \tfrac{1}{2}\left(2^{0}\right)$$

In general:

$$2^{n} = \tfrac{1}{2}(2^{n+1}) \quad \text{whenever} \quad n < 0$$

This is equivalent to (1 / base) * power(base, expo + 1).

12. **(C)** Each box in the diagram below represents a recursive call to doSomething. The numbers to the right of the boxes show the order of execution of the statements. Let D denote doSomething.

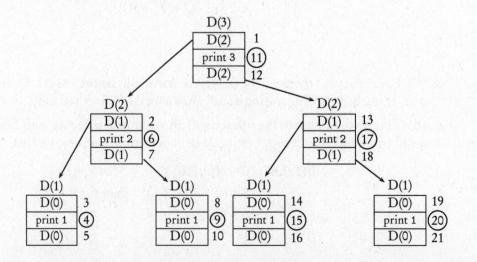

The numbers in each box refer to that method call only. D(0) is the base case, so the statement immediately following it is executed next. When all statements in a given box (method call) have been executed, backtrack along the arrow to find the statement that gets executed next. The circled numbers represent the statements that produce output. Following them in order, statements 4, 6, 9, 11, 15, 17, and 20 produce the output in choice C.

13. **(C)** Since even numbers are printed *before* the recursive call in segment I, they will be printed in the order in which they are read from the keyboard. Contrast this with the correct choice, segment III, in which the recursive call is made before the test for evenness. These tests will be stacked until the last number is read. Recall that the pending statements are removed from the stack in reverse order (most recent recursive call first), which leads to even numbers being printed in reverse order. Segment II is wrong because all numbers entered will be printed, irrespective of whether they are even or not. Note that segment II would work if the input list contained only even numbers.

14. **(A)** Let `mystery(3)` be denoted $m(3)$. Picture the execution of the method as follows:

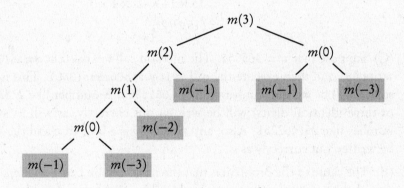

The base cases are shaded. Note that each of the six base case calls returns 2, resulting in a total of 12.

15. **(E)** The method generates a sequence. The first two terms, $t(1)$ and $t(2)$, are 2 and 4. Each subsequent term is generated by subtracting the previous two terms. This is the sequence: 2, 4, 2, −2, −4, −2, 2, 4, ... Thus, $t(5) = -4$. Alternatively,

$$t(5) = t(4) - t(3)$$
$$= [t(3) - t(2)] - t(3)$$
$$= -t(2)$$
$$= -4$$

16. **(D)** 15. Count them! (Note that you stop at $t(2)$ since it's a base case.)

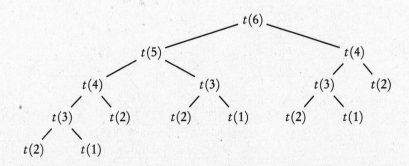

17. **(E)** This is an example of *mutual recursion*, where two methods call each other.

$$
\begin{aligned}
f_1(5,3) &= 5 + f_2(4,3) \\
&= 5 + (4 + f_1(2,3)) \\
&= 5 + (4 + (2 + f_2(1,3))) \\
&= 5 + (4 + (2 + 4)) \\
&= 15
\end{aligned}
$$

Note that $f_2(1,3)$ is a base case.

18. **(A)** foo(3) = 3 (This is a base case). Also, foo(4) = 4 × foo(3) = 12. So you need to find foo(foo(3) + foo(4)) = foo(15).

$$
\begin{aligned}
\text{foo}(15) &= 15 \times \text{foo}(14) \\
&= 15 \times (14 \times \text{foo}(13)) \\
&= \cdots \\
&= 15 \times 14 \times \cdots \times 4 \times \text{foo}(3) \\
&= 15 \times 14 \times \cdots \times 4 \times 3 \\
&= (15)!/(2!)
\end{aligned}
$$

19. **(C)** Suppose that $n = 365051$. The method call writeWithCommas(365051) will write 051 and then execute the call writeWithCommas(365). This is a base case, so 365 will be written out, resulting in 051,365. A number like 278278 (two sets of three identical digits) will be written out correctly, as will a "symmetrical" number like 251462251. Also, any $n < 1000$ is a base case and the number will be written out correctly as is.

20. **(B)** The cause of the problem is that the numbers are being written out with the sets of three digits in the wrong order. The problem is fixed by interchanging writeThreeDigits(n % 1000) and writeWithCommas(n / 1000). For example, here is the order of execution for writeWithCommas(365051).

    writeWithCommas(365) → Base case. Writes 365
    System.out.print(","); → 365,
    writeThreeDigits(051) → 365,051 which is correct

21. **(B)** Here is the "box diagram" for the recursive method calls, showing the order of execution of statements. Notice that the circled statements are the base case calls, the only statements that actually draw a line. Note also that the first time you reach a base case (see circled statement 6), you can get the answer: The picture in choice B is the only one that has a line segment joining (a,0) to (a,-a).

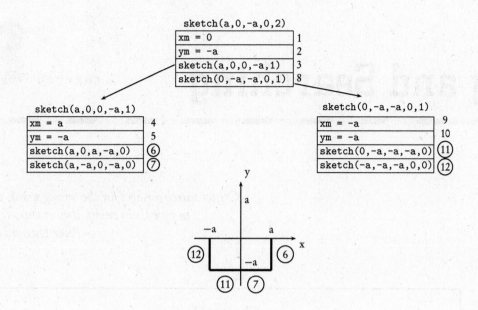

Sorting and Searching

Critics search for ages for the wrong word, which,
to give them credit, they eventually find.
—Peter Ustinov (1952)

Chapter Goals

- Java implementation of sorting algorithms

- Selection and insertion sorts

- Recursive sorts: mergesort and quicksort

- Sequential search and binary search

In each of the following sorting algorithms, assume that an array of *n* elements, a[0], a[1],..., a[n-1], is to be sorted in ascending order.

SORTS: SELECTION AND INSERTION SORTS

Selection Sort

This is a "search-and-swap" algorithm. Here's how it works.

Find the smallest element in the array and exchange it with a[0], the first element. Now find the smallest element in the subarray a[1] ... a[n-1] and swap it with a[1], the second element in the array. Continue this process until just the last two elements remain to be sorted, a[n-2] and a[n-1]. The smaller of these two elements is placed in a[n-2]; the larger, in a[n-1]; and the sort is complete.

Trace these steps with a small array of four elements. The unshaded part is the subarray still to be searched.

8	1	4	6	
1	8	4	6	after first pass
1	4	8	6	after second pass
1	4	6	8	after third pass

NOTE

1. For an array of n elements, the array is sorted after $n - 1$ passes.
2. After the kth pass, the first k elements are in their final sorted position.

Insertion Sort

Think of the first element in the array, a[0], as being sorted with respect to itself. The array can now be thought of as consisting of two parts, a sorted list followed by an unsorted list. The idea of insertion sort is to move elements from the unsorted list to the sorted list one at a time; as each item is moved, it is inserted into its correct position in the sorted list. In order to place the new item, some elements may need to be moved down to create a slot.

Here is the array of four elements. In each case, the boxed element is "it," the next element to be inserted into the sorted part of the list. The shaded area is the part of the list sorted so far.

8	1	4	6	
1	8	4	6	after first pass
1	4	8	6	after second pass
1	4	6	8	after third pass

NOTE

1. For an array of n elements, the array is sorted after $n - 1$ passes.
2. After the kth pass, a[0], a[1], ..., a[k] are sorted with respect to each other but not necessarily in their final sorted positions.
3. The worst case for insertion sort occurs if the array is initially sorted in reverse order, since this will lead to the maximum possible number of comparisons and moves.
4. The best case for insertion sort occurs if the array is already sorted in increasing order. In this case, each pass through the array will involve just one comparison, which will indicate that "it" is in its correct position with respect to the sorted list. Therefore, no elements will need to be moved.

> Both insertion and selection sorts are inefficient for large n.

RECURSIVE SORTS: MERGESORT AND QUICKSORT

Selection and insertion sorts are inefficient for large n, requiring approximately n passes through a list of n elements. More efficient algorithms can be devised using a "divide-and-conquer" approach, which is used in both the sorting algorithms that follow.

Mergesort

Here is a recursive description of how mergesort works:

If there is more than one element in the array
      Break the array into two halves.
      Mergesort the left half.
      Mergesort the right half.
      Merge the two subarrays into a sorted array.

> The main disadvantage of mergesort is that it uses a temporary array.

Mergesort uses a `merge` method to merge two sorted pieces of an array into a single sorted array. For example, suppose array `a[0] ... a[n-1]` is such that `a[0] ... a[k]` is sorted and `a[k+1] ... a[n-1]` is sorted, both parts in increasing order. Example:

a[0]	a[1]	a[2]	a[3]	a[4]	a[5]
2	5	8	9	1	6

In this case, `a[0] ...a[3]` and `a[4] ...a[5]` are the two sorted pieces. The method call `merge(a,0,3,5)` should produce the "merged" array:

a[0]	a[1]	a[2]	a[3]	a[4]	a[5]
1	2	5	6	8	9

The middle numerical parameter in `merge` (the 3 in this case) represents the index of the last element in the first "piece" of the array. The first and third numerical parameters are the lowest and highest index, respectively, of array a.

Here's what happens in mergesort:

1. Start with an unsorted list of n elements.
2. The recursive calls break the list into n sublists, each of length 1. Note that these n arrays, each containing just one element, are sorted!
3. Recursively merge adjacent pairs of lists. There are then approximately $n/2$ lists of length 2; then, approximately $n/4$ lists of approximate length 4, and so on, until there is just one list of length n.

An example of mergesort follows:

Break list into
n sublists of
length 1

5	−3	2	4	0	6

5	−3	2		4	0	6

5	−3	2		4	0	6

5	−3	2		4	0	6

Merge adjacent
pairs of lists

−3	5	2	0	4	6

−3	2	5	0	4	6

−3	0	2	4	5	6

Analysis of Mergesort:

1. The major disadvantage of mergesort is that it needs a temporary array that is as large as the original array to be sorted. This could be a problem if space is a factor.
2. Mergesort is not affected by the initial ordering of the elements. Thus, best, worst, and average cases have similar run times.

Quicksort

For large n, quicksort is, on average, the fastest known sorting algorithm. Here is a recursive description of how quicksort works:

> **Optional topic**

If there are at least two elements in the array
      Partition the array.
      Quicksort the left subarray.
      Quicksort the right subarray.

The `partition` method splits the array into two subarrays as follows: a *pivot* element is chosen at random from the array (often just the first element) and placed so that all items to the left of the pivot are less than or equal to the pivot, whereas those to the right are greater than or equal to it.

For example, if the array is 4, 1, 2, 7, 5, −1, 8, 0, 6, and `a[0]` = 4 is the pivot, the `partition` method produces

$$-1 \quad 1 \quad 2 \quad 0 \quad \boxed{4} \quad 5 \quad 8 \quad 7 \quad 6$$

Here's how the partitioning works: Let `a[0]`, 4 in this case, be the pivot. Markers up and down are initialized to index values 0 and $n - 1$, as shown. Move the up marker until a value less than the pivot is found, or down equals up. Move the down marker until a value greater than the pivot is found, or down equals up. Swap `a[up]` and `a[down]`. Continue the process until down equals up. This is the pivot position. Swap `a[0]` and `a[pivotPosition]`.

Notice that the pivot element, 4, is in its final sorted position.

> The main disadvantage of quicksort is that its worst case behavior is very inefficient.

Analysis of Quicksort:

1. For the fastest run time, the array should be partitioned into two parts of roughly the same size.

(continued)

2. If the pivot happens to be the smallest or largest element in the array, the split is not much of a split—one of the subarrays is empty! If this happens repeatedly, quicksort degenerates into a slow, recursive version of selection sort and is very inefficient.

3. The worst case for quicksort occurs when the partitioning algorithm repeatedly divides the array into pieces of size 1 and $n - 1$. An example is when the array is initially sorted in either order and the first or last element is chosen as the pivot. Some algorithms avoid this situation by initially shuffling up the given array (!) or selecting the pivot by examining several elements of the array (such as first, middle, and last) and then taking the median.

NOTE

For both quicksort and mergesort, when a subarray gets down to some small size m, it becomes faster to sort by straight insertion. The optimal value of m is machine-dependent, but it's approximately equal to 7.

SORTING ALGORITHMS IN JAVA

Unlike the container classes like `ArrayList`, whose elements must be objects, arrays can hold either objects or primitive types like `int` or `double`.

A common way of organizing code for sorting arrays is to create a sorter class with an array private instance variable. The class holds all the methods for a given type of sorting algorithm, and the constructor assigns the user's array to the private array variable.

Example

Selection sort for an array of `int`.

```
/* A class that sorts an array of ints from
 * largest to smallest using selection sort. */

public class SelectionSort
{
    private int[] a;

    public SelectionSort(int[] arr)
    { a = arr; }

    /** Swap a[i] and a[j] in array a.
     *   @param i an index for array a
     *   @param j an index for array a
     */
    private void swap(int i, int j)
    {
        int temp = a[i];
        a[i] = a[j];
        a[j] = temp;
    }
```

```
/** Sort array a from largest to smallest using selection sort.
 * Precondition: a is an array of ints.
 */
public void selectionSort()
{
    int maxPos, max;

    for (int i = 0; i < a.length - 1; i++)
    {
        //find max element in a[i+1] to a[a.length-1]
        max = a[i];
        maxPos = i;
        for (int j = i + 1; j < a.length; j++)
            if (max < a[j])
            {
                max = a[j];
                maxPos = j;
            }
        swap(i, maxPos); //swap a[i] and a[maxPos]
    }
}
```

Note that in order to sort *objects*, there must be a `compareTo` method in the class, since you need to be able to compare elements.

SEQUENTIAL SEARCH

Assume that you are searching for a key in a list of *n* elements. A sequential search starts at the first element and compares the key to each element in turn until the key is found or there are no more elements to examine in the list. If the list is sorted, in ascending order, say, stop searching as soon as the key is less than the current list element.

Analysis:

1. The best case has key in the first slot.
2. The worst case occurs if the key is in the last slot or not in the list. In the worst case, all *n* elements must be examined.
3. On average, there will be $n/2$ comparisons.

BINARY SEARCH

If the elements are in a *sorted* array, a divide-and-conquer approach provides a much more efficient searching algorithm. The following recursive pseudo-code algorithm shows how the *binary search* works.

Assume that a[low] ... a[high] is sorted in ascending order and that a method binSearch returns the index of key. If key is not in the array, it returns −1.

Binary search works only if the array is sorted on the search key.

```
    if (low > high)    //Base case. No elements left in array.
        return -1;
    else
    {
        mid = (low + high)/2;
        if (key is equal to a[mid])    //found the key
            return mid;
        else if (key is less than a[mid])  //key in left half of array
            < binSearch for key in a[low] to a[mid-1] >
        else    //key in right half of array
            < binSearch for key in a[mid+1] to a[high] >
    }
```

NOTE

When `low` and `high` cross, there are no more elements to examine, and `key` is not in the array.

Example: suppose 5 is the key to be found in the following array:

```
a[0]  a[1]  a[2]  a[3]  a[4]  a[5]  a[6]  a[7]  a[8]
 1     4     5     7     9    12    15    20    21
```

```
First pass:   mid = (8+0)/2 = 4.   Check a[4].
Second pass:  mid = (0+3)/2 = 1.   Check a[1].
Third pass:   mid = (2+3)/2 = 2.   Check a[2]. Yes! Key is found.
```

Analysis of Binary Search:

1. In the best case, the key is found on the first try (i.e., `(low + high)/2` is the index of `key`).
2. In the worst case, the key is not in the list or is at either end of a sublist. Here the n elements must be divided by 2 until there is just one element, and then that last element must be tested. An easy way to find the number of comparisons in the worst case is to round n up to the next power of 2 and take the exponent. For example, in the array above, $n = 9$. Suppose 21 were the key. Round 9 up to 16, which equals 2^4. Thus you would need four comparisons to find it. Try it!

Chapter Summary

You should not memorize any sorting code. You must, however, be familiar with the mechanism used in each of the sorting algorithms. For example, you should be able to explain how the merge method of mergesort works, or how many elements are in their final sorted position after a certain number of passes through the selection sort loop. You should know the best and worst case situations for each of the sorting algorithms.

Be familiar with the sequential and binary search algorithms. You should know that a binary search is more efficient than a sequential search, and that a binary search can only be used for an array that is sorted on the search key.

MULTIPLE-CHOICE QUESTIONS ON SORTING AND SEARCHING

1. The decision to choose a particular sorting algorithm should be made based on

    I Run-time efficiency of the sort
    II Size of the array
    III Space efficiency of the algorithm

    (A) I only
    (B) II only
    (C) III only
    (D) I and II only
    (E) I, II, and III

2. The following code fragment does a sequential search to determine whether a given integer, value, is stored in an array a[0] ... a[n-1].

```
int i = 0;
while (/* boolean expression */)
{
    i++;
}
if (i == n)
    return -1;    //value not found
else
    return i;     // value found at location i
```

    Which of the following should replace /* *boolean expression* */ so that the algorithm works as intended?
    (A) value != a[i]
    (B) i < n && value == a[i]
    (C) value != a[i] && i < n
    (D) i < n && value != a[i]
    (E) i < n || value != a[i]

3. A feature of data that is used for a binary search but not necessarily used for a sequential search is
    (A) length of list.
    (B) type of data.
    (C) order of data.
    (D) smallest value in the list.
    (E) median value of the data.

4. Array `unsortedArr` contains an unsorted list of integers. Array `sortedArr` contains a sorted list of integers. Which of the following operations is more efficient for `sortedArr` than `unsortedArr`? Assume the most efficient algorithms are used.

    I Inserting a new element
    II Searching for a given element
    III Computing the mean of the elements

    (A) I only
    (B) II only
    (C) III only
    (D) I and II only
    (E) I, II, and III

5. An algorithm for searching a large sorted array for a specific value x compares every third item in the array to x until it finds one that is greater than or equal to x. When a larger value is found, the algorithm compares x to the previous two items. If the array is sorted in increasing order, which of the following describes all cases when this algorithm uses fewer comparisons to find x than would a binary search?
    (A) It will never use fewer comparisons.
    (B) When x is in the middle position of the array
    (C) When x is very close to the beginning of the array
    (D) When x is very close to the end of the array
    (E) When x is not in the array

6. Assume that `a[0]` ... `a[N-1]` is an array of N positive integers and that the following assertion is true:

$$a[0] > a[k] \text{ for all } k \text{ such that } 0 < k < N$$

Which of the following *must* be true?
    (A) The array is sorted in ascending order.
    (B) The array is sorted in descending order.
    (C) All values in the array are different.
    (D) `a[0]` holds the smallest value in the array.
    (E) `a[0]` holds the largest value in the array.

7. The following code is designed to set `index` to the location of the first occurrence of `key` in array `a` and to set `index` to -1 if `key` is not in `a`.

```
index = 0;
while (a[index] != key)
    index++;
if (a[index] != key)
    index = -1;
```

In which case will this program *definitely* fail to perform the task described?
    (A) When key is the first element of the array
    (B) When key is the last element of the array
    (C) When key is not in the array
    (D) When key equals 0
    (E) When key equals `a[key]`

8. Consider the following class.

```java
/** A class that sorts an array of Integer objects from
 *  largest to smallest using a selection sort.
 */
public class Sorter
{
    private Integer[] a;

    public Sorter(Integer[] arr)
    { a = arr; }

    /** Swap a[i] and a[j] in array a. */
    private void swap(int i, int j)
    { /* implementation not shown */ }

    /** Sort array a from largest to smallest using selection sort.
     *  Precondition: a is an array of Integer objects.
     */
    public void selectionSort()
    {
        for (int i = 0; i < a.length - 1; i++)
        {
            //find max element in a[i+1] to a[n-1]
            Integer max = a[i];
            int maxPos = i;
            for (int j = i + 1; j < a.length; j++)
                if (max.compareTo(a[j]) < 0) //max less than a[j]
                {
                    max = a[j];
                    maxPos = j;
                }
            swap(i, maxPos);    //swap a[i] and a[maxPos]
        }
    }
}
```

If an array of Integer contains the following elements, what would the array look like after the third pass of selectionSort, sorting from high to low?

$$89 \quad 42 \quad -3 \quad 13 \quad 109 \quad 70 \quad 2$$

(A) 109 89 70 13 42 −3   2
(B) 109 89 70 42 13   2 −3
(C) 109 89 70 −3   2 13 42
(D)   89 42 13 −3 109 70   2
(E) 109 89 42 −3 13 70   2

9. Refer to method search.

```
/** @param v an initialized array of integers
 *  @param key the value to be found
 *  Postcondition:
 *   - Returned value k is such that -1 <= k <= v.length-1.
 *   - If k >= 0 then v[k] == key.
 *   - If k == -1, then key != any of the elements in v.
 */
public static int search(int[] v, int key)
{
    int index = 0;
    while (index < v.length && v[index] < key)
        index++;
    if (v[index] == key)
        return index;
    else
        return -1;
}
```

Assuming that the method works as intended, which of the following should be added to the precondition of search?
(A) v is sorted smallest to largest.
(B) v is sorted largest to smallest.
(C) v is unsorted.
(D) There is at least one occurrence of key in v.
(E) key occurs no more than once in v.

Questions 10–14 are based on the binSearch method and the private instance variable a for some class:

```
private int[] a;

/** Does binary search for key in array a[0]...a[a.length-1],
 *  sorted in ascending order.
 *  @param key the integer value to be found
 *  Postcondition:
 *   - index has been returned such that a[index]==key.
 *   - If key not in a, return -1.
 */
public int binSearch(int key)
{
    int low = 0;
    int high = a.length - 1;
    while (low <= high)
    {
        int mid = (low + high) / 2;
        if (a[mid] == key)
            return mid;
        else if (a[mid] < key)
            low = mid + 1;
        else
            high = mid - 1;
    }
    return -1;
}
```

A binary search will be performed on the following list.

a[0]	a[1]	a[2]	a[3]	a[4]	a[5]	a[6]	a[7]
4	7	9	11	20	24	30	41

10. To find the key value 27, the search interval *after* the first pass through the `while` loop will be
    (A) `a[0] ... a[7]`
    (B) `a[5] ... a[6]`
    (C) `a[4] ... a[7]`
    (D) `a[2] ... a[6]`
    (E) `a[6] ... a[7]`

11. How many iterations will be required to determine that 27 is not in the list?
    (A) 1
    (B) 3
    (C) 8
    (D) 27
    (E) An infinite loop since 27 is not found

12. What will be stored in y after executing the following?

    ```
    int y = binSearch(4);
    ```

    (A) 20
    (B) 7
    (C) 4
    (D) 0
    (E) -1

13. If the test for the `while` loop is changed to

    ```
    while (low < high)
    ```

    the `binSearch` method does not work as intended. Which value in the given list will not be found?
    (A) 4
    (B) 7
    (C) 11
    (D) 24
    (E) 30

14. For `binSearch`, which of the following assertions will be true following every iteration of the `while` loop?
    (A) key = a[mid] or key is not in a.
    (B) a[low] ≤ key ≤ a[high]
    (C) low ≤ mid ≤ high
    (D) key = a[mid], or a[low] ≤ key ≤ a[high]
    (E) key = a[mid], or a[low] ≤ key ≤ a[high], or key is not in array a.

15. A large sorted array containing about 30,000 elements is to be searched for a value key using an iterative binary search algorithm. Assuming that key is in the array, which of the following is closest to the smallest number of iterations that will guarantee that key is found? Note: $10^3 \approx 2^{10}$.
    - (A) 15
    - (B) 30
    - (C) 100
    - (D) 300
    - (E) 3000

For Questions 16–19 refer to the insertionSort method and the private instance variable a, both in a Sorter class.

```
private Integer[] a;

/** Precondition:  a[0],a[1]...a[a.length-1] is an unsorted array
 *                  of Integer objects.
 *  Postcondition: Array a is sorted in descending order.
 */
public void insertionSort()
{
    for (int i = 1; i < a.length; i++)
    {
        Integer temp = a[i];
        int j = i - 1;
        while (j >= 0 && temp.compareTo(a[j]) > 0)
        {
            a[j+1] = a[j];
            j--;
        }
        a[j+1] = temp;
    }
}
```

16. An array of Integer is to be sorted biggest to smallest using the insertionSort method. If the array originally contains

    1   7   9   5   4   12

    what will it look like after the third pass of the for loop?
    - (A) 9 7 1 5 4 12
    - (B) 9 7 5 1 4 12
    - (C) 12 9 7 1 5 4
    - (D) 12 9 7 5 4 1
    - (E) 9 7 12 5 4 1

17. When sorted biggest to smallest with insertionSort, which list will need the fewest changes of position for individual elements?
    - (A) 5, 1, 2, 3, 4, 9
    - (B) 9, 5, 1, 4, 3, 2
    - (C) 9, 4, 2, 5, 1, 3
    - (D) 9, 3, 5, 1, 4, 2
    - (E) 3, 2, 1, 9, 5, 4

18. When sorted biggest to smallest with `insertionSort`, which list will need the greatest number of changes in position?
    (A) 5, 1, 2, 3, 4, 7, 6, 9
    (B) 9, 5, 1, 4, 3, 2, 1, 0
    (C) 9, 4, 6, 2, 1, 5, 1, 3
    (D) 9, 6, 9, 5, 6, 7, 2, 0
    (E) 3, 2, 1, 0, 9, 6, 5, 4

19. While typing the `insertionSort` method, a programmer by mistake enters

    ```
    while (temp.compareTo( a[j]) > 0)
    ```

    instead of

    ```
    while (j >= 0 && temp.compareTo( a[j]) > 0)
    ```

    Despite this mistake, the method works as intended the first time the programmer enters an array to be sorted in descending order. Which of the following could explain this?

    I   The first element in the array was the largest element in the array.
    II The array was already sorted in descending order.
    III The first element was less than or equal to all the other elements in the array.

    (A) I only
    (B) II only
    (C) III only
    (D) I and II only
    (E) II and III only

20. The elements in a long list of integers are roughly sorted in decreasing order. No more than 5 percent of the elements are out of order. Which of the following is a valid reason for using an insertion sort rather than a selection sort to sort this list into decreasing order?

    I   There will be fewer comparisons of elements for insertion sort.
    II There will be fewer changes of position of elements for insertion sort.
    III There will be less space required for insertion sort.

    (A) I only
    (B) II only
    (C) III only
    (D) I and II only
    (E) I, II, and III

Optional topic

21. The code shown sorts array `a[0] ... a[a.length-1]` in descending order.

```
public static void sort(String[] a)
{
    for (int i = 0; i < a.length - 1; i++)
        for (int j = 0; j < a.length - i - 1; j++)
            if (a[j].compareTo(a[j+1]) < 0)
                swap(a, j, j + 1);  //swap a[j] and a[j+1]
}
```

    This is an example of
    (A) selection sort.
    (B) insertion sort.
    (C) mergesort.
    (D) quicksort.
    (E) none of the above.

22. Which of the following is a valid reason why mergesort is a better sorting algorithm than insertion sort for sorting long, randomly ordered lists?

    I   Mergesort requires less code than insertion sort.
    II Mergesort requires less storage space than insertion sort.
    III Mergesort runs faster than insertion sort.

    (A) I only
    (B) II only
    (C) III only
    (D) I and II only
    (E) II and III only

23. A large array of lowercase characters is to be searched for the pattern "pqrs." The first step in a very efficient searching algorithm is to look at characters with index
    (A) 0, 1, 2, ... until a "p" is encountered.
    (B) 0, 1, 2, ... until any letter in "p" ... "s" is encountered.
    (C) 3, 7, 11, ... until an "s" is encountered.
    (D) 3, 7, 11, ... until any letter in "p" ... "s" is encountered.
    (E) 3, 7, 11, ... until any letter other than "p" ... "s" is encountered.

24. The array `names[0]`, `names[1]`, ..., `names[9999]` is a list of 10,000 name strings. The list is to be searched to determine the location of some name X in the list. Which of the following preconditions is necessary for a binary search?
    (A) There are no duplicate names in the list.
    (B) The number of names N in the list is large.
    (C) The list is in alphabetical order.
    (D) Name X is definitely in the list.
    (E) Name X occurs near the middle of the list.

25. Consider the following method:

    ```
    /** Precondition: a[0],a[1]...a[n-1] contain integers. */
    public static int someMethod(int[] a, int n, int value)
    {
        if (n == 0)
            return -1;
        else
        {
            if (a[n-1] == value)
                return n - 1;
            else
                return someMethod(a, n - 1, value);
        }
    }
    ```

    The method shown is an example of
    (A) insertion sort.
    (B) mergesort.
    (C) selection sort.
    (D) binary search.
    (E) sequential search.

26. The `partition` method for quicksort partitions a list as follows:

    (i) A pivot element is selected from the array.
    (ii) The elements of the list are rearranged such that all elements to the left of the pivot are less than or equal to it; all elements to the right of the pivot are greater than or equal to it.

    Optional topic

    Partitioning the array requires which of the following?
    (A) A recursive algorithm
    (B) A temporary array
    (C) An external file for the array
    (D) A swap algorithm for interchanging array elements
    (E) A merge method for merging two sorted lists

27. Assume that mergesort will be used to sort an array `arr` of n integers into increasing order. What is the purpose of the `merge` method in the mergesort algorithm?
    (A) Partition `arr` into two parts of roughly equal length, then merge these parts.
    (B) Use a recursive algorithm to sort `arr` into increasing order.
    (C) Divide `arr` into n subarrays, each with one element.
    (D) Merge two sorted parts of `arr` into a single sorted array.
    (E) Merge two sorted arrays into a temporary array that is sorted.

28. A binary search is to be performed on an array with 600 elements. In the *worst* case, which of the following best approximates the number of iterations of the algorithm?
    (A) 6
    (B) 10
    (C) 100
    (D) 300
    (E) 600

29. A worst case situation for insertion sort would be

    I   A list in correct sorted order.
    II A list sorted in reverse order.
    III A list in random order.

    (A) I only
    (B) II only
    (C) III only
    (D) I and II only
    (E) II and III only

30. Consider a binary search algorithm to search an ordered list of numbers. Which of the following choices is closest to the maximum number of times that such an algorithm will execute its main comparison loop when searching a list of 1 million numbers?
    (A) 6
    (B) 20
    (C) 100
    (D) 120
    (E) 1000

31. Consider these three tasks:

    I   A sequential search of an array of n names
    II A binary search of an array of n names in alphabetical order
    III An insertion sort into alphabetical order of an array of n names that are initially in random order

    For large n, which of the following lists these tasks in order (from least to greatest) of their average case run times?

(A)	II	I	III
(B)	I	II	III
(C)	II	III	I
(D)	III	I	II
(E)	III	II	I

Questions 32 and 33 are based on the Sort interface and MergeSort and QuickSort classes shown below.

```java
public interface Sort
{
    void sort();
}

public class MergeSort implements Sort
{
    private String[] a;

    public MergeSort(String[] arr)
    { a = arr; }

    /** Merge a[lb] to a[mi] and a[mi+1] to a[ub].
     *  Precondition: a[lb] to a[mi] and a[mi+1] to a[ub] both sorted
     *                in increasing order.
     */
    private void merge(int lb, int mi, int ub)
    { /* Implementation not shown. */ }

    /** Sort a[first]..a[last] in increasing order using mergesort.
     *  Precondition: a is an array of String objects.
     */
    private void sort(int first, int last)
    {
        int mid;

        if (first != last)
        {
            mid = (first + last) / 2;
            sort(first, mid);
            sort(mid + 1, last);
            merge(first, mid, last);
        }
    }

    /** Sort array a from smallest to largest using mergesort.
     *  Precondition: a is an array of String objects.
     */
    public void sort()
    {
        sort(0, a.length - 1);
    }
}
```

(continued)

```
public class QuickSort implements Sort
{
    private String[] a;

    public QuickSort(String[] arr)
    { a = arr; }

    /** Swap a[i] and a[j] in array a. */
    private void swap(int i, int j)
    { /* Implementation not shown. */ }

    /** @return the index pivPos such that a[first] to a[last]
     *  is partitioned: a[first..pivPos] <= a[pivPos] and
     *  a[pivPos..last] >= a[pivPos]
     */
    private int partition(int first, int last)
    { /* Implementation not shown. */ }

    /** Sort a[first]..a[last] in increasing order using quicksort.
     *  Precondition: a is an array of String objects.
     */
    private void sort(int first, int last)
    {
        if (first < last)
        {
            int pivPos = partition(first, last);
            sort(first, pivPos - 1);
            sort(pivPos + 1, last);
        }
    }

    /** Sort array a in increasing order. */
    public void sort()
    {
        sort(0, a.length - 1);
    }
}
```

32. Notice that the `MergeSort` and `QuickSort` classes both have a private helper method that implements the recursive sort routine. For this example, which of the following is a valid reason for having a helper method?

    I The helper method hides the implementation details of the sorting algorithm from the user.

    II A method with additional parameters is needed to implement the recursion.

    III Providing a helper method increases the run-time efficiency of the sorting algorithm.

(A) I only
(B) II only
(C) III only
(D) I and II only
(E) I, II, and III

(continued)

33. A piece of code to test the `QuickSort` and `MergeSort` classes is as follows:

```
//Create an array of String values
String[] strArray = makeArray(strList);
writeList(strArray);
/* more code */
```

where `makeArray` creates an array of `String` from a list `strList`. Which of the following replacements for /* *more code* */ is reasonable code to test `QuickSort` and `MergeSort`? You can assume `writeList` correctly writes out an array of `String`.

(A)
```
Sort q = new QuickSort(strArray);
Sort m = new MergeSort(strArray);
q.sort();
writeList(strArray);
m.sort();
writeList(strArray);
```

(B)
```
QuickSort q = new Sort(strArray);
MergeSort m = new Sort(strArray);
q.sort();
writeList(strArray);
m.sort();
writeList(strArray);
```

(C)
```
Sort q = new QuickSort(strArray);
Sort m = new MergeSort(strArray);
String[] copyArray = makeArray(strList);
q.sort(0, strArray.length - 1);
writeList(strArray);
m.sort(0, copyArray.length - 1);
writeList(copyArray);
```

(D)
```
QuickSort q = new Sort(strArray);
String[] copyArray = makeArray(strList);
MergeSort m = new Sort(strArray);
q.sort();
writeList(strArray);
m.sort();
writeList(copyArray);
```

(E)
```
Sort q = new QuickSort(strArray);
String[] copyArray = makeArray(strList);
Sort m = new MergeSort(copyArray);
q.sort();
writeList(strArray);
m.sort();
writeList(copyArray);
```

Questions 34–36 refer to the Hi-Lo game described below.

Consider the problem of writing a Hi-Lo game in which a user thinks of an integer from 1 to 100 inclusive and the computer tries to guess that number. Each time the computer makes a guess, the user makes one of three responses:

- "lower" (i.e., the number is lower than the computer's guess)
- "higher" (i.e., the number is higher than the computer's guess)
- "you got it in *< however many >* tries!"

34. Suppose the game is programmed so that the computer uses a binary search strategy for making its guesses. What is the maximum number of guesses the computer could make before guessing the user's number?
    (A) 50
    (B) 25
    (C) 10
    (D) 7
    (E) 6

35. Suppose the computer used a *sequential search* strategy for guessing the user's number. What is the maximum number of guesses the computer could make before guessing the user's number?
    (A) 100
    (B) 99
    (C) 50
    (D) 25
    (E) 10

36. Using a sequential search strategy, how many guesses *on average* would the computer need to guess the number?
    (A) 100
    (B) 51
    (C) 50
    (D) 25
    (E) Fewer than 25

ANSWER KEY

---

1. E	13. A	25. E
2. D	14. E	26. D
3. C	15. A	27. D
4. B	16. B	28. B
5. C	17. B	29. B
6. E	18. A	30. B
7. C	19. D	31. A
8. A	20. A	32. D
9. A	21. E	33. E
10. C	22. C	34. D
11. B	23. D	35. A
12. D	24. C	36. C

ANSWERS EXPLAINED

---

1. **(E)** The time and space requirements of sorting algorithms are affected by all three of the given factors, so all must be considered when choosing a particular sorting algorithm.

2. **(D)** Choice B doesn't make sense: The loop will be exited as soon as a value is found that does *not* equal a[i]. Eliminate choice A because, if value is not in the array, a[i] will eventually go out of bounds. You need the i < n part of the boolean expression to avoid this. The test i < n, however, must precede value != a[i] so that if i < n fails, the expression will be evaluated as false, the test will be short-circuited, and an out-of-range error will be avoided. Choice C does not avoid this error. Choice E is wrong because both parts of the expression must be true in order to continue the search.

3. **(C)** The binary search algorithm depends on the array being sorted. Sequential search has no ordering requirement. Both depend on choice A, the length of the list, while the other choices are irrelevant to both algorithms.

4. **(B)** Inserting a new element is quick and easy in an unsorted array—just add it to the end of the list. Computing the mean involves finding the sum of the elements and dividing by n, the number of elements. The execution time is the same whether the list is sorted or not. Operation II, searching, is inefficient for an unsorted list, since a sequential search must be used. In sortedArr, the efficient binary search algorithm, which involves fewer comparisons, could be used. In fact, in a sorted list, even a sequential search would be more efficient than for an unsorted list: If the search item were not in the list, the search could stop as soon as the list elements were greater than the search item.

5. **(C)** Suppose the array has 1000 elements and x is somewhere in the first 8 slots. The algorithm described will find x using no more than five comparisons. A binary search, by contrast, will chop the array in half and do a comparison six

times before examining elements in the first 15 slots of the array (array size after each chop: 500, 250, 125, 62, 31, 15).

6. **(E)** The assertion states that the first element is greater than all the other elements in the array. This eliminates choices A and D. Choices B and C are incorrect because you have no information about the relative sizes of elements `a[1]...a[N-1]`.

7. **(C)** When `key` is not in the array, `index` will eventually be large enough that `a[index]` will cause an `ArrayIndexOutOfBoundsException`. In choices A and B, the algorithm will find `key` without error. Choice D won't fail if 0 is in the array. Choice E will work if `a[key]` is not out of range.

8. **(A)**

After 1st pass:	109	42	−3	13	89	70	2
After 2nd pass:	109	89	−3	13	42	70	2
After 3rd pass:	109	89	70	13	42	−3	2

9. **(A)** The algorithm uses the fact that array `v` is sorted smallest to largest. The `while` loop terminates—which means that the search stops—as soon as `v[index] >= key`.

10. **(C)** The first pass uses the interval `a[0]...a[7]`. Since `mid = (0+7)/2 = 3`, `low` gets adjusted to `mid + 1 = 4`, and the second pass uses the interval `a[4]...a[7]`.

11. **(B)** First pass: compare 27 with `a[3]`, since `low = 0` `high = 7` `mid = (0+7)/2 = 3`. Second pass: compare 27 with `a[5]`, since `low = 4` `high = 7` `mid = (4+7)/2 = 5`. Third pass: compare 27 with `a[6]`, since `low = 6` `high = 7` `mid = (6+7)/2 = 6`. The fourth pass doesn't happen, since `low = 6`, `high = 5`, and therefore the test (`low <= high`) fails. Here's the general rule for finding the number of iterations when `key` is not in the list: If n is the number of elements, round n up to the nearest power of 2, which is 8 in this case. $8 = 2^3$, which implies 3 iterations of the "divide-and-compare" loop.

12. **(D)** The method returns the index of the `key` parameter, 4. Since `a[0]` contains 4, `binSearch(4)` will return 0.

13. **(A)** Try 4. Here are the values for `low`, `high`, and `mid` when searching for 4:

> First pass: `low = 0`,   `high = 7`,   `mid = 3`
> Second pass: `low = 0`,   `high = 2`,   `mid = 1`

After this pass, `high` gets adjusted to `mid −1`, which is 0. Now `low` equals `high`, and the test for the `while` loop fails. The method returns −1, indicating that 4 wasn't found.

14. **(E)** When the loop is exited, either `key = a[mid]` (and `mid` has been returned) or `key` has not been found, in which case either `a[low]` ≤ `key` ≤ `a[high]` or `key` is not in the array. The correct assertion must account for all three possibilities.

15. **(A)** $30{,}000 = 1000 \times 30 \approx 2^{10} \times 2^5 = 2^{15}$. Since a successful binary search in the worst case requires $\log_2 n$ iterations, 15 iterations will guarantee that `key` is found. (Note that $30{,}000 < 2^{10} \times 2^5 = 32{,}768$.)

16. **(B)** Start with the second element in the array.

After 1st pass:	7	1	9	5	4	12
After 2nd pass:	9	7	1	5	4	12
After 3rd pass:	9	7	5	1	4	12

17. **(B)** An insertion sort compares a[1] and a[0]. If they are not in the correct order, a[0] is moved and a[1] is inserted in its correct position. a[2] is then inserted in its correct position, and a[0] and a[1] are moved if necessary, and so on. Since B has only one element out of order, it will require the fewest changes.

18. **(A)** This list is almost sorted in reverse order, which is the worst case for insertion sort, requiring the greatest number of comparisons and moves.

19. **(D)** j >= 0 is a stopping condition that prevents an element that is larger than all those to the left of it from going off the left end of the array. If no error occurred, it means that the largest element in the array was a[0], which was true in situations I and II. Omitting the j >= 0 test will cause a run-time (out-of-range) error whenever temp is bigger than all elements to the left of it (i.e., the insertion point is 0).

20. **(A)** Look at a small array that is almost sorted:

    10 8 9 6 2

    For <u>insertion sort</u> you need four passes through this array.
    The first pass compares 8 and 10—one comparison, no moves.
    The second pass compares 9 and 8, then 9 and 10. The array becomes
    10 9 8 6 2—two comparisons, two moves.
    The third and fourth passes compare 6 and 8, and 2 and 6—no moves.
    In summary, there are approximately one or two comparisons per pass and no more than two moves per pass.
    For <u>selection sort</u>, there are four passes too.
    The first pass finds the biggest element in the array and swaps it into the first position.
    The array is still 10 8 9 6 2—four comparisons. There are two moves if your algorithm makes the swap in this case, otherwise no moves.
    The second pass finds the biggest element from a[1] to a[4] and swaps it into the second position: 10 9 8 6 2—three comparisons, two moves.
    For the third pass there are two comparisons, and one for the fourth. There are zero or two moves each time.
    Summary: $4 + 3 + 2 + 1$ total comparisons and a possible two moves per pass.
    Notice that reason I is valid. Selection sort makes the same number of comparisons irrespective of the state of the array. Insertion sort does far fewer comparisons if the array is almost sorted. Reason II is invalid. There are roughly the same number of data movements for insertion and selection. Insertion may even have more changes, depending on how far from their insertion points the unsorted elements are. Reason III is wrong because insertion and selection sorts have the same space requirements.

Optional topic

21. **(E)** In the first pass through the outer for loop, the smallest element makes its way to the end of the array. In the second pass, the next smallest element moves to the second last slot, and so on. This is different from the sorts in choices A through D; in fact, it is a bubble sort.

22. **(C)** Reject reason I. Mergesort requires both a merge and a mergeSort method—

more code than the relatively short and simple code for insertion sort. Reject reason II. The merge algorithm uses a temporary array, which means *more* storage space than insertion sort. Reason III is correct. For long lists, the "divide-and-conquer" approach of mergesort gives it a faster run time than insertion sort.

23. **(D)** Since the search is for a four-letter sequence, the idea in this algorithm is that if you examine every fourth slot, you'll find a letter in the required sequence very quickly. When you find one of these letters, you can then examine adjacent slots to check if you have the required sequence. This method will, on average, result in fewer comparisons than the strictly sequential search algorithm in choice A. Choice B is wrong. If you encounter a "q," "r," or "s" without a "p" first, you can't have found "pqrs." Choice C is wrong because you may miss the sequence completely. Choice E doesn't make sense.

24. **(C)** The main precondition for a binary search is that the list is ordered.

25. **(E)** This algorithm is just a recursive implementation of a sequential search. It starts by testing if the last element in the array, a[n-1], is equal to value. If so, it returns the index n - 1. Otherwise, it calls itself with n replaced by n - 1. The net effect is that it examines a[n-1], a[n-2], ... The base case, if (n == 0), occurs when there are no elements left to examine. In this case, the method returns −1, signifying that value was not in the array.

26. **(D)** The partition algorithm performs a series of swaps until the pivot element is swapped into its final sorted position (see p. 327). No temporary arrays or external files are used, nor is a recursive algorithm invoked. The merge method is used for mergesort, not quicksort.

Optional topic

27. **(D)** Recall the mergesort algorithm:

> Divide arr into two parts.
> Mergesort the left side.
> Mergesort the right side.
> Merge the two sides into a single sorted array.

The merge method is used for the last step of the algorithm. It does not do any sorting or partitioning of the array, which eliminates choices A, B, and C. Choice E is wrong because merge starts with a *single* array that has two sorted parts.

28. **(B)** Round 600 up to the next power of 2, which is $1024 = 2^{10}$. For the worst case, the array will be split in half $\log_2 1024 = 10$ times.

29. **(B)** If the list is sorted in reverse order, each pass through the array will involve the maximum possible number of comparisons and the maximum possible number of element movements if an insertion sort is used.

30. **(B)** 1 million $= 10^6 = (10^3)^2 \approx (2^{10})^2 = 2^{20}$. Thus, there will be on the order of 20 comparisons.

31. **(A)** A binary search, on average, has a smaller run time than a sequential search. All of the sorting algorithms have greater run times than a sequential search. This is because a sequential search looks at each element once. A sorting algorithm, however, processes *other* elements in the array for each element it looks at.

32. **(D)** Reason I is valid—it's always desirable to hide implementation details from users of a method. Reason II is valid too—since QuickSort and MergeSort implement the Sort interface, they must have a sort method with no parameters. But parameters are needed to make the recursion work. Therefore each sort requires

Optional topic

(continued)

a helper method with parameters. Reason III is invalid in this particular example of helper methods. There are many examples in which a helper method enhances efficiency (e.g., Example 2 on p. 296), but the `sort` example is not one of them.

33. **(E)** Since `Sort` is an interface, you can't create an instance of it. This eliminates choices B and D. The `sort` methods alter the contents of `strArray`. Thus invoking `q.sort()` followed by `m.sort()` means that `m.sort` will always operate on a sorted array, assuming quicksort works correctly! In order to test both quicksort and mergesort on unsorted arrays, you need to make a copy of the original array or create a different array. Eliminate choice A (and B again!), which does neither of these. Choice C is wrong because it calls the *private* sort methods of the classes. The `Sort` interface has just a single *public* method, `sort`, with no arguments. The two classes shown must provide an implementation for this `sort` method, and it is this method that must be invoked in the client program.

34. **(D)** The computer should find the number in no more than seven tries. This is because the guessing interval is halved on each successive try:

$$
\begin{aligned}
&(1) &100 \div 2 = 50 \ \text{numbers left to try} \\
&(2) &50 \div 2 = 25 \ \text{numbers left to try} \\
&(3) &25 \div 2 = 13 \ \text{numbers left to try} \\
&(4) &13 \div 2 \ = 7 \ \text{numbers left to try} \\
&(5) &7 \div 2 \ = 4 \ \text{numbers left to try} \\
&(6) &4 \div 2 \ = 2 \ \text{numbers left to try} \\
&(7) &2 \div 2 \ = 1 \ \text{number left to try}
\end{aligned}
$$

Seven iterations of the loop leaves just 1 number left to try!

35. **(A)** The maximum number of guesses is 100. A sequential search means that the computer starts at the first possible number, namely 1, and tries each successive number until it gets to 100. If the user's number is 100, the computer will take 100 guesses to reach it.

36. **(C)** On average the computer will make 50 guesses. The user is equally likely to pick any number between 1 and 100. Half the time it will be less than 50; half the time, greater than 50. So on the average, the distance of the number from 1 is 50.

The AP Computer Science A Labs

I don't like museums, I like labs.
—Amit Kalantri

Chapter Goals

- The Magpie Lab
- The Elevens Lab
- The Picture Lab

The AP Computer Science A labs were developed as a replacement for the Grid-World case study. Starting in May 2015, there will be no exam questions on GridWorld. And there will be no specific questions that require knowledge of the content of the labs. Instead, new test questions will focus on concepts from the AP Java subset that are emphasized in the labs.

What follows below is a brief summary of the labs, the concepts they illustrate, the concepts they particularly emphasize, and some sample multiple-choice questions based on these concepts.

THE MAGPIE LAB

In this lab, students modify a chatbot, which is a computer program designed to simulate an intelligent conversation between a computer and a human user. Students enter phrases, the computer searches for keywords, then comes up with an intelligent-seeming response.

Student activities include:

- Working through the Magpie code (`if` statements)
- Using `Magpie` and `String` methods (`while` loops, strings, and Javadoc)
- Using an array of possible responses in generating a random response from the computer (arrays, `ArrayLists`, and random integers)
- Improving the search to find keywords that are complete words, not substrings buried in other strings (`String` methods)
- Transforming a computer response based on the format of the statement entered by the user (`String` methods)

Special Emphasis

STRING METHODS

The `String` methods `substring` and `indexOf` are used continually in this lab. Be sure that you recall

- The first index of a `String` is 0.
- The method call `s.substring(start, end)` returns the substring of `s` starting at index `start` but ending at index `end-1`.
- The method call `s.indexOf(sub)` returns the index of the first occurrence of `sub` in `s`.
- `s.indexOf(sub)` returns `-1` if `sub` is not in `s`.

You should be nimble and well practiced in processing strings.

The following type of code is used repeatedly in the lab to look for multiple occurrences of a substring in a given string:

```
int pos = s.indexOf(someSubstring);
while (pos >= 0)                 //the substring was found
{
    doSomething();
    s = s.substring(pos + 1);  //throw away all characters of s
                               //up to and including someSubstring

    pos = s.indexOf(someSubstring);  //Is there another occurrence
                                     //of someSubstring?
}
```

A modified version of the above code, using some combination of a loop, `indexOf`, and `substring`, can be used to

- count number of occurrences of `substring` in `str`.
- replace all occurrences of `substring` in `str` with `replacementStr`.
- remove all occurrences of `substring` in `str`.

On the AP exam, there will almost certainly be at least one free-response question that requires you to manipulate strings in this way.

RANDOM ELEMENT SELECTION

Another skill that is demonstrated in this lab is returning a random element from an array or `ArrayList`. For example, suppose `responses` is an `ArrayList<String>` of surprised responses the computer may make to a user's crazy input. If the contents of `responses` are currently

0	1	2	3	4	5
Oh my!	Say what?	No!	Heavens!	You're kidding me.	Jumping Jellybeans!

You should be able to randomly return one of these responses. The key is to select a random index from 0 to 5, inclusive, and then return the string in the `responses` list that is at that index.

Recall that the expression `(int)(Math.random()*howMany)` generates a random `int` in the range `0...howMany-1`. In the given example, `howMany` is 6. The piece of code that returns a random response is:

```
int randIndex = (int) (Math.random() * 6);
String response = responses.get(randIndex);
```

CONDITIONALS: `if...else` STATEMENT

The Magpie lab is loaded with conditionals, searching for keywords that will trigger different responses from the chatbot (computer). Using `if` and `if...else` should be second nature to you.

Example

The user will enter a `sentence` and the chatbot will produce a `chatBotReply`.

```
if (sentence.indexOf ("love") != -1)
{
    if (sentence.indexOf ("you") != -1)
        chatBotReply = "I'm in heaven!";
    else
        chatBotReply = "But do you love me?";
}
else
    chatBotReply = "My heart is in pieces on the floor.";
```

Here are some possible sentences that the user may enter, with the corresponding `chatBoxReply`:

Sentence	chatBoxReply
I love chocolate cake.	But do you love me?
I love chocolate cake; do you?	I'm in heaven.
I hate fudge.	My heart is in pieces on the the floor.

If the substring `"love"` isn't in the sentence, the opening test will be `false`, and execution skips to the `else` outside the braces, producing the `chatBotReply` `"My heart is in pieces on the floor"`. If sentence contains both `"love"` and `"you"`, the first test in the braces will be `true`, and the `chatBotReply` will be `"I'm in heaven!"` The middle response `"But do you love me?"` will be triggered by a sentence that contains `"love"` but doesn't contain `"you"`, causing the first test in the braces to be `false`, and the `else` part in the braces to be executed.

THE ELEVENS LAB

In this lab, students simulate a game of solitaire, Elevens, and a related game, Thirteens. A GUI is provided for the labs to make the game interesting and fun to play. You are not required to know about GUIs.

Student activities include:

- Creating a `Card` class (objects, classes, and `Strings`)
- Creating a `Deck` class (arrays, `ArrayLists`, conditionals, loops)
- Shuffling the deck (`Math.random`, list manipulation)
- Writing an `ElevensBoard` class, using an abstract `Board` class (inheritance, abstract classes)
- Testing and debugging
- Playing the game

Special Emphasis

SHUFFLING

Several different algorithms are discussed for shuffling an array of elements. A key ingredient of a good shuffle is generation of random integers. For example, to shuffle a deck of 52 cards in an array may require a random int from 0 to 51:

```
int cardNum = (int) (Math.random() * 52);
```

(Recall that the multiplier in parentheses is the number of possible random integers.) The following code for shuffling an array of Type elements is used often:

```
for (int k = arr.length - 1; k > 0; k--)
{
    //Pick a random index in the array from 0 to k
    int index = (int) (Math.random() * (k + 1));
    //Swap randomly selected element with element at position k
    Type temp = arr[k];
    arr[k] = arr[index];
    arr[index] = temp;
}
```

WRITING SUBCLASSES

On the AP exam, you will probably be asked to write a subclass of a given class. Don't forget the extends keyword:

```
public class Subclass extends Superclass
```

Recall that constructors are not inherited, and if you use the keyword super in writing a constructor for your subclass, the line containing it should precede any other code in the constructor.

Example

```
public class Dog
{
    private String name;
    private String breed;

    public Dog (String aName, String aBreed)
    {
        name = aName;
        breed = aBreed;
    }
        ...
}

public class Poodle extends Dog
{
    private boolean needsGrooming;

    public Poodle (String aName, String aBreed, boolean grooming)
    {
        super(aName, aBreed);
        needsGrooming = grooming;
    }
        ...
}
```

In the Elevens lab there's extensive discussion about using an abstract class, Board, to represent a game board on which the game of Elevens will be played.

The advantage of the abstract class is that its use can be extended for other solitaire games played on similar boards. In the Elevens lab, the subclass ElevensBoard is written, which is specific to the game of Elevens. Further on in the lab, another subclass ThirteensBoard is discussed, which applies to a different, but similar game, Thirteens.

The abstract Board class contains methods that are common to all games that would be played on a Board, like deal. But methods that would pertain to moves on the board, like isLegal, would be different for each of the specific games. These methods are therefore declared abstract in the superclass, but are overridden in the subclasses.

Note: If you're writing a concrete (nonabstract) subclass of an abstract superclass, you must be sure to write an implementation for every abstract method of the superclass.

POLYMORPHISM

Consider this hierarchy of classes, and the declarations that follow it:

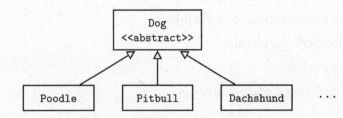

Suppose the Dog class has this method:

```
public abstract void eat();
```

And each of the subclasses, Poodle, PitBull, Dachshund, etc., has a different, overridden eat method. Now suppose that allDogs is an ArrayList<Dog> where each Dog declared above has been added to the list. Each Dog in the list will be processed to eat by the following lines of code:

```
for (Dog d: allDogs)
    d.eat();
```

Polymorphism is the process of selecting the correct eat method, during run time, for each of the different dogs.

TESTING AND DEBUGGING

In the Elevens lab, a lot of emphasis is placed on testing and debugging code as you write it. Here are some general principles:

- Start simple. For example, if writing a Deck class, start with a deck that contains just 2 or 3 cards.

- Always have a driver class (one with a main method) to test the current class you're writing.

- In your class, start with a constructor. You want to be sure you can create your object.

- After the constructor, write a toString method for clear and easy display. You want to be able to "see" the results of running your code.

SIMULATING RANDOM EVENTS

Flipping a coin, tossing a die, or picking a random card from a deck. Those random numbers again! If there are k possible outcomes, each of them equally likely, be sure you can generate a random int from 0 to k-1.

THE PICTURE LAB

In this lab, students manipulate digital pictures using two-dimensional arrays. Code for the GUI is provided in the lab.

The main concept emphasized is traversal of two-dimensional arrays. Other concepts used are UML diagrams, binary numbers, inheritance, interfaces, abstract methods, constants, and program analysis.

Student activities include:

- Learning how colors are stored in a program.
- Modifying a picture.
- Creating a mirror image of a picture.
- Mirroring part of a picture.
- Creating a collage.
- Detecting the edge of a picture.

Special Emphasis

PROCESSING A 2-D ARRAY

A matrix is stored as an array of rows, each of which is also an array. In the lab, a for-each loop is often used for traversal. Here is an example that traverses an array of int:

```
for (int[] row : matrix)        //for each row array in the matrix
    for (int num : row)         //for each int element in the current row
        doSomething();
```

Here is what doSomething can do:

- Access each element in the matrix (count, add, compare, etc.)

Here is what doSomething cannot do:

- Replace an element with another.

Suppose the matrix is an array of objects that can be changed with mutator methods. The for-each loop can be used not only to access elements, but also to modify them. (No replacing with new elements, however). The following code is OK.

```
for (Clock[] row : clockMatrix)
    for (Clock c : row)
        c.setTime(t);
```

MIRROR IMAGES

A large part of the lab is spent coming up with algorithms that create some kind of mirror image of a matrix. Students are asked to reflect across mirrors placed somewhere in the center of the matrix, horizontally, vertically, or diagonally.

Note that if a vertical mirror is placed down the center of a matrix, so that all elements to the left of the mirror are reflected across it, the element mat[row][col] reflects across to element mat[row][numCols-col-1].

You should teach yourself to trace the following type of code:

```
public static void matrixMethod(int[][] mat)
{
    int height = mat.length;
    int numCols = mat[0].length;
    for (int col = 0; col < numCols; col++)
        for (int row = 0; row < height/2; row++)
            mat[height - row - 1][col] = mat[row][col];
}
```

What does it do? How does it transform the matrix below?

```
2 3 4
5 6 7
8 9 0
1 1 1
```

Solution: The algorithm reflects the matrix from top to bottom across a horizontal mirror placed at its center.

```
height = 4, numCols = 3
col takes on values 0, 1, and 2
row takes on values 0 and 1
```

Here are the replacements that are made:

```
col = 0, row = 0: mat[3][0] = mat[0][0]
        row = 1: mat[2][0] = mat[1][0]

col = 1, row = 0: mat[3][1] = mat[0][1]
        row = 1: mat[2][1] = mat[1][1]

col = 2, row = 0: mat[3][2] = mat[0][2]
        row = 1: mat[2][2] = mat[1][2]
```

This transforms the matrix into

```
2 3 4
5 6 7
5 6 7
2 3 4
```

Note that a for-each loop was not used in the traversal, because elements in the matrix are being replaced.

BASE 2, BASE 8, BASE 16

Binary (base 2) and hexadecimal (base 16) numbers are discussed in the Picture lab as they apply to storage of colors. You need to be able to convert a given number in base b to a decimal (base 10) number (see p. 62).

Example

Convert the following octal (base 8) number to a decimal number: 123_{oct}
Solution:

$$123_{oct} = (1)(8^2) + (2)(8^1) + (3)(8^0)$$
$$= 64 + 16 + 3$$
$$= 83_{dec}$$

For a base 16 conversion, you'll be given that A, B, C, D, E, and F represent 10, 11, 12, 13, 14, and 15, respectively.

Example

Convert $A2B_{hex}$ to a decimal number.
Solution:

$$A2B_{hex} = (A)(16^2) + (2)(16^1) + (B)(16^0)$$
$$= 2560 + 32 + 11$$
$$= 2603_{dec}$$

Can you go in the other direction, namely, start with a decimal number and convert it to a different base?

Example

Convert 25 to a binary (base 2) number.
Solution:
Pull out the highest power of 2 less than or equal to 25, which is 16. Thus,

$$25 = 16 + 9$$

Now pull out the highest power of 2 less than or equal to 9, which is 8. Thus,

$$25 = 16 + 8 + 1$$

Now write 25 as a sum of powers of 2, making sure to include the missing powers that are less than the highest power in the first step of the solution:

$$25 = 16 + 8 + 1$$
$$= (1)(2^4) + (1)(2^3) + (0)(2^2) + (0)(2^1) + (1)(2^0)$$
$$= 11001_{bin}$$

Note: you must be careful to use 0's as place holders for the missing powers of 2.

Chapter Summary

String manipulation and matrix processing are the two big topics you should master. Review the meanings and boundary conditions of the parameters in the `String` methods `substring` and `indexOf`. For matrices, you should nail down both the row-column and for-each traversals. Remember, you cannot use a for-each loop for the replacement of elements.

Be sure you can hand-execute tricky matrix algorithms, like those used for modifying matrices using mirror images.

A matrix is an array of row-arrays, so familiarize yourself with the the use of a method with an array parameter to process the rows of a matrix.

Array manipulation is another big topic. Be sure you know how to shuffle the elements of an array.

Other concepts emphasized in the labs are inheritance and polymorphism, writing subclasses, abstract classes, simulation of events using random numbers, multi-base numbers, and conditional (`if...else`) statements. You should have all of these at your fingertips.

MULTIPLE-CHOICE QUESTIONS ON THE LAB CONCEPTS

1. For ticket-selling purposes, there are three categories at a certain theater:

Age	Category
65 or above	Senior
From 18 to 64 inclusive	Adult
Below 18	Child

Which of the following code segments will assign the *correct* string to `category` for a given integer age?

```
I   if (age >= 65)
        category = "Senior";
    if (age >= 18)
        category = "Adult";
    else
        category = "Child";

II  if (age >= 65)
        category = "Senior";
    if (18 <= age <= 64)
        category = "Adult";
    else
        category = "Child";

III if (age >= 65)
        category = "Senior";
    else if (age >= 18)
        category = "Adult";
    else
        category = "Child";
```

(A) I only
(B) II only
(C) III only
(D) II and III only
(E) I, II, and III

2. What is the output of the following code segment?

```
String s = "How do you do?";
int index = s.indexOf("o");
while (index >= 0)
{
    System.out.print(index + " ");
    s = s.substring(index + 1);
    index = s.indexOf("o");
}
```

(A) 1 3 2 3
(B) 2 4 3 4
(C) 1 5 8 12
(D) 1 5 8 11
(E) No output because of an IndexOutOfBoundsException

3. Consider the following method removeAll that creates and returns a string that has stripped its input phrase of all occurrences of its single-character String parameter ch.

```
Line 1: public static String removeAll(String phrase, String ch)
Line 2: {
Line 3:     String str = "";
Line 4:     String newPhrase = phrase;
Line 5:     int pos = phrase.indexOf(ch);
Line 6:     if (pos == -1)
Line 7:         return phrase;
Line 8:     else
Line 9:     {
Line 10:        while (pos >= 0)
Line 11:        {
Line 12:            str = str + newPhrase.substring(0, pos - 1);
Line 13:            newPhrase = newPhrase.substring(pos + 1);
Line 14:            pos = newPhrase.indexOf(ch);
Line 15:            if (pos == -1)
Line 16:                str = str + newPhrase;
Line 17:        }
Line 18:        return str;
Line 19:     }
Line 20: }
```

The method doesn't work as intended. Which of the following changes to the removeAll method will make it work as specified?
(A) Change Line 10 to
    while (pos >= -1)
(B) Change Line 12 to
    str = str + newPhrase.substring(0, pos);
(C) Change Line 13 to
    newPhrase = newPhrase.substring(pos);
(D) Change Line 14 to
    pos = phrase.indexOf(ch);
(E) Change Line 16 to
    str = str + newPhrase.substring(pos + 1);

4. A programmer has written a program that "chats" to a human user based on statements that the human inputs. The program contains a method `findKeyWord` that searches an input statement for a given keyword. The `findKeyWord` method contains the following line of code:

```
pos = statement.indexOf(word);
```

Suppose pos has a value >= 0, that is, word was found. The programmer now wants to test that an actual word was found, not part of another word. For example, if "cat" is the keyword, the programmer needs to check that it's not part of "catch" or "category." Here is the code that tests if word is a stand-alone word. (You may assume that statement is all lowercase and contains only letters and blanks.)

```
pos = statement.indexOf(word);
//Check for first or last word
if (pos == 0 || pos + word.length() == statement.length())
{
    before = " ";
    after = " ";
}
else
{
    before = statement.substring(pos - 1, pos);
    after = statement.substring(pos + word.length(),
            pos + word.length() + 1);
    if (/* test */)
        //then a stand-alone word was found ...
    else
        //word was part of a larger word
}
```

Which replacement for /* *test* */ will give the desired result?
(A) `(before < "a" || before > "z") && (after < "a" || after > "z")`
(B) `(before > "a" || before < "z") && (after > "a" || after < "z")`
(C) `(before.compareTo("a") < 0 && before.compareTo("z") > 0) ||`
    `(after.compareTo("a") > 0 && after.compareTo("z") < 0)`
(D) `(before.compareTo("a") > 0 && before.compareTo("z") < 0) &&`
    `(after.compareTo("a") > 0 && after.compareTo("z") < 0)`
(E) `(before.compareTo("a") < 0 || before.compareTo("z") > 0) &&`
    `(after.compareTo("a") < 0 || after.compareTo("z") > 0)`

5. A program that simulates a conversation between a computer and a human user generates a random response to a user's comment. All possible responses that the computer can generate are stored in an array of `String` called `allResponses`. The method given below, `getResponse`, returns a random response string from the array.

```
/** Precondition:  array allResponses is initialized with strings.
 *  Postcondition: returns a random response from allResponses.
 */
public String getResponse();
{ /* implementation */ }
```

Which is a correct /* *implementation* */?

(A) `int i = (int) (Math.random() * allResponses.length);`
    `return allResponses[i];`

(B) `return (String) (Math.random() * allResponses.length);`

(C) `int i = Math.random() * allResponses.length;`
    `return allResponses[i];`

(D) `int i = (int) (Math.random() * (allResponses.length - 1));`
    `return allResponses[i];`

(E) `return (int) (Math.random() * allResponses.length);`

Questions 6 and 7 refer to the Deck class described below.

A Deck class contains an array cards with an even number of Card values and a final variable NUMCARDS, which is an odd integer.

6. Here are two possible algorithms for shuffling the deck.

   Algorithm 1
   Initialize an array of Card called shuffled of length NUMCARDS.
   Set k to 0.
   For j=0 to NUMCARDS/2-1
   - Copy cards[j] to shuffled[k]
   - Set k to k+2
   Set k to 1.
   For j=NUMCARDS/2 to NUMCARDS-1
   - Copy cards[j] to shuffled[k]
   - Set k to k+2

   Algorithm 2
   Initialize an array of Card called shuffled containing NUMCARDS slots.
   For k=0 to NUMCARDS-1
   - Repeatedly generate a random integer j from 0 to NUMCARDS-1,
       until cards[j] contains a card not marked as empty
   - Copy cards[j] to shuffled[k]
   - Set cards[j] to empty

   Which is a *false* statement concerning Algorithms 1 and 2?
   (A) A disadvantage of Algorithm 1 is that it won't generate all possible deck permutations.
   (B) For Algorithm 2, to determine the last element shuffled requires an average of NUMCARDS calls to the random number generator.
   (C) Algorithm 2 will lead to more permutations of the deck than Algorithm 1.
   (D) In terms of run time, Algorithm 2 is more efficient than Algorithm 1.
   (E) If Algorithm 1 is repeated several times, it may return the deck to its original state.

7. The following `shuffle` method is used to shuffle the cards in the `Deck` class.

```
Line 1: public void shuffle()
Line 2: {
Line 3:     for (int k = NUMCARDS; k > 0; k--)
Line 4:     {
Line 5:         int randPos = (int) (Math.random() * (k + 1));
Line 6:         //swap randomly selected card with card at position k
Line 7:         Card temp = cards[k];
Line 8:         cards[k] = cards[randPos];
Line 9:         cards[randPos] = temp;
Line 10:     }
Line 11: }
```

The method does not work as intended. Which of the following changes should be made to correct the method?

(A) Replace Line 3 with
   ```
   for (int k = NUMCARDS; k >= 0; k--)
   ```

(B) Replace Line 3 with
   ```
   for (int k = NUMCARDS - 1; k > 0; k--)
   ```

(C) Replace Line 3 with
   ```
   for (int k = 1; k <= NUMCARDS; k++)
   ```

(D) Replace Line 5 with
   ```
   int randPos = (int) (Math.random() * k);
   ```

(E) Replace Lines 7 – 9 with
   ```
   Card temp = cards[randPos];
   cards[randPos] = cards[k];
   cards[k] = temp;
   ```

8. A programmer wants to simulate several different but related solitaire games, each of which uses a standard 52-card deck. Each game starts with 10 cards dealt face up on a table. The game types differ in the rules that allow groups of cards to be discarded from the table and new cards to be dealt from the remainder of the deck. For each of the solitaire games, a winning game occurs if there are no cards left in the pile or on the table. To represent the table for the games, the programmer will use the inheritance relationship shown below.

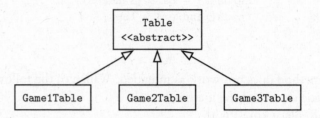

Which of the following methods should be abstract in the `Table` class?

   I `dealNextCard`, which provides the next card for the table

  II `checkForMove`, which returns `true` if a move is possible, `false` otherwise

 III `isWinningGame`, which returns `true` if both the table and deck of cards are empty

(A) I only
(B) II only
(C) III only
(D) I and II only
(E) II and III only

Questions 9 and 10 refer to the following.

A word creation game uses letter tiles, where each tile has a letter and a point value for scoring purposes. A `Tile` class is used to represent a letter tile.

```
public class Tile
{
    private String letter;
    private int pointValue;

    //Constructors and other methods are not shown.
}
```

9. The `Tile` class contains a `toString` method that creates a `String` containing the letter and point value of a `Tile`. The string should be in the following format:

```
Letter letter (point value = pointValue)
```

For example,

```
Letter A (point value = 1)
Letter Z (point value = 10)
```

Consider the `toString` method below:

```
public String toString()
{
    return /* code */
}
```

Which /* code */ leads to correct output?

(A) `Letter + "letter " + "(point value = " + pointValue + ")";`

(B) `"Letter " + letter + ("point value = " + pointValue);`

(C) `Letter + this.letter + " (point value = " + pointValue + ")";`

(D) `"Letter " + letter + " (point value = " + (String) pointValue + ")";`

(E) `"Letter " + letter + " (point value = " + pointValue + ")";`

10. Any two tiles in the word game that have the same letter also have the same point value, but the opposite is not necessarily true. For example, all the vowels have a point value of 1. Two tiles are said to match if they have the same letter. Consider the following `matches` method for the `Tile` class.

```
/** @return true if the letter on this tile equals the letter
 *  on otherTile */
public boolean matches(Tile otherTile)
{ return /* code */; }
```

Which replacements for /* *code* */ return the desired result? Note: You may *not* assume that the `Tile` class has its own `equals` method.

   I `letter == otherTile.letter`

  II `this.equals(otherTile)`

 III `letter.equals(otherTile.letter)`

(A) I only

(B) II only

(C) III only

(D) II and III only

(E) I and III only

11. Consider the following method.

```
public static void alterArray(int[] arr)
{
    int mid = arr.length/2;
    for (int i = 0; i < mid; i++)
    {
        int temp = arr[i];
        arr[i] = arr[arr.length - i - 1];
        arr[arr.length - i - 1] = temp;
    }
}
```

If the current state of a matrix mat is

```
2 7 9 5
8 1 4 3
6 5 0 9
```

which matrix will result from the method call `alterArray(mat[2])`?

(A) 2 7 9 5
     3 4 1 8
     6 5 0 9

(B) 2 7 0 5
     8 1 4 3
     6 5 9 9

(C) 5 9 7 2
     3 4 1 8
     9 0 5 6

(D) 2 7 9 5
     8 1 4 3
     9 0 5 6

(E) 5 9 7 2
     8 1 4 3
     6 5 0 9

12. Consider a program to manipulate images. The inheritance hierarchy is as follows:

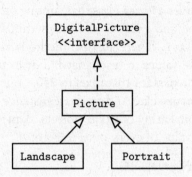

You may assume that Picture has a default (no-argument) constructor, but that Landscape and Portrait do not have any constructors. Which of the following declarations will compile?

I DigitalPicture p = new Portrait();

II Landscape p = new Picture();

III DigitalPicture p = new DigitalPicture();

(A) I only
(B) II only
(C) III only
(D) II and III only
(E) I, II, and III

13. The color of a pixel can be represented using the RGB (Red, Green, Blue) color model, which stores integer values for red, green, and blue, each ranging from 0 to 255. A value of 0 represents none of that color, while 255 represents the maximum. Consider a Pixel class that, among other methods, contains methods getRed, getGreen, and getBlue. These methods return integer values of those colors for that Pixel. There are also methods setRed, setGreen, and setBlue, which allow these values to be changed. For example, setBlue(250) would set the amount of blueness for that pixel to 250.

Consider a Picture class and a private instance variable pixels, where pixels is a two-dimensional array of Pixel objects. A method removeRed in the Picture class sets the red value of every pixel to zero:

```
public void removeRed()
{
    for (int row = 0; row < numRows; row++)
        for (int col = 0; col < numCols; col++)
        {
            /* code to set red value to 0 */
        }
}
```

Which is a correct replacement for /* *code to set red value to 0* */?

  I
```
Pixel p = pixels[row][col];
p.setRed(0);
```

  II
```
pixels[row][col].setRed(0);
```

  III
```
pixels[row][col].getRed() = 0;
```

(A) I only
(B) II only
(C) III only
(D) I and II only
(E) I, II, and III

14. Consider a class `MatrixStuff` that has a private instance variable

    ```
    private int[][] mat;
    ```

    The following method uses a vertical mirror down the center of a matrix to reflect the left half of the matrix onto the right. The following two examples show the result of mirroring a two-dimensional array of numbers from left to right vertically. (Another way of saying this is that the right half of the matrix is replaced by a vertical mirror image of the left half.)

    Example 1:

mat						mat after mirroring				
1	2	3	4	5		1	2	3	2	1
6	7	8	9	10		6	7	8	7	6
11	12	13	14	15		11	12	13	12	11

    Example 2:

mat					mat after mirroring			
1	2	3	4		1	2	2	1
5	6	7	8		5	6	6	5
9	10	11	12		9	10	10	9

    ```
    public static void mirrorVerticalLeftToRight(int[][] mat)
    {
        int width = mat[0].length;
        int numRows = mat.length;
        for (int row = 0; row < numRows; row++)
            for (int col = 0; col < width/2; col++)
                /*  element assignments */
    }
    ```

    Which replacement for /* *element assignments* */ will make the method work as intended?

    (A) `mat[row][col] = mat[row][width - col];`
    (B) `mat[row][width - col] = mat[row][col];`
    (C) `mat[row][width - 1 - col] = mat[row][col];`
    (D) `mat[row][col] = mat[row][width - 1 - col];`
    (E) `mat[row][width - 1 - col] = mat[col][row];`

15. Consider a square matrix in a class that has a private instance variable mat:

```
private int[][] mat;
```

Method alter in the class changes mat:

```
public void alter()
{
    for (int row = 1; row < mat.length; row++)
        for (int col = 0; col < row; col++)
            mat[col][row] = mat[row][col];
}
```

If mat has current value

```
{{1, 2, 3},
 {4, 5, 6},
 {7, 8, 9}}
```

what are the contents of mat after method alter has been executed?

(A) {{1, 4, 7},
    {4, 5, 8},
    {7, 8, 9}}

(B) {{1, 4, 7},
    {2, 5, 8},
    {3, 6, 9}}

(C) {{1, 2, 3},
    {2, 5, 6},
    {3, 6, 9}}

(D) {{9, 6, 3},
    {8, 5, 6},
    {7, 8, 9}}

(E) {{1, 2, 3},
    {4, 5, 2},
    {7, 4, 1}}

ANSWER KEY

1. C	6. D	11. D
2. A	7. B	12. A
3. B	8. B	13. D
4. E	9. E	14. C
5. A	10. C	15. A

ANSWERS EXPLAINED

1. **(C)** Segment III works because if you enter an age of 90, say, `category` will correctly be assigned `"Senior"`, and none of the other `else` pieces of code will be executed. Similarly, if you enter an age corresponding to an adult or a child, only the correct assignment is made. Segment I fails because if you enter an age of 90, `category` will be assigned `"Senior"`, but then will be changed to `"Adult"` when the age passes the second test. Segment II uses incorrect syntax. The segment will work if you change the second test to

   ```
   if (age >= 18 && age <= 64)
   ```

2. **(A)** The algorithm prints the current index of `"o"` in the string, then creates a new substring containing all remaining characters following that `"o"`. Here is the series of substrings and the corresponding output for each (the symbol ␣ denotes a blank character):

   ```
   How␣do␣you␣do?    1
   w␣do␣you␣do?      3
   ␣you␣do?          2
   u␣do?             3
   ```

3. **(B)** Here is a description of the algorithm:

   Make a copy of `phrase` in `newPhrase`.
   Find the first occurrence of `ch` in `newPhrase` (pos is the index).
   If you found it, concatenate to `str` the characters in `newPhrase` from 0 to pos-1.
   Change `newPhrase` to contain all characters from `ch` to the end, excluding `ch`.
   Repeat the process until there are no more occurrences of `ch` in `newPhrase`.

   So Line 12 is wrong because `newPhrase.substring(0,pos-1)` will not include the character at pos-1, which means that the string returned will lose a character that is *not* equal to `ch`.

4. **(E)** The program has found a stand-alone word if the characters `before` and `after` are both blank. Choice E tests that they are not letters between `"a"` and `"z"`, i.e., they must be blank. Choices A and B fail because you must use `compareTo` for inequality tests on strings. Choices C and D allow at least one of `before` and `after` to be a letter, which would mean that `word` was not a stand-alone word.

5. **(A)** The first line in choice A returns a random integer that lies between 0 and `allResponses.length-1`. This range corresponds to the range of the array indexes so it is correct. Choice B is garbage—you cannot cast a real number to a string. Choice C fails because `Math.random()` is type `double` and you require an `int`; you must do the cast to `int` shown in choice A. Choice D fails because the element `allResponses[allResponses.length-1]` will never be returned: `i` will contain a random `int` from 0 to `allResponses.length-2`. Choice E returns an `int`, not a `String`.

6. **(D)** The big defect of Algorithm 2 is that it eventually slows down. This is because every time it selects an empty element, it has to loop again. Each of the other choices is true. In choice A, for example, the element `cards[0]` always moves to `shuffled[0]`, eliminating all permutations that have `cards[0]` in a different slot. For choice B, by the time you get to assign the last element, all but two slots of the `cards` array are marked empty. So, on average, you will need to go through NUMCARDS tries to find one of those two nonempty slots. For choice C, even though Algorithm 2 is slow, in theory every element in `cards` could land in any given slot in `shuffled`. This is not true for Algorithm 1, where the first element never budges out of the first slot. For choice E, because of the precise ordering of elements in Algorithm 1, the array will always eventually return to its original state, assuming there are sufficient iterations.

7. **(B)** If `k` starts with the value NUMCARDS, the method encounters `cards[NUMCARDS]` on Line 7 and throws an `ArrayIndexOutOfBoundsException`.

8. **(B)** Since `dealNextCard` and `isWinningGame` have the same code irrespective of which game is being played, they should be regular methods in the `Table` class. Method II, `checkForMove`, is unique to each game and therefore should be abstract in the superclass and overridden in each subclass.

9. **(E)** The actual letter and its point value must not be in quotes because their *values* must be printed. Everything else, including the parentheses, must be in quotes. (All text in quotes is printed literally, as is.) Choices A and C fail because they don't place the opening word, `Letter`, in quotes. Choice B doesn't have the parentheses in quotes. Choice D incorrectly tries to cast an `int` to a `String`.

10. **(C)** Segment I will only be true if an object and its parameter are the same reference, which is not necessarily true for two matching tiles. Segment II fails similarly if the `Tile` class doesn't have its own `equals` method. (The inherited method from `Object` compares references.)

11. **(D)** The matrix `mat` consists of an array of rows, `mat[0]`, `mat[1]`, `mat[2]`, each of which is an array. The method `alterArray` swaps the first and last element of an array, then the second and second-last elements, and so on, until it reaches the middle of the array. The method call `alterArray(mat[2])` performs this series of swaps on row 2 of the matrix, resulting in the matrix in choice D.

12. **(A)** Declaration I works because a `Portrait` *is-a* `DigitalPicture`, and it will be assigned the default constructor from `Picture`, its superclass. Declaration II fails because a `Picture` is *not* a `Landscape`. Declaration III fails because you can't create an instance of an interface.

13. **(D)** Segment I works because `p` is a reference to the element `pixels[row][col]`. Changing `p` with a mutator method will change the array. Segment II changes the two-dimensional array directly. Segment III is garbage: you cannot assign a value

through an accessor method.

14. **(C)** Look at Example 2 for this question:

mat					mat after mirroring			
1	2	3	4		1	2	2	1
5	6	7	8		5	6	6	5
9	10	11	12		9	10	10	9

Now consider one element, 12 say. It must be replaced by its vertical mirror image 9, i.e., mat[2][3]=mat[2][0]. The value of width is 4. See which expression in the answer choices correctly makes this assignment. Eliminate choices A and D right away because col can only have the values 0 and 1 in this algorithm, so mat[2][3] will not be assigned. In choice B, when col has value 1, mat[2][3]=mat[2][1], an incorrect assignment. Choice C works: when row is 2 and col is 0, mat[2][3]=mat[2][0]. In choice E, when row is 2 and col is 0, the assignment mat[2][3]=mat[0][2] is incorrect.

15. **(A)** Method alter places a mirror along the major diagonal and reflects the elements from left to right across this diagonal.

$$
\begin{array}{ccc}
1 & 2 & 3 \\
4 & 5 & 6 \\
7 & 8 & 9
\end{array}
$$

In this algorithm, when row is 1, col can only be 0, and when row is 2, col takes on the values 0 and 1. Thus, only 3 elements are altered: mat[0][1], mat[0][2], and mat[1][2]. (Note that the method assigns values to mat[col][row].) These elements are all to the right of the diagonal. Choice A is the only choice that leaves elements to the left of the diagonal unchanged.

Practice
Exams

Answer Sheet: Practice Exam Two

1. Ⓐ Ⓑ Ⓒ Ⓓ Ⓔ
2. Ⓐ Ⓑ Ⓒ Ⓓ Ⓔ
3. Ⓐ Ⓑ Ⓒ Ⓓ Ⓔ
4. Ⓐ Ⓑ Ⓒ Ⓓ Ⓔ
5. Ⓐ Ⓑ Ⓒ Ⓓ Ⓔ
6. Ⓐ Ⓑ Ⓒ Ⓓ Ⓔ
7. Ⓐ Ⓑ Ⓒ Ⓓ Ⓔ
8. Ⓐ Ⓑ Ⓒ Ⓓ Ⓔ
9. Ⓐ Ⓑ Ⓒ Ⓓ Ⓔ
10. Ⓐ Ⓑ Ⓒ Ⓓ Ⓔ
11. Ⓐ Ⓑ Ⓒ Ⓓ Ⓔ
12. Ⓐ Ⓑ Ⓒ Ⓓ Ⓔ
13. Ⓐ Ⓑ Ⓒ Ⓓ Ⓔ
14. Ⓐ Ⓑ Ⓒ Ⓓ Ⓔ

15. Ⓐ Ⓑ Ⓒ Ⓓ Ⓔ
16. Ⓐ Ⓑ Ⓒ Ⓓ Ⓔ
17. Ⓐ Ⓑ Ⓒ Ⓓ Ⓔ
18. Ⓐ Ⓑ Ⓒ Ⓓ Ⓔ
19. Ⓐ Ⓑ Ⓒ Ⓓ Ⓔ
20. Ⓐ Ⓑ Ⓒ Ⓓ Ⓔ
21. Ⓐ Ⓑ Ⓒ Ⓓ Ⓔ
22. Ⓐ Ⓑ Ⓒ Ⓓ Ⓔ
23. Ⓐ Ⓑ Ⓒ Ⓓ Ⓔ
24. Ⓐ Ⓑ Ⓒ Ⓓ Ⓔ
25. Ⓐ Ⓑ Ⓒ Ⓓ Ⓔ
26. Ⓐ Ⓑ Ⓒ Ⓓ Ⓔ
27. Ⓐ Ⓑ Ⓒ Ⓓ Ⓔ
28. Ⓐ Ⓑ Ⓒ Ⓓ Ⓔ

29. Ⓐ Ⓑ Ⓒ Ⓓ Ⓔ
30. Ⓐ Ⓑ Ⓒ Ⓓ Ⓔ
31. Ⓐ Ⓑ Ⓒ Ⓓ Ⓔ
32. Ⓐ Ⓑ Ⓒ Ⓓ Ⓔ
33. Ⓐ Ⓑ Ⓒ Ⓓ Ⓔ
34. Ⓐ Ⓑ Ⓒ Ⓓ Ⓔ
35. Ⓐ Ⓑ Ⓒ Ⓓ Ⓔ
36. Ⓐ Ⓑ Ⓒ Ⓓ Ⓔ
37. Ⓐ Ⓑ Ⓒ Ⓓ Ⓔ
38. Ⓐ Ⓑ Ⓒ Ⓓ Ⓔ
39. Ⓐ Ⓑ Ⓒ Ⓓ Ⓔ
40. Ⓐ Ⓑ Ⓒ Ⓓ Ⓔ

How to Calculate Your (Approximate) AP Computer Science Score

Multiple Choice

Number correct (out of 40) = _____ ⟸ Multiple-Choice Score

Free Response

Question 1 _____
          (out of 9)

Question 2 _____
          (out of 9)

Question 3 _____
          (out of 9)

Question 4 _____
          (out of 9)

Total _____ × 1.11 = _____ ⟸ Free-Response Score
                                                                (Do not round.)

Final Score

_____ + _____ = _____
Multiple-   Free-   Final Score
Choice   Response   (Round to nearest
Score   Score   whole number.)

Chart to Convert to AP Grade
Computer Science

Final Score Range	AP Grade[a]
62–80	5
47–61	4
37–46	3
29–36	2
0–28	1

[a]The score range corresponding to each grade varies from exam to exam and is approximate.

Practice Exam Two
COMPUTER SCIENCE
SECTION I

Time—1 hour and 30 minutes
Number of questions—40
Percent of total grade—50

Directions: Determine the answer to each of the following questions or incomplete statements, using the available space for any necessary scratchwork. Then decide which is the best of the choices given and fill in the corresponding oval on the answer sheet. Do not spend too much time on any one problem.

Notes:
- Assume that the classes in the Quick Reference have been imported where needed.
- Assume that variables and methods are declared within the context of an enclosing class.
- Assume that method calls that have no object or class name prefixed, and that are not shown within a complete class definition, appear within the context of an enclosing class.
- Assume that parameters in method calls are not `null` unless otherwise stated.

---

1. A large Java program was tested extensively, and no errors were found. What can be concluded?
   (A) All of the preconditions in the program are correct.
   (B) All of the postconditions in the program are correct.
   (C) The program may have bugs.
   (D) The program has no bugs.
   (E) Every method in the program may safely be used in other programs.

Questions 2–4 refer to the Worker class below:

```
public class Worker
{
    private String name;
    private double hourlyWage;
    private boolean isUnionMember;

    public Worker()
    { /* implementation not shown */ }

    public Worker(String aName, double anHourlyWage, boolean union)
    { /* implementation not shown */ }

    //Accessors getName, getHourlyWage, getUnionStatus are not shown.

    /** Permanently increase hourly wage by amt.
     *  @param amt the amount of wage increase
     */
    public void incrementWage(double amt)
    { /* implementation of incrementWage */ }

    /** Switch value of isUnionMember from true to false and
     *  vice versa.
     */
    public void changeUnionStatus()
    { /* implementation of changeUnionStatus */ }
}
```

2. Refer to the incrementWage method. Which of the following is a correct
   /* *implementation of* incrementWage */?
   (A) return hourlyWage + amt;
   (B) return getHourlyWage() + amt;
   (C) hourlyWage += amt;
   (D) getHourlyWage() += amt;
   (E) hourlyWage = amt;

GO ON TO THE NEXT PAGE.

3. Consider the method changeUnionStatus. Which is a correct
   /* *implementation of* changeUnionStatus */?

   I if (isUnionMember)
          isUnionMember = false;
   else
          isUnionMember = true;

   II isUnionMember = !isUnionMember;

   III if (isUnionMember)
          isUnionMember = !isUnionMember;

   (A) I only
   (B) II only
   (C) III only
   (D) I and II only
   (E) I, II, and III

4. A client method computePay will return a worker's pay based on the number of hours worked.

   ```
   /** Precondition:  Worker w has worked the given number of hours.
    *  @param w a Worker
    *  @param hours the number of hours worked
    *  @return amount of pay for Worker w
    */
   public static double computePay(Worker w, double hours)
   { /* code */ }
   ```

   Which replacement for /* *code* */ is correct?
   (A) return hourlyWage * hours;
   (B) return getHourlyWage() * hours;
   (C) return w.getHourlyWage() * hours;
   (D) return w.hourlyWage * hours;
   (E) return w.getHourlyWage() * w.hours;

5. Consider this program segment. You may assume that wordList has been declared as ArrayList<String>.

   ```
   for (String s : wordList)
       if (s.length() < 4)
           System.out.println("SHORT WORD");
   ```

   What is the maximum number of times that SHORT WORD can be printed?
   (A) 3
   (B) 4
   (C) wordList.size()
   (D) wordList.size() - 1
   (E) s.length()

6. Refer to the following method.

```
public static int mystery(int n)
{
    if (n == 1)
        return 3;
    else
        return 3 * mystery(n - 1);
}
```

What value does mystery(4) return?
(A) 3
(B) 9
(C) 12
(D) 27
(E) 81

7. Refer to the following declarations:

```
String[] colors = {"red", "green", "black"};
List<String> colorList = new ArrayList<String>();
```

Which of the following correctly assigns the elements of the colors array to colorList? The final ordering of colors in colorList should be the same as in the colors array.

```
 I for (String col : colors)
       colorList.add(col);

 II for (String col : colorList)
       colors.add(col);

III for (int i = colors.length - 1; i >= 0; i--)
       colorList.add(i, colors[i]);
```

(A) I only
(B) II only
(C) III only
(D) II and III only
(E) I, II, and III

8. Often the most efficient computer algorithms use a divide-and-conquer approach, for example, one in which a list is repeatedly split into two pieces until a desired outcome is reached. Which of the following use a divide-and-conquer approach?

    I Mergesort
    II Insertion sort
    III Binary search

    (A) I only
    (B) II only
    (C) III only
    (D) I and III only
    (E) I, II, and III

9. An Insect class is to be written, containing the following data fields:
    age, which will be initialized to 0 when an Insect is constructed.
    nextAvailableID, which will be initialized to 0 outside the constructor and incremented each time an Insect is constructed.
    idNum, which will be initialized to the current value of nextAvailableID when an Insect is constructed.
    position, which will be initialized to the location in a garden where the Insect is placed when it is constructed.
    direction, which will be initialized to the direction the Insect is facing when placed in the garden.
    Which variable in the Insect class should be static?

    (A) age
    (B) nextAvailableID
    (C) idNum
    (D) position
    (E) direction

Questions 10 and 11 refer to the classes `Address` and `Customer` given below.

```java
public class Address
{
    private String street;
    private String city;
    private String state;
    private int zipCode;

    public Address(String aStreet, String aCity, String aState,
            int aZipCode)
    { /* implementation not shown */ }

    public String getStreet()
    { /* implementation not shown */ }

    public String getCity()
    { /* implementation not shown */ }

    public String getState()
    { /* implementation not shown */ }

    public int getZipCode()
    { /* implementation not shown */ }

    //Other methods are not shown.
}

public class Customer
{
    private String name;
    private String phone;
    private Address address;
    private int ID;

    public Customer(String aName, String aPhone, Address anAddr,
            int anID)
    { /* implementation not shown */ }

    public Address getAddress()
    { /* implementation not shown */ }

    public String getName()
    { /* implementation not shown */ }

    public String getPhone()
    { /* implementation not shown */ }

    public int getID()
    { /* implementation not shown */ }

    //Other methods are not shown.
}
```

GO ON TO THE NEXT PAGE.

10. Which of the following correctly creates a Customer object c?

```
 I Address a = new Address("125 Bismark St", "Pleasantville",
       "NY", 14850);
   Customer c = new Customer("Jack Spratt", "747-1674", a, 7008);

II Customer c = new Customer("Jack Spratt", "747-1674",
       "125 Bismark St, Pleasantville, NY 14850", 7008);

III Customer c = new Customer("Jack Spratt", "747-1674",
       new Address("125 Bismark St", "Pleasantville", "NY", 14850),
       7008);
```

(A) I only
(B) II only
(C) III only
(D) I and II only
(E) I and III only

11. Consider an AllCustomers class that has private instance variable

```
private Customer[] custList;
```

Given the ID number of a particular customer, a method of the class, locate, must find the correct Customer record and return the name of that customer. Here is the method locate:

```
/** Precondition: custList contains a complete list of Customer objects.
 *  @param idNum the ID number for a Customer
 *  @return the name of the customer with the specified idNum
 */
public String locate(int idNum)
{
    for (Customer c : custList)
        if (c.getID() == idNum)
            return c.getName();
    return null;      //idNum not found
}
```

A more efficient algorithm for finding the matching Customer object could be used if
(A) Customer objects were in alphabetical order by name.
(B) Customer objects were sorted by phone number.
(C) Customer objects were sorted by ID number.
(D) the custList array had fewer elements.
(E) the Customer class did not have an Address data member.

12. The following shuffling method is used to shuffle an array arr of int values. The method assumes the existence of a swap method, where swap(arr,i,j) interchanges the elements arr[i] and arr[j].

```
public static void shuffle (int[] arr)
{
    for (int k = arr.length - 1; k > 0; k--)
    {
        int randIndex = (int) (Math.random() * (k + 1));
        swap(arr, k, randIndex);
    }
}
```

Suppose the initial state of arr is 1 2 3 4 5, and when the method is executed the values generated for randIndex are 3, 2, 0, and 1, in that order. What will be the final state of arr?
(A) 5 2 1 3 4
(B) 1 2 5 3 4
(C) 5 4 1 3 2
(D) 4 5 1 3 2
(E) 2 5 1 3 4

GO ON TO THE NEXT PAGE.

13. Refer to method `removeWord`.

```
/** @param wordList an ArrayList of String objects
 *  @param word the word to be removed
 *  Postcondition: All occurrences of word have been removed
 *                 from wordList.
 */
public static void removeWord(ArrayList<String> wordList,
                                             String word)
{
    for (int i = 0; i < wordList.size(); i++)
        if ((wordList.get(i)).equals(word))
            wordList.remove(i);
}
```

The method does not always work as intended. Consider the method call

```
removeWord(wordList, "cat");
```

For which of the following lists will this method call fail?
(A) `The cat sat on the mat`
(B) `The cat cat sat on the mat mat`
(C) `The cat sat on the cat`
(D) `cat`
(E) `The cow sat on the mat`

14. A `Clock` class has hours, minutes, and seconds represented by `int` values. It also has each of the following methods: `setTime` to change the time on a `Clock` to the hour, minute, and second specified; `getTime` to access the time; and `toString` to return the time as a `String`. The `Clock` class has a constructor that allows a `Clock` to be created with three `int` parameters for hours, minutes, and seconds. Consider a two-dimensional array of `Clock` values called `allClocks`. A code segment manipulating `allClocks` is as follows:

```
for (Clock[] row : allClocks)
    for (Clock c : row)
        /* more code */
```

Assuming the `Clock` class works as specified, which replacement for */* more code */* will cause an error?

I `System.out.print(c);`

II `c.setTime(0, 0, 0);`

III `c = new Clock(0, 0, 0);`

(A) I only
(B) II only
(C) III only
(D) II and III only
(E) I and II only

15. Consider the following method that will access a square matrix mat:

```
/** Precondition: mat is initialized and is a square matrix.
 */
public static void printSomething(int[][] mat)
{
    for (int r = 0; r < mat.length; r++)
    {
        for (int c=0; c<=r; c++)
            System.out.print(mat[r][c] + " ");
        System.out.println();
    }
}
```

Suppose mat is originally

```
0 1 2 3
4 5 6 7
3 2 1 0
7 6 5 4
```

After the method call printSomething(mat) the output will be

(A) 0 1 2 3
     4 5 6 7
     3 2 1 0
     7 6 5 4

(B) 0
     4 5
     3 2 1
     7 6 5 4

(C) 0 1 2 3
     4 5 6
     3 2
     7

(D) 0
     4
     3
     7

(E) There will be no output. An ArrayIndexOutOfBoundsException will be thrown.

16. Consider two different ways of storing a set of nonnegative integers in which there are no duplicates.

    Method One: Store the integers explicitly in an array in which the number of elements is known. For example, in this method, the set {6, 2, 1, 8, 9, 0} can be represented as follows:

0	1	2	3	4	5
6	2	1	8	9	0

    6 elements

    Method Two: Suppose that the range of the integers is 0 to MAX. Use a boolean array indexed from 0 to MAX. The index values represent the possible values in the set. In other words, each possible integer from 0 to MAX is represented by a different position in the array. A value of true in the array means that the corresponding integer is in the set, a value of false means that the integer is not in the set. For example, using this method for the same set above, {6, 2, 1, 8, 9, 0}, the representation would be as follows (T = true, F = false):

0	1	2	3	4	5	6	7	8	9	10	...	MAX
T	T	T	F	F	F	T	F	T	T	F	...	F

    The following operations are to be performed on the set of integers:

    I Search for a target value in the set.
    II Print all the elements of the set.
    III Return the number of elements in the set.

    Which statement is *true*?
    (A) Operation I is more efficient if the set is stored using Method One.
    (B) Operation II is more efficient if the set is stored using Method Two.
    (C) Operation III is more efficient if the set is stored using Method One.
    (D) Operation I is equally efficient for Methods One and Two.
    (E) Operation III is equally efficient for Methods One and Two.

17. An algorithm for finding the average of N numbers is

    $$average = \frac{sum}{N}$$

    where N and sum are both integers. In a program using this algorithm, a programmer forgot to include a test that would check for N equal to zero. If N is zero, when will the error be detected?
    (A) At compile time
    (B) At edit time
    (C) As soon as the value of N is entered
    (D) During run time
    (E) When an incorrect result is output

GO ON TO THE NEXT PAGE.

Practice Exam 2

18. What is wrong with this interface?

```
public interface Bad
{
    void someMethod(String password)
    {
        System.out.println("Psst! The password is " + password);
    }
}
```

(A) A method in an interface should be declared `public`.
(B) A method in an interface should be declared `abstract`.
(C) There should not be a method implementation as shown.
(D) There should be a class implementation provided.
(E) There should not be any method parameters.

19. Consider method getCount below:

```
public static int getCount(String s, String sub)
{
    int count = 0;
    int pos = s.indexOf(sub);
    while (pos >= 0)
    {
        s = s.substring(pos);
        count++;
        pos = s.indexOf(sub);
    }
    return count;
}
```

What will the method call getCount("a carrot and car", "car") return?
(A) 0
(B) 1
(C) 2
(D) 3
(E) No value returned. The method is in an infinite loop.

20. Consider a program that deals with various components of different vehicles. Which of the following is a reasonable representation of the relationships among some classes that may comprise the program? Note that an open up-arrow denotes an inheritance relationship and a down-arrow denotes a composition relationship.

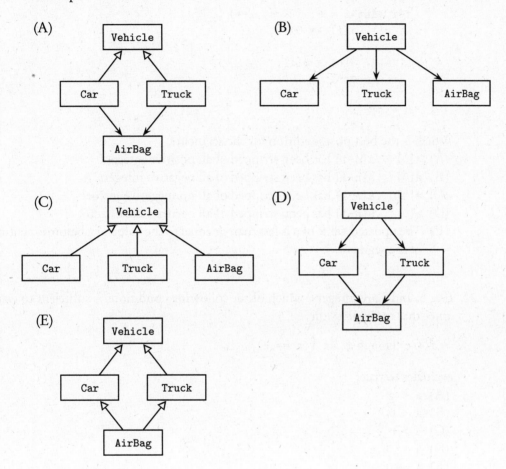

21. Consider the following program segment:

```
/** Precondition: a[0]...a[n-1] is an initialized array of integers,
 *                and 0 < n <= a.length.
 */
    int c = 0;
    for (int i = 0; i < n; i++)
        if (a[i] >= 0)
        {
            a[c] = a[i];
            c++;
        }
    n = c;
```

Which is the best postcondition for the segment?
(A) a[0]...a[n-1] has been stripped of all positive integers.
(B) a[0]...a[n-1] has been stripped of all negative integers.
(C) a[0]...a[n-1] has been stripped of all nonnegative integers.
(D) a[0]...a[n-1] has been stripped of all occurrences of zero.
(E) The updated value of n is less than or equal to the value of n before execution of the segment.

22. If a, b, and c are integers, which of the following conditions is sufficient to *guarantee* that the expression

```
a < c || a < b && !(a == c)
```

evaluates to true?
(A) a < c
(B) a < b
(C) a > b
(D) a == b
(E) a == c

23. Airmail Express charges for shipping small packages by integer values of weight. The charges for a weight w in pounds are as follows:

$$0 < w \le 2 \qquad \$4.00$$
$$2 < w \le 5 \qquad \$8.00$$
$$5 < w \le 20 \qquad \$15.00$$

The company does not accept packages that weigh more than 20 pounds. Which of the following represents the best set of data (weights) to test a program that calculates shipping charges?
(A) 0, 2, 5, 20
(B) 1, 4, 16
(C) −1, 1, 2, 3, 5, 16, 20
(D) −1, 0, 1, 2, 3, 5, 16, 20, 22
(E) All integers from −1 through 22

24. Consider the following instance variable and methods in the same class.

```
private int[][] matrix;

/** Precondition: array.length > 0.
  * @return the largest integer in array
  */
private int max(int[] array)
{  /* implementation not shown */  }

/** @return num1 if num1 >= num2; otherwise return num2
  */
public int max(int num1, int num2)
{  /* implementation not shown */  }
```

Suppose matrix has a current value of

```
2 1 4 8
6 0 3 9
5 7 7 6
1 2 3 4
```

What will be returned by the following method call in the same class?

```
max(max(matrix[2]), max(matrix[3]))
```

(A) 9
(B) 8
(C) 7
(D) 4
(E) Compile-time error. No value returned.

Questions 25–26 are based on the following class declaration:

```
public class AutoPart
{
    private String description;
    private int partNum;
    private double price;

    public AutoPart(String desc, int pNum, double aPrice)
    { /* implementation not shown */ }

    public String getDescription()
    { return description; }

    public int getPartNum()
    { return partNum; }

    public double getPrice()
    { return price; }

    //Other methods are not shown.
    //There is no compareTo method.
}
```

25. This question refers to the `findCheapest` method below, which occurs in a class that has an array of `AutoPart` as one of its private data fields:

```
private AutoPart[] allParts;
```

The `findCheapest` method examines an array of `AutoPart` and returns the part number of the `AutoPart` with the lowest price whose description matches the `partDescription` parameter. For example, several of the `AutoPart` elements may have "headlight" as their description field. Different headlights will differ in both price and part number. If the `partDescription` parameter is "headlight", then `findCheapest` will return the part number of the cheapest headlight.

```
/** Precondition:  allParts contains at least one element whose
 *                 description matches partDescription.
 *  @param partDescription the description of a part in allParts
 *  @return the part number of the cheapest AutoPart
 *  whose description matches partDescription
 */
public int findCheapest(String partDescription)
{
    AutoPart part = null;       //AutoPart with lowest price so far
    double min = LARGE_VALUE;   //larger than any valid price
    for (AutoPart p : allParts)
    {
        /* more code */
    }
    return part.getPartNum();
}
```

Which of the following replacements for /* *more code* */ will find the correct part number?

```
 I if (p.getPrice() < min)
   {
       min = p.getPrice();
       part = p;
   }

II if (p.getDescription().equals(partDescription))
       if (p.getPrice() < min)
       {
           min = p.getPrice();
           part = p;
       }

III if (p.getDescription().equals(partDescription))
        if (p.getPrice() < min)
            return p.getPartNum();
```

(A) I only
(B) II only
(C) III only
(D) I and II only
(E) I and III only

26. Consider the following method:

    ```
    /** Precondition: st1 and st2 are distinct String objects.
     * @return smaller of st1 and st2
     */
    public static String min(String st1, String st2)
    {
        if (st1.compareTo(st2) < 0)
            return st1;
        else
            return st2;
    }
    ```

    A method in the same class has these declarations:

    ```
    AutoPart p1 = new AutoPart(<suitable values>);
    AutoPart p2 = new AutoPart(<suitable values>);
    ```

    Which of the following statements will cause an error?

    I `System.out.println(min(p1.getDescription(),`
       `p2.getDescription()));`

    II `System.out.println(min(((String) p1).getDescription(),`
       `((String) p2).getDescription()));`

    III `System.out.println(min(p1, p2));`

    (A) None
    (B) I only
    (C) II only
    (D) III only
    (E) II and III only

27. This question is based on the following declarations:

    ```
    String strA = "CARROT", strB = "Carrot", strC = "car";
    ```

    Given that all uppercase letters precede all lowercase letters when considering alphabetical order, which is true?
    (A) `strA.compareTo(strB) < 0 && strB.compareTo(strC) > 0`
    (B) `strC.compareTo(strB) < 0 && strB.compareTo(strA) < 0`
    (C) `strB.compareTo(strC) < 0 && strB.compareTo(strA) > 0`
    (D) `!(strA.compareTo(strB) == 0) && strB.compareTo(strA) < 0`
    (E) `!(strA.compareTo(strB) == 0) && strC.compareTo(strB) < 0`

28. A programmer has a file of names. She is designing a program that sends junk mail letters to everyone on the list. To make the letters sound personal and friendly, she will extract each person's first name from the name string. She plans to create a parallel file of first names only. For example,

fullName	firstName
Ms. Anjali DeSouza	Anjali
Dr. John Roufaiel	John
Mrs. Mathilda Concia	Mathilda

Here is a method intended to extract the first name from a full name string.

```
/** Precondition:
 *    - fullName starts with a title followed by a period.
 *    - A single space separates the title, first name, and last name.
 * @param fullName a string containing a title, period, blank,
 * and last name
 * @return the first name only in fullName
 */
public static String getFirstName(String fullName)
{
    final String BLANK = " ";
    String temp, firstName;

    /* code to extract first name */

    return firstName;
}
```

Which represents correct /* *code to extract first name* */?

```
 I  int k = fullName.indexOf(BLANK);
    temp = fullName.substring(k + 1);
    k = temp.indexOf(BLANK);
    firstName = temp.substring(0, k);

 II int k = fullName.indexOf(BLANK);
    firstName = fullName.substring(k + 1);
    k = firstName.indexOf(BLANK);
    firstName = firstName.substring(0, k);

III int firstBlank = fullName.indexOf(BLANK);
    int secondBlank = fullName.indexOf(BLANK);
    firstName = fullName.substring(firstBlank + 1, secondBlank + 1);
```

(A) I only
(B) II only
(C) III only
(D) I and II only
(E) I, II, and III

Questions 29–31 refer to the ThreeDigitInteger and ThreeDigitCode classes below.

```
public class ThreeDigitInteger
{
    private int hundredsDigit;
    private int tensDigit;
    private int onesDigit;
    private int value;

    /** @param aValue a 3-digit int */
    public ThreeDigitInteger(int aValue)
    { /* implementation not shown */ }

    /** @return the sum of digits for this ThreeDigitInteger */
    public int digitSum()
    { /* implementation not shown */ }

    /** @return the sum of the hundreds digit and tens digit */
    public int twoDigitSum()
    { /* implementation not shown */ }

    //Other methods are not shown.
}

public class ThreeDigitCode extends ThreeDigitInteger
{
    private boolean isValid;

    /** @param aValue a 3-digit int */
    public ThreeDigitCode(int aValue)
    { /* implementation code */ }

    /** A ThreeDigitCode is valid if and only if the remainder when
     *  the sum of the hundreds and tens digits is divided by 7 equals
     *  the ones digit. Thus 362 is valid while 364 is not.
     *  @return true if ThreeDigitCode is valid, false otherwise
     */
    public boolean isValid()
    { /* implementation not shown */ }
}
```

GO ON TO THE NEXT PAGE.

29. Which is a *true* statement about the classes shown?
    (A) The `ThreeDigitInteger` class inherits the `isValid` method from the class `ThreeDigitCode`.
    (B) The `ThreeDigitCode` class inherits all of the public accessor methods from the `ThreeDigitInteger` class.
    (C) The `ThreeDigitCode` class inherits the constructor from the class `ThreeDigitInteger`.
    (D) The `ThreeDigitCode` class can directly access all the private variables of the `ThreeDigitInteger` class.
    (E) The `ThreeDigitInteger` class can access the `isValid` instance variable of the `ThreeDigitCode` class.

30. Which is correct /* *implementation code* */ for the `ThreeDigitCode` constructor?

    ```
    I  super(value);
       isValid = isValid();

    II super(value, valid);

    III super(value);
        isValid = twoDigitSum() % 7 == onesDigit;
    ```

    (A) I only
    (B) II only
    (C) III only
    (D) I and III only
    (E) I, II, and III

31. Refer to these declarations in a client program:

    ```
    ThreeDigitInteger code = new ThreeDigitCode(127);
    ThreeDigitInteger num = new ThreeDigitInteger(456);
    ```

    Which of the following subsequent tests will *not* cause an error?

    ```
    I   if (code.isValid())
           ...

    II  if (num.isValid())
           ...

    III if (((ThreeDigitCode) code).isValid())
           ...
    ```

    (A) I only
    (B) II only
    (C) III only
    (D) I and II only
    (E) I and III only

GO ON TO THE NEXT PAGE.

32. Consider the following hierarchy of classes:

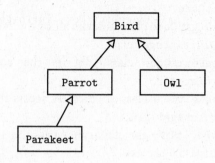

Assuming that each class has a valid default constructor, which of the following declarations in a client program are correct?

```
I  Bird b1 = new Parrot();
   Bird b2 = new Parakeet();
   Bird b3 = new Owl();

II Parakeet p = new Parrot();
   Owl o = new Bird();

III Parakeet p = new Bird();
```

(A) I only
(B) II only
(C) III only
(D) II and III only
(E) I, II, and III

33. Consider an array arr and a list list that is an ArrayList<String>. Both arr and list are initialized with string values. Which of the following code segments correctly appends all the strings in arr to the end of list?

```
I  for (String s : arr)
       list.add(s);

II for (String s : arr)
       list.add(list.size(), s);

III for (int i = 0; i < arr.length; i++)
       list.add(arr[i]);
```

(A) I only
(B) II only
(C) III only
(D) I and III only
(E) I, II, and III

34. Refer to the nextIntInRange method below:

```
/** @return a random integer in the range low to high, inclusive */
public int nextIntInRange(int low, int high)
{
    return /* expression */
}
```

Which /* *expression* */ will always return a value that satisfies the postcondition?

(A) `(int) (Math.random() * high) + low;`

(B) `(int) (Math.random() * (high - low)) + low;`

(C) `(int) (Math.random() * (high - low + 1)) + low;`

(D) `(int) (Math.random() * (high + low)) + low;`

(E) `(int) (Math.random() * (high + low - 1)) + low;`

35. Consider the following mergeSort method and the private instance variable a both in the same Sorter class:

```
private int[] a;

/** Sorts a[first] to a[last] in increasing order using mergesort. */
public void mergeSort(int first, int last)
{
    if (first != last)
    {
        int mid = (first + last) / 2;
        mergeSort(first, mid);
        mergeSort(mid + 1, last);
        merge(first, mid, last);
    }
}
```

Method mergeSort calls method merge, which has this header:

```
/** Merge a[lb] to a[mi] and a[mi+1] to a[ub].
 * Precondition: a[lb] to a[mi] and a[mi+1] to a[ub] both
 *               sorted in increasing order.
 */
private void merge(int lb, int mi, int ub)
```

If the first call to mergeSort is mergeSort(0,3), how many *further* calls will there be to mergeSort before an array b[0]...b[3] is sorted?

(A) 2
(B) 3
(C) 4
(D) 5
(E) 6

36. A large hospital maintains a list of patients' records in no particular order. To find the record of a given patient, which represents the most efficient method that will work?
   (A) Do a sequential search on the name field of the records.
   (B) Do a binary search on the name field of the records.
   (C) Use insertion sort to sort the records alphabetically by name; then do a sequential search on the name field of the records.
   (D) Use mergesort to sort the records alphabetically by name; then do a sequential search on the name field of the records.
   (E) Use mergesort to sort the records alphabetically by name; then do a binary search on the name field of the records.

Use the following information for Questions 37 and 38.

Here is a diagram that shows the relationship between some of the classes that will be used in a program to draw a banner with block letters.

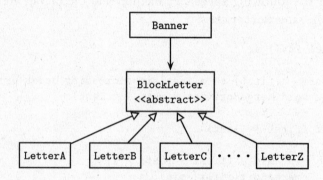

The diagram shows that the `Banner` class uses `BlockLetter` objects, and that the `BlockLetter` class has 26 subclasses, representing block letters from A to Z.

The `BlockLetter` class has an abstract `draw` method

```
public abstract void draw();
```

Each of the subclasses shown implements the `draw` method in a unique way to draw its particular letter. The `Banner` class gets an array of `BlockLetter` and has a method to draw all the letters in this array.

Here is a partial implementation of the `Banner` class:

```
public class Banner
{
    private BlockLetter[] letters;
    private int numLetters;

    /** Constructor. Gets the letters for the Banner. */
    public Banner()
    {
        numLetters = < some integer read from user input >
        letters = getLetters();
    }
```

```
    /** @return an array of block letters */
    public BlockLetter[] getLetters()
    {
        String letter;
        letters = new BlockLetter[numLetters];
        for (int i = 0; i < numLetters; i++)
        {
            < read in capital letter >

            if (letter.equals("A"))
                letters[i] = new LetterA();
            else if (letter.equals("B"))
                letters[i] = new LetterB();
                    ...            //similar code for C through Y
            else
                letters[i] = new LetterZ();
        }
        return letters;
    }

    /** Draw all the letters in the Banner. */
    public void drawLetters()
    {
        for (BlockLetter letter : letters)
            letter.draw();
    }

    //Other methods are not shown.
}
```

37. You are given the information that BlockLetter is an abstract class that is used
    in the program. Which of the following can you conclude about the class?

    I All of its methods *must* be abstract.

    II It *must* have at least one subclass.

    III No instances of BlockLetter can be created.

    (A) I only
    (B) II only
    (C) III only
    (D) II and III only
    (E) I, II, and III

38. Which is a *true* statement about method drawLetters?
    (A) It is an overloaded method in the Banner class.
    (B) It is an overridden method in the Banner class.
    (C) It uses polymorphism to draw the correct letters.
    (D) It will cause a compile-time error because draw is not implemented in the
        BlockLetter class.
    (E) It will cause a run-time error because draw is not implemented in the
        BlockLetter class.

GO ON TO THE NEXT PAGE.

39. Consider `method1` and `method2` below, which are identical except for the second last line of code. Each method returns a new matrix based on the input matrix `mat`.

```
public static int[][] method1(int[][] mat)
{
    int numRows = mat.length;
    int numCols = mat[0].length;
    int[][] newMat = new int[numRows][numCols];
    for (int row = 0; row < numRows; row++)
        for (int col = 0; col < numCols; col++)
            newMat[numRows - row -1][col] = mat[row][col];
    return newMat;
}

public static int[][] method2(int[][] mat)
{
    int numRows = mat.length;
    int numCols = mat[0].length;
    int[][] newMat = new int[numRows][numCols];
    for (int row = 0; row < numRows; row++)
        for (int col = 0; col < numCols; col++)
            newMat[row][col] = mat[numRows - row - 1][col];
    return newMat;
}
```

Suppose the same input matrix is used for `method1` and `method2`, and the output for `method1` is `matrix1` while the output for `method2` is `matrix2`. Which is a true statement about `matrix1` and `matrix2`?

(A) `matrix1` is identical to `matrix2`.

(B) The rows of `matrix1` are the columns of `matrix2`.

(C) `matrix1` is a reflection of `matrix2` across a vertical line on the edge of either matrix.

(D) `matrix1` is a reflection of `matrix2` across a horizontal line on the bottom or top edge of either matrix.

(E) The rows of `matrix1` are the rows of `matrix2` in reverse order.

40. Consider an `ArrayList` cards of `Card` objects that needs to be shuffled. The following algorithm is used for shuffling:

> Create a temporary `ArrayList<Card>`
> Do the following `cards.size()` number of times
> — Generate a random integer r that can index any card in `cards`
> — Remove the card found at position r in `cards` and add it to the end of the temporary `ArrayList`
> Set `cards` to the temporary `ArrayList`

Here is the method that implements this algorithm.

```
Line 1: public void shuffle()
Line 2: {
Line 3:     int size = cards.size();
Line 4:     List<Card> temp = new ArrayList<Card>();
Line 5:     for (int j = 1; j < size; j++)
Line 6:     {
Line 7:         int index = (int) (Math.random() * size);
Line 8:         temp.add(cards.get(index));
Line 9:     }
Line 10:    cards = temp;
Line 11: }
```

The method does not work as intended. Which of the following changes to `shuffle` would ensure that it works correctly?

I Replace Line 5 with

```
for (int j = 0; j < size; j++)
```

II Replace Line 7 with

```
int index = (int) (Math.random() * cards.size());
```

III Replace Line 8 with

```
temp.add(cards.remove(index));
```

(A) I only
(B) II only
(C) III only
(D) I and III only
(E) I, II, and III

END OF SECTION I

COMPUTER SCIENCE
SECTION II

Time—1 hour and 30 minutes
Number of questions—4
Percent of total grade—50

Directions: SHOW ALL YOUR WORK. REMEMBER THAT
PROGRAM SEGMENTS ARE TO BE WRITTEN IN Java.

Write your answers in <u>pencil only</u> in the booklet provided.

Notes:

- Assume that the classes in the Quick Reference have been imported where needed.

- Unless otherwise stated, assume that parameters in method calls are not `null` and that methods are called only when their preconditions are satisfied.

- In writing solutions for each question, you may use any of the accessible methods that are listed in classes defined in that question. Writing significant amounts of code that can be replaced by a call to one of these methods may not receive full credit.

---

1. Consider a system for processing names and addresses from a mailing list. A `Recipients` class will be used as part of this system. The lines in the mailing list are stored in an `ArrayList<String>`, a private instance variable in the `Recipients` class. The blank line that separates recipients in the mailing list is stored as the empty string in this list, and the final element in the list is an empty string.
A portion of the mailing list is shown below, with the corresponding part of the `ArrayList`.

```
Mr. J. Adams
6 Rose St.
Ithaca, NY 14850

Jack S. Smith
12 Posy Way
Suite 201
Glendale, CA 91203

Ms. M.K. Delgado
2 River Dr.
New York, NY 10013
```

    ...

GO ON TO THE NEXT PAGE.

	0	1	2	3	4
	"Mr. J. Adams"	"6 Rose St."	"Ithaca, NY 14850"	""	"Jack S. Smith"

	5	6	7	8	9
	"12 Posy Way"	"Suite #201"	"Glendale, CA 91023"	""	"Ms. M.K. Delgado"

	10	11	12	
	"2 River Dr."	"New York, NY 10013"	""	...

The Recipients class that processes this data is shown below.

```
public class Recipients
{
    /** The list of lines in the mailing list */
    private List<String> lines;

    /** Constructor. Fill lines with mailing list data.
     *  Postcondition:
     *    - Each element in lines is one line of the mailing list.
     *    - Lines appear in the list in the same order
     *      that they appear in the mailing list.
     *    - Blank line separators in the mailing list are stored
     *      as empty strings.
     */
    public Recipients()
    { /* implementation not shown */ }

    /** Postcondition: Returns the city contained in the cityZip
     *                 string of an address.
     *  @param  cityZip contains the city, state, and zipcode
     *  line of an address
     *  @return the city substring contained in cityZip
     */
    public String extractCity(String cityZip)
    { /* to be implemented in part (a) */ }

    /** Precondition:  The recipient name is the first line of each
     *                 label on the mailing list.
     *  Postcondition: Prints a list of recipient names to console,
     *                 one per line.
     */
    public void printNames()
    { /* to be implemented in part (b) */ }
```

```
/** Postcondition: Returns the address of the recipient with
 *                 the specified name.
 * @param name a name in the lines ArrayList
 * @return the address of the recipient with the given name
 */
public String getAddress(String name)
{/* to be implemented in part (c) */}

//Other methods are not shown.
}
```

(a) Write the `extractCity` method of the `Recipients` class. In the `cityZip` parameter the city is followed by a comma, then one blank space, then two capital letters for a state abbreviation, then a space and 5-digit zip code. For example, if `cityZip` is `"Ithaca, NY 14850"`, the method call `extractCity(cityZip)` should return `"Ithaca"`.

Information repeated from the beginning of the question

`public class Recipients`

```
private List<String> lines
public Recipients()
public String extractCity(String cityZip)
public void printNames()
public String getAddress(String name)
```

Complete method `extractCity` below.

```
/** Postcondition: Returns the city contained in the cityZip
 *                 string of an address.
 * @param  cityZip contains the city, state, and zipcode
 * line of an address
 * @return the city substring contained in cityZip
 */
public String extractCity(String cityZip)
```

(b) Write the `printNames` method of the `Recipients` class. Method `printNames` prints the names of all recipients to the console, one per line. For the sample part of the mailing list shown at the beginning of the question, the output for `printNames` would be:

```
Mr. J. Adams
Jack S. Smith
Ms. M.K. Delgado
```

Complete method printNames below.

```
/** Precondition:  The recipient name is the first line of each
 *                 label on the mailing list.
 * Postcondition: Prints a list of recipient names to console,
 *                 one per line.
 */
public void printNames()
```

(c) Write the getAddress method of the Recipients class. This method should return a string that contains only the address of the corresponding name parameter. For example, if name is "Jack S. Smith", a string containing the three subsequent lines of his address should be returned. This string should contain line breaks in appropriate places, including after the last line of the address. This ensures that the address will have the proper address format when printed by a client class.

Complete method getAddress below.

```
/** Postcondition: Returns the address of the recipient with
 *                 the specified name.
 * @param name a name in the lines ArrayList
 * @return the address of the recipient with the given name
 */
public String getAddress(String name)
```

2. A WordSet, whose partial implementation is shown in the class declaration below, stores a set of String objects in no particular order and contains no duplicates. Each word is a sequence of capital letters only.

```java
public class WordSet
{
    /** Constructor initializes set to empty. */
    public WordSet()
    { /* implementation not shown */ }

    /** @return the number of words in set */
    public int size()
    { /* implementation not shown */ }

    /** Adds word to set (no duplicates).
     *  @param word the word to be added
     */
    public void insert(String word)
    { /* implementation not shown */ }

    /** Removes word from set if present, else does nothing.
     *  @param word the word to be removed
     */
    public void remove(String word)
    { /* implementation not shown */ }

    /** Returns kth word in alphabetical order, where 1 <= k <= size().
     *  @param k position of word to be returned
     *  @return the kth word
     */
    public String findkth(int k)
    { /* implementation not shown */ }

    /** @return true if set contains word, false otherwise */
    public boolean contains(String word)
    { /* implementation not shown */ }

    //Other instance variables, constructors, and methods are not shown.
}
```

GO ON TO THE NEXT PAGE.

The findkth method returns the *k*th word in alphabetical order in the set, even though the implementation of WordSet may not be sorted. The number *k* ranges from 1 (corresponding to first in alphabetical order) to *N*, where *N* is the number of words in the set. For example, if WordSet s stores the words {"GRAPE", "PEAR", "FIG", "APPLE"}, here are the values when s.findkth(k) is called.

k	values of s.findkth(k)
1	APPLE
2	FIG
3	GRAPE
4	PEAR

(a) Write a client method countA that returns the number of words in WordSet s that begin with the letter "A." In writing countA, you may call any of the methods of the WordSet class. Assume that the methods work as specified.

Complete method countA below.

```
/** @param s the current WordSet
 *  @return the number of words in s that begin with "A"
 */
public static int countA(WordSet s)
```

(b) Write a client method removeA that removes all words that begin with "A." If there are no such words in s, then removeA does nothing. In writing removeA, you may call method countA specified in part (a). Assume that countA works as specified, regardless of what you wrote in part (a).

```
Information repeated from the beginning of the question

public class WordSet

public WordSet()
public int size()
public void insert(String word)
public void remove(String word)
public String findkth(int k)
public boolean contains(String word)
```

Complete method removeA below:

```
/** @param s the current WordSet
 *  Postcondition: WordSet s contains no words that begin with
 *                 "A", but is otherwise unchanged.
 */
public static void removeA(WordSet s)
```

GO ON TO THE NEXT PAGE.

(c) Write a client method `commonElements` that returns the `WordSet` containing just those elements occurring in both of its `WordSet` parameters.

For example, if `s1` is `{"BE", "NOT", "AFRAID"}` and `s2` is `{"TO", "BE", "OR", "NOT"}`, then `commonElements(s1, s2)` should return the `WordSet` `{"BE", "NOT"}`. (If you are familiar with mathematical set theory, `commonElements` returns the intersection of s1 and s2.)

Complete method `commonElements` below.

```
/** @param s1 the first given set
 *  @param s2 the second given set
 *  @return the WordSet containing only the elements that occur
 *          in both s1 and s2
 */
public static WordSet commonElements(WordSet s1, WordSet s2)
```

3. A puzzle-solving competition is held in a large hall with a two-dimensional arrangement of contestants. Each square below represents one contestant.

Since contestants may be moved around during the competition, each contestant keeps track of his or her location, which is the row number and column number. A `Location` object is represented by the class below.

GO ON TO THE NEXT PAGE.

```
public class Location
{
    private int rowNumber;
    private int colNumber;

    /** Create a new Location.
     *  @param row the row number
     *  @param col the column number  */
    public Location (int row, int col)
    {
        rowNumber = row;
        colNumber = col;
    }

    /** @return the row number of this Location */
    public int getRowNumber()
    { return rowNumber; }

    /** @return the column number of this Location */
    public int getColNumber()
    { return colNumber; }

    public String toString()
    { /* implementation not shown */}
}
```

A contestant in the contest can be represented by a Contestant class, whose partial implementation is shown below.

```
public class Contestant
{
    private String name;
    private int score;
    private Location loc;

    /** @return the name of this contestant */
    public String getName()
    { return name; }

    /** @return the score of this contestant */
    public int getScore()
    { return score; }

    /** @return the location of this contestant */
    public Location getLocation()
    { return loc; }

    /** Changes the location of this contestant to a new row
     *  and column.
     *  @param newRow the new row
     *  @param newCol the new column  */
    public void updateLocation(int newRow, int newCol)
    { /* to be implemented in part (a) */ }

    //Constructor and other methods are not shown.
}
```

GO ON TO THE NEXT PAGE.

(a) Write the `Contestant` method `updateLocation`, which changes the contestant's location to have the new row and column numbers.

Complete method `updateLocation` below.

```
/** Changes the location of this contestant to a new row
 *  and column.
 *  @param newRow the new row
 *  @param newCol the new column
 */
public void updateLocation(int newRow, int newCol)
```

In parts (b) and (c) you will write two methods of a `ContestOrganizer` class, whose partial implementation is shown below. A contest organizer keeps track of contestants in a two-dimensional array.

```
public class ContestOrganizer
{
    /** the number of rows of contestants */
    public static final int NUM_ROWS = < some integer >;

    /** the number of columns of contestants */
    public static final int CONTESTANTS_PER_ROW = < some integer >;

    /** The two-dimensional array of contestants */
    private Contestant[][] contestants;

    /** Sorts arr in increasing order by score.
     *  Postcondition:
     *     - arr sorted in increasing order by score.
     *     - Location of each contestant correctly updated such that
     *       column number matches contestant's position in arr.
     *  @param arr the array to be sorted
     */
    private void sort(Contestant[] arr)
    { /* implementation not shown */ }

    /** Sorts each row of contestants into increasing order by score.
     *  Postcondition: Contestant with highest score in row[k] is
     *                 in the rightmost column of row[k], 0<=k<NUM_ROWS.
     */
    public void sortAllRows()
    { /* to be implemented in part(b) */ }

    /** Returns name of contestant with highest score.
     *  Precondition:
     *     - Contestants have not been sorted by score.
     *     - Top score is unique.
     *     - Only one contestant has the highest score.
     *  @return name of contestant with highest score
     */
    public String findWinnerName()
    { /* to be implemented in part(c) */ }
}
```

GO ON TO THE NEXT PAGE.

(b) Write the `ContestOrganizer` method `sortAllRows`. This method should sort the contestants by score in each row, from lowest to highest.

Example: Suppose contestants are as shown below:

	0	1	2
0	John 160 (0,0)	Mary 185 (0,1)	Jay 22 (0,2)
1	Harry 190 (1,0)	Ted 100 (1,1)	Joan 88 (1,2)

Here is what contestants will be after a call to `sortAllRows`:

	0	1	2
0	Jay 22 (0,0)	John 160 (0,1)	Mary 185 (0,2)
1	Joan 88 (1,0)	Ted 100 (1,1)	Harry 190 (1,2)

In writing `sortAllRows`, your method *must* use the `ContestantOrganizer` method `sort`. You may assume that `sort` works as specified.

Complete method `sortAllRows` below.

```
/** Sorts each row of contestants into increasing order by score.
 *  Postcondition: Contestant with highest score in row[k] is
 *                 in the rightmost column of row[k], 0<=k<NUM_ROWS.
 */
public void sortAllRows()
```

(c) Write the `Contestant` method `findWinnerName`, which returns the name of the contestant with the highest score. For example, if the contestants are as shown above, a call to `findWinnerName` should return `"Harry"`.

When writing `findWinnerName`, you should assume that the contestants have not yet been sorted by score, and that there is only one contestant with the highest score. In writing your solution, you *must* use method `sortAllRows`. You may assume that `sortAllRows` works as specified, regardless of what you wrote in part (b).

Complete method `findWinnerName` below.

```
/** Returns name of contestant with highest score.
 *  Precondition:
 *    - Contestants have not been sorted by score.
 *    - Top score is unique.
 *    - Only one contestant has the highest score.
 *  @return name of contestant with highest score
 */
public String findWinnerName()
```

GO ON TO THE NEXT PAGE.

4. Consider the hierarchy of classes shown for a small part of a bird sanctuary.

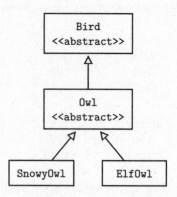

Notice that an `Owl` *is-a* `Bird`, a `SnowyOwl` *is-a* `Owl`, and an `ElfOwl` *is-a* `Owl`. The class `Bird` is specified as an abstract class as shown in the following implementation. Each `Bird` has a name and a noise that are specified when it is constructed.

```
public abstract class Bird
{
    private String name;
    private String noise;

    /** Constructor for objects of class Bird */
    public Bird(String birdName, String birdNoise)
    {
        name = birdName;
        noise = birdNoise;
    }

    public String getName()
    { return name; }

    public String getNoise()
    { return noise; }

    public abstract String getFood();
}
```

An `Owl` is a `Bird` whose noise is `"hoot"`. The food it eats depends on the type of `Owl`, which means that `getFood` cannot be implemented in the `Owl` class. Here is the implementation for the `Owl` class.

```
public abstract class Owl extends Bird
{
    //Constructor
    public Owl(String owlName)
    { super(owlName, "hoot"); }
}
```

GO ON TO THE NEXT PAGE.

(a) A SnowyOwl is an Owl whose name is always "Snowy owl". A SnowyOwl will randomly eat a hare, a lemming, or a small bird (depending on what's available!), where each type of food is equally likely. The SnowyOwl class should use a random number to determine which food the SnowyOwl will eat. Assuming that the Owl class has been correctly defined, and given the class hierarchy shown previously, write a complete declaration of the class SnowyOwl, including implementation of its constructor and method(s).

(b) Consider the following partial declaration of class BirdSanctuary.

```
public class BirdSanctuary
{
    /** The list of birds */
    private Bird[] birdList;

    /** Precondition:  Each Bird in birdList has a getFood
     *                 method implemented for it.
     *  Postcondition: For each Bird in the birdList array, its name
     *     followed by the result of a call to its getFood
     *     method has been printed, one line per Bird.
     */
    public void allEat()
    { /* to be implemented in this part */ }.

    //The constructor and other methods are not shown.
}
```

Write the BirdSanctuary method allEat. For each Bird in BirdSanctuary, allEat prints a line with the name of the Bird followed by the result of a call to its getFood method, one line per Bird.

Complete method allEat below.

```
/** Precondition:  Each Bird in birdList has a getFood
 *                 method implemented for it.
 *  Postcondition: For each Bird in the birdList array, its name
 *     followed by the result of a call to its getFood
 *     method has been printed, one line per Bird.
 */
public void allEat()
```

END OF EXAMINATION

ANSWER KEY (Section I)

1. C	15. B	29. B
2. C	16. C	30. A
3. D	17. D	31. C
4. C	18. C	32. A
5. C	19. E	33. E
6. E	20. A	34. C
7. A	21. B	35. E
8. D	22. A	36. A
9. B	23. D	37. D
10. E	24. C	38. C
11. C	25. B	39. A
12. A	26. E	40. E
13. B	27. C	
14. C	28. D	

ANSWERS EXPLAINED

Section I

1. **(C)** Testing a program thoroughly does not prove that a program is correct. For a large program, it is generally impossible to test every possible set of input data.

2. **(C)** The private instance variable `hourlyWage` must be incremented by `amt`. Eliminate choice E, which doesn't *increment* `hourlyWage`; it simply *replaces* it by `amt`. Choice D is wrong because you can't use a method call as the left-hand side of an assignment. Choices A and B are wrong because the `incrementWage` method is void and should not return a value.

3. **(D)** The value of the boolean instance variable `isUnionMember` must be changed to the opposite of what it currently is. Segments I and II both achieve this. Note that `!true` has a value of `false` and `!false` a value of `true`. Segment III fails to do what's required if the current value of `isUnionMember` is `false`.

4. **(C)** `computePay` is a client method and, therefore, cannot access the private variables of the class. This eliminates choices A and D. The method `getHourlyWage()` must be accessed with the dot member construct; thus, choice B is wrong, and choice C is correct. Choice E is way off base—hours is not part of the `Worker` class, so `w.hours` is meaningless.

5. **(C)** If `s.length() < 4` for all strings in `wordList`, then `SHORT WORD` will be printed on each pass through the `for` loop. Since there are `wordList.size()` passes through the loop, the maximum number of times that `SHORT WORD` can be printed is `wordList.size()`.

6. **(E)**

$$\text{mystery}(4) = 3 * \text{mystery}(3)$$
$$= 3 * 3 * \text{mystery}(2)$$
$$= 3 * 3 * 3 * \text{mystery}(1)$$
$$= 3 * 3 * 3 * 3$$
$$= 81$$

7. **(A)** The declaration of the `colors` array makes the following assignments: `colors[0] = "red"`, `colors[1] = "green"`, and `colors[2] = "black"`. The loop in segment I adds these values to `colorList` in the correct order. Segment II fails because `colors` is an array and therefore can't use the get method. The code also confuses the lists. Segment III, in its first pass through the loop, attempts to add `colors[2]` to index position 2 of `colorList`. This will cause an `IndexOutOfBoundsException` to be thrown, since index positions 0 and 1 do not yet exist!

8. **(D)** Mergesort repeatedly splits an array of *n* elements in half until there are *n* arrays containing one element each. Now adjacent arrays are successively merged until there is a single merged, sorted array. A binary search repeatedly splits an array into two, narrowing the region that may contain the key. Insertion sort, however, does no array splitting. It takes elements one at a time and finds their insertion point in the sorted piece of the array. Elements are shifted to allow correct insertion of each element. Even though this algorithm maintains the array in two parts—a sorted part and yet-to-be-sorted part—this is not a divide-and-conquer approach.

9. **(B)** A static variable is shared by all instances of the class. "Static" means that there will be just one memory slot allocated, no matter how many `Insects` are constructed. All instances of `Insect` access the same information stored in that slot. When an `Insect` is created, it will get tagged with the current value of `nextAvailableID` for that memory slot, which will then be incremented for the next `Insect` created. All of the other variables—`age`, `idNum`, `position`, `direction`—are specific to one instance of `Insect` and should therefore be private instance variables in the class.

10. **(E)** A new `Address` object must be created, to be used as the `Address` parameter in the `Customer` constructor. To do this correctly requires the keyword `new` preceding the `Address` constructor. Segment II omits `new` and does not use the `Address` constructor correctly. (In fact, it inserts a new `String` object in the `Address` slot of the `Customer` constructor.)

11. **(C)** The algorithm used in method `locate` is a sequential search, which may have to examine all the objects to find the matching one. A binary search, which repeatedly discards a chunk of the array that does not contain the key, is more efficient. However, it can only be used if the values being examined—in this case customer ID numbers—are sorted. Note that it doesn't help to have the array sorted by name or phone number since the algorithm doesn't look at these values.

12. **(A)** The values of `k` are consecutively 4, 3, 2, and 1. The values of `randIndex` are consecutively 3, 2, 0, and 1. Thus, the sequence of swaps and corresponding states of `arr` will be:

```
swap arr[4] and arr[3]          1 2 3 5 4
swap arr[3] and arr[2]          1 2 5 3 4
swap arr[2] and arr[0]          5 2 1 3 4
swap arr[1] and arr[1]          5 2 1 3 4
```

13. **(B)** The `remove` method of `ArrayList` removes the indicated element, shifts the remaining elements down one slot (i.e., it does not leave gaps in the list), and adjusts the size of the list. Consider the list in choice B. The index values are shown:

```
The cat cat sat on the mat mat
 0   1   2   3   4  5   6   7
```

After the first occurrence of cat has been removed:

```
The cat sat on the mat mat
 0   1   2  3   4   5   6
```

The value of `i`, which was 1 when `cat` was removed, has now been incremented to 2 in the `for` loop. This means that the word to be considered next is `sat`. The second occurrence of `cat` has been missed. Thus, the given code will fail whenever occurrences of the word to be removed are consecutive. You fix it by not allowing the index to increment when a removal occurs:

```
int i = 0;
while (i < wordList.size())
{
    if ((wordList.get(i)).equals(word))
        wordList.remove(i);
    else
        i++;
}
```

14. **(C)** You cannot use a for-each loop to replace elements, only to access (as in segment I) or modify using a mutator method (as in segment II). Note that segment III will compile and execute, but won't replace the clocks in `allClocks` as intended.

15. **(B)** When `r` is 0, `c` goes from 0 to 0, and just one element, `mat[0][0]`, will be printed. When `r` is 1, `c` goes from 0 to 1, and two elements, `mat[1][0]` and `mat[1][1]`, will be printed, and so on. When `r` is 3, all four elements of row 3 will be printed.

16. **(C)** To return the number of elements in the set for Method One requires no more than returning the number of elements in the array. For Method Two, however, the number of cells that contain true must be counted, which requires a test for each of the MAX values. Note that searching for a target value in the set is more efficient for Method Two. For example, to test whether 2 is in the set, simply check if `a[2] == true`. In Method One, a sequential search must be done, which is less efficient. To print all the elements in Method One, simply loop over the known number of elements and print. Method Two is less efficient because the whole array must be examined: Each cell must be tested for true before printing.

17. **(D)** An `ArithmeticException` will be thrown at run time. Note that if *N* were of type `double`, no exception would be thrown. The variable `sum` would be assigned the value `Infinity`, and the error would only be detected in the output.

18. **(C)** In general, an interface provides method declarations only. No implementations! The methods are automatically `public` and `abstract`, so there is no need to specify this explicitly. Note, however, that in Java 8 *default* methods that have implementations *in the interface* are allowed, but only if the `default` keyword is used at the beginning of the method signature. Default methods will not be tested on the AP exam.

19. **(E)** The first value of `pos` is 2, the index of the first occurrence of `"car"` in `"a carrot and car"`. Then `s` gets assigned `"carrot and car"` and `pos` is now 0. Since `pos` is not advanced, it is stuck with a value of 0 and the method has an infinite loop. Notice that you can fix this problem by changing `s=s.substring(pos);` to `s=s.substring(pos+1);`.

20. **(A)** The correct diagram uses two up arrows to show that a `Car` *is-a* `Vehicle` and a `Truck` *is-a* `Vehicle` (inheritance relationship). The two down arrows indicate that a `Car` *has-a* `AirBag` and a `Truck` *has-a* `AirBag` (composition relationship). In each of the incorrect choices, at least one of the relationships does not make sense. For example, in choice B a `Vehicle` *has-a* `Truck`, and in choice E an `AirBag` *is-a* `Car`.

21. **(B)** The postcondition should be a true assertion about the major action of the segment. The segment overwrites the elements of array `a` with the nonnegative elements of `a`. Then `n` is adjusted so that now the array `a[0]...a[n-1]` contains just nonnegative integers. Note that even though choice E is a correct assertion about the program segment, it's not a good postcondition because it doesn't describe the main modification to array `a` (namely all negative integers have been removed).

22. **(A)** Note the order of precedence for the expressions involved: (1) parentheses, (2) `!`, (3) `<`, (4) `==`, (5) `&&`, (6) `||`. This means that `a < c`, `a < b`, and `!(a == b)` will all be evaluated before `||` and `&&` are considered. The given expression then boils down to `value1 || (value2 && value3)`, since `&&` has higher precedence than `||`. Notice that if `value1` is true, the whole expression is true since `(true || any)` evaluates to true. Thus, `a < c` will guarantee that the expression evaluates to true. None of the other conditions will guarantee an outcome of true. For example, suppose `a < b` (choice B). If `a == c`, then the whole expression will be false because you get `F || F`.

23. **(D)** Test data should always include a value from each range in addition to all boundary values. The given program should also handle the cases in which weights over 20 pounds or any negative weights are entered. Note that choice E contains redundant data. There is no new information to be gained in testing two weights from the same range—both 3 and 4 pounds, for example.

24. **(C)** The `max` methods shown are overloaded methods (same name but different parameter types). In the given statement, `matrix[2]` and `matrix[3]` refer to row 2 and row 3 of the matrix, respectively, each of which is an array of `int`. `max(matrix[2])` is the largest element in row 2, namely 7, and `max(matrix[3])` is the largest element in row 3, namely 4. The given statement is therefore equivalent to `max(7,4)`, which will return 7.

25. **(B)** Segment II correctly checks that the part descriptions match and keeps track of the current part with minimum price. If this is not done, the part whose number must be returned will be lost. Segment I is incorrect because it doesn't check that `partDescription` matches the description of the current part being examined in the array. Thus, it simply finds the `AutoPart` with the lowest price, which is not what was required. Segment III incorrectly returns the part number of the first part it finds with a matching description.

26. **(E)** Statement I is fine: The parameters are `String` objects and can be compared. Statement II will throw a `ClassCastException` because an `AutoPart` cannot be cast to a `String`. Statement III will fail because p1 and p2 are not `String` objects and min applies to strings. Also, the `AutoPart` class as currently written does not have a `compareTo` method, so `AutoPart` objects cannot be compared.

27. **(C)** Ordering of strings involves a character-by-character comparison starting with the leftmost character of each string. Thus, strA precedes strB (since "A" precedes "a") or `strA.compareTo(strB) < 0`. This eliminates choices B and D. Eliminate choices A and E since strB precedes strC (because "C" precedes "c") and therefore `strB.compareTo(strC) < 0`. Note that `string1.compareTo(string2) == 0` if and only if string1 and string2 are equal strings.

28. **(D)** Suppose `fullName` is Dr. John Roufaiel. In segment I the expression `fullName.indexOf(BLANK)` returns 3. Then temp gets assigned the value of `fullName.substring(4)`, which is John Roufaiel. Next k gets assigned the value `temp.indexOf(BLANK)`, namely 4, and firstName gets assigned `temp.substring(0, 4)`, which is all the characters from 0 to 3 inclusive, namely John. Note that segment II works the same way, except firstName gets assigned John Roufaiel and then reassigned John. This is not good style, since a variable name should document its contents as precisely as possible. Still, the code works. Segment III fails because indexOf returns the *first* occurrence of its `String` parameter. Thus, firstBlank and secondBlank will both contain the same value, 3.

29. **(B)** ThreeDigitCode is a subclass of ThreeDigitInteger and therefore inherits all the public methods of ThreeDigitInteger except constructors. All of the statements other than B are false. For choice A, ThreeDigitInteger is the superclass and therefore cannot inherit from its subclass. For choice C, constructors are never inherited (see p. 135). For choice D, a subclass can access private variables of the superclass through accessor methods only (see p. 135). For choice E, a superclass cannot access any additional instance variables of its subclass.

30. **(A)** Implementation II is wrong because the constructor has no boolean validity parameter. Implementation III is wrong because a subclass cannot access a private instance variable of its superclass.

31. **(C)** A compile-time error will occur for both tests I and II because at compile time the types of code and num are both ThreeDigitInteger, and the class ThreeDigitInteger does not have an isValid method. To avoid this error, the code object must be cast to ThreeDigitCode, its actual type. Note that if you try to cast num to ThreeDigitCode, you'll get a run-time error (`ClassCastException`) because num is not an instance of ThreeDigitCode.

32. **(A)** The *is-a* relationship must work from right-to-left: a Parrot *is-a* Bird, a Parakeet *is-a* Bird, and an Owl *is-a* Bird. All are correct. This relationship fails in declarations II and III: a Parrot is not necessarily a Parakeet, a Bird is not necessarily an Owl, and a Bird is not necessarily a Parakeet.

33. **(E)** All three segments traverse the array, accessing one element at a time, and appending it to the end of the `ArrayList`. In segment II, the first parameter of the add method is the position in list where the next string s will be added. Since `list.size()` increases by one after each insertion, this index is correctly updated in each pass through the for-each loop.

34. **(C)** Suppose you want random integers from 2 to 8, that is, `low = 2` and `high = 8`. This is 7 possible integers, so you need

    ```
    (int) (Math.random() * 7)
    ```

    which produces 0, 1, 2, ..., or 6. Therefore the quantity

    ```
    (int) (Math.random() * 7) + 2
    ```

    produces 2, 3, 4, ..., or 8. The only expression that yields the right answer with these values is

    ```
    (int) (Math.random() * (high - low + 1)) + low;
    ```

35. **(E)** Here is a "box diagram" for `mergeSort(0,3)`. The boldface numbers 1–6 show the order in which the `mergeSort` calls are made.

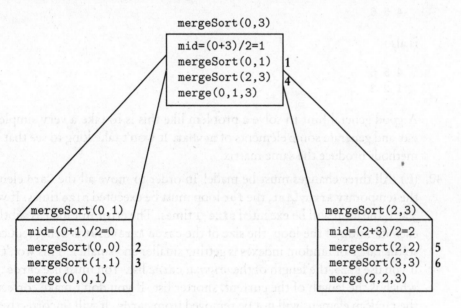

    The `mergeSort` calls in which `first == last` are base case calls, which means that there will be no further method calls.

36. **(A)** Since the records are not sorted, the quickest way to find a given name is to start at the beginning of the list and sequentially search for that name. Choices C, D, and E will all work, but it's inefficient to sort and then search because all sorting algorithms take longer than simply inspecting each element. Choice B won't work: A binary search can only be used for a sorted list.

37. **(D)** Statement I is false: An abstract class may have *no* abstract methods. The point about an abstract class is that it represents an abstract concept, and no instance of it will ever be created. The only instances that will be created are instances of its subclasses. Statement II *must* be true, since you are told the abstract class is actually used in the program. Statement III is true because an abstract class cannot be instantiated.

38. **(C)** The `draw` method is polymorphic, which means that it is a superclass method that is overridden in at least one of its subclasses. During run time, there is dynamic binding between the calling object and the method, that is, the actual instance is bound to its particular overridden method. In the `drawLetters` method, the correct version of `draw` is called during each iteration of the `for` loop, and a banner with the appropriate letters is drawn.

39. **(A)** method1 creates a mirror image of its parameter mat across a horizontal line placed under mat. If mat is the matrix

```
1 2 3
4 5 6
```

then the mirror image created below it is

```
4 5 6
1 2 3
```

method2 also creates a mirror image, this time with the mirror placed *above* its parameter mat. Note that the reflection across a horizontal line above

```
1 2 3
4 5 6
```

is also

```
4 5 6
1 2 3
```

A good general hint to solve a problem like this is to take a very simple matrix mat and generate some elements of newMat. It won't take long to see that the two methods produce the same matrix.

40. **(E)** All three changes must be made! In order to move all the Card elements to the temporary ArrayList, the for loop must be executed size times. If you start j at 1, the loop will be executed size-1 times. The error in Line 7 is subtle. With each iteration of the loop, the size of the cards ArrayList is being reduced by 1, so the range of random indexes is getting smaller and smaller. This won't happen if you use size, the length of the *original* cards list. You must use cards.size(), which is the length of the current, shorter list. If you don't make correction III, the random element will not be removed from cards. It will (incorrectly) remain there while a copy of it will be added to temp. If this error isn't corrected, execution of the method is likely to cause the temp list to hold more than one copy of a given card!

Section II

1. (a)
```
public String extractCity(String cityZip)
{
    int commaPos = cityZip.indexOf(",");
    return cityZip.substring(0, commaPos);
}
```

(b)
```
public void printNames()
{
    System.out.println(lines.get(0));
    int index = 1;
    while(index < lines.size() - 1)
    {
        if (lines.get(index).equals(""))
            System.out.println(lines.get(index + 1));
        index++;
    }
}
```

(c)
```
public String getAddress(String name)
{
    int index = 0;
    while(index < lines.size() && !name.equals(lines.get(index)))
        index++;
    index++;
    String s = "";
    while (!(lines.get(index).equals("")))
    {
        s += lines.get(index) + "\n";
        index++;
    }
    return s;
}
```

NOTE

- In part (b), the empty string signals that the next element in the list will be a name. This is why you should be careful that you don't miss the first name in the list, which is at index 0. Notice, too, that you can avoid the empty string at the end of the list by having

  ```
  index < lines.size() - 1
  ```

  as the test in the while loop. If you don't do this, the final

  ```
  lines.get(index + 1)
  ```

  will cause an IndexOutOfBoundsException.
- Part (c) first finds the name that matches the parameter, and then builds a string out of the next two or three lines that comprise the address. Again, the empty string signals that the end of the address has been reached.
- The escape character string, "\n", inserts a line break into the string.

2. (a)
```
public static int countA(WordSet s)
{
    int count = 0;
    while (count < s.size() &&
            s.findkth(count + 1).substring(0, 1).equals("A"))
        count++;
    return count;
}
```

Alternatively,

```
public static int countA(WordSet s)
{
    boolean done = false;
    int count = 0;
    while (count < s.size() && !done)
    {
        String nextWord = s.findkth(count + 1);
        if (nextWord.substring(0,1).equals("A"))
            count++;
        else
            done = true;
    }
    return count;
}
```

(b)
```
public static void removeA(WordSet s)
{
    int numA = countA(s);
    for (int i = 1; i <= numA; i++)
        s.remove(s.findkth(1));
}
```

Alternatively,

```
public static void removeA(WordSet s)
{
    while (s.size() != 0 &&
            s.findkth(1).substring(0, 1).equals("A"))
        s.remove(s.findkth(1));
}
```

(c)
```
public static WordSet commonElements(WordSet s1, WordSet s2)
{
    WordSet temp = new WordSet();
    for (int i = 1; i <= s1.size(); i++)
    {
        String nextWord = s1.findkth(i);
        if (s2.contains(nextWord))
            temp.insert(nextWord);
    }
    return temp;
}
```

NOTE

- To test whether a word starts with "A", you must compare the first letter of word, that is, word.substring(0,1), with "A".
- In part (a), you must check that your solution works if s is empty. For the given algorithm, count < s.size() will fail and short circuit the test, which is desirable since s.findkth(1) will violate the precondition of findkth(k), namely that k cannot be greater than size().
- The parameter for s.findkth must be greater than 0. Hence the use of s.findkth(count+1) in part (a).
- For the first solution in part (b), you get a subtle intent error if your last step is s.remove(s.findkth(i)). Suppose that s is initially {"FLY", "ASK", "ANT"}. After the method call s.remove(s.findkth(1)), s will be {"FLY", "ASK"}. After the statement s.remove(s.findkth(2)), s will be {"ASK"}!! The point is that s is adjusted after each call to s.remove. The algorithm that works is this: If *N* is the number of words that start with "A", simply remove the first element in the list *N* times. Note that the alternative solution avoids the pitfall described by simply repeatedly removing the first element if it starts with 'A.' The alternative solution, however, has its own pitfall: The algorithm can fail if a test for s being empty isn't done for each iteration of the while loop.
- Part (c) could also be accomplished by going through each element in s2 and checking if it's included in s1.

3. (a)
```
public void updateLocation(int newRow, int newCol)
{
    loc = new Location(newRow, newCol);
}
```

(b)
```
public void sortAllRows()
{
    for(Contestant[] row: contestants)
        sort(row);
}
```

(c)
```
public String findWinnerName()
{
    sortAllRows();
    int max = contestants[0][0].getScore();
    String winner = contestants[0][0].getName();
    for(int k = 0; k < NUM_ROWS; k++)
    {
        Contestant c = contestants[k][CONTESTANTS_PER_ROW - 1];
        if (c.getScore() > max)
        {
            winner = c.getName();
            max = c.getScore();
        }
    }
    return winner;
}
```

NOTE

- In part (a), since the `Location` class does not contain mutator methods to set a new row and new column, you need to use the constructor of `Location` to set those new values.
- Part (b) uses the Java feature that a two-dimensional array is an array of arrays. Thus, each row, which is an array of `Contestant`, can be sorted using the helper method `sort`.
- Part (c) uses the fact that after you sort all the rows of contestants, the winning contestant will be in the last column of the matrix of contestants. When you go through the loop, searching for a score that's higher than the current max, be sure to store the name that goes with that score!

4. (a)
```java
public class SnowyOwl extends Owl
{
    //Constructor
    public SnowyOwl()
    { super ("Snowy owl"); }

    //Returns type of food for this SnowyOwl
    public String getFood()
    {
        int num = (int)(Math.random()*3);
        if (num == 0)
            return "hare";
        else if (num == 1)
            return "lemming";
        else
            return "small bird";
    }
}
```

   (b)
```java
public void allEat()
{
    for (Bird b: birdList)
        System.out.println(b.getName() + " " + b.getFood());
}
```

NOTE

- The `Owl` class inherits the abstract `getFood` method. Since the food type for an `Owl` depends on the type of `Owl`, the `Owl` class does not provide implementation code for `getFood`. This is the reason that the `Owl` class is an abstract class.
- In part (a), since `SnowyOwl` is a concrete (nonabstract) class, it must provide implementation code for `getFood`.
- In part (a), `super` must be used in the constructor because there is no direct access to the private instance variables of the `Bird` class.
- Note that the noise for `Owl` will always be "hoot". Thus, noise does not need to be provided as a parameter in the `SnowyOwl` constructor.

The statement `super(owlName, "hoot")` will use the superclass—namely `Bird`—constructor to automatically assign `"hoot"` as an `SnowyOwl`'s noise. Similarly, the `SnowyOwl` does not need any parameters in its constructor: using the superclass (`Owl`) constructor will automatically provide it with its name through the statement `super("Snowy owl")`.

- In part (b), polymorphism will determine which `getFood` method to print for the actual instance of each `Bird` in `birdList`.

Answer Sheet: Practice Exam Three

1. Ⓐ Ⓑ Ⓒ Ⓓ Ⓔ
2. Ⓐ Ⓑ Ⓒ Ⓓ Ⓔ
3. Ⓐ Ⓑ Ⓒ Ⓓ Ⓔ
4. Ⓐ Ⓑ Ⓒ Ⓓ Ⓔ
5. Ⓐ Ⓑ Ⓒ Ⓓ Ⓔ
6. Ⓐ Ⓑ Ⓒ Ⓓ Ⓔ
7. Ⓐ Ⓑ Ⓒ Ⓓ Ⓔ
8. Ⓐ Ⓑ Ⓒ Ⓓ Ⓔ
9. Ⓐ Ⓑ Ⓒ Ⓓ Ⓔ
10. Ⓐ Ⓑ Ⓒ Ⓓ Ⓔ
11. Ⓐ Ⓑ Ⓒ Ⓓ Ⓔ
12. Ⓐ Ⓑ Ⓒ Ⓓ Ⓔ
13. Ⓐ Ⓑ Ⓒ Ⓓ Ⓔ
14. Ⓐ Ⓑ Ⓒ Ⓓ Ⓔ

15. Ⓐ Ⓑ Ⓒ Ⓓ Ⓔ
16. Ⓐ Ⓑ Ⓒ Ⓓ Ⓔ
17. Ⓐ Ⓑ Ⓒ Ⓓ Ⓔ
18. Ⓐ Ⓑ Ⓒ Ⓓ Ⓔ
19. Ⓐ Ⓑ Ⓒ Ⓓ Ⓔ
20. Ⓐ Ⓑ Ⓒ Ⓓ Ⓔ
21. Ⓐ Ⓑ Ⓒ Ⓓ Ⓔ
22. Ⓐ Ⓑ Ⓒ Ⓓ Ⓔ
23. Ⓐ Ⓑ Ⓒ Ⓓ Ⓔ
24. Ⓐ Ⓑ Ⓒ Ⓓ Ⓔ
25. Ⓐ Ⓑ Ⓒ Ⓓ Ⓔ
26. Ⓐ Ⓑ Ⓒ Ⓓ Ⓔ
27. Ⓐ Ⓑ Ⓒ Ⓓ Ⓔ
28. Ⓐ Ⓑ Ⓒ Ⓓ Ⓔ

29. Ⓐ Ⓑ Ⓒ Ⓓ Ⓔ
30. Ⓐ Ⓑ Ⓒ Ⓓ Ⓔ
31. Ⓐ Ⓑ Ⓒ Ⓓ Ⓔ
32. Ⓐ Ⓑ Ⓒ Ⓓ Ⓔ
33. Ⓐ Ⓑ Ⓒ Ⓓ Ⓔ
34. Ⓐ Ⓑ Ⓒ Ⓓ Ⓔ
35. Ⓐ Ⓑ Ⓒ Ⓓ Ⓔ
36. Ⓐ Ⓑ Ⓒ Ⓓ Ⓔ
37. Ⓐ Ⓑ Ⓒ Ⓓ Ⓔ
38. Ⓐ Ⓑ Ⓒ Ⓓ Ⓔ
39. Ⓐ Ⓑ Ⓒ Ⓓ Ⓔ
40. Ⓐ Ⓑ Ⓒ Ⓓ Ⓔ

How to Calculate Your (Approximate) AP Computer Science Score

Multiple Choice

Number correct (out of 40) = _____ ⟸ Multiple-Choice Score

Free Response

Question 1 _____
(out of 9)

Question 2 _____
(out of 9)

Question 3 _____
(out of 9)

Question 4 _____
(out of 9)

Total _____ × 1.11 = _____ ⟸ Free-Response Score
(Do not round.)

Final Score

_____ + _____ = _____
Multiple-   Free-   Final Score
Choice   Response   (Round to nearest
Score   Score   whole number.)

Chart to Convert to AP Grade
Computer Science

Final Score Range	AP Grade[a]
62–80	5
47–61	4
37–46	3
29–36	2
0–28	1

[a]The score range corresponding to each grade varies from exam to exam and is approximate.

Practice Exam Three
COMPUTER SCIENCE
SECTION I

Time—1 hour and 30 minutes
Number of questions—40
Percent of total grade—50

Directions: Determine the answer to each of the following questions or incomplete statements, using the available space for any necessary scratchwork. Then decide which is the best of the choices given and fill in the corresponding oval on the answer sheet. Do not spend too much time on any one problem.

Notes:
- Assume that the classes in the Quick Reference have been imported where needed.
- Assume that variables and methods are declared within the context of an enclosing class.
- Assume that method calls that have no object or class name prefixed, and that are not shown within a complete class definition, appear within the context of an enclosing class.
- Assume that parameters in method calls are not `null` unless otherwise stated.

---

1. What output is produced by the following line of code?

```
System.out.println("\"This is\n very strange\"");
```

(A) \This is\n very strange\

(B) "This is very strange"

(C) This is
     very strange

(D) \"This is
     very strange\"

(E) "This is
     very strange"

2. A certain class, `SomeClass`, contains a method with the following header:

   ```
   public int getValue(int n)
   ```

   Suppose that methods with the following headers are now added to `SomeClass`:

   I `public int getValue()`

   II `public double getValue(int n)`

   III `public int getValue(double n)`

   Which of the above headers will cause an error?
   (A) None
   (B) I only
   (C) II only
   (D) III only
   (E) I and III only

3. Consider the following statement:

   ```
   int num = /* expression */;
   ```

   Which of the following replacements for `/* expression */` creates in `num` a random integer from 2 to 50, including 2 and 50?
   (A) `(int)(Math.random() * 50) - 2`
   (B) `(int)(Math.random() * 49) - 2`
   (C) `(int)(Math.random() * 49) + 2`
   (D) `(int)(Math.random() * 50) + 2`
   (E) `(int)(Math.random() * 48) + 2`

4. Consider the following code segment.

   ```
   int num = 0, score = 10;
   if (num != 0 && score / num > SOME_CONSTANT)
       statement1;
   else
       statement2;
   ```

   What is the result of executing this statement?
   (A) An `ArithmeticException` will be thrown.
   (B) A syntax error will occur.
   (C) *statement1*, but not *statement2*, will be executed.
   (D) *statement2*, but not *statement1*, will be executed.
   (E) Neither *statement1* nor *statement2* will be executed; control will pass to the first statement following the `if` statement.

5. The following shuffle algorithm is used to shuffle an array of int values, nums.

```
public void shuffle ()
{
    for (int k = nums.length - 1; k > 0; k--)
    {
        int randPos = (int) (Math.random() * (k + 1));
        int temp = nums[k];
        nums[k] = nums[randPos];
        nums[randPos] = temp;
    }
}
```

Suppose the initial state of nums is 8, 7, 6, 5, 4, and when the method is executed the values generated for randPos are 3, 2, 0, 0, in that order. What element will be contained in nums[2] after execution?

(A) 8
(B) 7
(C) 6
(D) 5
(E) 4

6. Consider the following instance variables and method assignValues in the same class:

```
private int numRows;
private int numCols;
private int[][] mat;

/** arr has numCols elements */
private void assignValues(int[] arr, int value)
{
    for (int k = 0; k < arr.length; k++)
        arr[k] = value;
}
```

Which of the following code segments will correctly assign mat to have the value 100 in each slot? You may assume that the instance variables have all been correctly initialized.

```
 I for (int row = 0; row < numRows; row++)
        assignValues(mat[row], 100);

 II for (int col = 0; col < numCols; col++)
        assignValues(mat[col], 100);

III for (int[] row: mat)
        for (int num: row)
            num = 100;
```

(A) I only
(B) II only
(C) III only
(D) I and II only
(E) I and III only

7. Consider the following inheritance hierarchy.

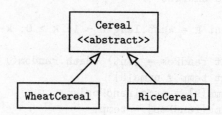

Which of the following declarations will *not* cause an error? You may assume that each of the classes above has a default constructor.

I   WheatCereal w = new Cereal();

II   Cereal c1 = new Cereal();

III   Cereal c2 = new RiceCereal();

(A) I only
(B) II only
(C) III only
(D) I and III only
(E) I, II, and III

Questions 8 and 9 refer to the following class definitions.

```
public interface Class1
{ void method1(); }

public class Class2 implements Class1
{
    public void method1()
    { /* implementation not shown */ }

    //Private instance variables and other methods are not shown.
}

public class Class3 extends Class2
{
    public void method2(Class3 other)
    { /* implementation not shown */ }

    //Private instance variables and other methods are not shown.
}
```

8. Assuming that both Class2 and Class3 have default constructors, which is (are) valid in a client class?

     I Class1 c1 = new Class2();

    II Class2 c2 = new Class3();

   III Class1 c3 = new Class3();

   (A) I only
   (B) II only
   (C) III only
   (D) I and II only
   (E) I, II, and III

9. Consider the following declarations in a client class.

```
     Class3 ob3 = new Class3();
     Class2 ob2 = new Class2();
```

   Which method calls would be legal?

     I ob3.method1();

    II ob2.method2(ob3);

   III ob3.method2(ob2);

   (A) I only
   (B) II only
   (C) III only
   (D) II and III only
   (E) I, II, and III

10. Refer to the following program segment.

```
for (int n = 50; n > 0; n = n / 2)
    System.out.println(n);
```

How many lines of output will this segment produce?
(A) 50
(B) 49
(C) 7
(D) 6
(E) 5

11. Let `list` be an `ArrayList<String>` containing only these elements:

```
"John", "Mary", "Harry", "Luis"
```

Which of the following statements will cause an error to occur?

```
 I list.set(2, "6");

 II list.add(4, "Pat");

III String s = list.get(4);
```

(A) I only
(B) II only
(C) III only
(D) II and III only
(E) I, II, and III

12. Consider the following static method.

```
public static int compute(int n)
{
    for (int i = 1; i < 4; i++)
        n *= n;
    return n;
}
```

Which of the following could replace the body of `compute`, so that the new version returns the identical result as the original for all n?
(A) return 4 * n;
(B) return 8 * n;
(C) return 64 * n;
(D) return (int) Math.pow(n, 4);
(E) return (int) Math.pow(n, 8);

13. Consider the following instance variable and method.

```
private int[] nums;

/** Precondition: nums contains int values in no particular order.
 */
public int getValue()
{
    for (int k = 0; k < nums.length; k++)
    {
        if (nums[k] % 2 != 0)
            return k;
    }
    return -1;
}
```

Suppose the following statement is executed:

```
int j = getValue();
```

If the value returned in j is a positive integer, which of the following best describes the contents of nums?

(A) The only odd int in nums is at position j.
(B) All values in positions 0 through j-1 are odd.
(C) All values in positions 0 through j-1 are even.
(D) All values in positions nums.length-1 down to j+1 are odd.
(E) All values in positions nums.length-1 down to j+1 are even.

14. Consider the following method.

```
public int mystery (int n)
{
    if (n == 0)
        return 0;
    else if (n % 2 == 1)
        return n;
    else
        return n + mystery(n - 1);
}
```

What will be returned by a call to mystery(6)?
(A) 6
(B) 11
(C) 12
(D) 27
(E) 30

15. Consider the following code segment.

```
int num1 = value1, num2 = value2, num3 = value3;
while (num1 > num2 || num1 > num3)
{
    /* body of loop */
}
```

You may assume that value1, value2, and value3 are int values. Which of the following is sufficient to guarantee that /* *body of loop* */ will never be executed?

(A) There is no statement in /* *body of loop* */ that leads to termination

(B) num1 < num2

(C) num1 < num3

(D) num1 > num2 && num1 > num3

(E) num1 < num2 && num1 < num3

16. Consider the following two classes.

```
public class Performer
{
    public void act()
    {
        System.out.print(" bow");
        perform();
    }

    public void perform()
    {
        System.out.print(" act");
    }
}

public class Singer extends Performer
{
    public void act()
    {
        System.out.print(" rise");
        super.act();
        System.out.print(" encore");
    }

    public void perform()
    {
        System.out.print(" aria");
    }
}
```

Suppose the following declaration appears in a class other than `Performer` or `Singer`:

```
Performer p = new Singer();
```

What is printed as a result of the call `p.act();`?
- (A) rise bow aria encore
- (B) rise bow act encore
- (C) rise bow act
- (D) bow act aria
- (E) bow aria encore

GO ON TO THE NEXT PAGE.

Use the program description below for Questions 17–19.

A car dealer needs a program that will maintain an inventory of cars on his lot. There are three types of cars: sedans, station wagons, and SUVs. The model, year, color, and price need to be recorded for each car, plus any additional features for the different types of cars. The program must allow the dealer to

- Add a new car to the lot.
- Remove a car from the lot.
- Correct any data that's been entered.
- Display information for any car.

17. The programmer decides to have these classes: `Car`, `Inventory`, `Sedan`, `SUV`, and `StationWagon`. Which statement is *true* about the relationships between these classes and their attributes?

> I There are no inheritance relationships between these classes.
> II The `Inventory` class *has-a* list of `Car` objects.
> III The `Sedan`, `StationWagon`, and `SUV` classes are independent of each other.

(A) I only
(B) II only
(C) III only
(D) I and II only
(E) II and III only

18. Suppose that the programmer decides to have a `Car` class and an `Inventory` class. The `Inventory` class will maintain a list of all the cars on the lot. Here are some of the methods in the program:

```
addCar          //adds a car to the lot
removeCar       //removes a car from the lot
displayCar      //displays all the features of a given car
setColor        //sets the color of a car to a given color
                //May be used to correct data
getPrice        //returns the price of a car
displayAllCars  //displays features for every car on the lot
```

In each of the following, a class and a method are given. Which is the *least* suitable choice of class to be responsible for the given method?
(A) `Car, setColor`
(B) `Car, removeCar`
(C) `Car, getPrice`
(D) `Car, displayCar`
(E) `Inventory, displayAllCars`

19. Suppose Car is a superclass and Sedan, StationWagon, and SUV are subclasses of Car. Which of the following is the most likely method of the Car class to be overridden by at least one of the subclasses (Sedan, StationWagon, or SUV)?
    (A) setColor(newColor)   //sets color of Car to newColor
    (B) getModel()   //returns model of Car
    (C) displayCar()   //displays all features of Car
    (D) setPrice(newPrice)   //sets price of Car to newPrice
    (E) getYear()   //returns year of Car

20. Consider the following segment of code.

    ```
    String word = "conflagration";
    int x = word.indexOf("flag");
    String s = word.substring(0, x);
    ```

    What will be the result of executing the above segment?
    (A) A syntax error will occur.
    (B) String s will be the empty string.
    (C) String s will contain "flag".
    (D) String s will contain "conf".
    (E) String s will contain "con".

21. Consider the following class declaration:

    ```
    public abstract class AClass
    {
        private int v1;
        private double v2;

        //methods of the class
            ...
    }
    ```

    Which is *true* about AClass?
    (A) Any program using this class will have an error: An abstract class cannot contain private instance variables.
    (B) AClass *must* have a constructor with two parameters in order to initialize v1 and v2.
    (C) At least one method of AClass must be abstract.
    (D) A program that uses AClass must have another class that is a subclass of AClass.
    (E) In a program that uses AClass, more than one instance of AClass can be created.

22. A class of 30 students rated their computer science teacher on a scale of 1 to 10 (1 means awful and 10 means outstanding). The responses array is a 30-element integer array of the student responses. An 11-element array `freq` will count the number of occurrences of each response. For example, `freq[6]` will count the number of students who responded 6. The quantity `freq[0]` will not be used.

Here is a program that counts the students' responses and outputs the results.

```
public class StudentEvaluations
{
    public static void main(String args[])
    {
        int[] responses = {6,6,7,8,10,1,5,4,6,7,
                           5,4,3,4,4,9,8,6,7,10,
                           6,7,8,8,9,6,7,8,9,2};
        int[] freq = new int[11];
        for (int i = 0; i < responses.length; i++)
            freq[responses[i]]++;
        //output results
        System.out.print("rating" + "   " + "frequency\n");
        for (int rating = 1; rating < freq.length; rating++)
            System.out.print(rating + "   " +
                freq[rating] + "\n");
    }
}
```

Suppose the last entry in the initializer list for the `responses` array was incorrectly typed as 12 instead of 2. What would be the result of running the program?
(A) A rating of 12 would be listed with a frequency of 1 in the output table.
(B) A rating of 1 would be listed with a frequency of 12 in the output table.
(C) An `ArrayIndexOutOfBoundsException` would be thrown.
(D) A `StringIndexOutOfBoundsException` would be thrown.
(E) A `NullPointerException` would be thrown.

Questions 23–25 are based on the three classes below:

```
public class Employee
{
    private String name;
    private int employeeNum;
    private double salary, taxWithheld;

    public Employee(String aName, int empNum, double aSalary,
        double aTax)
    { /* implementation not shown */ }

    /** @return pre-tax salary */
    public double getSalary()
    { return salary; }

    public String getName()
    { return name; }

    public int getEmployeeNum()
    { return employeeNum; }

    public double getTax()
    { return taxWithheld; }

    public double computePay()
    { return salary - taxWithheld; }
}

public class PartTimeEmployee extends Employee
{
    private double payFraction;

    public PartTimeEmployee(String aName, int empNum, double aSalary,
        double aTax, double aPayFraction)
    { /* implementation not shown */ }

    public double getPayFraction()
    { return payFraction; }

    public double computePay()
    { return getSalary() * payFraction - getTax();}
}

public class Consultant extends Employee
{
    private static final double BONUS = 5000;

    public Consultant(String aName, int empNum, double aSalary,
        double aTax)
    { /* implementation not shown */ }

    public double computePay()
    { /* implementation code */ }
}
```

23. The `computePay` method in the `Consultant` class redefines the `computePay` method of the `Employee` class to add a bonus to the salary after subtracting the tax withheld. Which represents correct /* *implementation code* */ of `computePay` for `Consultant`?

    I   `return super.computePay() + BONUS;`

    II   `super.computePay();`
         `return getSalary() + BONUS;`

    III   `return getSalary() - getTax() + BONUS;`

    (A) I only
    (B) II only
    (C) III only
    (D) I and III only
    (E) I and II only

24. Consider these valid declarations in a client program:

    ```
    Employee e = new Employee("Noreen Rizvi", 304, 65000, 10000);
    Employee p = new PartTimeEmployee("Rafael Frongillo", 287, 40000,
        7000, 0.8);
    Employee c = new Consultant("Dan Lepage", 694, 55000, 8500);
    ```

    Which of the following method calls will cause an error?
    (A) `double x = e.computePay();`
    (B) `double y = p.computePay();`
    (C) `String n = c.getName();`
    (D) `int num = p.getEmployeeNum();`
    (E) `double g = p.getPayFraction();`

GO ON TO THE NEXT PAGE.

25. Consider the `writePayInfo` method:

```
/** Writes Employee name and pay on one line. */
public static void writePayInfo(Employee e)
{ System.out.println(e.getName() + " " + e.computePay()); }
```

The following piece of code invokes this method:

```
Employee[] empList = new Employee[3];
empList[0] = new Employee("Lila Fontes", 1, 10000, 850);
empList[1] = new Consultant("Momo Liu", 2, 50000, 8000);
empList[2] = new PartTimeEmployee("Moses Wilks", 3, 25000, 3750,
    0.6);
for (Employee e : empList)
    writePayInfo(e);
```

What will happen when this code is executed?
   (A) A list of employees' names and corresponding pay will be written to the screen.
   (B) A `NullPointerException` will be thrown.
   (C) A `ClassCastException` will be thrown.
   (D) A compile-time error will occur, with the message that the `getName` method is not in the `Consultant` class.
   (E) A compile-time error will occur, with the message that an instance of an `Employee` object cannot be created.

26. Consider an array arr that is initialized with int values. The following code segment stores in count the number of positive values in arr.

```
int count = 0, index = 0;
while (index < arr.length)
{
    if (arr[index] > 0)
        count++;
    index++;
}
```

Which of the following is equivalent to the above segment?

```
I  int count = 0;
   for (int num : arr)
   {
       if (arr[num] > 0)
           count++;
   }

II int count = 0;
   for (int num : arr)
   {
       if (num > 0)
           count++;
   }

III int count = 0;
    for (int i = 0; i < arr.length; i++)
    {
        if (arr[i] > 0)
            count++;
    }
```

(A) I only
(B) II only
(C) III only
(D) II and III only
(E) I and III only

27. A square matrix is declared as

    ```
    int[][] mat = new int[SIZE][SIZE];
    ```

    where SIZE is an appropriate integer constant. Consider the following method:

    ```
    public static void mystery(int[][] mat, int value, int top, int left,
        int bottom, int right)
    {
        for (int i = left; i <= right; i++)
        {
            mat[top][i] = value;
            mat[bottom][i] = value;
        }
        for (int i = top + 1; i <= bottom - 1; i++)
        {
            mat[i][left] = value;
            mat[i][right] = value;
        }
    }
    ```

    Assuming that there are no out-of-range errors, which best describes what method mystery does?
    (A) Places value in corners of the rectangle with corners (top, left) and (bottom, right).
    (B) Places value in the diagonals of the square with corners (top, left) and (bottom, right).
    (C) Places value in each element of the rectangle with corners (top, left) and (bottom, right).
    (D) Places value in each element of the border of the rectangle with corners (top, left) and (bottom, right).
    (E) Places value in the topmost and bottommost rows of the rectangle with corners (top, left) and (bottom, right).

28. Which of the following statements about a class SomeClass that implements an interface is (are) true?

    I It is illegal to create an instance of SomeClass.

    II Any superclass of SomeClass must also implement that interface.

    III SomeClass must implement every method of the interface.

    (A) None
    (B) I only
    (C) II only
    (D) III only
    (E) II and III only

29. Assume that a `Book` class has a `compareTo` method where, if `b1` and `b2` are `Book` objects, `b1.compareTo(b2)` is a negative integer if `b1` is less than `b2`, a positive integer if `b1` is greater than `b2`, and 0 if `b1` equals `b2`. The following method is intended to return the index of the "smallest" book, namely the book that would appear first in a sorted list of `Book` objects.

```
/** Precondition:
 *    - books is initialized with Book objects.
 *    - books.length > 0.
 */
public static int findMin(Book[] books)
{
    int minPos = 0;
    for (int index = 1; index < books.length; index++)
    {
        if ( /* condition */ )
        {
            minPos = index;
        }
    }
    return minPos;
}
```

Which of the following should be used to replace /* *condition* */ so that `findMin` works as intended?

(A) `books[minPos] > books[index]`
(B) `books[index] > books[minPos]`
(C) `books[index].compareTo(books[minPos]) > 0`
(D) `books[index].compareTo(books[minPos]) >= 0`
(E) `books[index].compareTo(books[minPos]) < 0`

30. Refer to the static method `removeNegs` shown below.

```
/** Precondition: list is an ArrayList<Integer>.
 * Postcondition: All negative values have been removed from list.
 * @param list the list of Integer objects
 */
public static void removeNegs(List<Integer> list)
{
    int index = 0;
    while (index < list.size())
    {
        if (list.get(index).intValue() < 0)
        {
            list.remove(index);
        }
        index++;
    }
}
```

For which of the following lists will the method *not* work as intended?

(A) `6 -1 -2 5`
(B) `-1 2 -3 4`
(C) `2 4 6 8`
(D) `-3`
(E) `1 2 3 -8`

GO ON TO THE NEXT PAGE.

31. A sorted list of 120 integers is to be searched to determine whether the value 100 is in the list. Assuming that the most efficient searching algorithm is used, what is the maximum number of elements that must be examined?
    - (A) 7
    - (B) 8
    - (C) 20
    - (D) 100
    - (E) 120

32. Consider a sorted array `arr` of n elements, where n is large and n is even. Under which conditions will a sequential search of `arr` be faster than a binary search?

    I The target is not in the list.

    II The target is in the first position of the list.

    III The target is in `arr[1 + n/2]`.

    - (A) I only
    - (B) II only
    - (C) III only
    - (D) I and III only
    - (E) II and III only

33. Refer to the following data field and method.

```
private int[] arr;

/** Precondition: arr.length > 0 and index < arr.length. */
public void remove(int index)
{
    int[] b = new int[arr.length - 1];
    int count = 0;
    for (int i = 0; i < arr.length; i++)
    {
        if (i != index)
        {
            b[count] = arr[i];
            count++;
        }
    }
    /* assertion */
    arr = b;
}
```

Which of the following assertions is true when the /* *assertion* */ line is reached during execution of remove?

(A) `b[k] == arr[k]` for `0 <= k < arr.length`.

(B) `b[k] == arr[k + 1]` for `0 <= k < arr.length`.

(C) `b[k] == arr[k]` for `0 <= k <= index`, and
    `b[k] == arr[k + 1]` for `index < k < arr.length - 1`.

(D) `b[k] == arr[k]` for `0 <= k < index`, and
    `b[k] == arr[k + 1]` for `index <= k < arr.length - 1`.

(E) `b[k] == arr[k]` for `0 <= k < index`, and
    `b[k] == arr[k + 1]` for `index <= k < arr.length`.

34. When an integer is represented in base 16 (hexadecimal), the digits 0, 1, 2, 3, 4, 5, 6, 7, 8, 9, A, B, C, D, E, F are used, where A–F represent the numbers 10–15. If base 16 is represented with the subscript $_{hex}$ and base 10 is represented with the subscript $_{dec}$, then the decimal number 196 could be represented in hexadecimal as shown below:

$$196_{dec} = C4_{hex}$$

Which of the following is equal to $2AF_{hex}$?

(A) 27_{dec}

(B) 300_{dec}

(C) 687_{dec}

(D) 4002_{dec}

(E) 6896_{dec}

GO ON TO THE NEXT PAGE.

Questions 35–37 refer to the `TennisPlayer`, `GoodPlayer`, and `WeakPlayer` classes below. These classes are to be used in a program to simulate a game of tennis.

```java
public abstract class TennisPlayer
{
    private String name;

    public TennisPlayer(String aName)
    { name = aName; }

    public String getName()
    { return name; }

    public abstract boolean serve();
    public abstract boolean serviceReturn();
}

public class GoodPlayer extends TennisPlayer
{
    public GoodPlayer(String aName)
    { /* implementation not shown */ }

    /** @return true if serve is in (80% probability),
     *  false if serve is out (20% probability)
     */
    public boolean serve()
    { /* implementation not shown */ }

    /** @return true if service return is in (70% probability),
     *  false if service return is out (30% probability)
     */
    public boolean serviceReturn()
    { /* implementation not shown */ }
}

public class WeakPlayer extends TennisPlayer
{
    public WeakPlayer(String aName)
    { /* implementation not shown */ }

    /** @return true if serve is in (45% probability),
     *  false if serve is out (55% probability)
     */
    public boolean serve()
    { /* implementation not shown */ }

    /** @return true if service return is in (30% probability),
     *  false if service return is out (70% probability)
     */
    public boolean serviceReturn()
    { /* implementation not shown */ }
}
```

35. Which of the following declarations will cause an error? You may assume all the constructors are correctly implemented.
    (A) `TennisPlayer t = new TennisPlayer("Smith");`
    (B) `TennisPlayer g = new GoodPlayer("Jones");`
    (C) `TennisPlayer w = new WeakPlayer("Henry");`
    (D) `TennisPlayer p = null;`
    (E) `WeakPlayer q = new WeakPlayer("Grady");`

36. Refer to the serve method in the `WeakPlayer` class:

    ```
    /** @return true if serve is in (45% probability),
     *  false if serve is out (55% probability)
     */
    public boolean serve()
    { /* implementation */ }
    ```

    Which of the following replacements for /* *implementation* */ satisfy the post-condition of the serve method?

    ```
    I  double value = Math.random();
       return value >= 0 || value < 0.45;
    ```

    ```
    II double value = Math.random();
       return value < 0.45;
    ```

    ```
    III int val = (int) (Math.random() * 100);
        return val < 45;
    ```

    (A) I only
    (B) II only
    (C) III only
    (D) II and III only
    (E) I, II, and III

37. Consider the following class definition:

```
public class Beginner extends WeakPlayer
{
    private double costOfLessons;

    //methods of Beginner class
        ...
}
```

Refer to the following declarations and method in a client program:

```
TennisPlayer g = new GoodPlayer("Sam");
TennisPlayer w = new WeakPlayer("Harry");
TennisPlayer b = new Beginner("Dick");

public void giveEncouragement(WeakPlayer t)
{ /* implementation not shown */ }
```

Which of the following method calls will *not* cause an error?
(A) `giveEncouragement((WeakPlayer) g);`
(B) `giveEncouragement((WeakPlayer) b);`
(C) `giveEncouragement((Beginner) w);`
(D) `giveEncouragement(w);`
(E) `giveEncouragement(b);`

38. A matrix class that manipulates matrices contains the following declaration:

    ```
    private int[][] mat = new[numRows][numCols];
    ```

    Consider the following method that alters matrix mat.

    ```
    public void doSomething()
    {
        int width = mat[0].length;
        int numRows = mat.length;
        for (int row = 0; row < numRows; row++)
            for (int col = 0; col < width/2; col++)
                mat[row][col] = mat[row][width - 1 - col];
    }
    ```

    If mat has current value

    ```
    1 2 3 4 5 6
    1 3 5 7 9 11
    ```

    what will the value of mat be after a call to doSomething?

    (A) 1 2 3 3 2 1
        1 3 5 5 3 1

    (B) 6 5 4 4 5 6
        11 9 7 7 9 11

    (C) 6 5 4 3 2 1
        11 9 7 5 3 1

    (D) 1 2 3 4 5 6
        1 2 3 4 5 6

    (E) 1 3 5 7 9 11
        1 3 5 7 9 11

GO ON TO THE NEXT PAGE.

Questions 39 and 40 refer to the following information.

Consider an array `arr` that is sorted in increasing order, and method `findMost` given below. Method `findMost` is intended to find the value in the array that occurs most often. If every value occurs exactly once, `findMost` should return -1. If there is more than one value that occurs the most, `findMost` should return any one of those. For example, if `arr` contains the values `[1,5,7,7,10]`, `findMost` should return 7. If `arr` contains `[2,2,2,7,8,8,9,9,9]`, `findMost` should return 2 or 9. If `arr` contains `[1,2,7,8]`, `findMost` should return -1.

```
Line 1: /** Precondition: arr sorted in increasing order.
Line 2: */
Line 3: public static int findMost(int[] arr)
Line 4: {
Line 5:     int index = 0;
Line 6:     int count = 1;
Line 7:     int maxCountSoFar = 1;
Line 8:     int mostSoFar = arr[0];
Line 9:     while (index < arr.length - 1)
Line 10:    {
Line 11:        while (index < arr.length - 1 &&
Line 12:                arr[index] == arr[index + 1])
Line 13:        {
Line 14:            count++;
Line 15:            index++;
Line 16:        }
Line 17:        if (count > maxCountSoFar)
Line 18:        {
Line 19:            maxCountSoFar = count;
Line 20:            mostSoFar = arr[index];
Line 21:        }
Line 22:        index++;
Line 23:    }
Line 24:    if (maxCountSoFar == 1)
Line 25:        return -1;
Line 26:    else
Line 27:        return mostSoFar;
Line 28: }
```

39. The method `findMost` does not always work as intended. An *incorrect* result will be returned if `arr` contains the values
    - (A) `[1,2,3,4,5]`
    - (B) `[6,6,6,6]`
    - (C) `[1,2,2,3,4,5]`
    - (D) `[1,1,3,4,5,5,5,7]`
    - (E) `[2,2,2,4,5,5]`

40. Which of the following changes should be made so that method `findMost` will work as intended?
    - (A) Insert the statement count = 1; between Lines 20 and 21.
    - (B) Insert the statement count = 1; between Lines 21 and 22.
    - (C) Insert the statement count = 1; between Lines 16 and 17.
    - (D) Insert the statement count = 0; between Lines 23 and 24.
    - (E) Insert the statement count = 1; between Lines 23 and 24.

END OF SECTION I

COMPUTER SCIENCE
SECTION II

Time—1 hour and 30 minutes
Number of questions—4
Percent of total grade—50

Directions: SHOW ALL YOUR WORK. REMEMBER THAT
PROGRAM SEGMENTS ARE TO BE WRITTEN IN Java.

Write your answers in pencil only in the booklet provided.

Notes:

- Assume that the classes in the Quick Reference have been imported where needed.

- Unless otherwise stated, assume that parameters in method calls are not null and that methods are called only when their preconditions are satisfied.

- In writing solutions for each question, you may use any of the accessible methods that are listed in classes defined in that question. Writing significant amounts of code that can be replaced by a call to one of these methods may not receive full credit.

---

1. Consider the problem of keeping track of the available seats in a theater. Theater seats can be represented with a two-dimensional array of integers, where a value of 0 shows a seat is available, while a value of 1 indicates that the seat is occupied. For example, the array below shows the current seat availability for a show in a small theater.

	[0]	[1]	[2]	[3]	[4]	[5]
[0]	0	0	1	1	0	1
[1]	0	1	0	1	0	1
[2]	1	0	0	0	0	0

The seat at slot [1] [3] is taken, but seat [0] [4] is still available.
A show can be represented by the Show class shown below.

Practice Exam 3

```
public class Show
{
    /** The seats for this show */
    private int[][] seats;

    private final int SEATS_PER_ROW = <some integer value>;
    private final int NUM_ROWS = <some integer value>;

    /** Returns true if the seat with the specified row and seat
     *  number is an aisle seat, false otherwise.
     *  @param row the row number
     *  @param seatNumber the seat number
     *  @return true if an aisle seat, false otherwise
     */
    public boolean isAisleSeat (int row, int seatNumber)
    { /* to be implemented in part (a) */ }

    /** Reserve two adjacent seats and return true if this was
     *  successfully done.
     *  If two adjacent seats could not be found, leave the state
     *  of the show unchanged, and return false.
     *  @return true if two adjacent seats were found, false
     *  otherwise
     */
    public boolean twoTogether()
    { /* to be implemented in part (b) */ }

    /** Return the lowest seat number in the specified row for a
     *  block of empty adjacent seats. If no such block exists,
     *  return -1.
     *  @param row the row number
     *  @param seatsNeeded the number of adjacent empty seats needed
     *  @return lowest seat number for a block of needed adjacent
     *  seats or -1 if no such block exists
     */
    public int findAdjacent(int row, int seatsNeeded)
    { /* to be implemented in part (c) */ }

    //There may be instance variables, constructors, and methods
    //that are not shown.
}
```

(a) Write the Show method isAisleSeat, which should return true if the seat with the specified row and seat number is an aisle seat, false otherwise. Aisle seats are the first and the last columns of the two-dimensional array representing the theater. For example, in the diagram shown above, if show is a Show variable, here are some results of calling the isAisleSeat method.

Method call	Return value
show.isAisleSeat(2,5)	true
show.isAisleSeat(0,4)	false
show.isAisleSeat(1,0)	true

Complete method isAisleSeat below.

GO ON TO THE NEXT PAGE.

```
/** Returns true if the seat with the specified row and seat
 *  number is an aisle seat, false otherwise.
 *  @param row the row number
 *  @param seatNumber the seat number
 *  @return true if an aisle seat, false otherwise
 */
public boolean isAisleSeat (int row, int seatNumber)
```

(b) Write the Show method twoTogether, which reserves two adjacent seats and returns true if this was successfully done. If it is not possible to find two adjacent seats that are unoccupied, the method should leave the show unchanged and return false. For example, suppose this is the state of a show.

	[0]	[1]	[2]	[3]	[4]	[5]
[0]	0	0	1	1	0	1
[1]	0	1	0	1	0	1
[2]	1	0	0	0	1	1

A call to twoTogether should return true, and the final state of the show could be any one of the following three configurations.

	[0]	[1]	[2]	[3]	[4]	[5]
[0]	1	1	1	1	0	1
[1]	0	1	0	1	0	1
[2]	1	0	0	0	1	1

OR

	[0]	[1]	[2]	[3]	[4]	[5]
[0]	0	0	1	1	0	1
[1]	0	1	0	1	0	1
[2]	1	1	1	0	1	1

OR

	[0]	[1]	[2]	[3]	[4]	[5]
[0]	0	0	1	1	0	1
[1]	0	1	0	1	0	1
[2]	1	0	1	1	1	1

For the following state of a show, a call to twoTogether should return false and leave the two-dimensional array as shown.

	[0]	[1]	[2]	[3]	[4]	[5]
[0]	0	1	0	1	1	0
[1]	1	1	0	1	0	1
[2]	0	1	1	1	1	1

GO ON TO THE NEXT PAGE.

```
Information repeated from the beginning of the question

public class Show

private int[][] seats
private final int SEATS_PER_ROW
private final int NUM_ROWS
public boolean isAisleSeat (int row, int seatNumber)
public boolean twoTogether()
public int findAdjacent(int row, int seatsNeeded)
```

Complete method twoTogether below.

```
/** Reserve two adjacent seats and return true if this was
 *  successfully done.
 *  If two adjacent seats could not be found, leave the state
 *  of the show unchanged, and return false.
 *  @return true if two adjacent seats were found, false
 *  otherwise
 */
public boolean twoTogether()
```

(c) Write the Show method findAdjacent, which finds the lowest seat number
in the specified row for a block of empty adjacent seats. If no such block
exists, the findAdjacent method should return -1. No changes should be
made to the state of the show, irrespective of the value returned.
For example, suppose the diagram of seats is as shown.

	[0]	[1]	[2]	[3]	[4]	[5]
[0]	0	1	1	0	0	0
[1]	0	0	0	0	1	1
[2]	1	0	0	1	0	0

The following table shows some examples of calling findAdjacent for show.

Method call	Return value
show.findAdjacent(0,3)	3
show.findAdjacent(1,3)	0 or 1
show.findAdjacent(2,2)	1 or 4
show.findAdjacent(1,5)	-1

Complete method findAdjacent below.

```
/** Return the lowest seat number in the specified row for a
 *  block of empty adjacent seats. If no such block exists,
 *  return -1.
 *  @param row the row number
 *  @param seatsNeeded the number of adjacent empty seats needed
 *  @return lowest seat number for a block of needed adjacent
 *  seats or -1 if no such block exists
 */
public int findAdjacent(int row, int seatsNeeded)
```

GO ON TO THE NEXT PAGE.

2. A company sends a form letter to all of its potential customers. In order to personalize each letter, various tokens (symbols) in the form letter are replaced by either the customer's name, city, or state, depending on the token. A customer can be represented by a `Customer` class, whose partial implementation is shown below.

```
public class Customer
{
    private String name;
    private String city;
    private String state;

    /** @return the name of this customer */
    public String getName()
    { return name; }

    /** @return the city of this customer */
    public String getCity()
    { return city; }

    /** @return the state of this customer */
    public String getState()
    { return state; }

    //Constructor and other methods are not shown.
}
```

A `FormLetter` object has a list of lines that make up the letter, and a list of customers who will receive the letter. In this question you will be asked to write two methods of the `FormLetter` class, whose partial implementation is shown below.

```
public class FormLetter
{
    /** The list of lines that make up this form letter */
    private List<String> lines;

    /** The list of customers */
    private List<Customer> customers;

    /** @return a copy of lines */
    public List<String> makeCopy()
    {
        List<String> newLines = new ArrayList<String>();
        for (String line: lines)
            newLines.add(line);
        return newLines;
    }
```

```
    /** Replace all occurrences of sub in line with replacement
     *  string, repl.
     *  @param line a String
     *  @param sub a substring to be replaced
     *  @param replacement the replacement string
     *  Precondition: sub is not a substring of repl,
     *                the replacement string.
     *  @return line with each occurrence of sub replaced by replacement
     */
    public String replaceAll(String line, String sub, String repl)
    { /* to be implemented in part (a) */ }


    /** Write letter for one customer, using personalized lines
     *  contained in customerLines.
     *  @param customerLines the personalized lines for one customer
     */
    public void writeLetter(List<String> customerLines)
    { /* implementation not shown */ }


    /** Creates and prints a personalized form letter for each
     *  customer in the customers list.
     *  Postcondition: In each customer letter:
     *   - every occurrence of "@" is replaced by the customer's name;
     *   - every occurrence of "&" is replaced by the customer's city;
     *   - every occurrence of "$" is replaced by the customer's state.
     *   - A letter with the replacements is printed for each customer.
     */
    public void createPersonalizedLetters()
    { /* to be implemented in part (b) */ }


//Constructors and other methods are not shown.
}
```

(a) Write the FormLetter method replaceAll, which examines a given string and replaces all occurrences of a specified substring with a replacement string. In writing your solution, you may not use the replace, replaceAll, or replaceFirst methods in the Java String class.

Suppose f is a FormLetter. The following table shows the result of calling f.replaceAll(line,substring,replacement).

line	substring	replacement	string returned
oh me oh my	oh	aah	aah me aah my
sing to me a sin	sin	brin	bring to me a brin
ooh la la	ah	oh	ooh la la

GO ON TO THE NEXT PAGE.

Complete method `replaceAll` below.

```
/** Replace all occurrences of sub in line with replacement
 *  string, repl.
 *  @param line a String
 *  @param sub a substring to be replaced
 *  @param replacement the replacement string
 *  Precondition: sub is not a substring of repl,
 *                the replacement string.
 *  @return line with each occurrence of sub replaced by replacement
 */
public String replaceAll(String line, String sub, String repl)
```

(b) Write the `FormLetter` method `createPersonalizedLetters`. For each customer in the customers list, method `createPersonalizedLetters` should create then print a letter that

- replaces all occurrences of @ in `lines`, with the customer's name
- replaces all occurrences of & in `lines`, with the customer's city
- replaces all occurrences of $ in `lines`, with the customer's state

For example, suppose the first five lines in the form letter are:

```
Dear @,
If you buy a garden gnome you will
have the best-looking house in &,
heck, @, in the whole state of $!
@, @, @, don't delay.
```

The letter generated for a customer Joan from Glendale, California, should have these replacement lines:

```
Dear Joan,
If you buy a garden gnome you will
have the best-looking house in Glendale,
heck, Joan, in the whole state of California!
Joan, Joan, Joan, don't delay.
```

In writing method `createPersonalizedLetters`, you *must* use the method `replaceAll` that you wrote in part (a). Assume that `replaceAll` works as specified, regardless of what you wrote in part (a).

Complete method `createPersonalizedLetters` below.

```
/** Creates and prints a personalized form letter for each
 *  customer in the customers list.
 *  Postcondition: In each customer letter:
 *    - every occurrence of "@" is replaced by the customer's name;
 *    - every occurrence of "&" is replaced by the customer's city;
 *    - every occurrence of "$" is replaced by the customer's state.
 *    - A letter with the replacements is printed for each customer.
 */
public void createPersonalizedLetters()
```

3. A clothing store sells shoes, pants, and tops. The store also allows a customer to buy an "outfit," which consists of three items: one pair of shoes, one pair of pants, and one top.

Each clothing item has a description and a price. The four types of clothing items are represented by the four classes `Shoes`, `Pants`, `Top`, and `Outfit`. All four classes implement the following `ClothingItem` interface.

```
public interface ClothingItem
{
    /** @return the description of the clothing item */
    String getDescription();

    /** @return the price of the clothing item */
    double getPrice();
}
```

The following diagram shows the relationship between the `ClothingItem` interface and the `Shoes`, `Pants`, `Top`, and `Outfit` classes.

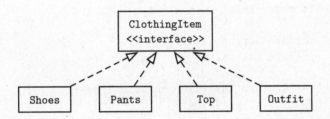

The store allows customers to create `Outfit` clothing items each of which includes a pair of shoes, pants, and a top. The description of the outfit consists of the description of the shoes, pants, and top, in that order, separated by "/" and followed by a space and "outfit". The price of an outfit is calculated as follows. If the sum of the prices of any two items equals or exceeds $100, there is a 25% discount on the sum of the prices of all three items. Otherwise there is a 10% discount.

For example, an outfit consisting of sneakers ($40), blue jeans ($50), and a T-shirt ($10), would have the name "sneakers/blue jeans/T-shirt outfit" and a price of $0.90(40 + 50 + 10) = \$90.00$. An outfit consisting of loafers ($50), cutoffs ($20), and dress-shirt ($60), would have the description "loafers/cutoffs/dress-shirt outfit" and price $0.75(50 + 20 + 60) = \$97.50$. Write the `Outfit` class that implements the `ClothingItem` interface. Your implementation must include a constructor that takes three parameters representing a pair of shoes, pants, and a top.

The code segment below should have the following behavior.

```
Shoes shoes;
Pants pants;
Top top;
/* Code to initialize shoes, pants, and top */

ClothingItem outfit =
    new Outfit (shoes, pants, top); //Compiles without error
ClothingItem outfit =
    new Outfit (pants, shoes, top); //Compile-time error
ClothingItem outfit =
    new Outfit (shoes, top, pants); //Compile-time error
```

Write your solution below.

4. A word creation game uses letter tiles, each of which has a letter and numerical value printed on it. A partial implementation of the Tile class is shown below.

```
public class Tile
{
    private String letter;
    private int value;

    /** @return the value on this Tile */
    public int getValue()
    { return value; }

    /** @return the letter on this Tile */
    public String getLetter()
    { return letter; }

    //Constructor and other methods are not shown.
}
```

All tiles for the word game are called the tile set, which is represented by the TileSet class, whose partial implementation is shown below.

GO ON TO THE NEXT PAGE.

```
public class TileSet
{
    /** tiles contains all the tiles in the word game,
     *  both used and not-yet-used.
     */
    private List<Tile> tiles;

    /** unusedSize is the number of tiles that are not yet used. */
    private int unusedSize;

    /** Determines if there are still unused tiles.
     *  @return true if all the tiles have been used; false otherwise
     */
    public boolean allUsed()
    { return unusedSize == 0; }

    /** @return the number of unused tiles in this tile set */
    public int getUnusedSize()
    { return unusedSize; }

    /** Shuffles the tiles in the tile set, and
     *  resets unusedSize to the total number of tiles in the set.
     */
    public void shuffle()
    { /* to be implemented in part (a) */ }

    /** Get an unused tile from this tile set.
     *  @return an unused tile, or null if all tiles have been used
     */
    public Tile getNewTile()
    { /* implementation not shown */ }

//Constructors and other methods are not shown.
}
```

(a) Write the shuffle method for the TileSet class. Your method should use
the following algorithm.

> for k starting at the end of the tiles list and going down to 1:
>   pick a random index in $0, 1, 2, \ldots, k$
>   swap the tiles at position index and position k
> Reset unusedSize to the number of tiles in the tile set.

Complete method shuffle below.

```
/** Shuffles the tiles in the tile set, and resets
 *  unusedSize to the total number of tiles in the set.
 */
public void shuffle()
```

GO ON TO THE NEXT PAGE.

For parts (b) and (c) you will write methods from the Player class, whose partial implementation is shown below. A player in the word game has NUM_LETTERS tiles in front of her. After she makes a word, she helps herself to unused tiles to maintain NUM_LETTERS tiles, if possible.

```
public class Player
{
    /** NUM_LETTERS is the number of letter tiles a player should
     * have (if tiles have not yet all been used) at the start of
     * her turn. */
    public static final int NUM_LETTERS = < some integer >;

    /** playerTiles is the list of tiles for this player. */
    private List<Tile>playerTiles;

    /** Adds a sufficient number of unused tiles from tileSet t
     * to playerTiles so that this player has NUM_LETTERS tiles.
     * If there are insufficient unused tiles, the player should
     * take all of the remaining available tiles.
     * Precondition: playerTiles.size() < NUM_LETTERS.
     * Postcondition: playerTiles.size() <= NUM_LETTERS.
     * @param t the tile set for the word game
     */
    public void replaceTiles(TileSet t)
    { /* to be implemented in part (b) */ }

    /** Returns the score a player receives for using tiles from
     * his playerTiles at his turn. The score is the sum of values
     * on each tile used. Indexes of tiles used are contained in
     * the indexes array. If index[0] is -1, the player
     * has used no tiles at his turn and the method returns a
     * score of 0. If the player uses all of the tiles in
     * playerTiles, a bonus of 20 points is added to his score.
     * @param indexes the array of positions of tiles in
     *     playerTiles that the player uses at his turn
     * Precondition:
     *   - playerTiles contains NUM_LETTERS tiles.
     *   - indexes[0 .. n] is sorted in increasing order,
     *     n < NUM_LETTERS.
     */
    public int getWordScore(int[] indexes)
    { /* to be implemented in part (c) */ }
}
```

(b) Write the Player method replaceTiles. This method should, if possible, add unused tiles to the player's playerTiles list, until playerTiles contains NUM_LETTERS tiles. If there are insufficient unused tiles in the tile set, the player should take all of the remaining tiles.

Complete method `replaceTiles` below.

```
/** Adds a sufficient number of unused tiles from tileSet t
 *  to playerTiles so that this player has NUM_LETTERS tiles.
 *  If there are insufficient unused tiles, the player should
 *  take all of the remaining available tiles.
 *  Precondition:  playerTiles.size() < NUM_LETTERS.
 *  Postcondition: playerTiles.size() <= NUM_LETTERS.
 *  @param t the tile set for the word game
 */
public void replaceTiles(TileSet t)
```

(c) Write the `Player` method `getWordScore`. This method returns the total of the values of tiles in `playerTiles` whose positions are indicated in the `indexes` parameter. If `indexes` contains {0,1,4}, this means that the player will use the tiles at positions 0, 1, and 4 in his `playerTiles` list at his turn, and his score will be the sum of values of those tiles. If the player uses all of his tiles at his turn, a bonus of 20 points is added to his score. If the only value in the `indexes` array is -1, this means that the player passes at his turn, and `getWordScore` should return a value of 0.

For example, suppose `NUM_LETTERS` is 5, and `playerTiles` has the following state before the method call.

	0	1	2	3	4
	"O"	"C"	"V"	"E"	"N"
	1	3	4	1	1

State of indexes array	Result of getWordScore(indexes)
{0,2,3,4}	7
{0,1,2,3,4}	30
{0,1,4}	5
{-1}	0

Complete method `getWordScore` below.

```
/** Returns the score a player receives for using tiles from
 *  his playerTiles at his turn. The score is the sum of values
 *  on each tile used. Indexes of tiles used are contained in
 *  the indexes array. If index[0] is -1, the player
 *  has used no tiles at his turn and the method returns a
 *  score of 0. If the player uses all of the tiles in
 *  playerTiles, a bonus of 20 points is added to his score.
 *  @param indexes the array of positions of tiles in
 *     playerTiles that the player uses at his turn
 *  Precondition:
 *  - playerTiles contains NUM_LETTERS tiles.
 *  - indexes[0 .. n] is sorted in increasing order,
 *    n < NUM_LETTERS.
 */
public int getWordScore(int[] indexes)
```

END OF EXAMINATION

ANSWER KEY (Section I)

1. E	15. E	29. E
2. C	16. A	30. A
3. C	17. E	31. A
4. D	18. B	32. B
5. A	19. C	33. D
6. A	20. E	34. C
7. C	21. D	35. A
8. E	22. C	36. D
9. A	23. D	37. B
10. D	24. E	38. B
11. C	25. A	39. E
12. E	26. D	40. B
13. C	27. D	
14. B	28. A	

ANSWERS EXPLAINED

Section I

1. **(E)** The string parameter in the line of code uses two escape characters:
\", which means print a double quote.
\n, which means print a newline character (i.e., go to the next line).

2. **(C)** The intent of the programmer is to have overloaded `getValue` methods in `SomeClass`. Overloaded methods have different signatures, where the signature of a method includes the name and parameter types only. Thus, the signature of the original method is `getValue(int)`. The signature in header I is `getValue()`. The signature in header II is `getValue(int)`. The signature in header III is `getValue(double)`. Since the signature in header II is the same as that of the given method, the compiler will flag it and say that the method already exists in `SomeClass`. Note: The return type of a method is not included in its signature.

3. **(C)** The expression `(int)(Math.random() * 49)` produces a random integer from 0 through 48. (Note that 49 is the number of possibilities for `num`.) To shift this range from 2 to 50, add 2 to the expression.

4. **(D)** Short-circuit evaluation of the boolean expression will occur. The expression `(num != 0)` will evaluate to `false`, which makes the entire boolean expression `false`. Therefore the expression `(score/num > SOME_CONSTANT)` will not be evaluated. Hence no division by zero will occur, and there will be no `ArithmeticException` thrown. When the boolean expression has a value of `false`, only the `else` part of the statement, *statement2*, will be executed.

5. **(A)** The values of k are, consecutively, 4, 3, 2, and 1. The values of randPos are, consecutively, 3, 2, 0, and 0. Thus, the sequence of swaps and corresponding states of nums will be:

swap nums[4] and nums[3]	8 7 6 4 5
swap nums[3] and nums[2]	8 7 4 6 5
swap nums[2] and nums[0]	4 7 8 6 5
swap nums[1] and nums[0]	7 4 8 6 5

Thus, the element in nums[2] is 8.

6. **(A)** A matrix is stored as an array of arrays, that is, each row is an array. Therefore it is correct to call a method with an array parameter for each row, as is done in Segment I. Segment II fails because mat is not an array of columns. The segment would cause an error, since mat[col] refers to a *row*, not a column. (If the number of rows were less than the number of columns, the method would throw an ArrayIndexOutOfBoundsException. If the number of rows were greater than the number of columns, the method would correctly assign the value 100 to the first n rows, where n is the number of columns. The rest of the rows would retain the values before execution of the method.) Segment III fails because you cannot assign new elements in a for-each loop. The matrix remains unchanged.

7. **(C)** Declarations I and II fail because you can't create an instance of an abstract class. Additionally, declaration I fails this test: Cereal *is-a* WheatCereal? No. Notice that declaration III passes this test: RiceCereal *is-a* Cereal? Yes.

8. **(E)** All satisfy the *is-a* test! Class2 *is-a* Class1. Class3 *is-a* Class2. Class3 *is-a* Class1. Note: Since Class3 is a subclass of Class2, it automatically implements any interfaces implemented by Class2, its superclass.

9. **(A)** Method call I works because Class3 inherits all the methods of Class2. Method call II fails because Class2, the superclass, does not inherit the methods of Class3, its subclass. Method call III uses a parameter that fails the *is-a* test: ob2 is *not* a Class3, which the parameter requires.

10. **(D)** After each execution of the loop body, n is divided by 2. Thus, the loop will produce output when n is 50, 25, 12, 6, 3, and 1. The final value of n will be 1 / 2, which is 0, and the test will fail.

11. **(C)** Statement III will cause an IndexOutOfBoundsException because there is no slot 4. The final element, "Luis", is in slot 3. Statement I is correct: It replaces the string "Harry" with the string "6". It may look peculiar in the list, but the syntax is correct. Statement II looks like it may be out of range because there is no slot 4. It is correct, however, because you must be allowed to add an element to the end of the list.

12. **(E)** The effect of the given algorithm is to raise n to the 8th power.
When $i = 1$, the result is $n * n = n^2$.
When $i = 2$, the result is $n^2 * n^2 = n^4$.
When $i = 3$, the result is $n^4 * n^4 = n^8$.

13. **(C)** The method traverses nums, starting at position 0, and returns the current position the first time it finds an odd value. This implies that all values in positions 0 through the current index $- 1$ contained even numbers.

14. **(B)** Since n == 6 fails the two base case tests, method call mystery(6) returns 6 + mystery(5). Since 5 satisfies the second base case test, mystery(5) returns 5, and there are no more recursive calls. Thus, mystery(6) = 6 + 5 = 11.

15. **(E)** In order for /* *body of loop* */ not to be executed, the test must be false the first time it is evaluated. A compound OR test will be false if and only if both pieces of the test are false. Thus, choices B and C are insufficient. Choice D fails because it guarantees that both pieces of the test will be *true*. Choice A is wrong because /* *body of loop* */ may be executed many times, until the computer runs out of memory (an infinite loop!).

16. **(A)** When p.act() is called, the act method of Singer is executed. This is an example of polymorphism. The first line prints rise. Then super.act() goes to the act method of Performer, the superclass. This prints bow, then calls perform(). Again, using polymorphism, the perform method in Singer is called, which prints aria. Now, completing the act method of Singer, encore is printed. The result?

    rise bow aria encore

17. **(E)** Statement I is false: The Sedan, StationWagon, and SUV classes should all be subclasses of Car. Each one satisfies the *is-a* Car relationship. Statement II is true: The main task of the Inventory class should be to keep an updated list of Car objects. Statement III is true: A class is independent of another class if it does not require that class to implement its methods.

18. **(B)** The Inventory class is responsible for maintaining the list of all cars on the lot. Therefore methods like addCar, removeCar, and displayAllCars must be the responsibility of this class. The Car class should contain the setColor, getPrice, and displayCar methods, since all these pertain to the attributes of a given Car.

19. **(C)** Each subclass may contain additional attributes for the particular type of car that are not in the Car superclass. Since displayCar displays all features of a given car, this method should be overridden to display the original plus additional features.

20. **(E)** The expression word.indexOf("flag") returns the index of the first occurrence of "flag" in the calling string, word. Thus, x has value 3. (Recall that the first character in word is at index 0.) The method call word.substring(0, x) is equivalent to word.substring(0, 3), which returns the substring in word from 0 to 2, namely "con". The character at index 3 is not included.

21. **(D)** A program that uses an abstract class must have at least one subclass that is *not* abstract, since instances of abstract classes cannot be created. Thus, choice E is false. Choice A is false: An abstract class can contain any number of private instance variables. Choice B is wrong—for example v1 and v2 could be initialized in a default constructor (constructor with no parameters). Choice C is incorrect: The point of an abstract class is that no instances of it will be created. The class does not need to contain any abstract methods.

22. **(C)** If the responses array contained an invalid value like 12, the program would attempt to add 1 to freq[12]. This is out of bounds for the freq array.

23. **(D)** Implementation I calls super.computePay(), which is equivalent to the computePay method in the Employee superclass. The method returns the quantity (salary - taxWithheld). The BONUS is then correctly added to this expression, as required. Implementation III correctly uses the public accessor methods getSalary and getTax that the Consultant class has inherited. Note that the Consultant class does not have direct access to the private instance variables salary and taxWithheld. Implementation II incorrectly returns the salary plus

BONUS—there is no tax withheld. The expression `super.computePay()` returns a value equal to salary minus tax. But this is neither stored nor included in the `return` statement.

24. **(E)** Note that `p` is declared to be of type `Employee`, and the `Employee` class does not have a `getPayFraction` method. To avoid the error, `p` must be cast to `PartTimeEmployee` as follows:

```
double g = ((PartTimeEmployee) p).getPayFraction();
```

25. **(A)** The code does exactly what it looks like it should. The `writePayInfo` parameter is of type `Employee` and each element of the `empList` array *is-a* `Employee` and therefore does not need to be downcast to its actual instance type. There is no `ClassCastException` (choice C) since nowhere is there an attempt made to cast an object to a class of which it is not an instance. None of the array elements is null; therefore, there is no `NullPointerException` (choice B). Choice D won't happen because the `getName` method is inherited by both the `Consultant` and `PartTimeEmployee` classes. Choice E would occur if the `Employee` superclass were abstract, but it's not.

26. **(D)** Segment I is incorrect because `num` is not an index in the loop: It is a value in the array. Thus, the correct test is `if (num > 0)`, which is correctly used in segment II. Segment III is a regular `for` loop, exactly equivalent to the given `while` loop.

27. **(D)** The first `for` loop places `value` in the top and bottom rows of the defined rectangle. The second `for` loop fills in the remaining border elements on the sides. Note that the `top + 1` and `bottom - 1` initializer and terminating conditions avoid filling in the corner elements twice.

28. **(A)** Statement I is false: An *interface* may not be instantiated, but a class that implements the interface can be instantiated, provided it is not an abstract class. Statement II is false: Any subclass of `SomeClass` will automatically implement the interface, but not necessarily the superclass. For example, suppose a superclass `Animal` has a subclass `Bird`. And suppose `Bird` implements `CanFly`, which is an interface with a single method, `fly`. Clearly, `Animal` shouldn't implement `CanFly`—not all animals fly. Statement III appears to be true: This is what it means for a class to implement an interface—it's a promise that the class will contain all methods of that interface. This is not true, however, if `SomeClass` is an abstract class. Any method of the interface that is not implemented in `SomeClass` then automatically becomes an abstract method of `SomeClass` and must be implemented by any nonabstract subclass of `SomeClass`.

29. **(E)** Eliminate choices A and B: When comparing `Book` objects, you cannot use simple inequality operators; you *must* use `compareTo`. For the calling object to be *less than* the parameter object, use the *less than* 0 test (a good way to remember this!).

30. **(A)** Method `removeNegs` will not work whenever there are consecutive negative values in the list. This is because removal of an element from an `ArrayList` causes the elements to the right of it to be shifted left to fill the "hole." The index in the given algorithm, however, always moves one slot to the right. Therefore in choice A, when -1 is removed, -2 will be passed over, and the final list will be 6 -2 5.

31. **(A)** If the list is sorted, a binary search is the most efficient algorithm to use. Binary search chops the current part of the array being examined in half, until you have found the element you are searching for, or there are no elements left to look at. In the worst case, you will need to divide by 2 seven times:

$$120/2 \rightarrow 60$$
$$60/2 \rightarrow 30$$
$$30/2 \rightarrow 15$$
$$15/2 \rightarrow 7$$
$$7/2 \rightarrow 3$$
$$3/2 \rightarrow 1$$
$$1/2 \rightarrow 0$$

32. **(B)** For a sequential search, all n elements will need to be examined. For a binary search, the array will be chopped in half a maximum of $\log_2 n$ times. When the target is in the first position of the list, a sequential search will find it in the first comparison. The binary search, which examines a middle element first, will not. Condition I is a worst case situation for both the sequential search and binary search. Condition III is approximately the middle of the list, but it won't be found on the first try of the binary search. (The first try examines `arr[n/2]`.) Still, the target *will* be located within fewer than $\log n$ tries, whereas the sequential search will need more than $n/2$ tries.

33. **(D)** The `remove` method removes from `arr` the element `arr[index]`. It does this by copying all elements from `arr[0]` up to but not including `arr[index]` into array `b`. Thus, `b[k] == arr[k]` for `0 <= k < index` is true. Then it copies all elements from `arr[index + 1]` up to and including `arr[arr.length - 1]` into `b`. Since no gaps are left in `b`, `b[k] == arr[k + 1]` for `index <= k < arr.length - 1`. The best way to see this is with a small example. If `arr` is 2, 6, 4, 8, 1, 7, and the element at `index` 2 (namely the 4) is to be removed, here is the picture:

```
         0   1  [2]  3   4   5
arr  →  | 2 | 6 | 4 | 8 | 1 | 7 |

         0   1  [2]  3   4
  b  →  | 2 | 6 | 8 | 1 | 7 |
```

```
b[0] == arr[0]
b[1] == arr[1]
b[2] == arr[3]
b[3] == arr[4]
b[4] == arr[5]
```

Notice that `arr.length` is 6, but k ends at 4.

34. **(C)**
$$2AF_{hex} = (F)(16^0) + (A)(16^1) + (2)(16^2)$$
$$= (15)(1) + (10)(16) + (2)(256)$$
$$= 15 + 160 + 512$$
$$= 687_{dec}$$

35. **(A)** Choice A is illegal because you cannot create an instance of an abstract class.

36. **(D)** The statement

    ```
    double value = Math.random();
    ```

    generates a random `double` in the range $0 \leq$ `value` < 1. Since random doubles are uniformly distributed in this interval, 45 percent of the time you can expect `value` to be in the range $0 \leq$ `value` < 0.45. Therefore, a test for `value` in this range can be a test for whether the serve of a `WeakPlayer` went in. Since `Math.random()` never returns a negative number, the test in implementation II, `value < 0.45`, is sufficient. The test in implementation I would be correct if `||` were changed to `&&` ("or" changed to "and"—both parts must be true). Implementation III also works. The expression

    ```
    (int) (Math.random() * 100)
    ```

    returns a random integer from 0 to 99, each equally likely. Thus, 45 percent of the time, the integer `val` will be in the range $0 \leq$ `val` ≤ 44. Therefore, a test for `val` in this range can be used to test whether the serve was in.

37. **(B)** Choice B is fine: `b`, the `Beginner`, *is-a* `WeakPlayer`. Choices A and C will each cause a `ClassCastException` to be thrown: You can't cast a `GoodPlayer` to a `WeakPlayer`, and you can't cast a `WeakPlayer` to a `Beginner`. Choices D and E will each cause a compile-time error: The parameter must be of type `WeakPlayer`, but `w` and `b` are declared to be of type `TennisPlayer`. Each of these choices can be corrected by casting the parameter to `WeakPlayer`.

38. **(B)** The method copies the elements from columns 3, 4, and 5 into columns 2, 1, and 0, respectively, as if there were a vertical mirror down the middle of the matrix. To see this, here are the values for the given matrix: `width` = 6, `width/2` = 3, `numRows` = 2. The variable `row` goes from 0 to 1 and `column` goes from 0 to 2. The element assignments are

    ```
    mat[0][0] = mat[0][5]
    mat[0][1] = mat[0][4]
    mat[0][2] = mat[0][3]
    mat[1][0] = mat[1][5]
    mat[1][1] = mat[1][4]
    mat[1][2] = mat[1][3]
    ```

39. **(E)** In choice E, `findMost` returns the value 5. This is because `count` has not been reset to 1, so that when 5 is encountered, the test `count>maxCountSoFar` is true, causing `mostSoFar` to be incorrectly re-assigned to 5. In choices A, B, and C, the outer `while` loop is not entered again, since a second run of equal values doesn't exist in the array. So `mostSoFar` comes out with the correct value. In choice D, when the outer loop is entered again, the test `count>maxCountSoFar` just happens to be true anyway and the correct value is returned. The algorithm fails whenever a new string of equal values is found whose length is shorter than a previous string of equal values.

40. **(B)** The `count` variable must be reset to 1 as soon as `index` is incremented in the outer `while` loop, so that when a new run of equal values is found, `count` starts out as 1.

Section II

1. (a)
```
public boolean isAisleSeat (int row, int seatNumber)
{
    return seatNumber == 0 || seatNumber == SEATS_PER_ROW - 1;
}
```

(b)
```
public boolean twoTogether()
{
    for (int r = 0; r < NUM_ROWS; r++)
        for (int c = 0; c < SEATS_PER_ROW-1; c++)
            if (seats[r][c] == 0 && seats[r][c+1] == 0)
            {
                seats[r][c] = 1;
                seats[r][c+1] = 1;
                return true;
            }
    return false;
}
```

(c)
```
public int findAdjacent(int row, int seatsNeeded)
{
    int index = 0, count = 0, lowIndex = 0;
    while (index < SEATS_PER_ROW)
    {
        while (index < SEATS_PER_ROW && seats[row][index] == 0)
        {
            count++;
            index++;
            if (count == seatsNeeded)
                return lowIndex;
        }
        count = 0;
        index++;
        lowIndex = index;
    }
    return -1;
}
```

NOTE

- In part (a), the seat numbers go from 0 to `SEATS_PER_ROW - 1`.
- In part (b), you need the test `c < SEATS_PER_ROW-1`, because when you refer to `seats[r][c+1]`, you must worry about going off the end of the row and causing an `ArrayIndexOutOfBounds` exception.
- In part (c), every time you increment `index`, you need to test that it is in range. This is why you need this test twice: `index < SEATS_PER_ROW`.
- In part (c), every time you reset the count, you need to reset the `lowIndex`, because this is the value you're asked to return.
- In parts (b) and (c), the final return statements are executed only if all rows in the show have been examined unsuccessfully.

2. (a)
```
public String replaceAll(String line, String sub, String repl)
{
    int pos = line.indexOf(sub);
    while (pos >= 0)
    {
        line = line.substring(0, pos) + repl +
                line.substring(pos + sub.length());
        pos = line.indexOf(sub);
    }
    return line;
}
```

(b)
```
public void createPersonalizedLetters()
{
    for (int i = 0; i < customers.size(); i++)
    {
        List<String> tempLines = makeCopy();
        Customer c = customers.get(i);
        for (int j = 0; j < tempLines.size(); j++)
        {
            tempLines.set(j,
                replaceAll(tempLines.get(j), "@", c.getName()));
            tempLines.set(j,
                replaceAll(tempLines.get(j), "&", c.getCity()));
            tempLines.set(j,
                replaceAll(tempLines.get(j), "$", c.getState()));
        }
        writeLetter(tempLines);
    }
}
```

NOTE

- In part (a), each time you encounter sub in line, you simply create a new line that concatenates the "before" substring, the replacement, and the "after" substring. This guarantees termination of the loop: Eventually sub won't be found in line because all occurrences have been replaced, and line.indexOf(sub) will return -1 (sub not found in line).
- In part (b), you need a nested loop: for each customer, loop through all the lines and do the replacements.
- In part (b), one of the tricky lines of code is

```
List<String> tempLines = makeCopy();
```

You need a fresh, unchanged copy of lines for each customer. If, by mistake, you use the line

```
List<String> tempLines = lines;
```

then tempLines and lines will be the same reference, so any changes to tempLines will also be made to lines, and the second (and all subsequent) customers won't have a fresh copy of lines with the tokens. Instead, lines will contain the first customer's information.

```
3.    public class Outfit implements ClothingItem
      {
          private Shoes shoes;
          private Pants pants;
          private Top top;

          public Outfit (Shoes aShoes, Pants aPants, Top aTop)
          {
              shoes = aShoes;
              pants = aPants;
              top = aTop;
          }

          public String getDescription()
          {
              return shoes.getDescription() + "/" + pants.getDescription()
                      + "/" + top.getDescription() + " outfit";
          }

          public double getPrice()
          {
              if (shoes.getPrice() + pants.getPrice() >= 100
                      ||shoes.getPrice() + top.getPrice() >= 100
                      ||top.getPrice() + pants.getPrice() >= 100)
                  return 0.75 * (shoes.getPrice() + pants.getPrice() +
                          top.getPrice());
              else
                  return 0.90 * (shoes.getPrice() + pants.getPrice() +
                          top.getPrice());
          }
      }
```

NOTE

- To access the price and descriptions of items that make up an outfit, your class needs to have variables of type Shoes, Pants, and Top.

```
4.    (a) public void shuffle()
          {
              for (int k = tiles.size() - 1; k > 0; k--)
              {
                  int randIndex = (int) (Math.random() * (k + 1));
                  Tile temp = tiles.get(k);
                  tiles.set(k,  tiles.get(randIndex));
                  tiles.set(randIndex, temp);
              }
              unusedSize = tiles.size();
          }
```

(b)
```
    public void replaceTiles(TileSet t)
    {
        int numTiles = NUM_LETTERS - playerTiles.size();
        if (numTiles <= t.getUnusedSize())
        {
            for (int i = 1; i <= numTiles; i++)
                playerTiles.add(t.getNewTile());
        }
        else
        {
            for (int i = 1; i <= t.getUnusedSize(); i++)
                playerTiles.add(t.getNewTile());
        }
    }
```

Alternatively

```
    while (NUM_LETTERS > playerTiles.size() && !t.allUsed())
        playerTiles.add(t.getNewTile());
```

(c)
```
    public int getWordScore(int[] indexes)
    {
        if (indexes[0] == -1)
            return 0;
        int total = 0;
        if (indexes.length == NUM_LETTERS)
            total += 20;
        for (int i = 0; i < indexes.length; i++)
        {
            total += playerTiles.get(indexes[i]).getValue();
        }
        return total;
    }
```

NOTE

- In part (a), the line

  ```
  int randIndex = (int) (Math.random() * (k + 1));
  ```

  returns a random integer in the range $0, 1, 2, \ldots, k$.
- In part (b), there are two things to check:

  1. How many new tiles does the player need?
  2. Are there enough unused tiles available?

- In part (c), notice that indexes[i] are the positions of the tiles whose scores you need to access.

Appendix: Glossary of Useful Computer Terms

I hate definitions.
—*Benjamin Disraeli,* Vivian Grey *(1826)*

API library: Applications Program Interface library. A library of classes for use in other programs. The library provides standard interfaces that hide the details of the implementations.

Applet: A graphical Java program that runs in a web browser or applet viewer.

Application: A stand-alone Java program stored in and executed on the user's local computer.

Binary number system: Base 2.

Bit: From "binary digit." Smallest unit of computer memory, taking on only two values, 0 or 1.

Buffer: A temporary storage location of limited size. Holds values waiting to be used.

Byte: Eight bits. Similarly, megabyte (MB, 10^6 bytes) and gigabyte (GB, 10^9 bytes).

Bytecode: Portable (machine-independent) code, intermediate between source code and machine language. It is produced by the Java compiler and interpreted (executed) by the Java Virtual Machine.

Cache: A small amount of "fast" memory for the storage of data. Typically, the most recently accessed data from disk storage or "slow" memory is saved in the main memory cache to save time if it's retrieved again.

Compiler: A program that translates source code into object code (machine language).

CPU: The central processing unit (computer's brain). It controls the interpretation and execution of instructions. It consists of the arithmetic/logic unit, the control unit, and some memory, usually called "on-board memory" or cache memory. Physically, the CPU consists of millions of microscopic transistors on a chip.

Debugger: A program that helps find errors by tracing the values of variables in a program.

Decimal number system: Base 10.

GUI: Graphical user interface.

Hardware: The physical components of computers. These are the ones you can touch, for example, the keyboard, monitor, printer, CPU chip.

Hertz (Hz): One cycle per second. It refers to the speed of the computer's internal clock and gives a measure of the CPU speed. Similarly, megahertz (MHz, 10^6 Hz) and gigahertz (GHz, 10^9 Hz).

Hexadecimal number system: Base 16.

High-level language: A human-readable programming language that enables instructions that require many machine steps to be coded concisely, for example, Java, C++, Pascal, BASIC, FORTRAN.

HTML: Hypertext Markup Language. The instructions read by web browsers to format web pages, link to other websites, and so on.

IDE: Integrated Development Environment. Provides tools such as an editor, compiler, and debugger that work together, usually with a graphical interface. Used for creating software in a high-level language.

Interpreter: A program that reads instructions that are not in machine language and executes them one at a time.

Javadoc: A program that extracts comments from Java source files and produces documentation files in HTML. These files can then be viewed with a web browser.

JavaScript: (Not to be confused with Java, the programming language.) A dynamic programming language most commonly used as part of web browsers.

JVM (Java Virtual Machine): An interpreter that reads and executes Java bytecode on any local machine.

Linker: A program that links together the different modules of a program into a single executable program after they have been compiled into object code.

Low-level language: Assembly language. This is a human-readable version of machine language, where each machine instruction is coded as one statement. It is translated into machine language by a program called an assembler. Each different kind of CPU has its own assembly language.

Mainframe computer: A large computer, typically used by large institutions, such as government agencies and big businesses.

Malware: (Short for malicious software.) Any software designed to disrupt computer operation or gain access to private computer systems. For example, viruses, spyware, etc.

Microcomputer: Personal computer.

Minicomputer: Small mainframe.

Modem: A device that connects a computer to a phone line or TV cable.

Network: Several computers linked together so that they can communicate with each other and share resources.

Object code: Machine language. Produced by compiling source code.

Octal number system: Base 8.

Operating system: A program that controls access to and manipulation of the various files and programs on the computer. It also provides the interface for user interaction with the computer. Some examples: Windows, MacOS, and Linux.

Primary memory: RAM. This gets erased when you turn off your computer.

RAM: Random Access Memory. This stores the current program and the software to run it.

ROM: Read Only Memory. This is permanent and nonerasable. It contains, for example, programs that boot up the operating system and check various components of the hardware. In particular, ROM contains the BIOS (Basic Input Output System)—a program that handles low-level communication with the keyboard, disk drives, and so on.

SDK: Sun's Java Software Development Kit. A set of tools for developing Java software.

Secondary memory: Hard drive, disk, magnetic tapes, CD-ROM, and so on.

Server: The hub of a network of computers. Stores application programs, data, mail messages, and so on, and makes them available to all computers on the network.

Software: Computer programs written in some computer language and executed on the hardware after conversion to machine language. If you can install it on your hard drive, it's software (e.g., programs, spreadsheets, word processors).

Source code: A program in a high-level language like Java, C++, Pascal, or FORTRAN.

Swing: A Java toolkit for implementing graphical user interfaces.

Transistor: Microscopic semiconductor device that can serve as an on-off switch.

URL: Uniform Resource Locator. An address of a web page.

USB flash drive: A removable and rewritable device that fits into a USB port of a computer.

Virus: A computer program that can replicate itself and spread from one computer to another. A form of malware.

Workstation: Desktop computer that is faster and more powerful than a microcomputer.

Index

How to Use the CD-ROM

The software is not installed on your computer; it runs directly from the CD-ROM. Barron's CD-ROM includes an "autorun" feature that automatically launches the application when the CD is inserted into the CD-ROM drive. In the unlikely event that the autorun feature is disabled, follow the manual launching instructions below.

Windows®

1. Click on the Start button and choose "My Computer."
2. Double-click on the CD-ROM drive, which is named **AP_Computer Science**.
3. Double-click **AP_Computer Science** to launch the program.

MAC®

1. Double-click the CD-ROM icon.
2. Double-click the **AP_Computer Science** icon to start the program.

SYSTEM REQUIREMENTS

Microsoft® Windows®
2.33GHz or faster x86-compatible processor, or Intel Atom™ (1.6GHz or faster processor for netbook class devices) Microsoft® Windows® XP, Windows Server 2008, Windows Vista® Home Premium, Business, Ultimate, or Enterprise (including 64 bit editions) with Service Pack 2, Windows 7, or Windows 8 Classic 512MB of RAM (1GB recommended)

MAC® OS X
Intel® Core™ Duo 1.83GHz or faster processor Mac OS X v10.6, v10.7, v10.8, or v10.9 512MB of RAM (1GB recommended)